Chris Thrall was born in southeast London. At eighteen, he joined the Royal Marine Commandos. Following active service in the Northern Ireland conflict and Arctic warfare and survival training, he earned his parachutist's 'wings' and went on to serve in a high-security detachment on board an aircraft carrier.

In 1995, Chris moved to Hong Kong to oversee the Asia-Pacific expansion of a successful marketing operation he'd built, part-time, while serving in the Forces. A year later, he was homeless, in psychosis from crystal meth addiction and working for the 14K, a Hong Kong triad society, as a doorman in the infamous Wan Chai red-light district.

Eating Smoke is a moving yet humorous first book. It is not a memoir of regret.

———————————————

"Among the best of the newcomers." – *The Star*

"Exemplary pacing, completely engaging tone, wealth of winning detail. Thrall uses such verve, enthusiasm and faultless comic timing that it is hard not to be swept along." – *South China Morning Post*

"… a colourful cast of characters from the sewers of Hong Kong."
– *Loaded*

"This city can be dizzyingly fast-paced and hard to grasp even when one is straight and sober. Try living and working here on a daily diet of crystal methamphetamine. … Thrall's disoriented narrative has found a substantial audience in the city; for weeks, it has been riding on Hong Kong's best-seller list." – *Asia Times*

"This year's best book." – *Time Out Hong Kong*

EATING SMOKE

Chris Thrall

BLACKSMITH BOOKS

For a true friend, Rob Bailey.

Eating Smoke
ISBN 978-988-19002-9-6

Published by Blacksmith Books
Unit 26, 19/F, Block B, Wah Lok Industrial Centre,
37-41 Shan Mei Street, Fo Tan, Hong Kong
Tel: (+852) 2877 7899
www.blacksmithbooks.com

Edited by Alan Sargent
Map by Katy Hung

First printed August 2011
Reprinted 2012, 2013
Revised and reprinted September 2016

Also by Chris Thrall
The Drift
The Trade

Author's note: Names and other identifying details of individuals,
places and books have been changed.

Contents

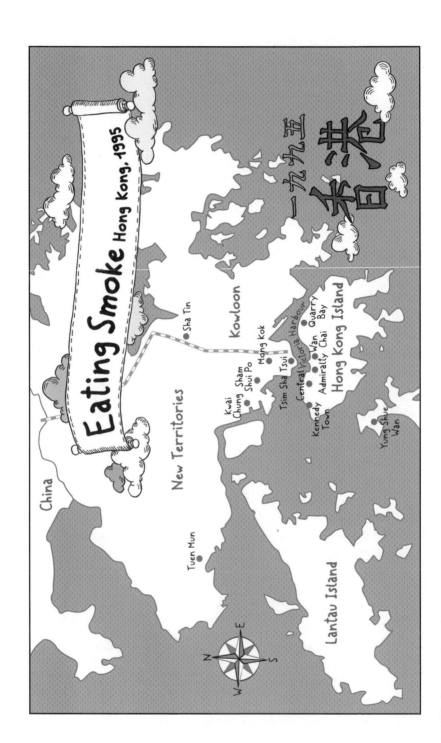

Prologue

IN 2004, I WORKED IN A MENTAL HEALTH UNIT. People often asked, 'How can you stand it with all those nutters?' I'd quote from the textbook: 'It's a misunderstood condition affecting one in four people at some stage in their lives.' I never told the real reason. I worried knowledge might confuse them. You see, in 1996, I went mad.

Now, this isn't necessarily as bad as it sounds. The UK has plenty of systems in place to help people who throw wobblers – doctors, medicine, hospitals, not to mention Incapacity Benefit and God. Unfortunately, these comforts were in short supply for me. Therefore, I must warn you: If your mind is planning on playing an away game, taking a sabbatical or simply fucking off, you're in for quite a ride if you happen to be working as a nightclub doorman in Hong Kong…

The Man in the Mirror

I STARED INTO THE LARGEST SHARD of blood-splashed glass.

'Do I know you...?'

'You've never known him at all...'

Sitting on the filthy concrete, I convulsed occasionally and whimpered like a sick dog. I hadn't slept for days, the crystal meth pulsing through my veins denying all refuge from the madness enveloping me.

Now the anger had passed, I found myself suspended in a ghostly calm, trying to piece together a life as fragmented as the mirror I'd smashed. I needed to make sense of what happened and put a stop to the Voice.

I leant forward, slowly, to examine the claw marks in my scalp and a haunted face I hardly recognised.

'Is this *me...?*'

The only thing familiar was the eyes – now bloodshot and yellow, with pupils raging deep and menacing. Would these black abysses dilate further, triumphing over the turquoise rings around them, heralding the madness had claimed my soul?

I was in my flat, the Killing House, with its strange blood splats on the walls, not knowing whose blood it was or how it got there.

The Voice named it that after the Special Air Service's anti-terrorist training house at Hereford Camp, back in England. I'd seen it in the film *Who Dares Wins* and on a visit to the base during my own military career.

In my mind, people surely suffered a terrible death up here, the top-floor apartment of a decaying tenement in a run-down part of Wan Chai.

As a mosquito whined in the glow of an underrated bulb, the sound of cats wailing, dogs barking and the hustle on the street below hardly made its way up to the solitude of my smashed-up hovel.

It may have been squalid, but I called it home, a humble abode by day but one that came alive at night. A place I loved far more than the two-bedroom new-build I owned in Plymouth. It was a fleapit with character, my very own piece of Hong Kong.

'Where's it all gone…?'

'I don't know… I don't know where.'

Memories of better days floated up out of the insanity like bubbles of clarity rising to burst atop a glass of mad soda… dining on top of the World Trade Center with Dan as teenage marines on our first proper holiday. Windows on the World they called that place, its lift shaking as it travelled up a hundred floors already swaying in the downtown Manhattan breeze, then the ritziness of gold, marble, glass, and satin tablecloths, with lobster followed by strawberries and more of New York's awesome skyline.

I'd chuckled as the elderly toilet attendant ran gold-plated taps and, with a respectful smile, handed me soap and a towel – three days earlier we'd been lying armed to the teeth and covered in shit in a ditch in the Belfast countryside.

After our meal, the evening just got better. A limousine picked us up with the girls from Texas and we drank a load more champagne.

'Great night… eh?'

'Yeah… a great night.'

I'd left the Forces to run my own business in Hong Kong – or *Heung Gong*, to use the colony's rightful title, the Fragrant Harbour. But all that was bullshit now. I had to think about my family. Despite the difficulties over the years, they were always there for me, my friends too – my real friends, not the superficial ones struggling to understand themselves in this ego-fuelled city. There was no way I would go home, though, a failure with a bankrupt dream. How could I do that?

None of them would recognise me anyway. They certainly wouldn't like the dump I lived in, the amount of drugs I took, or that triads followed me home *again* the other morning. I knew they were tailing me – hardly surprising after the bizarre chain of events unfolding that night…

An inch from rock bottom, I'd taken a job as doorman in Club Nemo. As with many nightclubs in Asia, although owned by a local businessman, the dominant crime syndicate organised the security, bar, prostitutes and drug deals. In Wan Chai, this was the 14-K, the most ruthless brotherhood in existence.

'Paul' Eng, a cross-eyed psychopath, invited me to work for them. He was the resident *Dai Lo*, or 'Big Brother', a middle-ranking triad who managed Nemo's and the mobsters who ran it.

I was leaving the club the night they set me up. I hadn't been scared… *okay…* a little, but I wasn't going to show those cowards that.

I laughed at them – fucking gangsters with their expat cronies and weird secret hand signs. I was still laughing when glancing over my shoulder I noticed a sleek black Mercedes stalking me slowly through the morning-after litter adorning Jaffe Road.

I was heading to the sanctuary of my flat, off my face on the meth I'd smoked the night before and looking forward to smoking some more, wondering if this would be another twenty-four hours without any sleep.

As the terror took hold, I decided to give them the slip by scooting up a back alley – a dark stinking shortcut crawling with fat rats thriving on scraps thrown out of restaurants. These dirt-matted mutants only scurried away so they could watch with contempt as you passed through their turf, jeering as stale water dripped down from antiquated air conditioners.

I ducked into one of the dirt-grey buildings and shot up the back stairs, heart pounding and breathing frenetic. After several attempts at smashing through the ageing exit door, I found myself out on the roof, desperate for a place to hide and fumbling in the leather pouch around my waist for the Mini Maglite and chain.

Illumination I didn't need, only the blunt force the torch delivered when connecting with someone's head. I'd never had cause to use it in the club – at least not as a weapon. It had come in handy at the end of the night, though, for scouring the disco's dirt-caked floor for any drugs and valuables the customers dropped – a trick I learnt from Dai Su, the 'Violent Hand' assassin.

They may be coming with meat cleavers – a triad's prerogative – but it wouldn't faze me. Not much does when you're a mental ex-marine flying high on ice. I would do my utmost to fuck 'em up. There are no Queensberry Rules in Wan Chai.

Still, a hiding place might prove worthwhile.

Scanning around I spied a recess set into the roof like some kind of utility shaft. I grabbed the rusting ladder but only got a foot on a rung before slipping, falling headlong into the darkness and – *'Umph!'* – landing on some god-awful mess below.

Something broke my fall, but it was far from pleasant. I felt hair and cold, hardened flesh and smelt a stench – *'Urrrh!'* – that would have been unbearable in anything less than a crisis.

It wasn't just rancid, dead and decomposing... it was *human*, my mind flashing back to a corpse I'd stumbled upon on a riverbank in Cairo.

The next thing I knew the Maglite was on, and because this was Hong Kong, where situations can always get worse, I believed what I saw.

I don't know if it was a mother and *her* baby, or a woman and *a* baby. Nor what she'd done or why. What I did know was she'd been hacked to pieces as a result.

Her face – what was left of it – still contorted with fear, as if she'd realised death was imminent, grimaced and, after the chopper sliced from crown to ear, her features stayed that way.

I wondered if the victim's tormentor lopped her arms and legs off before or after that fatal blow, as they now lay awkwardly against her torso.

The little boy was on his back, draped across her midriff, eyes gently closed and mouth slightly ajar, as if in peaceful sleep.

His tiny belly wasn't so composed. Through a single slash, a rainbow of entrails spilled onto the woman's emaciated chest, time and bodily fluid welding them together.

I tried to back into a corner but could barely move my own limbs. Bodies or no bodies, I would lie low until the danger passed. Although the meth had stolen it all, I still respected myself and could sit in the darkness next to two corpses and say, 'Fuck 'em! *Fuck 'em all!*'

The Chinese have an expression: *Life is meat*, explaining how the country can lose a hundred people in a coal mining accident, hide it from the world and carry on business as usual. Well, I had my own saying as I listened to my heartbeat in overdrive: *Meat is life*.

Besides, waiting shit out in adverse conditions is what the Royal Marines do best. Lying up all night in an ambush position in the Arctic has that effect on you. I could wait. I could wait as long as necessary...

I awoke on the Hawaiian-pattern mattress covering my rickety bamboo bunk – one I'd built to make use of the room space I didn't have. Cold in the tropical heat, ravenous and shivering with exhaustion, I gathered my thoughts. It slowly dawned it was dark and I should have been back at work by now. I checked the Casio G-Shock.

'*Shit!*'

It had gone 10pm. I was over two hours late. Along with pawning my treasured Swiss watch, it was another reason to feel crap.

I threw off the rough blanket lying across my chest and eased my legs over the edge of the bed, hopping the five-foot drop to land unsteady on my feet.

In amongst the junk littering my gone-to-pot attempt at tatami flooring was a crumpled page from a yellowing newspaper. As I shoved a Marlboro between my lips and set it alight, an aerial photograph caught my eye.

It was a brick construction set into the roof of one of the colony's tower blocks. Filling the recess, as well as my attention, was the picture's focus. It looked as though someone had created a grotesque Picasso using real people... although in reality, the woman and baby had been hacked to death in signature triad revenge.

An eerie *déjà vu* spread through every cell in my body, like a banshee's wail building to a crescendo that chilled and electrified my being. Frantically I scanned for the date on the newspaper... *15 May 1995...* was *three days* before I'd arrived in Hong Kong...

About Turn!

'CORPORAL THRALL, I'VE HEARD you're slightly unhappy upon leaving the Royal Marines?' probed the commanding officer, horn rims halfway down his nose.

I was twenty-five and had enjoyed my seven-year stint with this elite commando force, but this last year and a half as I got a business off the ground in my spare time I'd met with obstinacy and scorn from certain 'career-minded' individuals.

Now, standing before the boss on my final day of service, I sensed that he too had jumped on the bandwagon.

'*No*, Sir!' I replied. 'I've had a great time in the Royal Marines. I just take issue with you sending Corporal Johns to prison for two months for having his hair half an inch too long, especially as he has a wife and kids *and* a clean conduct record, Sir.' I referred to a recent disciplinary – one instigated by our regimental sergeant major (RSM), who happened to be standing three feet away.

'*Hmmh?* I hear what you're saying,' the CO replied – rather generously as I don't think anyone had been so frank since the formation of the Corps in 1664.

I waited for the standard military issue '*However…*'

'*However…* This *is* the *Royal Marines*, Corporal Thrall. We have to have that discipline, you understand?'

'Yes, Sir – that's why I'm leaving.'

It was a fitting answer when 'discipline' equates to kangaroo-court logic and fifty-year-old colonels can't come up with anything better than 'however' speeches.

'Well, I wish you the very best of luck outside, *Mister* Thrall. You're dismissed.'

'Thank you, Sir. Goodbye,' I replied, the provost sergeant giving me the order to about-turn and leave the room.

As I walked towards the door I could feel the RSM's eyes burning into the back of my head.

'*Mister* Thrall! If you think doing two months inside is harsh for having your hair too long, *you* don't belong in the Royal Marines!' he barked. 'But good luck in Civvy Street.' Then he scowled at me as I walked out of Stonehouse Barracks' huge iron gates for the last time.

He just had to get that in, but I didn't mind. I'd built a multinational sales organisation from humble beginnings in Plymouth, and after all my hard work it had been pulling in the big bucks in Hong Kong.

The personal attack alarm sold me on becoming an 'independent distributor' for Quorum International – a network-marketing venture already achieving success in the States. I knew on a camp of five hundred marines, many of whom saw their partners infrequently, selling the concept of security via pocket-sized I-don't-want-the-missus-to-be-attacked alarms would be a doddle.

By my third week, I'd sold enough plastic spouse-protectors to scale the promotion ladder, reaching the dizzy heights of senior executive.

While serving out my notice, I continued to sell Quorum's products but unfortunately had to give refunds for all the home alarms. The supersonic booms of Concorde were setting off their pressure sensors. This didn't stop me from sponsoring a significant number of distributors into my network, which now spanned the UK and Europe.

Yet despite my promotion to 'silver' executive, two positions away from financial freedom for life, I slid further into debt. It cost a fortune holding meetings in lavish hotels and making trips abroad. Then six months prior to my leaving the military, my creation, the Max*Tech* Group, witnessed a miracle, an eleventh-hour redemption in the form of Lee Han Keung – or 'Vance' Lee, as I would come to know him.

Having invited Wayne 'Flash' Gordon to a business presentation, his reply had been frank: 'I'm not interested, but I met a guy in the Hong Kong Army who will be. Is your company opening up there?'

'No, mate,' I told Flash, 'but if it does you'll be the first to know.'

When I arrived back at my office – a part of the kitchen I'd upgraded with a desk, fax machine and hand-held electric whisk – I picked up a fax announcing: QUORUM'S HONG KONG LAUNCH!

Attention caught, I read on '…so if any of our European distributors have connections in Hong Kong, you should contact them right away.'

'Well I never!' I thought, stopping short of the Orwellian innuendo that followed.

During a telephone call to Vance, he declared, from his ever-loyal disposition and without asking what it was really about, he would start straight away. True to his word, he built Quorum's largest network in Hong Kong and China. It was only the start of the Asia Pacific operation and I was receiving three percent of a monthly turnover that was already US$100,000.

The RSM was right: I definitely thought I was right. I belonged elsewhere… in Hong Kong, the business capital of the world.

Goodbye, Great Britain

AS THE TRAIN SLID OUT of Plymouth Station, something wasn't right – and not just the prices in the buffet car. Although happy to leave the Forces, I knew in my heart the business was failing.

I'd been to Hong Kong twice before, my initial visit pure fortuity, a fellow marine announcing, 'All the lads are going on an indulgence flight for Christmas. Do you want in?'

Indulgence was a perk of the job. Only as opposed to a company fuel card, this kickback got you, the aspiring Columbus, to any British military interest worldwide with either the Royal Air Force or a civilian airline, simply by paying a token administration fee.

Not surprisingly, 'all the lads' cried off our Hong Kong odyssey, opting to spend leave '…with the missus,' or '…down the pub.' But I couldn't wait to jet off to the Orient, amigoed-up or not.

I would be visiting the place I'd seen in the film *Double Impact*. As Jean-Claude Van Damme escaped a respectable number of psychopaths by skipping across the junks lining Aberdeen Harbour, I dreamt of visiting this unique enclave myself.

I drank enough of British Airways' in-flight drink to recover my forty quid and didn't let my feet hit the ground having landed. I blasted around the colony sucking up all the sights and sounds and then flew to Thailand to see if one night in Bangkok really does make hard men humble. Back in Hong Kong a week later, sporting a broken nose and five stitches, I took the hydrofoil to Macau to check out the casinos, even managing a visit to mainland China – no mean feat for a British serviceman, China being our supposed red enemy.

But in the land of sleeping dragons, you don't want to be around when one of them stirs.

In Sai Wan District, a gun battle broke out on the street I was on, instigated by a mainland triad gang who'd smuggled foot soldiers across the border to rob an exclusive jewellery store. A few days later, I left Mad Dogs in Lan Kwai Fong to find twenty-one people dead or dying in a nearby street, crushed in a panic during the traditional New Year's countdown. There were blue flashing lights everywhere and people collapsed in doorways with paramedics trying to resuscitate them. 'Why are there shoes scattered down the street?' I wondered.

Travelling over to Kowloon the next day on a Star ferry, I happened to glance at someone's copy of the *South China Morning Post*. As we chugged across the busy harbour, the pleasant rays of sunlight rebounding off the water and doing wonders for my hangover, the true horror of what had happened sunk in.

I'd visited Hong Kong a second time to meet Vance. Only this time it was different. 'Officially' I had a month left to serve as part of my resettlement leave, so I still had my ID card and was able to get an indulgence flight. But this trip wasn't about self-gratification – more gambling of self.

I'd just said goodbye to the security blanket I'd taken for granted all my adult life. The possibility of getting your arse shot off in faraway places may not seem the securest of blankets to some, but in comparison to your civilian counterpart, getting paid 24/7 in sickness and in health, with the only requisite being you kept yourself fit and said 'Yes, *Sir!*' even when you didn't mean it, was in reality a ten-tog duvet to make an Eskimo proud.

No longer did I have a BMW to park free of charge in the military spaces outside Gatwick's Terminal Four, my fuel warrant paid for by the British taxpayer. I wouldn't be waltzing through Immigration wearing shorts and a smile, and even the novelty of seating myself down in BA comfort on a Boeing 747 seemed somewhat estranged. Winging my way towards the throbbing metropolis I had it all on the line and my anxiety levels continued to rise.

For a start I was seven grand in debt to the bank and credit card companies. Also, I'd rented my house out to a dizzy blonde friend-of-a-friend and I just knew there'd be a problem with the rent and she'd take half my furnishings with her when she moved in with the first joker she met out on Plymouth's Union Street. And the crucial issue was the product supply on which I'd founded my networking success. It was turning into a consumer-electronic joke.

The personal attack alarm continued to be a big seller, but the burglar alarms still insisted on informing homeowners that the passengers and crew of Concorde were only thirty thousand feet away – so ready the baseball bat. The garden shed alarm was so crap you could guarantee it would be the only item left behind after your shed was broken into and all your possessions – including the shed itself – stolen. And the Quorum Bicycle Alarm intended to set off firecrackers in the Chinese market cost eight times more there than an actual bike.

As the distributors in my receding empire became reluctant to sell the products, the Max *Tech* Group's turnover dropped to a laughable low. At this rate, it wouldn't be long before I made Barings Bank's end-of-year returns look as sexy as a swimsuit model with a fridge full of beer. Sitting on the train, I felt like a replacement captain rowing out to the *Titanic* – *after* it hit the iceberg.

Determined to take decisive action in these adverse circumstances, I went to the nearest exit window to smoke a joint. If I were a top athlete, I pondered, drugs would serve to enhance my performance, perhaps tipping the balance between silver and gold. But as an aspiring leader of commerce, one ready to capitalise on China's fear of burglary by Concorde or having their garden hoes stolen, I couldn't help thinking I wasn't doing myself any favours.

Standing there chugging away, trying to get the hash smoke to go out the window, I clocked my old school chum, Bob Horten, bouncing off the seats down the aisle towards me.

'Hi, Chris! Is that a joint?'

'Yeah, mate. Want some?' I replied, as our approach to Exeter St Davids came over the tannoy and the train slowed.

'Thanks, man!'

Bob's need became self-evident as he told me all that had happened since we last met and had played for an afternoon in a Status Quo tribute band we'd formed. I'd strummed my heart out using every single one of the three chords I knew, before the pressure of international stardom got to us – there in the church hall – and we split up.

Not only did Bob live penniless in a squat, not only had he just been released from the police cells for not paying his poll tax bill, *and* not only had he featured on the front page of *The Sun*, having been arrested for going through a red light, drunk, while travelling in a shopping trolley, but he'd also been apprehended by the ticket inspector for not paying his fare.

As the train picked up speed, I leant out the window to muse on my own problems. A ten-pound note fluttered across the platform... the white line fizzled and disappeared... the edgy feeling came rushing back... I felt I was out of it, flying high and looking down on myself.

There was Bob, dressed in shabby-with-holes, gothic attire, and here was I on my way to do business in Hong Kong, with a dress-bag filled with a smart suit, shirts, ties and a blazer. Bob had a résumé suiting any supermarket seeking a drink-driving trolley boy who blatantly ignores traffic signals in a quest for celebrity, and I'd gone through the toughest infantry course in the world, earned a medal for serving my country and gone on to build an international marketing organisation. The irony was, as we sparked up another spliff, I felt our prospects were even – or if push came to shove... I felt willing to concede.

Hello, Hong Kong

AS THE PLANE CAME IN TO KAI TAK, it was *HELLO, HONG KONG!* and a landing like no other. The pilot initiated a diving turn over the emerald-green South China Sea to fly by the skyscrapers hugging the knuckle-whitening approach – so low I could make out the Asiatic features of locals hanging washing out to dry on iron frames bolted to the buildings. Flashing my military ID, I passed straight through the residents' channel at Immigration.

Immersed in the heat, I navigated the vibrant throng to nab a seat on the A2 bus heading to Admiralty District, where HMS *Tamar*, the Royal Naval Barracks, stood on the island's magnificent waterfront.

As I boarded the bus, an overly made-up crone stinking of booze thrust a business card at me. Printed in fortune-enhancing gold letters was *Chungking Mansions, Bamboo Guesthouse.*

'You stay *heeya!*' she ordered, more eyes than mouth.

While the bus forged through Kowloon's bustling traffic – signature red taxis, Rolls-Royces, souped-up hatchbacks and triad-driven minibuses – heading for the harbour tunnel, I turned my thoughts to securing free accommodation in this expensive city, kindly dismissing Chungking Mansions' tropical-grass-themed offer.

On previous visits, I'd show my ID to the Gurkha rifleman at the base's pristine white gates. He'd salute me together with '*Sahb!*' – for my white face and not my lowly rank – an endearing quality I'd always admired when working with the regiment of mountain men.

Now, I threw him an appreciative smile and breezed on in to enquire at the guardroom, 'Are there any bootnecks around, Corporal?'

Several marines from the speedboat squadron were relaxing in the accommodation block congratulating themselves on a haul of cocaine they'd seized the previous day from a junk in the sound. I resisted the temptation of asking if they had any of the good stuff put aside, instead introducing myself and enquiring about a room.

I soon settled into a well-worn one with a spectacular view over Victoria Harbour, its blue-green waters ruffled gently by the breeze, and the giant towers of commerce reaching greedily up into the delicate azure above Central District. I threw my military bergen onto the faded orange bedcover, then ducked under a shower, all the time looking forward to meeting Vance in the nearby tube station.

My inner child flew down the steps four at a time into the spotlessly clean underground to find my business partner standing by the turnstiles with a grin that said it all. Stocky, handsome, and slightly shorter than my five foot eight, Vance had a kind face never far from a smile. Everything he said or did was unassuming and genuine.

'Hallo, mayte!' he said, using the term 'mate' the way foreigners do when they don't *quite* get the endearment.

'*Lee San* (Mister Lee),' I replied. '*Lei ho ma?* (You good, yeah?)'

Mr Lee laughed. He loved it when this *gweilo*, 'devil man', got to grips with his language and culture. 'Well, the bissniss,' he began, and I smiled. Vance, true to the ethos of Hong Kong life, always began a conversation with a summary of the 'bissniss'.

Hong Kong is a convoluted yet fascinating society. Hidden from the process of modernisation behind a huge mountain range, a vast ocean and a great wall, China, 'The Middle Kingdom', was a land ruled by feudalism and dynasty, its peasants having no knowledge of the outside world.

Then the British arrived in trading ships brimming with opium leached from the poppy plants of India. They soon realised the Fragrant Harbour provided a gateway for supplying the drug to the mainland in return for silver, silk, porcelain, tea, and other goods in demand in Europe.

Under the Convention of Chuen Pi in January 1841, the Chinese ceded Hong Kong to the British. So in the short space of 154 years, the psyche of the people had adapted to uphold the culture of the motherland and the profit-seeking mindset of the new British masters, creating the lucrative entrepôt now famously known as Hong Kong.

'The bissniss quiet at the moment,' Vance continued, with veritable Asian diplomacy. 'But how abou' we eat?'

Eating is Hong Kong's second major institution and dining with Vance was always a treat, the steaming platters cooked fresh from the market making a mockery of the takeaways back home.

On my previous trip, we'd travelled to the mainland to conduct a meeting with some of our distributors. Vance, fluent in English, Cantonese and Mandarin, suggested it might be boring for me, so I'd gone to sit at a street-side eating place and indulge in the exotic fare on offer.

An amicable Chinese gent and his partner were tucking into plates piled with snails, and sipping beer. Wang insisted on a guided tour of the cuisine, openly displayed in blue plastic tubs. Giant crabs filled one, greeny-blue eels the next and massive wart-covered toads after that. The last bucket contained a writhing mass of three-foot-long brown fat-bellied snakes.

Wang dared me to pick one up, so I grabbed the least ferocious-looking wriggler and held the varmint up, to the applause of our fellow gastronomes.

After ploughing through a good many molluscs and guzzling more local *bair chau*, I spied Vance making his way from the meeting.

'The bissniss—'

'Vance! I just picked up a snake!'

'Where?'

'*There*, mate,' I said, pointing into the viper pool.

Without hesitation, he shoved his arm into the writhing entanglement, picked up the meanest-looking brute and began swinging the ugly asp's face right past his own. 'I used to collect these,' he said, 'when we eat them in the orphanage.'

'M'goy!' came the frantic shout of 'excuse me', interrupting thoughts of admiration for my new partner. *'Pu' it down!'* said the restaurant's owner. 'Sometime get da *wrong* one!'

Having travelled over to Kowloon on the Mass Transit Railway, we sat down in one of Tsim Sha Tsui's plush eating parlours, resplendent in cream satin tablecloths, walls curtained in crimson velvet, and minarets portraying characters from ancient mythology set on pedestals all around us.

Sitting in exquisitely carved redwood chairs, sipping jasmine tea in the ambience created by the lanterns overhead, beautiful in red with their decorative ideographic soliloquies, Vance addressed the issue of the *bissniss...* or the lack of it.

He explained how he'd put our distributors on hold, saying better products were in the pipeline, adding, 'The peepall only bash their head against the wall so many time before they don't come to the wall anymore.'

He was right, and I would go and confront 'Winston' Wong, the director of Quorum Asia Pacific, right after our meal.

When I got up to leave to go back over to the island, Vance grabbed my arm. 'Quiss'a, you *promise* to me... *that this bissniss would work.*'

'I'm sorry, Vance... I really thought it would, mate.'

I took the MTR three stops to Causeway Bay. The city is two sprawling metropolises, one on the Kowloon Peninsula and the other on Hong Kong Island. If you're new to the place, you go into a station nested amongst towering edifices and chaotic street life and come out to another, not realising you've crossed beneath a mile of busy harbour.

I entered an imposing skyscraper and took the lift to the twelfth floor. The woman at reception said Winston was looking forward to meeting me but presently engaged and would I like to sit in Quorum's swish cinema and watch a promotional video.

Fifteen-or-so smartly dressed distributors were already in there, all from my network. 'Michael' Keung introduced me to 'Sally' Ling, saying they worked in publishing.

The film was Hollywood in style and grandeur, jawing gold- and diamond-level distributors from America elucidating on how they'd achieved their rags-to-riches plan and how we could do likewise. As it ended, Michael said, 'Errh, Quiss'a. We have presentation of our own tonight. You wanna come?'

Sally looked a little coy, muttering something I couldn't understand, before Michael jumped in, saying, 'Find out more later, okay?'

Having accepted their business cards with customary two-handed politeness, I went to meet the big tofu in his swanky room with a view.

Following introductions, Winston said the Asia Pacific operation was going well, but when I probed him on the quality of the recent products, he said, '*You* and *your* distributors don' work hard enough!' So without saying another word to this rhetoric-soaked jackass I stood up and walked out, leaving Quorum International never to return.

I met Michael and Sally at a noodle shop in Causeway Bay. After downing a bowl of vermicelli swimming in chicken stock alongside a fried egg and lettuce, using chopsticks to pick out the tidbits and a plastic spoon to scoop up the broth, we made our way to the basement of a nearby building.

As expected, it was a Christian affair, with warm-hearted American missionaries persuading the locals to move from their Taoist and Buddhist principles aimed at truth and enlightenment to the other scenario in which an old boy sits on a cloud, knocking up stone tablets and virgins.

A little way into the talk, I began to feel uncomfortable – not with the spiel of these Bible-loving cats from the Belt, but in my nether regions. They weren't coping with the heat as well as I was. It was as if I had a knot tied in my towrope and someone was using it for target practice with an air rifle. I apologised to Michael and Sally and left for the base.

Ignoring the breathtaking view, I lay on the bed, but in no time at all the pain morphed into a thudding sensation, as if someone had stuck me in the lumbar region with a pitchfork and then invited a few friends over to kick me for the hell of it.

Writhing in agony, I got up and made my way down the corridor, bouncing off the walls. Upon reaching the guardroom, trembling and tripping out, I had to cling to the counter.

The Gurkha listened wide-eyed to my instruction to 'Do something, quickly!' and then got on the blower to the duty sergeant, who was no doubt lounging in the mess. He reeled off some disarming command to which my tenacious mountain man replied, '*No, Sahb!* Iss one of the marine. I fink he abou' to *die!*'

I don't remember arriving at the British Military Hospital in Kowloon, just lying on ward's primrose floor tiles throwing up at the feet of two nurses from the Women's Royal Army Nursing Corps.

'Don't worry,' one of the Nightingales assured me.

'Where's the doctor?' I rasped.

'*Don't worry!* He's been paged,' she replied, yet forty-five minutes later, he'd yet to make an appearance.

'What floor are we on?'

'Why?' asked the other nurse.

'Because I'm going to jump out the window.'

'There's *no* need for that!' she said, in a haughty, matron-esque tone.

'Can I get some painkillers then... *please?*'

'Not until the doctor's had a look at you.'

'Great!' I thought, as dark green bile accrued on the Dettol-scented floor.

One of them went away and returned with a bottle of laughing gas. It didn't achieve anything, though – not even a giggle.

The doctor finally arrived, looking half-asleep. 'So, what are *you* doing in Hong Kong, Royal?' he asked with genuine interest.

'*Fuck* Hong Kong, Doc! What about some fucking painkillers?'

'All in good time, marine!' he chuckled.

His examination was swift, and before I knew it, one of the nurses was injecting opiate into my backside and feeding me a pinkish concoction to dissolve the *kidney stones* left in my body. Then they left me watching a pop concert on the television by my bed.

Checking out my new surroundings, I noticed the nitrous oxide nearby. Never one to preclude a good party, or a laugh, I took a good few sucks, and drifting into a dreamlike, somewhat more ecstatic, state, I marvelled at how good this Michael Jackson lad was.

When I awoke the next morning, it felt good to be alive, the dazzling sunlight entering through the bay windows ricocheting around my soul. It felt even better when the hospital's happy-go-lucky Chinese orderly appeared. 'Wha' kin'a foo' you wan'?'

'What kind of food is there?' I asked, expecting the same overcooked slop masquerading as nutrition in the UK's sick houses.

'We got *wha'ever* you wan'!' he replied, the intonation in his voice suggesting I'd just asked the dumbest question in the hospital's proud history. Then he handed me an eight-page menu listing English, Cantonese, Nepalese and Indian dishes.

'So are you telling me I can have… *errh*… a cheese omelette and chips? And some geezer is gonna cook that especially for me?'

'*Speshooley for yoooo!*' He grinned from ear to ear, delighted to be a party to this English simpleton's arrival in food heaven.

'In that case I'll have… a cheese omelette and chips, please!'

As I lay back, bathing in the clean and pressed comfort of my crib, Florence One and Two appeared, looking as sexy as sirens in their nurse's outfits… *uniforms*, I mean.

'Here he is!' said the voluptuous strawberry-blonde. 'Here's the one with the sexy bum!'

'*Ooh!* You can say that again!' said the attractive brunette.

I *frickin'* knew it! Even when I'd been lying on the floor with vomit drooling from my gob, I *knew* they'd both fancied me… or at least I would have liked to think so.

The truth was a *wee* bit different. Despite having ample gratification in that department over the years, I still had a problem believing women might fancy me – not the ones I wanted to do so, that is.

I also had to remind myself I was in an on-off relationship with a girl in Plymouth. As a young marine, I'd met Sarah on a night out on Union Street and asked, 'Do you fancy my mate Dan, then?'

'No!' she replied. 'I like you.'

On day three, my recovery took a downturn. The orderly approached, looking a little concerned, saying I had to call the adjutant at the naval base right away.

'*Ah!* Our *mysterious* marine!' he boomed. 'What in God's name do you think you're doing, *stowing away* on our camp? You're to report to me *right away*. You understand?'

'Yes, Sir.' Of course I understood. Reporting to him right away was a separate issue as far as I was concerned.

'Don't you *know* that any serviceman entering the territory has to ask for *Crown* permission *first?*' He slammed the phone down.

'*Crown permission?* What's that colonial crap all about? *Report to me right away?* Not bloody likely!' I thought, getting dressed as quickly as I could.

On arrival at my ill-gotten abode, I grabbed my gear then bugged out of the Crown's property, waxing lyrical about the Queen of England, wishing she had nothing to do with my life choices. In a telephone call to Vance, he came to my rescue once more, offering me a room in his apartment.

Taking the MTR to Mong Kok over on Kowloon Side, I couldn't help thinking my Hong Kong venture hadn't got off to the best of starts. My business had died an ugly – albeit dignified – death, my health had taken a hit *and* I didn't get either of the Florence's phone numbers. Now I was on the UK's Most Wanted list and in danger, if caught, of having bits ripped off and shoved into orifices.

I had no idea as we passed below *Gau Lung's* crowded streets – 'Nine Dragons', as Kowloon literally means – my problems hadn't begun.

Mong Kok

I STEPPED OUT OF THE STATION into Mong Kok, the most heavily populated square mile on the planet, and began to make my way past the myriad of shops lining Nathan Road, a six-lane highway stemming the length of Kowloon's sky-scraped peninsula like an artery flowing with corpuscles of bright red taxis.

Steering a course through what seemed a frenetic mass of pedestrians, I soon realised it wasn't the people that were chaotic – they moved surprisingly slowly – it was the surroundings. The sights, sounds and smells of Cantonese exchange bombarded my senses as elaborate façades sold everything from Rolex watches to dried tiger penis, steam poured out of noodle shops and a cacophony of traffic noise complemented the vivid clashing colours of signs anchored to the buildings' walls. Worded in English, Chinese or both, they fought for line of sight to announce the services on offer and the mindset behind them. 'Happy Lucky Golden Company' announced one optimist, 'Golden Fortune Company' another.

After turning into Argyle Street and then Victory Avenue, I skipped up the small flight of steps into Hing Tak Mansion, bidding '*Ngh on* (Good afternoon)' to the security guard – a slight old man, dressed in shorts, vest and flip-flops, who sat grinning by the grilled gateway.

Vance's apartment was on the ground floor. I smiled, as it was the only one without a shrine outside housing a revered mythological figure amongst a cluster of joss sticks. Typical of Vance – no time for sentiment, only for the *bissniss*.

Answering the door with gusto, he looked pleased I'd arrived. 'How'is going, mayte?'

'Not *too* bad. You?' I felt exhausted.

'Well, the *bissniss*—'

'Vance, fff… *sod* the business.' I had to be mindful of my profanity, as Vance never swore. 'Winston's an idiot, and Quorum's going nowhere.'

'Well, we can wait 'til the product get better—'

'Nah, Vance. It ain't gonna happen,' I replied, knowing we'd have better luck signing people up for cholera.

As usual, his place was brimming with characters, many of them Filipinas from Hong Kong's service community, befriended by Vance through his marketing ventures. Other individuals included two Gurkhas, friends of the girls, and some of our Chinese distributors hankering to use the telephone and fax in Vance's office. His good-natured wife, Lim, appeared to be the only one missing, Vance saying she was at the local pool, giving kids swimming lessons.

Vance ushered me through a tiny antiquated kitchen and into a shoddily erected office tacked onto the back of the apartment. Hing Tak Mansion had a fortress-shaped design surrounding an open-air quadrangle the size of a tennis court. The other ground-floor tenants had built similar do-it-yourself affairs to capitalise on the extra space.

'This is your room,' said Vance. 'This used to be the office for my Amway distributors before I tell them to move over to the Quorum *bissniss.*' He frowned.

Vance had been a successful Emerald-level distributor for Amway's long-established Hong Kong operation, but following our initial success he'd focussed his efforts on Quorum, giving notice for his job as police sergeant in the Hong Kong Army.

'How much do I pay you, Vance?'

'Ah, juss something for the air-con,' he replied, and left me to settle in amongst the desks and chairs.

Sitting down on a flimsy camp bed, I heard a voice around the door: '*Halloo…* Can I com'een?'

'Yeah, come in!' I looked over to see the large, beaming mug of 'Benny' Tsang enter the room. Wearing a smart suit, and with kind eyes behind silver-framed spectacles, he seemed the same age as me.

'How you doin', *Quiss'a?*' he asked softly, perching on the bed. 'A'm one of your distributor, do you know?'

'*Oh!* How do you do, Benny?' I was pleased to see a friendly soul in these unfamiliar surroundings.

'So how you like your room?' he enquired, adding with a look of concern, 'You know that there is very *big* problem heeya?'

'Why's that, Benny?'

'Is's the ghost!' he said, eyes wide with conviction. 'This room is full of dem.'

'*Really*, mate?'

'*Really! Many* time me an' Mister Kong sit *heeya*, discuss how to get rid of the spirits. We very *worried* abou' you.'

'*Wow!*' I replied – taking Benny's cultural beliefs seriously and noting a variety of creaks coming from the roof as it swayed in the wind whistling down around the tropical flora beautifying the courtyard. But it wasn't *just* the wind. I swore I heard something moving around above the polystyrene ceiling tiles. Perhaps we *weren't* alone...

'Quiss'a, you wanna go for a walk?' He looked at me in earnest, his narrow-cut eyes appearing bigger through pebbled lenses.

'Sure, mate.' I was pleased to have such a pleasant tour guide.

Not long into our stroll down through the lively activity on Nathan Road, he said, 'See the guy there selling the newspaper?'

I clocked the chap, sat on a wooden crate by a rack of newssheets. 'Yeah, I see him.'

'This my brother!'

'Great!' I said, looking to my host for the expected introduction – only he kept his eyes fixed ahead and walked right by.

'*Benny!* You don't say hello to your own brother?'

'Oh, we *say* hallo...' Benny replied.

The following afternoon, Jayne, a young and pretty Filipina, took me on another interesting meander, to Mong Kok's open-air food market.

Arriving there the intensity took me aback, as locals jostled for space to prepare and sell their fare. The place was alive with the sounds of market barter and bathed in exciting colours. Pak choi, a tasty green leaf, clashed for exposure alongside pineapples, coconuts and lychees, and a mass of poultry hung off metal racks on S-shaped spikes next to their beef and pork competition.

But what really caught my attention was an old wizened chap, three long white wispy appendages sprouting from top lip and chin, sat on a rattan mat on the detritus-strewn floor, plucking dark green snakes – still very much alive – out of a wicker basket. After making a cut behind the reptile's head with a penknife, his nimble fingers ripped the creature's skin off in a single movement. Then he casually dropped it back, still squirming and now *pink*, into the creel to clash colour with its soon-to-be-on-the-block compadres.

When we arrived back at Hing Tak Mansion, Jayne asked, 'Have you any plan this evening, Creese?'

'Not really. How about you?'

'We're going to *Kangaroo* Pub!'

'*Kangaroo Pub! Kangaroo Pub!*' her friends twittered like gremlins.

'Well, *Kangaroo Pub* it is, then!'

Just being in Hong Kong was exhilarating, let alone taking the MTR again. This super-fast ride would see you to any destination on the island or peninsula within fifteen minutes. I was also thrilled at the prospect of a night out in Tsim Sha Tsui, especially with these friendly and attractive Filipinas.

Exiting the station, the level of my hostesses' fever-pitched chatter matched that of the sight greeting us – an onslaught of flashing neon announcing fervent disco experiences: Ned Kelly's Last Stand, Bottoms Up (featured in *The Man with the Golden Gun*) and many more. They took precedent over the now seemingly ordinary daytime signs such as Kwan Lee Batteries, Lee Hing Clothing and the luck-obsessed Midas contingent.

Upon arrival at the Australian-themed pub, the girls were ushered inside while the guys had to queue up and pay, a tactic employed in Clubland. It brought in the young Filipinas, who sent most of their hard-earned dollars home, thus enticing sailors swarming off ships hove-to in Hong Kong's deep-water harbour into the place.

Many of the clubs operated a 'number' system. If a female regular wanted to earn extra cash, the bar allocated her a code. When someone treated her to a drink, she got a percentage of the profit.

A few hours into my marsupial-flavoured experience, I must have drunk enough for everyone – in Australia, the Philippines and Hong Kong – yet unease burgeoned in my stomach. I had no idea how to support myself here, let alone make my fortune. Time to sleep on it, I left the girls bopping to the cover band and staggered into the street.

I made my way to the nearest MTR entrance through a mass of *gaai bin dong* vendors, their garishly painted handbarrows full of delicious-smelling wares – skewered beef, curried fish balls, roasted chestnuts, congee, noodles and tofu – lit in eerie beauty by flickering paraffin lamps.

Bidding *'Jou tau'* (Good night) to the ever-beaming security guard, little did I know supporting myself financially wasn't to be my biggest challenge in the coming months.

38 Lines

I AWOKE EARLY ON THE KHAKI COT. Sleeping had proved difficult anyway. The air-con swapped tropic for Baltic, was as noisy as a lawnmower, and turning it off saw you needing a lifebelt.

Also, I kept hearing those weird scurrying noises coming from the false ceiling, reminding me of the film *Alien*, where the crew of the stricken starship keep hearing weird scurrying noises coming from the false ceiling. Now daylight had arrived, I wondered if I'd dreamt it.

Entering the living room, I heard more strange sounds – frantic huffing and puffing. I hesitated for fear I might interrupt a Filipina bumping uglies with a one-night stand from the Kangaroo Pub but it turned out to be Vance in the middle of a rigorous press-up routine.

'Jou san, Lee San!'

'Morning, mayte. I juss come back from swimming.' He smiled, looking under-satisfied as he concentrated on his dips.

'*Wha!* You been swimming *already* this morning?'

'*No!* Already this morning, I take the army recruits for fife-mile run.'

'*Whoa,* Vance! You gotta be careful at your age,' I joked, Vance being early thirties. 'Can you keep up with those youngsters?'

'*No!*' he shot back, grinning between lunges. 'Youngsta have problem to keep up with me!'

Showered and suited, we left the air-conditioned apartment to hit the heat and humidity of Hong Kong's hectic streets in the rainy season.

Vance had an appointment in Yau Ma Tei, one stop on the MTR, so he suggested a quick McDonald's as opposed to delicious dim sum in one of the upmarket eating palaces further down the peninsula. Concerned about my finances, I happily agreed.

Having finished his food, Vance took up a newspaper. A photograph on the front page grabbed my attention. It was the blood-and-guts coverage of a shark attack at a Sai Kung beach the previous day.

As friends manhandled the mutilated swimmer from the surf, he screamed in terror, his limbs shredded into multi-coloured ribbons, his blood dripping to form thick puddles at their feet. The utter shock on their faces said it all.

'*Vance*! Does that happen here *often?*'

'Yeah,' he replied casually. 'When the shakk come, peepall get attack.'

'And are these kind'a pictures normal?' I asked, knowing they'd be censored back home – not that Plymouth has that many shark attacks.

'*Yeaah*! Hong Kong peepall very *animal*,' he said, the noun befitting as an adjective. 'You *wanna* read?' He pushed the English daily through the tomato sauce smears on the yellow plastic table.

I noted the inane and bravado-soaked quotes of those who bore witness to the tiger shark's feeding frenzy and the subsequent rescue from its razor-laden jaws.

'I do not worry to swim in the sea with the shark…' said one hero. 'It is my destiny,' another.

I turned the page and read an equally horrific account.

> The diver missing during a night dive has been found. Police recovered his body yesterday morning where it washed ashore. His right leg had been bitten off at the waist.

'*Hell*.' A scuba-diver myself, I couldn't imagine anything more horrific than being chomped on while swimming *alone*, *underwater*, in the *dark*!

'Vance, I need to look for a job,' I said, back at the apartment.

'You can look in the paper.' He handed it to me once more.

I flicked past the Piscean horror to find the job sheets. One post caught my attention:

> Bodyguard required to protect well-known and likeable Hong Kong celebrity…

I quickly knocked up a résumé – *former Royal Marine, well versed with small arms.*

Then I screwed it up and threw it in the bin. I didn't want the likeable celebrity to think I was an accomplished poet with malformed limbs.

…former Royal Marine, adept at 9mm pistol, martial arts and Cantonese…

This sounded better – although the part about martial arts and Cantonese was a slight exaggeration. I only spoke a few words of *Gwongdungwa* and my accomplishment in the Oriental fighting skills was limited to a few judo lessons at school and an afternoon of taekwondo during commando training.

The latter part of my ninja past involved our physical training instructor asking for '…another volunteer, *please!*'

All his demonstrations began with 'Right, fellas! If some bloke comes up to you in the pub… like *this*… yeah?'

Which I took to mean: 'If you ever find yourself behind enemy lines with no weapon and only three hours unarmed combat training and your body parts to protect you, you're *fucked*, lads. Better to use the taxpayer's money to teach you how to keep your end up in the boozer!'

The second advertisement I read was even more intriguing.

> Foreign English-speaking people with white faces, American, English, French, for your example, required to work in successful computer company in Sheung Wan. Good rates of pay. Gung Wan Hong. 38 lines.

It went on to list *all* thirty-eight telephone numbers.

'What's all that about?' I selected one at random.

A daintily speaking female answered.

I asked if they were still recruiting and if I needed to send a résumé.

'*No!*' she replied. 'Juss come 2pm, meet Fang *San* – errh, *Mister* Fang.'

I arrived at Wing Wo Street drenched in sweat, located the building and took the lift to the seventh floor, stepping out to plush surrounds of gilt, glass, polished stone and the smiles of *four* young women sat behind a maroon-leather-fronted and marble-topped reception desk. Three chunky gold characters were set high up on the wall. I assumed they read

'Gung Wan Hong' and that these four charmers had the onerous task of answering the thirty-eight phone lines.

'What if they all ring at the same time?' I wondered.

Ushered through a door, I was surprised at the chaotic environment. Western and Chinese workers buzzed about with stacks of papers, while others sat at desks or queued for the water cooler, photocopier and a row of chattering fax machines. Everyone was in animated conversation on the telephone or with a colleague. Files were stacked on every surface alongside coffee-stained mugs and dated office equipment.

A stunning Eurasian stepped forward, introducing herself as Jenny from Canada. Her miniskirt was so ridiculously succinct that when she leant over Fang's desk to tell him I'd arrived, the world saw the length of her well-formed pins *and* the saving on fabric her underwear company made. It wasn't hard to see where Fang *San* was at – dirty old dog, I thought, with a pang of envy.

In his late sixties, he wore a lurid Japanese motor-racing shirt covered in advertising patches exalting the virtues of various oil-based products and custom racing parts. Below this, three-quarter-length ice-white jeans and dazzling sports shoes, and wrapped around him, three weighty gold necklaces, a bracelet and a Rolex. Wearing brown-framed browsers the size of a juggernaut's windscreen, he sat there, snakelike, a super-length Marlboro smoking in the corner of his mouth.

'Fang *San,* errh… *Mister* Fang doesn't speak mush English, so I will interpret,' announced Jenny.

'That's fine by me,' I assured her, happy not to converse directly with this scary reptilian who dressed like Jimmy Savile.

Our exchange was to the point and began with her explaining the company traded in computer chips and peripherals. Fang *San* made no eye contact with me, preferring to fix his gaze on his saucy assistant. Through her, he probed me with blunt enquiry. 'What have you sold?' was the first question.

I showed him photographs of mock-antique advertising signs proclaiming the benefits in 1938 of using Dr Mackenzie's smelling-salts, drinking Coca-Cola, and mixing up Bisto granules to add a special something to your Sunday roast. They were a sideline of mine in England, something to boost the Max *Tech* Group's profits… the only issue being, I hadn't managed to sell any.

He seemed easily impressed, questioning me as to the mark-up on these items and my turnover. I waffled a few statistics, which seemed to do the trick.

I swear – albeit fleetingly – I caught a glimpse of human as he flashed a smile before whispering something to Jenny. 'Mister Fang likes you,' she said, 'and because you have *previous* sales experience, you can start right away on twelve thousand a month.'

Back at the apartment, I found my business partner staring at the floor with a furrowed brow.

'Everything alright, Vanc—?'

'The problem is Miss Lim… Miss Lim say the shower smell very terrible.' He raised an eyebrow.

'*Oh!* Sorry, Vance.' I wondered if this direct approach was a Chinese thing, feeling awful because I knew what it was.

In this tropical environment, my feet were sweating like crazy. As I stood under the spray that morning, I hoped I wouldn't stink the bathroom out – obviously, I had.

Feeling embarrassed, I nipped down to the Ladies Market on Tung Choi Street to buy a pair of sandals, figuring I could pick up a boogie box while I was there.

Locals and foreigners packed the place, hemmed in by stalls flying green tarpaulins and selling every type of clothing imaginable. I wandered through a gigantic kaleidoscope created by the colourful goods of capitalism, the smell of fresh denim a reminder of the invasive traders changing the face of Hong Kong long before I arrived.

As I ambled along, capitalising on the wake of a large German tourist, touts piped up with, 'Hambag', 'Sunglass', 'Wrollex', shooting it out the sides of their mouths like agents in a spy thriller.

A fake Rolex I didn't need. One evening, my local pub landlord had peeled the Rolex Oyster Sea Dweller from his wrist and given me a run-down on the model, explaining that the Swiss-jewelled diver's watch could go to a depth of 1,220 metres, achieving the ultimate accolade, *Officially Certified Superlative Chronometer,* as well as a great deal of celebrity.

Mercedes Gleitze wore one in 1927 when she became the first British woman to swim the English Channel. After fourteen hours and fifteen minutes immersed in the choppy waters of the Anglo-French divide, both her heart and watch ticked away without problem.

On 29 May 1953, Edmund Hillary wore his when he and Sherpa Tenzing Norgay became the first men to summit Everest.

A few years later, Jacques Piccard descended 10,916 metres to the bottom of the Pacific Ocean's Marianas Trench in the bathysphere *Trieste*, the Rolex Oyster strapped to the outside surviving the one ton per square centimetre put upon it.

Chuck Yeager, the US fighter pilot, had one on his arm in 1941 when he became the first person to break the sound barrier.

And as for James Bond, well, he refused to be seen on Her Majesty's Secret Service without one.

Knowing this watch had swum further, climbed higher, dived deeper and flown faster than any other in clockwork history, *and* it had a licence to kill, sold me on it – hypothetically, that is. A Sea Dweller cost £1,348 in 1989, £6,400 in today's prices.

Over the next two years, whenever I was in Plymouth's city centre, I would stare into Ballan's window display, dreaming of the day I'd buy the Sea Dweller nestled amongst the other Rolexes.

And then that day arrived.

I'd gone to the bank to withdraw the savings I'd made during a five-month tour of duty in Northern Ireland. Intending to buy a car, I couldn't resist a visit to the Rolex shop.

As I gazed at the greatest watch ever made, a surge of adrenalin took control of my legs. Into the ostentatious atmosphere I plunged – much to the disgust of the shop assistant standing behind the jewellery-laden cabinets. I saw her eyes flick over my tracksuit bottoms and training shoes and read a mind that said, 'Look what the cat's dragged in!' and, 'Would the cat mind dragging him out again, please?'

With reluctance and disdain, she showed me the Sea Dweller.

When I went back in a second time, having been outside to think, she got shirty with me. 'But I've *already* shown it to you!'

'Yeah, but I'd like to buy it, please… If that's alright?'

'*Oh!* Why didn't you say? Sit down, *please*. Can I get you a coffee?'

Gung Wan Hong

I RETURNED TO WING WO STREET wearing my new sandals on the commute through the rain. My Next loafers I had tucked away in a nylon briefbag – one I'd bought at a three-day Eric Jansen seminar, the world-famous American personal-development coach, at Earls Court in London. The military paid for 'Break Through the Barriers Inside' as part of my resettlement package.

It was an unbelievable experience, Eric using his larger-than-life persona to impart get-what-you-want-out-of-life skills. He also taught us to walk over red-hot coals to sharpen our decision-making skills.

Waiting for the lift, I watched a Chinese gent tap the UP button rat-a-tat-tat fashion like a game in an amusement arcade – as if this technique would make the ageing tin can arrive sooner – while wondering what Gung Wan Hong and Fang *San* had in store for me.

After wishing *'Jou san'* to the girls in the extravagant foyer, who replied in unison, followed by a fit of giggles, I went through the not-so-auspicious glass-paned door into the office itself. Fang *San's* desk was directly opposite, but he didn't appear willing to greet me.

Instead, Dennis Chang, a young English-born Chinese, pounced, and even at this early stage, something told me this gofer was a creep. He showed me to a desk with an electronic ribbon-fed typewriter and said to sit down and wait.

'Wait for what?'

'Just wait,' he tutted.

So there I sat, unsure why most people had a computer and I had this outmoded machine. I wanted a computer. I had no idea how to use one, but that wasn't the point.

My thumbs twiddled while telephones rang and business deals were conducted in English and Cantonese. I wondered if I should be doing something – sharpening pencils or nipping out to grab the boss a coffee. It didn't feel right. I thought *time* was *money*.

Finally, Fang *San* rustled something into the ear of Chang, who corrupted the Chinese whispers by speaking to a Westerner, who made his way over.

John was a laid-back English chap wearing horn-rimmed glasses, an easy smile and a loose tie. He led me to the boardroom for my induction into the art of selling computer chips.

As we entered the elaborate setting, with its long French-polished table and smoked-glass windows, Adam, an overweight and zitty-faced Brit, joined us. With juvenile pride, he announced he would be co-instructing.

John showed me a motherboard and began explaining the functions of the microchips plugged into it – Dynamic Random-Access Memory (D-RAM) being the company's core business. Holding up a price list for the chips and other hardware, he elucidated on the dealers ringing up to buy them.

Then the meeting took on an informal tone, the guys asking why I'd come to Hong Kong and what I'd done back home.

I had a few questions of my own, John's business card stating: *John Taylor, BSc (Hons), International Sales Manager.*

'John, how did you become international sales manager and what's your degree?'

'I didn't do a degree,' he chuckled, 'and I'm not an international sales manager.' He made eye contact with an amused Adam. 'Up until six months ago, I worked in McDonald's.'

'What's all this stuff on the card, then?' I pressed.

'That's because we design our *own* business cards. And what would you want million-dollar buyers to think? That they're dealing with the *international sales manager* with an elite education *or* an uneducated speccy twat who used to fry Big Macs?'

'But you must have *some* experience…?'

'You don't get it, mate. Fang just wants clients to see a shitload of white faces so it makes Gung Wan Hong look like the biggest cheese trading D-RAM in Asia.'

'Is that the reason for the thirty-eight phone lines? Is that bullshit?'

'*Exactly!* It's why it says on the business card that Gung Wan Hong owns the *whole* of the seventh floor and *three rooms* on the third!'

'Well, shoot me!' I reckoned in my own quest for financial freedom I might be able to employ this art of misrepresentation – although the 'three rooms' thing made Fang *San* sound like a right box of plonkers.

As if reading my mind, John added, 'When you get to know the customers it's possible do a few deals at home… become the middleman. All you need is a phone and a fax.'

The discussion moved onto office anthropology. Fang *San*, the most eccentric personality, had amassed his first million in the seventies by trading in quartz crystal movements, made popular when the digital watch came onto the scene. His business acumen being far more advanced than his dress sense, he'd recognised the niche market for memory chips when the personal computer craze kicked off. These small black chunks of silicon with intricate gold-veined architecture were actually worth their weight in gold, and because electronics giants, like Samsung, purposely restricted production, they traded in the same way gold does. Fang grabbed a massive piece of the pie, multiplying his million several times over.

Fang's struggle to keep hold of his wealth had seen him develop an erratic and egocentric demeanour, in addition to being a paranoid old bastard. He insisted staff be in for work at eight and not leave until seven at night, figuring they couldn't then play the market in their own time.

He was old-school Hong Kong, not a guy to mess with as he despised and distrusted *gweilos*. With our freakish-coloured hair, strange eyes and disgusting habits, he viewed us the way his ancestors did five hundred years before when the first European visitor, Jorge Álvares, dropped anchor here.

Sandra, his wife, was senior manager. Pretty and demure, she was the opposite of her oddball husband, even sitting in a separate office to him… and his nubile assistant. Half Fang's age, she seemed more concubine than consort. You had to wonder if Cupid was tripping on mushrooms when he let loose those arrows.

Dennis Chang was general manager. Despite the privacy of the boardroom, John and Adam spoke in hushed tones, explaining that being English presented Chang with an identity conflict.

Ken Kwok was an affable twenty-four-year-old Canadian. A real workhorse, he constituted the lungs of Fang's operation. Unlike Chang, he dealt with the East-West conundrum without sweat and was always willing to have a laugh with us Brits when he wasn't hammering out lucrative deals to all four corners of the globe.

I began familiarising myself with the literature scattered about the place, such as the *Hong Kong Trade Development Council Catalogue* touting products made by Original Equipment Manufacturers (OEMs) in China. Of particular interest were the fake Rolexes, and laser-pens. I wondered if I could ship a load back to Britain and make a killing.

My attention turned to the faxes John dropped on my desk. He'd explained that after an OEM produces a product – a few hundred thousand musical keyboards, for example – they put the chips, transistors, capacitors and diodes left over up for sale. It seemed a simple job of matching components listed as WANTED with those being OFFERED. But with a TI093457B serving a completely different function to a TI093457C, it was harder than it looked.

Just as I was sorting out the world's electronic needs, the telephone rang. Hesitantly, I picked up the handset. '*Goood* afternoon! Gung Wung, *errh… Wung* Gung, *errm… lucky… golden… very happy* computer company!'

'*Hallo!* Ziss'is Mizsta Bigsta from Taiwan. Can you give me a prize on a mudderboard?' the customer enquired – rather strangely, as the Taiwanese appeared to speak English with a weird Slavic accent.

'*Oh shit! Price on a motherboard!*' I said to myself, cupping a hand over the mouthpiece.

'And, Mizsta *Creese*, what about the prize of furty-four megabyte D-RAM?' the mysterious gent continued… into *both* my ears.

I suddenly realised Mr 'Big Star's' *true* identity, turning to see Adam in fits. 'Just want to keep you on your toes!' he said.

Fang *San* didn't appear to make sales either. Instead, he sauntered around the office, Marlboro smoking away in one hand, can of beer in the other, calling out 'Teeee, coffeeee, whiskeeee, beeaaar, miwlk' whenever a client visited.

Just as I thought things couldn't get any weirder, an old man dressed in traditional Chinese labourer's clothing of coarse black-cloth top, three-quarter length trousers, wide-brimmed straw hat and sandals appeared in the office doorway. Hunched over, he hefted three red-white-and-blue-check nylon-weave holdalls, Fang's staff busying themselves clearing desks and covering them in newspaper.

The old boy opened the bags and began placing stacks of yellow-plastic-plated meals wrapped in tea towels on the *Hong Kong Commercial* and *Sing Pao Daily* tablecloths.

The food came from a backstreet *dai pai dong* kitchen. It was delicious and all paid for by Mr Fang. My favourites were pork strips fried in crispy sugared-batter, shrimp omelette with garlic, and steamed pak choi in oyster sauce. Eating them with chopsticks off a bed of perfectly cooked rice while catching up on the office gossip became a part of the day I looked forward to the most. It certainly catered to the Confucian ethic that workers must respect boss and, in return, boss must provide for all.

This approach didn't work on Ken Kwok, though. He would stuff down Kentucky Fried Chicken, laughing and asking, 'How can you *eat* that shit?'

Adam also bought food out, favouring Délifrance until Mitterrand began blowing up the innocent atolls of the South Pacific with nuclear missiles. Then he decided a boycott was in order.

Later in the day, Andrew McEvoy, a young British backpacker, joined in the microchip mayhem. He was staying in the legendary Chungking Mansions. John and Adam had mentioned this place, saying it was something of a roach palace but popular with shoestring travellers and Hong Kong's émigré community.

'I don't s'pose you're staying in the Bamboo Guesthouse, Andy?'

He shot me a look. 'How did you know *that*?'

'Some woman at the airport!' we choroused, both laughing at the thought of the old gal homing in on every cheap-arsed arrival.

'Yeah, I'm in one of the dormitories.'

'What's that like... sharing a room, I mean?'

'It's fuckin' mad, Chris. There's this one bloke, yeah. 'Ard as nails Essex boy. Only cares about gangstering, drugs, German motors, and birds – in that *fackin'* order. *Know what I mean?*'

I chuckled.

'He's working as a doorman in Tsim Sha Tsui. One night a van pulled up and a gang of triads attacked him with *meat cleavers!*'

'Fuck!'

'Nah!' That ain't all, mate. His face was a right mess, slashed to bits, and his thumb was sliced off when he put his hands up to protect himself. It was hanging down by the side of his *wrist!*'

'Fuuu—!'

'But get this! The geezer was only back working the door *three* days later, like nothing 'ad happened!'

'You're *joking!* Who says British hooligans aren't the best in the world, hey!'

'Yeah, but here's the crazy part. It was a case of mistaken identity!'

'No!'

Andy went on to say he'd been smoking weed with a girl in the backpackers, so I asked if he could get me some.

'Nah, mate, but just go to Chungking. You'll easily get hold of it.'

I returned to Hing Tak to find Vance deep in conversation with two businessmen discussing a joint venture selling electric massage beds from a shopping centre in Tsim Sha Tsui.

'Larry' Kong was the friend Benny discussed the exorcism with. A hearty personality, his existing business was importing gadgets from the mainland.

The second guy didn't look the type to flirt with cute Western appellation, Vance introducing him as Liu *San*. Something told me not to trust him, and I think the feeling was mutual.

Having changed into jeans, T-shirt and sandals, I rushed out for my appointment with Chungking Mansions. But I never made it through the ageing monstrosity's deceptive marble façade, for standing on the escalator out of Tsim Sha Tsui MTR I had a stroke of the most wonderfully timed luck.

I happened to glance down and right there between my feet, pressed into the aluminium footplate, was a brown putty-like lump. Talk about *perfect* timing! I bent down and prized up an eighth of an ounce of squidgy black. Delighted with my find, I continued out of the station, ducking through an iron gateway into the beauty and tranquillity of Kowloon Park.

I found a secluded bench set amongst lush bamboo stands, their black-ringed yellow shoots and drooping lime fingers pure sensory pleasure, combining with a rock-and-water feature and a soft green carpet to create an oasis of calm – a perfect glade in the concrete jungle.

Contented, I sat undisturbed by the rain and the lovebirds strolling by, skinning up using papers brought from England and tobacco from Chinese cigarettes, samples given to Vance on a trip to the Mainland.

Just as my musing turned to Tarzan – whether that's a cool name to call a kid – the dope took effect. Good stuff, it knocked my socks off, so I decided against rolling another and steered my mashed self towards the nearest MTR.

On board the train, I felt as sideways as a Space Invader. My fellow passengers morphed, like some chimeric experiment, from passive commuters conversing in subdued tones into chattering chimpanzees. It was so intriguing, I *couldn't* stop staring. I knew it was the hash talking, that the Planet of the Apes wasn't on the tube route... but I did feel somewhat *alienated* from Hong Kong life for a moment.

Over the next few days after work, I sat on a bench in a quiet side street near Hing Tak and smoked the rest of the gear. When I'd crumbled the last of it into a spliff, I decided a trip to Chungking was on the cards.

I approached a young triad. The Mallen-like streak bleached into his fringe made him stand out amongst Hong Kong's pedestrians, yet his lowly position in the criminal fraternity saw him hawk fake watches on the street. The set of laminated-plastic sheets he held up sandwiched photographs of the imitation timepieces, which jumped out at you alluringly, but to skirt his pitch, I showed him the real McCoy and cut to the chase.

After a suspicious glance up and down the pavement, he hid his brochure under a pile of magazines on a nearby newsstand and beckoned me to follow him into Chungking.

We entered a busy concourse lined with enough Bollywood video rentals to supply entertainment to the whole of the Indian subcontinent – in addition to the mansion's 4,000 inhabitants – passing curry houses, African bistros, sari shops and other outlets catering to the comforts of faraway homes. He took me down a flight of stairs and into a basement office. With the exception of a metal desk and a roller chair, it was empty of furniture.

Sitting in the chair was an older triad with an equally far-out hairdo. Leaning against the walls were several younger accomplices in tracksuit tops and similar punkish quiffs, reminiscent of a scene from *Scarface*, though the characters a mix of *Bugsy Malone*, *Enter the Dragon*, Ziggy Stardust and the sportswear page from a clothing catalogue.

The guy pulled open a drawer stuffed with see-through-plastic bags, some containing fake watches, others *pillow-sized* clumps of weed. 'How mush you wan'?' he asked.

'Enough for a few joints… please,' I replied, feeling a slight stupid.

He cracked a joke with his understudies, who looked at me and laughed – I guess they thought I was a real player – then ripped a few buds from one of the bagged-up bushes, wrapped them in newspaper and thrust the package across the tabletop. I paid a HK$100, bid a communal goodbye and headed for Kowloon Park's shrub solacing hideaway.

A few days later, I wished I'd asked the mobsters for more, my resolution not to smoke in Hong Kong going further towards Fantasy Land. I set out on another pilgrimage to the decadence of Chungking and hung around in the masses milling on the pavement – Indians, Pakistanis, Bangladeshis, Nepalese, Africans, the odd Westerner too.

I threw a nod to a couple of fast-walking hush-talking Nepalis who looked as though they were on a mission of their own. Begrudgingly, I broke a golden rule by giving them HK$100, then watched as they disappeared with a nonchalant wave and a promise to come right back.

A rubbed-shiny railing ran along the pavement to prevent people wandering out of the mansion's deceivingly impressive frontage – a maw of polished marble embossed with gold characters – and into Nathan Road's traffic. Hopping up onto it, I waited in hope.

Next to me, a long-grey-haired-and-bearded dude leant against the railing. He introduced himself as Pepi, a guest in Chungking, and dressed in the sort of white cotton robe you'd expect to see wrapped around Hindu holy men, not a Californian in downtown Hong Kong.

Pepi had turned his back on the American Dream and sold his engineering business to become a Child of the Rainbow – an itinerant hippy clique. Each year, they all met somewhere on the planet for a spiritually enlightening event, the Rainbow Gathering.

'The Rainbow is *not* about drugs,' he said, keen to assure me. 'It's a community where people take their kids to be at one with nature. There are workshops where you can learn meditation and juggling and singing. It's *not* about drugs…

'What are you waiting for, anyway?'

'Oh, *errm*… I'm buying… *drugs*.' Explaining my rendezvous, I felt I was letting this gentle man down.

'*Hmmh?* Them *Nepali* boys…' He frowned. 'You *gotta* watch out for them Nepali boys.'

He knew that ethnic minorities often struggle to survive legitimately in Hong Kong. The labour pool for the most menial of tasks was brimming with both the colonisers and the colonised. And if a hard core of old-school Hong Kongers thought little of us *gweilos*, they disliked the other immigrants even more, particularly black people, who they called *haak gwei*, 'black devils'. It wasn't uncommon to see a local move to the end of the MTR carriage to avoid sitting next to a Westerner, let alone a colourful cousin.

Just as I was about to lose hope, I spotted my Himalayan friends attempting to make a discreet exit, so I caught their attention. The shorter member of the already short two thrust something into my palm, gave me an acknowledging wink, then grabbed his mate's arm and steered him off through the crowd.

Happy I'd got away with breaking one rule and would soon be breaking another, I said goodbye to Pepi, thinking I would take up my spot in the park. '*No!*' he said. 'Come up to my room and smoke that.'

I knew it was a gesture of friendship, because Pepi didn't partake, so I accepted the offer, pleased to have his company for a while longer.

The torture of the lift journey was far superior to the agony spent waiting for it – stopped at every floor by people pushing both buttons in vain, the ascent worsened by Chungking's trademark odour, which increased threefold once the doors closed. Ordinarily, the smell of curry and garlic would have been inviting, but mixed with that of hair ointment, cheap aftershave and body odour, urine, faeces and rotting pest life, it created a miasma of suffocating proportions.

We stepped out of one claustrophobic atmosphere and entered another. Pepi's room had a single bed, a foot of space alongside and an electric fan mounted on the wafer-thin wall – the latter only blowing the stifling air around the tiny digs. His sole luggage was the sackcloth bag he'd been carrying when I met him.

We sat on the bed with its clean yet heavily stained linen and Pepi switched off the blower so I could roll a joint with my recently scored blim. I sparked it up, took a few puffs, but didn't feel the anticipated euphoria sweeping my body.

Pepi took a closer look at the piece of black and raising it to his nose went on to clarify what I'd worked out for myself – that I'd bought ten cents' worth of *incense*… which had started to mask Chungking's pungent whiff with a seductive bouquet of jasmine.

'*Fuck it*, Pepi! I was *dying* for a smoke.' I punched the mattress.

Pepi tilted his head back and chuckled. Then bringing his gracious laughter lines and deep tan closer, he said, 'You know what *this* means?'

'Nope, what does this mean, Pepi?'

'This means we're gonna have to take a trip to *Lamma Island*!'

Lamma Island

I WOKE UP EARLY AND EXCITED the next day, still curious as to what the strange scurrying sounds were coming from the roof space.

I'd heard about this mysterious place, Lamma Island, and Sunday being my only full day off, I finally had the chance to visit.

I was also in anticipation mode because I knew there would be an opportunity to take drugs, a pathway I started to tread – somewhat unsuccessfully – back in my mod days. At thirteen, me and my mate Lucas tried to emulate the Beat Generation's bad habits by smoking anything that might get us high: dried banana skins, tea leaves, oregano, basil. You name it, and if it tastes good in a casserole, we probably tried it.

One time we even gulped down some of his mum's hormone-replacement tablets, thinking because of their shape and colour they might have been purple hearts – luckily we didn't get a buzz off them or I'd be sporting a huge pair of jugs now.

As opposed to Lantau Island, which has prized accommodation, a high-speed catamaran service, costly condominiums and private moorings for the world's most expensive watercraft, Lamma is different.

Together with a sprinkling of locals, it's mainly members of the Hippy Trail, artistic types and other free-spirited *gweilos* who inhabit the tiny island – most working in the city but wanting to withdraw from its chaotic environment and relax during their evenings and weekends.

With its fair share of dope smokers, Lamma has a bad name with the Chinese community, whose cultural identity, I would learn, sees them despise drugs and the people who do them.

I met Pepi by the people-polished railings outside Chungking. We took a Star ferry across to Hong Kong Island and made our way towards the Outlying Islands Terminal. En route, Pepi took it upon himself to show his Passepartout a key trick of the shoestring traveller, pulling a heavily stained McDonald's cup from his bag and going into a franchise to refill the drink he hadn't bought in the first place.

Following our free caffeine fix, we headed for the terminal. In amongst its docks mooring state-of-the-art cruisers ready to whisk passengers across the wave tops to Lantau we spotted our dilapidated barge – one travelling at half the speed of the modern Sea Cats.

This wasn't a problem for Lamma's inhabitants, though, as the subsequent hour-long journey put off any old Tom, Dick and Harriet from moving there, thus sustaining a tightly-knit bohemian community, a retreat for painters, writers, poets and musicians.

We had the choice of two ferries with different ports of call, Pepi opting for a longer chug through the green water of the East Lamma Channel to a picturesque fishing village.

Sok Kwu Wan nestled between verdant-topped cliffs, its bay packed with floating fish farms and brightly painted fishing craft and circuited by equally vivid shack-like restaurants full of day-trippers enjoying five-star seafood platters.

From there we walked two miles across the top of the island, enjoying its heath landscape, unique rock formations and fresh-tasting air, before descending into Yung Shue Wan, the primary port. With its 4,000-strong population, the village's relaxed atmosphere seemed more Mediterranean than South Pacific – especially as the monsoon rain had yet to put in an appearance.

It was a real awakener, like arriving in a non-conformist's paradise. The only exceptions to the ban on motorised transport were the electric carts buzzing around, carrying trade goods and building materials.

Dressed in saris, shorts or sarongs, and flip-flops, the people walked or cycled everywhere, stopping to exchange pleasantries as they moved between the beach, restaurants and bars. The latter, decorated with fluorescent cartoon-style graffiti, created quite a sight. With Bob Marley crooning his philanthropic vibe in the background, it was hedonism at its best.

I saw people disappearing inland towards smart three-storey maisonettes and wondered if they were nipping home for a smoke. As if reading my mind, Pepi invited me up to some friends he knew, saying they worked in construction on the new airport.

We spent a relaxing afternoon on their patio roof. The sun finally dropped below the palette of red and yellow brushstrokes it had painted across the horizon and an orchestra of a billion crickets initiated their rhythmic chorus, simultaneously, from the dense green scrub. While I enjoyed a last reefer with one of the guys, Pepi let out a sigh of utter contentment... *'Boy...* this place is *real* Rainbow...'

During the week, as I struggled to get to grips with the international D-RAM market, a host of *gweilos* turned up for interview. I smiled as I overheard them telling Fang, through his sexy assistant Jenny, all about their 2:1 degrees in completely irrelevant subjects.

When I arrived the next day, a short, stocky chap with curly, fair hair was already at his desk. He stood up immediately and, with an idiotic grin spreading a ridiculous amount of freckles around sky-blue eyes, bounded over like an excited puppy.

'Hi!' he announced – flamboyance at its best and breaking Fang's rule about chitchat in the office. *'I'm* Neil Diamond! *I'm* a paranoid schizophrenic!'

'Pleased to meet you both,' I replied, taking an immediate liking to this chap.

Neil's story was both incredible and bloody hilarious. His condition developed in the 1970s, a time when the medical community had yet to get to grips with the complexity of the illness and the behaviour of those experiencing it and when anti-psychotic drugs were still in their infancy. In those days, plugged into mainstream schooling, you'd likely be lumped into a remedial learning class as opposed to somewhere that met your unique needs – although this wasn't so for Neil, who proudly informed me he had a bachelor's degree in geography and soil science.

Born in Kenya to British parents, Neil's favourite pastime was investigating all things creepy-crawly. With deep sincerity, he told me he enjoyed lifting up rocks to investigate the fragile ecosystems beneath.

While living in the UK he'd been exploring a ditch behind his parents' home. His neighbour approached, accusing Neil of spying on his wife. 'No, Sir! I'm just looking for slugs!' he said – not realising this may have sounded odd, coming from a grown man.

'Don't be daft!' the guy replied. 'I'm calling the police.' As he spoke, the tree branch he was holding to steady himself snapped.

Neil said, matter-of-factly, 'I thought he was going to hit me with it… so I broke his jaw…' as if this was an inevitable course of action.

Not yet diagnosed with schizophrenia, Neil received a conviction for GBH and ended up in Strangeways, in time for the massive riot in 1990 when prisoners set it on fire to protest against the squalid conditions.

He didn't intend to join in the mayhem created by Britain's hardest criminals. When a fellow inmate unlocked Neil's cell, all he wanted to do was find his civilian clothes. 'When I put them on it felt *great*!' said this sweet lad, drawing an inordinate amount of satisfaction from such an insignificant event. After this, he knocked out some ceiling tiles with a broom handle to let out the choking smoke. Another prisoner shouted, '*Good idea,* mate! *Let's get on the roof!*' and the infamous mutiny broadcast on news channels around the world had begun.

The next person awarded the title of director of international sales was Gary King. Short of stature, slight of build and blond-haired, Gary wore silver-framed specs in front of eyes like a cartoon worm. He came from London's East End, and true to his tough upbringing was out to pull the Oriental rug from under the 'plates of meat' of egocentric bigheads like Fang by ripping them off any way he could.

The funniest, most likeable and happy-go-lucky Cockney character you could ever meet, he kicked off our friendship by telling me how, growing up in poverty in Bethnal Green, his dad routinely sent him sneaking into the local coalyard to fill his school bag with fuel for the family's fire. One time the yard's staff rumbled Gary, so he did a runner, leaving his Adidas bag behind on the coal pile. The police arrived at his house to enquire, 'Is this *your* son's bag?'

'*No!*' his father replied.

'How come it's got his *bloody* name in it, then?'

We burst into further hysterics when he said his old man had to lean across the doorway to prevent the coppers seeing the hearth roaring away in the background.

Gary and I soon realised the best way to kill the monotony of the Hong was to go up on the roof and smoke a big fat joint, our lunchtime topic soon turning to the subject of drugs. The mate he lived with on Lamma survived by selling ecstasy tablets smuggled from the UK.

One afternoon, as we chuffed away, watching people on the street below, he asked if I had '…ever tried ice?'

'No, mate, what is it?'

Crystal meth, he explained, was a drug manufactured in underground labs in the Philippines and smuggled into Hong Kong in abundance. It was speed refined to a crystalline form – hence the name. Hong Kong Customs recently intercepted a shipment and tests showed it to be ninety-nine percent pure. Gary said it was the most addictive drug ever produced… *and* it sent people loony tunes.

Another showbiz name joining our expat party was David Niven, whose upbringing and Oxford education led him to speak like his namesake. David was a laid-back, enigmatic character, standing six foot three, with brown curly hair, boyish good looks and steel-blue eyes.

On top of life, he'd spent the last two years travelling around China, teaching, writing magazine articles and incorporating a great sex life along the way by the sound of it.

Then into the fray came Ronald Dennison – or Old Ron, as he would become. He was also English, but unlike the other expats, he came across as a *weird* biscuit.

Late-thirties, Ron was a gangly individual, with black balding hair slicked-back above nervous brown eyes set into the gaunt sockets of an ashen face. He dressed in an expensive pinstriped suit, but it was far too big, flapping around his skinny frame to give the impression of a flimflammer.

Ron took every opportunity to present as Mr Big Shot, saying that running a successful finance company in London had become boring so he'd moved to Hong Kong for a change of scene. 'Why've you taken a job in this circus,' I asked. 'Haven't you got, like… better options?'

'On the contrary,' he replied. 'It's a great opportunity to launch my own venture in the D-RAM market.'

Ron also launched an annoying habit of calling me Marine Boy, when he wasn't busy saying *'Jaldi! Jaldi!'* in a Hindi accent, which I assumed meant 'hurry up'.

So that was our expatriated clique: John, Adam, Andrew, Neil, Gary, David, Ron and me – only Andy announced he couldn't stand the hours and had found himself a job in an advertising company run by a dodgy Londoner in Admiralty District.

It was just as well, as Chang, after a conspiratorial chat with Fang, came to speak to us. With his usual smugness, he said Fang no longer wanted us to focus on sales and from now on we would be writing to potential buyers informing them of Gung Wan Hong's products – leads forwarded by the Trade Development Council.

Our mind-numbing task saw us typing our name and baloney title onto the company's information letter and posting it off. And the way the letter was composed proved a constant source of amusement – in a similar vein to the instructions that come with a product made in China. 'Place with good correct direction 2 x AA batteries in Singing, Dancing, Cuddly Fun Bear… Remember this product is not a toy.'

Well, Fang's literary masterpiece was just as convoluted and full of his cringeworthy ego, but he got upset if anyone dared change it, especially one of us *gweilos*.

Typing one address after another was excruciating – but not for Old Ron, who took it so bloody seriously, hammering at the keys of his typewriter for hours. 'That's thirty-four letters I've sent!' he stated with pride one morning. 'How many have you done, *Marine* Boy… *eh…. eh?*'

'Ron, I'll make it *really* simple for you,' I replied. 'I've done *fuck* all, mate. What do you think you're playin' at, anyway? You ain't gonna get paid more. You're only here for your white face.'

'Yeah, but when Fang sees how hard I work, I'll be promoted. And when I've built a client base, I'll start my own company.'

'Ha! In *Cuckoo* Land, Ron! And stop calling me Marine Boy.'

'No problem, *Marine* Boy.'

Not for the first time, I turned to Gary and we mouthed, *'Wanker!'*

Yet despite his constant harassment, *something* hinted that he did actually like me. I had a sneaking suspicion he might have been a little envious – of what, I wasn't sure.

Both John and Adam left the Hong, landing jobs in similar organisations but with better prospects. John and I would stay in touch and hopefully do some business on the side.

By now the letter writing had turned into a joke. Having mailed out the first hundred, Gary and I turned our attention to far more fulfilling endeavours, such as how many sachets of Nescafé we could drink in a day and jokes about the Fang.

We began to fantasise we were in the classic police series, *Starsky and Hutch* – where two bad boys work out of a crappy office, drink loads of coffee while being shouted at by a stressed-out boss.

It wasn't hard to guess who the irate boss was – the Fangster, as we called him. On TV an over-the-hill and always-angry black dude played his character. Gary would slam a fist down on my desk and shout, 'Can't you *damn* jokers get *anything* right? *Ahh* want diss case *closed! Ahh* got da *DA* on ma *ass!*'

After work, we'd taken to visiting a nearby *dai pai dong*. One evening as we perused the delicious-looking food on offer, two local men invited us to their table. 'Help yourselves!' they said cheerily, indicating with their chopsticks to a veritable banquet. In reciprocation, we bought the beers.

As we were getting to know our hosts, one of them said they were policemen. With pride, he presented me with a business card: *Tseung Lai Kwong, Triad Police.*

I was intrigued, for as a young marine exploring some of the world's dodgier ports of call, I'd suffered the wrath of such criminal organisations myself. Together with seeing newspaper coverage of a recent police raid in which they arrested fifty or so men in a factory then led them in handcuffs to waiting trucks, I couldn't wait to hear the Triad Police's take. These guys took on the Sun Yee On, the 14-K and the Wo Shing Wo – to name a few of the violent clans – and these are not people you mess around with without reprisals.

Dipping chopsticks into the exotic treats, and with the *bair chau* flowing, I asked 'Barry' Tseung Lai Kwong and his partner 'Martin' Chen Lee Wing whether in the course of their work they ever felt scared.

'*Nooo!*' was Martin's reply. 'This our *job!*'

The next day at the Hong, I spotted Old Ron chuckling away behind his crappy typewriter.

'What's up, Ron?' I asked, but he continued to giggle. 'Come on, Ronald!'

'Are you *scaaared?*' he said, pulling a face like a twisted lemon. 'Didn't you see those policemen's faces when you asked that?'

Ron seemed to think it was funny. I'm glad something tickled him.

We only met our police hosts once more. When we did, Martin Chen introduced us to Old Man Lee with an element of grandeur. Dressed in a traditional *changshan* and black skullcap, Old Man Lee was your archetypal Chinese, a man more of thought than words.

Upon hearing Mr Lee was a chemist, I immediately pictured him mixing up a herbal remedy, the knowledge of which long since lost to the West, although looking at his business card, it appeared he worked in a modern pharmacy.

Partway into our meal Martin leant over, asking with measured sincerity, '*Errh,* Quiss'a, Mister Lee wan' to know if he can read your hand?'

'Sure!' I replied, intrigued at having my fortune told and why he'd chosen me out of our group of *gweilos*. 'What has he seen that I need to know?' I wondered.

Old Man Lee knew exactly what he'd seen and I reckon he wanted to use my open hand as a medium to impart this ancient wisdom. Interpreting the old man's, Martin said, '*Errh,* Quiss'a, Mister Lee say you have some difficult year ahead.'

I smiled at this observation plucked from thin air.

'But, Quiss'a, Mister Lee also say don't worry too mush about that, becoss, *errh,* when you are reaching thirty years old, you will be the *happiess* man you know!'

章
九

Ice

I SAW LESS OF VANCE as the weeks flew by. As the loneliness increased, I spent my free time with English friends or on the secluded bench near Hing Tak, smoking weed and getting lost in thought.

Lim, his wife, I hardly saw at all. They weren't getting on too well, which explained why she often stayed at her parents' place. It was a shame as chatting to this dainty creature with her short-cropped hair and delicate bronze skin was always fun.

'Do you have one eyelip or two eyelip?' she asked me once, bringing her face close and staring with intent.

'Eh?'

'*Ah!* You have *two* eyelip!' she said. 'You kno', Chiniss have one or two eyelip. I have two!' As she pulled on her eyelash, it became clear what she meant.

'*Oh!*' It had never occurred to me some people only have one eyelid on each eye.

Despite the pressure, Vance was unrelenting in his quest for financial freedom. He spent his time with Benny Tsang, Larry Kong and Mr Liu, working on their massage bed venture.

Occasionally, when Mr Liu wasn't around, we would play cards and drink Chinese wine. Benny and Larry delighted in teaching me Cantonese, listening intently as I repeated the phrases, laughing when I got them right.

Pok gai, they explained, was something you must never say. It meant 'fuck you', but unlike in the West where you can get away with such expletives, *pok gai* is the highest form of insult. It's fine saying it to yourself – if you'd spilt your coffee, perhaps – but otherwise taboo.

I noticed that not many expats learned the language, most satisfied with being able to say *cheesin gweilo*, 'crazy devil man', in a piss-taking accent.

During one of our card games, Mr Liu arrived, so I retired to my room. I decided to find out what the weird noises were – the ones plaguing my sleep from the roof space. Standing on the army cot, I used a mop handle to knock out one of the polystyrene panels.

'*Urrh!*'

A shower of black pellets rained down. Bloody rat shit! I'd been host to members of the rodent community. They must have infested the place for years as there was a four-inch layer of droppings. 'At least I have an explanation for Benny and Larry's ghosts!' I chuckled.

As I stood there, I heard the scraping of tiny – or not-so-very tiny – feet clawing their way up inside a piece of metal conduit bolted to the wall. Appearing out of the top of the duct and peering with curiosity at me was the head of an enormous rat.

A few minutes later, Vance entered the room, laughing to find me lying in ambush, ready to grab my unwanted guest. Unperturbed, he said he would call the Rat Police and ask them to lay down some poison.

Vance didn't drink often. I think he was a little inebriated from the wine because his mood was melancholic. He began to talk about the business, hinting he was out of pocket and into the last of his savings.

I apologised again. I was well aware the majority of network marketers fail miserably and most companies go the way of the pear. But we'd have succeeded if the product line held up – which it hadn't.

'No problem,' said Vance, then showing a sentimental side I'd not seen before, he said, 'You know, Quiss, I hope that one day we can make our fortune together... an' we can sail our yacht through Hong Kong harbour without a care in the world an' really start to enjoy life.'

'Ah, *Vance! Me too*!' I pictured it in my mind... *cruising through the sound in ocean-going splendour... Vance and I cutting a dash in the cockpit, the epitome of frivolity, our white shirts and slacks immaculate beneath captain's epaulettes and important peaks... Benny in the stern clinking a glass of champers with Lim and my Sarah, the 'spirits' the furthest thing from his mind... and all the time the sun beating down, the sea spraying us with salty confetti...*

'You know, Quiss... you are very special person... I can juss feel it. The way you are with peepall... is *very* special. You know, I *like* the English, but they different to you... I feel you can do *anything*!'

It was a kind thing to say to a lost young man a long way from home.

A fax arrived at Vance's office, sent by a business acquaintance of mine, another Chris, from Plymouth. He wanted me to source redwood furniture, saying his client was interested in buying a container load. Vance arranged a meet with 'Cantu' Lau, an army friend, who owned a workshop in China.

I went off to my Gung Wan Hong duties – or the lack of them – with fingers crossed. Finally, I might do some business in the Pearl of the Orient.

The day began uneventfully for us *gweilos*. A cocktail-in-Kabul's chance of making sales, our security lay in looking the international executive part and sending out the ludicrous letters. Then a bizarre occurrence took place.

Ken Kwok was conducting one of his loud telephone conversations with a client overseas, the type generating up to a million Hong Kong dollars for the company, when Fang *San* flipped his lid. He stormed up to Ken and let rip with a string of abuse, which I'm sure, even from my understanding, contained a liberal sprinkling of *pok gai*.

The office fell into such stunned silence you could have heard a fly cough. Poor Ken just sat there like a rabbit caught in headlights and then, true to the Confucian ethic of employee respects boss, said, '*Hai, Fang San,*' picked up his briefcase and walked out.

'What was that about?' I wondered, slipping over to see 'Peter' Liu, a likeable local lad, with pebbled glasses and a big toothy grin.

Pete said Ken had gone with some of the girls for karaoke the night before, something Fang forbid – going with the girls, that is. Even this fruitcake didn't have a problem with karaoke.

Ken's dismissal demonstrated how deep ethical principles ran in this society. We were stunned Fang could so easily say goodbye to all that cash.

Back behind the desk, I drummed my fingers, wondering how to break up the soul-sucking boredom. I decided a trip to the toilet would add a full-on-and-mental bent to the day… and I wasn't wrong.

Standing at the urinal, I wondered what the unusual smell was coming from the cubicle, turning to see Neil Diamond step out of it.

'*Chris!* Come in here!' he said, his eyes glinting like the Child Catcher in *Chitty Chitty Bang Bang*.

A tad excited, I duly obeyed.

He took a square of folded-up foil from his trouser pocket, smoothed it into a V-shaped chute and asked, 'Have you ever tried *ice*?'

'Nah, mate... heard about it, though.'

Groping in his underpants, he retrieved a small plastic wrap containing a gram of white crystals and then handed me a rolled-up banknote. After sprinkling a few chunks onto his creation, he held it at a tilt and began heating from underneath with a lighter.

'Well, smoke some of this!'

He didn't have to twist my arm – quite the contrary. If this was the drug sending people round the bend, then I wanted in.

As the crystals liquefied and journeyed down the silver chute, vaporising into sweet-tasting wisps, I hoovered them up, making sure not to miss a single molecule, and as Neil carefully tilted the foil the other way, I knew I'd reunited with a long-lost friend... one, funnily enough, with the same name as me.

Sat at my desk for the afternoon, one that for all I cared could go on as long as it wanted, I found it hard to believe I'd walked through a toilet door and come back out to Paradise. I experienced an amazing sense of wellbeing, a real nirvana, as if slowly becoming drunk on fine Champagne but without the clouded thoughts that alcohol induces. It far surpassed any high of the party prescriptions peddled in dance clubs back home. Shivers flowed up and down my spine, nerves tingled all over and supreme confidence and positivity radiated from every cell within.

As the day at the Hong drew to a close, me receiving *nil point* the day's effort, I didn't want the sensation to end. The moment Hong Kong struck 7pm I was out of my seat and on a mission – a trip into Chungking's labyrinth to find Mark.

Mark was a Ghanaian immigrant who scratched a living selling drugs out of the seediest part of the most decrepit tower block. He lived in a tiny room with nicotine-stained paint peeling off its walls and a black-and-white television atop a small chest of drawers in the corner.

I'd met him before when Neil suggested we score some grass. Only, having introduced me, Neil vanished to get his rocks off with the young Indian woman standing all-expectant in her doorway, wearing a filthy nightdress, decayed buckteeth and an obvious need for cash.

On that occasion, as he told me what it was like for a black African with basic education trying to survive in Hong Kong, Mark rolled a huge spliff, took a couple of puffs and passed it to me. As I put it to my lips, he said, 'That was up a Nigerian's arse this morning!' throwing his head back with a '*Heeeeeeeeeeee!*' as I absorbed scenario, weed and God knows what.

Morocco and Egypt being the furthest I'd ventured into Africa, Mark took offence when I asked if there were lions or elephants in Ghana. After apologising, I visited the adjacent bathroom – a filth-emblazoned germ hole with a waterlogged concrete floor, stench, and paint as tarnished as next door. The iron tub had most of its ceramic missing, the glaze left on it discoloured, yellow and brown, by water dripping from a sole working tap and a myriad of other fluids – most of them bodily, by the look of it.

The toilet had seen better days too. With half its rim smashed off, the flush mechanism substituted for a grime-coated bucket and the cistern top missing, it also had its own share of unsaintly blemishes, laid down with such intricacy over the years you could no longer see the white porcelain beneath. It was certainly a contrast to the Peninsula Hotel's gleaming five-star receptacles just across Nathan Road.

On this occasion, with the vestiges of meth still working wonders, I located the squalid corridor and knocked on Mark's door.

Receiving a cautionary challenge of '*Who is it?*' ventured in a way that makes it obvious the enquirer is up to no good, I resisted replying with what I'd heard someone say in Plymouth: '*Open up!* It's the *fucking* police! And you're *all* under arrest for taking *drugs!*' – not that there's anything even remotely similar to Chungking Mansions in my home city. This place must stand as the world's all-time greatest craphouse, minus five stars in *The Least Good Places to Stay Guide*, a real lone wolf, and a rabid flea-bitten canine at that. Instead, I went for the softer option: '*Mark*, it's me, *Chris!*'

Mark sat on his bed with two American lads crammed on plastic chairs beside him. Busy rolling a reefer, they looked to be of high school age. Astute though, they introduced themselves as Brad and Cliff, but seemed the last two people you'd expect to find in this devil-forsaken dump. I guess looking at me suited and booted, they thought the same.

I asked Mark if he had any ice – gutted when this stocky Ghanaian with a Mike Tyson crew cut said he'd just sold his last HK$100 deal.

'*Bollocks!*' I almost shouted my frustration aloud, which rang alarm bells – I wouldn't feel like that in a supermarket if they'd run out of eggs.

'I got some number four?' he said, punting his other wares.

'*Number four…?*'

'*Heroin!*' Brad and Cliff replied, Mark's eyes flicking to the door as he cautioned them to keep it down.

'Have you guys tried it?'

'Oh *yeah*!' they chorused.

'We used to do it all the time, but got bored,' said Brad.

'What's it like?'

'It's alright,' said Cliff. 'But these days we stick to weed or ice.'

'*What!* You guys take ice?' I was amazed at how indifferent these sixteen-year-olds were when it came to dabbling with drugs – ones with a reputation for screwing people right up.

'Yeah,' said Brad. 'It's great for school when you got like assignments to hand in an' you have to stay up all night.'

Cliff passed him some drops, explaining they got rid of bloodshot eyes. An image of these reprobates standing like choirboys in front of their parents came to my mind – deviant little bastards!

'So how do I take this number four, then?' Being a good role model, I thought it only proper to empower the teenagers.

While they explained, Mark set up the tinfoil as Neil had done earlier and then did the tilty-slidy thing. I sucked the smoke deep into my lungs… wondering if this was a Rubicon I should really be crossing.

The Big Apple

TO HEAL THE TEDIUM at Gung Wan Hong, I taught myself more of the language using *The Right Word in Cantonese*, by Kwan Choi Wah, and a small dictionary. I practised my repertoire on the girls in the office, who broke out into giggles, until Sandra Fang sent the flunky Dennis Chang over to tell me to keep it down.

Each night I would arrive at Hing Tak Mansion drinking a coconut milkshake, chosen from the variety of flavours on offer in a nearby shopfront, and ask the small security guard, '*Sik jo faan may'a?* (Eaten rice, not yet?)' – an ancient pleasantry, the back-to-frontness of which not a difficult concept to grasp.

I'd also ask the old boy – not his fellow guard, a middle-aged man with prematurely white hair who I felt didn't like me – if I could get him anything from the 7-Eleven. He'd always grin and reply, '*M'hai, dojeh* (No, thank you very much).' I'd buy him an iced tea all the same, but he always tried to insist I keep it.

Vance knocked on my door to tell me there was a call from 'Miss Sarah' in England. I jumped out of bed, not having slept well anyway, despite my hashish nightcap.

In the night, something jumped on me. You didn't need to be Hercule Poirot to work out what. I'd fumbled for the bedside light to find a rat perched on my knee – obviously the exterminator's poison had no effect on these mega hamsters.

I watched the little blighter for a few seconds then flicked it high into the air, where it executed a magnificent triple salco before landing on the bedside table. Then it sat there, its beady black orbs staring at me.

If I hadn't been so tired, I'd have scored it 9.6 across the board. Instead, I went back to sleep. I didn't mind. Up for the full Hong Kong experience, I'd started to appreciate the patter of tiny feet.

I picked up the receiver and heard Sarah's voice for the first time in ages. It must have been midnight in the UK – maybe she'd had a drink and got a bit sentimental.

Nineteen when we met in Plymouth, we went out for three years. She thought the world of me, and I her, only after a stupid drunken argument I'd let her disappear from my life. Later that evening, I'd found myself asking, 'Just how many people *have* doted on you?' With the exception of my kid brother, Ben, the conclusion I came to was one.

Growing up, my life had been as stable as a stick of gelignite, with countless parental separations, divorces and remarriages, and eleven homes – in addition to life-scarring abuse suffered at one of my five primary schools. I was homeless and wandering the streets at fifteen, having punched my stepfather as he tried to lay his hands on me, moved in with my dad but had to leave when he married a woman with issues of her own. I slept in my car until a friend put me up, and joined the Marines shortly after.

Then along came Sarah, a girl who completely accepted me, even loved me, and I'd let her walk off down Union Street. It wasn't one of my better moves.

I didn't see Sarah for a few years then bumped into her in a pub. After a few seconds, both of us speechless, our relationship took off again, only I left for Hong Kong three weeks later. I said goodbye, thinking I would never see her again.

Yet here she was on the phone, telling me her mum, who worked for British Airways, could get her a standby ticket and she wanted to come and live with me. Things were looking up.

That evening I met Cantu Lau, the furniture guy. He came to Hing Tak with an elderly and unassuming gent he introduced as Mr Chan, saying, 'Mister Chan is the greatest woodcavver in China.'

I thought Cantu was just blowing smoke, but looking at photos of Chan *San's* work – chairs, tables, dining suites, mirror frames, footstools, intricately-carved screens – all fashioned in redwood, it truly was that of master craftsmen.

I sent a set of pictures to Chris in the UK, who faxed back to say his client was putting in an order for a container load and would spend a whole lot more if everything went to plan.

I never heard from him again. I didn't even call his office, knowing it was yet another bitter disappointment.

It was at this point I realised I had a problem. Returning from work, two or three times a week, I couldn't get home on the MTR.

It wasn't that the super-fast shuttle kept breaking down – far from it. I mean *I* couldn't get home. I would board the train at Sheung Wan, change trains at Admiralty for the harbour tunnel to Kowloon, all the time saying, *'Mong Kok! Come on, Chrissy! We're going to Mong Kok!'*

And what would happen? As soon as the train doors opened at Tsim Sha Tsui my feet would walk my body off the train and straight to Chungking Mansions to score a HK$100 bag of ice.

If Ghanaian Mark didn't have any substances for sale, I would knock on the next door and ask a Chinese guy called Alan. Smartly dressed, intelligent and with an excellent grasp of English, he shifted large quantities of number four.

Mark told me he would hear footsteps in the corridor in the early hours as triad foot soldiers arrived with a shipment. Alan would split it into small deals, then rush out and stash it in less than the half an hour it took for the Drug Squad to arrive, should someone notify them.

Unlike Mark, Alan knew to cover his tracks as a middleman. Only two things gave his relationship with heroin away: his girlfriend, who gouged out on the bed all day, hardly able to lift her head and say, *'Urhh?'* when a visitor arrived, and the Nepali boys. I'd heard them hammering on his door, screaming in agonised withdrawal and begging for credit. They shared a single blunt syringe covered in bloody dabs and stored on top of the doorframe in the filthy bathroom. It was a desperate state of affairs. Alan would tell them a firm *'No!'* and to come back when they had money.

If Mark and Alan weren't around, I had a source in a small, tree-lined park in Mong Kok. I'd come across a group of homeless people there trading in counterfeit cigarettes smuggled in from China. I'd begun to buy several packs at a time to knock out to my workmates. Once, while conducting a transaction, I'd asked the rough-sleeping Chinese if he knew where I could buy *houhmah sei*, 'number four'. He wandered over to an associate, returning with an inch of drinking straw that had its ends melted together with a cigarette lighter to seal in the powder. Taking a hundred bucks, he indicated I should stick it in my mouth, so if the cops busted me I could swallow the evidence.

Now, I don't think I'm a stupid guy. I'm just an average guy who does stupid things. I'm smart enough to know the difference between right and wrong, but dense enough to choose the latter – at least that would be the explanation a stack of people not kicked from pillar to post throughout their formative years would queue up to ratify.

'Damn the nature-nurture debate! God makes good 'uns and he makes wrong 'uns, and if that boy would put a little more effort in, he too could become a success – just like me!'

But that's not how it works.

You see, I'd put effort in and got good results. I'd seen a fair bit of the world and had a great time in the Forces. I got to throw myself out of helicopters, helium balloons and C-130s, sometimes into the pitch-black wearing only parachute silk and a kamikaze grin, and I always made sure I was the first man out the door. And despite the way things were going, I'd managed to work my way into the business capital of the world.

Outward confidence and ability, I had plenty of. It was on the inside something was missing, and if I had to proffer my thesis, I'd say it had been that way for a while.

Standing on the platform in Tsim Sha Tsui for the third time in a week, unable to stop myself going to buy meth, I knew I was addicted. Of that, I was never in denial. I didn't bother with phoney resolutions either. Deep inside something told me this was one ride I'd see through to the end.

I opened Mark's door to find two girls in place of Brad and Cliff. The replacements had a lot in common with the replaced, though – same age, same expensive school, same penchant for smoking ice.

But the biggest difference between Brad and Cliff and Cindy and Carrie, other than the obvious gender distinction, was that Cindy and Carrie were *bloody* stunning! These two were a pair of Barbie dolls. And good-looking teenage blondes from private schools, whose parents hold esteemed positions in the territory, smoking drugs with Ghanaian Mark in Chungking's dilapidated rat trap, meant one thing: *BIG FUCKING TROUBLE!*

I gestured for Mark to leave the room and, diplomatically, tried to ask what the fuck he thought he was playing at and did he want to see the inside of a Hong Kong prison. But he refused to listen. It seemed Mark was smitten with the presence of these rich kids in his life and unable to see where it would lead.

I could see it, though. I don't think the writing could be any clearer on Chungking's manky walls. The second a snooping mom got wind of what her little angel was up to shit would fly. With the threat of being sent back to school in the States, these youngsters would grass Mark up quicker than beans.

It was fun talking to the girls, but I could see Mark's agitation increasing, so I stuck the ice down my sock and said goodbye.

Checking around the door – '*Shit!*' – I knew the guy coming out of the lift was a cop. If you wear a polo shirt, jeans, chukka boots and walk as though you have a rolled-up carpet under each arm, it doesn't matter how long you have your hair now you're undercover, you're British Forces.

I only had time to whisper, '*Cops! Fucking cops!*' before the door smashed in and our uninvited incognito-haired fashion victim shouted, '*Hong Kong Police! Stay where you are!*'

The rest of the Drug Squad closed in, as I sat back on the bed thinking, 'Oh dear!' and imagining the consequences of upsetting the CID, Chung King, Corporate America, three consulate generals and a certain head teacher. Hopefully it would be an after-school detention and a hundred lines:

I must not take drugs in shitholes.
I must not take drugs in shitholes.
I must not take drugs in shitholes.
I must not take…

More likely, the detaining would take place in the Hong Kong Hilton – the one with the en-suite bars but no room service.

But just as I was wondering if it's possible to eat yourself, the copper turned and said, 'Were you getting up to go, mate?'

'*Yeah*… I was.'

'Let's have a look in your bag then?' he continued, more sweetness than Sweeney.

'Certainly, *Officer*,' I volunteered, laying on the politeness.

Then, for a reason known only to him, he allowed me to breeze on out. Thankfully, as it all happened so fast, the lift doors were still open. Instead of descending, I went up a floor and made for the back stairway, taking the eight flights four steps at a time, in case it was a trap. Taking a side exit into the back alley, I ran away… *very* fast!

Fortunately, we all got away with it. In a split-second movement, Mark flicked his bag of gear under the blanket. And as luck would have it, the Undercover didn't think to look under the cover, and the girls didn't have anything on them… but there could always be a next time.

Preparing for lift-off back in my little out-quarter, I revelled in the process – rolling the toot, smoothing the silver foil, sprinkling a few tiny translucent chips onto it and smoking them up.

The resultant experience – complete relaxation blended with utter euphoria – was not one to see you sit back and take it easy. It combined with total awareness and control and an immense surge of energy, making you feel razor-sharp and ready to tackle anything. In this hyperactive state, I craved intellectual stimulation – *something to do.*

I discovered 'abilities' I never knew I had or was told I was a failure at in school. I'd while away the night hours teaching myself how to draw Japanese *manga* characters or writing poetry and song lyrics.

One night, in view of the nightmare I felt to be looming on the horizon, I resolved to write a sort of creed, something to keep my aspirations alive, if not my lifestyle on track.

Long, Tall and Sort It
Every now and again comes a time in my life
When decision comes a knocking at the door
When I walk a well-worn path and I come to a fork
I'll take the one less worn, that's for sure
When I talk the talk, I'll walk the walk
Soar like an eagle, won't dive like a hawk
Shortcuts to a high mean a deep-cutting low
High on life's where it's at, that's the way I wanna go
There's always accommodation for all things in moderation
But when you face a liberation of money, health and relations
Then you gotta call time out for some serious consideration
You gotta know when to quit, quit when you know
Coz when you quit knowing, it's a bad way to go
You walked a worn-out path, now you gotta take the heat
End up in the rehab, or roughin' it on the street
And roughin' it on the street, ain't no mean feat
Coz you're gonna have to dance to a whole new beat
So when people all around you are losing their heads
Stay cool, calm, collected, and start using yours instead
Fuel up your body with what you know is right
Train it real good, so you can win the fight
Coz in the ring of life it ain't always so polite
So don't wait for round ten when two is quite alright
Treat brothers and sisters in the way you want them to treat you
They may one day be on a door that you're needin' to go through
Coz I remember this, in everything I do
I only see the sky, not this world as being blue
The world will change in time, believe me it's true
And that's work for someone else, ain't a worry for you
So live your life to the full, and rearrange the rules
Be a shoulder to cry on and a best friend to all
Never be afraid of failure or of taking a fall
Just get yourself back up and get over that wall

For on the other side you will hear success call
It's waiting for you and it's having a ball…

As I finished my *magnum opus*, and with the sunshine pouring into Hing Tak's courtyard and through my tiny frosted window, I knew I'd just written a load of horseshit. I reckon even the rats were splitting their furry sides – or pissing themselves, their favourite pastime. Although there was no denying the message in my lyrics, I wasn't in charge of my life. Who was I trying to kid?

I showered, suited up and left for the MTR, still with a good deal of buzz rushing around my body. At work, I'd swapped desks and pinched Adam's old computer. Screened off from the room by rows of filing cabinets, I opted to spend the day chain-smoking, drinking coffee and playing pinball on my new machine.

More *gweilos* turned up for interview, slipping through Fang's rigorous recruitment process and into their seats the next day.

Pete and Emily Sax, a friendly English couple, had just arrived in Hong Kong from the beaches of Thailand. Pete, a welder back home, loved to smoke weed and soon joined our lunchtime session. Emily and I also had something in common – she'd recently recovered from kidney stones. 'More painful than getting pregnant,' she said.

'Uh?'

'…*Giving* birth, I mean.' She looked away, blushing.

Antoine du Maurier was a young, well-to-do English graduate born to French parents. A touch gangly, with red hair, silver-rimmed glasses and a conk like Concorde, he dropped numerous hints about his heterosexuality, making me wonder if he was gay, shy, or both. Easy to get on with, he told me about this thing called e-mail, saying you could use it to keep in touch people. It sounded *awfully* cutting edge.

A few of us *gweilos* decided on a night out, Old Ron suggesting the Big Apple in Wan Chai. We knew he liked the place as he often arrived at work absolutely mingbats, proudly announcing he'd been in there all night, before savaging his typewriter while under the influence.

One day, he let slip a demon, saying he had to be careful when drunk because he got a bit loose with the old vocabulary. 'I once told a barmaid she looked like my sister… ' His crest rose at the mention of his sister, before falling again. 'Apparently, what I actually said was, "You're a big fat slag."'

'And?'

'She slapped me…'

We'd be keeping an eye on him tonight.

I met up with Ron, Neil and David Niven at Wan Chai MTR Station's northwest exit. As we cut through the heavy traffic on Lockhart Road, the sky opened up and all the rain fell out – most of it on us.

After walking a block to Luard Road, we found ourselves surrounded by multicoloured neon – Joe Bananas, Rick's Café, Club Neptune, Big Apple – and thumping disco sound.

Locals, expats, tourists, sailors, Nepalis, Indians and Filipinas flowed along the pavements, all moving with different gaits and paces and in varying states of inebriation. Some were completely sober – either going to work, coming back from work or having to work later – some were completely pissed and not working very well at all.

At the bottom of the steep staircase into the Big Apple, the large, smiling Chinese door attendant let our party inside for free.

It wasn't a big place. In fact, it was comfortably small. You came through the door onto a dance floor the size of a badminton court, its alcoved walls housing red U-shaped sofas, and tables. The bar area was to the right. Staffed by a couple of Chinese lads, it had space for twenty people. A chest-high drinks table separated the two areas along with the DJ box set against the far wall, which at this time pumped out European dance tunes.

Still early for Wan Chai, many of the discos staying open until ten in the morning – this one twenty-four hours at weekends – the Apple was near empty. It had that pathetic feel a club has when the music blares away redundantly, the staff look bored and the few punters present are hesitant to dance. We bought beers and stood tapping our feet to the beat while regaling one other with anecdotes from our experience at the Hong – mostly at the expense of Fang, his dress sense and behaviour.

I got talking to a fellow dance music fan, an English chap named Tom, who stood chatting to the DJ. A touch chubby, he had unassuming features and wore a miniature red snooker ball on a thong around his neck. 'I'm a DJ too,' he told me. 'I'm in Hong Kong looking for work.'

'Haven't found any, then?' I asked, a little envious of his vocation.

'Nah, all the slots are full. There's plenty in the clubs in China, but you have to sell your soul to work there.'

'Why's that?'

'The Chinese crowd only want to hear tacky dance-pop shit. Jive freakin' Bunny, that sort of thing.'

'Not much of a rave scene then?'

'Nah, mate. Hardcore whisky drinkers.'

'Have you ever tried this drug ice?'

'Only once but it made me feel *weird*. Not my cup of tea at all. It's bad shit, twists people right up.'

'*Hmmh?*' I pondered. He wasn't the first person to warn me of meth's side effects. But it made me feel great and if school kids were taking it to do their homework, it couldn't be that bad.

I told Tom, if things got desperate, there was always a position at Gung Wan Hong. 'Will you have a word with this Fang bloke?' he asked.

'No need, mate,' I assured him. 'If you've got a white face and can count up to ten… not necessarily in the right order, the job's yours.'

I had a chat with the Apple's sole bouncer, Colin – but he soon put me straight. 'I'm not a *doorman*,' he said. 'I'm a *slob*. They just pay me to be a doorman.'

He told me his boss had not long left the Forces, grabbing his attention and introducing me as a former marine.

'I'm Ray,' he said. 'Good to meet you, Chris.' At six foot five, he was something of a giant, although with his short-cropped blond hair, smiling blue eyes and youthful face he wasn't scary like a real giant.

By sheer happenstance, he'd served with the Coldstream Guards, in the patch in Belfast my unit, 42 Commando, had in 1989. As Ray and I cracked on, it felt good to have a thicker-than-water bond with the manager of a popular Hong Kong club.

Unable to tempt the others, I was content to groove away to 'Missing' by Everything But The Girl on my own, pleasantly surprised when a curvaceous Filipina joined me.

With her permanent smile, it was easy to see how much wiggling a slipper meant to Nicole too. From this moment, whenever we met in the Apple her face would light up and we'd get deep down and funky.

Whirling around each other in our theatre of dance, I noticed a Chinese gent, who must have been late seventies, sat at the long drinks table watching us. He stood up smiling and made his way over, gyrating his hips and waving his arms around, while fluttering his fingers like butterflies.

I shook hands with 'Mr Lu', thinking, 'What a player!' It was wonderful to see someone letting it all hang loose, especially at his age.

By midnight, Old Ron was flopping towards pissed. Knowing we had to work in the morning, we called the evening short, but he insisted on staying. I said my goodbyes to Nicole and Lu *San*, Ray, and Colin, the phoney but likeable doorman, shook hands with the DJ, wished the guy at the door '*Jeurk lei ho wun* ('Appoint' you good luck),' and left for home.

The next day at the Hong, as the Big Applers sat nursing hangovers and sorting out jack shit from bugger all, Old Ron arrived – *absolutely slaughtered!* He was at that stage where you've drunk yourself into oblivion but managed to stay awake all night. Then miraculously as the sun rises you start to feel on-top-of-the-world sober... when you're still *really* pissed.

The guy even wore one of those tacky fancy-dress accoutrements – the Chinese skullcap with fake, plaited queue hanging down the back.

Well, Ronald might have been soaked in good spirit, but the Fangster sure as hell wasn't. He stormed up to where Ron sat, telling us how many people he'd upset and took a dive off the deep end.

I'd never seen anything like it. Standing by Old Ron's desk, he screamed like a jet engine (strangely at the Chinese, not at Ron), expelling insults even I could work out: '*Diu lei lo mo!* (Fuck your mother!)' and '*Pok gai, gweilo!*' to name a few.

Bang on cue, Dennis Chang appeared to tell the dumbfounded Ron to take his headwear off – something he'd worked out for himself.

Poor Old Ronster, we'd been getting away with so much shit in this place, but he'd taken it too far. Humiliated and embarrassed, he began to write a formal resignation letter. Having grown fond of Ron and his *jaldi jaldis*, me especially, we tried to persuade him not to until he found another job.

But he typed his letter, placed it on Fang's desk and said to Jenny, 'Tell Mister Fang thank you very much for having me here.'

I don't think the Fangaroo had ever seen a resignation letter. Either he sparked people or they simply buggered off. He sat bewildered, looking at the letter and Old Ron. Then as Ron left, his Gung Wan Hong experience over, Fang got the message and went bally hoo-ha again.

A few days later, I visited Ron in Tsim Sha Tsui in the room he rented from a local woman who lived in the apartment with her two daughters.

Neil Diamond had turned up at Hing Tak, carrying two bags. One, hidden down his pants, was the small Ziploc type and contained half a gram of those highly addictive crystals.

The other, made from khaki fabric, he carried in his hand. It was similar to the bag you took your gym kit to junior school in. Only, Neil's bag didn't have plimsolls in it – nothing remotely close and certainly not a thing you'd give a child… unless you were mental.

'What's in the bag, Neil?'

'Oh, a highly venomous snake,' he replied, as if it's the accepted protocol to bring a poisonous viper into your friend's home. 'I found it on the common.'

'*Neil!* Why the *fuck* are you carrying a *snake* around Hong Kong? Did you bring it on the MTR?'

'Yeah… I brought it on the MTR. *You know?*'

'No, Neil! I *don't* know! Please explain?'

'…I like snakes.' He looked a little hurt.

'Oh… fair one.'

We smoked some ice, chatting away in increasingly excited banter and getting to know one another better.

It was a wee bit unsettling he chose to tuck his trousers into his shin-high Timberlands, like in the military, and that when I asked what he'd been listening to on his Walkman on the way from his parents' house in Pok Fu Lam, he grinned, childlike, and replied, 'Rick Astley!'

When I had probed him on his choices, he got defensive.

'But I *like* Rick Astley!' he said, and went on, rather crossly, to say he didn't need any fashion tips. After all, in 1985, he was the *first* person to wear a trilby in Hong Kong *and* it had a feather stuck in it *and* the angle he wore it made him look *rather* jaunty, and I should have seen the looks he got parading the streets as a leading fashion icon.

'Fashion *victim* more like!' I thought. With his trouser legs inside his boots, you could tell Neil thought he was an urban commando.

He probably did too. I didn't know much about mental illness. I took Neil at face value because he was a mate, good fun and intelligent. No schizoid psycho-nonsense seemed to apply to him.

Ron's landlady let us into the apartment as she was leaving. He was in his room, sitting on a single bed next to an open wardrobe.

A queer fish, you couldn't help but feel for him. He wore a well-worn white T-shirt with 'Budweiser' written across it, the kind of shorts your dad wears at the beach, and traveller-type sandals, their black-felt straps making them look even cheaper than mine. He appeared content to stare at his limited possessions: suit, shirt, tie, shoes, jeans, socks, underwear, towel and washbag.

'Not much stuff you've got, Ron?' I shook him from his muse.

'Oh! Errh… *nope!* I came to Hong Kong with that and I'm leaving with that. I like to travel light.' He looked pleased. 'I'm going on the day of the handover.'

He referred to 1997, when the Chinese would take back control of Hong Kong, a somewhat sad occasion in Britain's colonial history and one many feared would initiate the demise of this prosperous enclave.

'I'm going to swim from Hong Kong to the mainland.'

'Why's that, Ron?' I smiled.

'Symbolic… gesture of defiance.'

'But, Ron, if you swim to the mainland, you'll end up here in Kowloon, and this'll be a part of China too.'

'Oh…'

He hadn't thought of that.

Neil piped up, asking if we wanted anything from the 7-Eleven, before disappearing to buy cigarettes.

Ron looked down and asked, 'What's in the bag, Chris?'

'Oh… just a highly venomous snake, Ron.'

'*Wha!*' came the expected reply, so I told him how Neil and the snake had met, romance blossomed and it ended up in his bedroom.

'Shall we have a look?' I tempted, feeling like a naughty schoolchild.

'Hee-hee!' Ron giggled. 'Let's open it in the bath!'

We laid the bag in the cast-iron tub and used a broom handle to pry apart its neck. No sooner had we done so than a wicked-looking asp shot out, its head moving from side to side as it attempted to squirm up over the side.

'Fuck me, Ron! It's escaping!'

I panicked, imagining having to explain to Neil we'd lost his pet viper and to Ron's landlady that a poisonous reptile was on the loose in her family home. It was a bright yellowy-green one too, with a diamond-shaped head – the kind years of evolution tells you not to play the shit around with.

Old Ron jumped up and down, waving his arms and screaming, *'Don't let it get out!'* as I ran around the bath, knocking it back in with the broom like a contestant on a Japanese game show.

With Ron bravely holding the bag open, I hooked the little devil up and dropped it in, just as its owner returned.

'Everything alright?' Neil asked, as we tried not to smirk.

'Fine, mate,' I replied. 'But I think David Attenborough and I could do with a beer.'

Sarah Comes to Stay

ALBEIT TINGED WITH LONELINESS and a lack of direction, life in Hong Kong continued to be exciting. Even Gung Wan Hong had its moments as the situations I found myself in became increasingly bizarre.

Tom, the DJ, turned up for interview, still wearing the little red snooker ball around his neck. Having his shoes on the right feet and operating his eyelids correctly, he landed the job as I said he would.

He did incredibly well, despite having to listen to Fang *San's* rants, managing forty-five minutes before shouting to everyone in the room, 'How the *fuck* can you work for that *wanker*?' Then he walked out.

I got on well with David Niven – all six foot three inches of his Britishness. Unlike Old Ron, who'd asked, 'Chris, those stories about being in the Marines, they're *not* true, are they?' David was far more secure and found my tales amusing.

Dave bunked in with an old varsity mate who lived in the Mid-Levels, an exclusive retreat set halfway up the Peak, the island's prominent mountain landmark. The striking ice-white condominiums enjoy a magnificent view over the territory, with the business district's Hongkong and Shanghai Banking Corporation Tower and fellow edifices in the foreground.

At night, these mega-structures are lit by spotlights, each with a vibrant colour choice, and huge neon advertising hoardings on their roofs and sides, all of which synch to create the spectacular effect of an iridescent space-age metropolis. Air raid-like searchlights atop the bigger players shoot revolving fingers of light into clouds tinged with yellow and pink, like believers attempting to contact far-distant life.

Over the tops of the buildings, you can watch the iconic green-and-white Star ferries chug across the busy harbour, oblivious to the container ships, junks and hydrofoils running across their snub-nosed bows. In the distance, gigantic cranes offload seaborne goods on Kowloon's cramped waterfront, the towering robots more suited to a futuristic battlefield in a war of machines.

David and I often discussed business. I would tell him some of my ideas, and he would say, '*Bloody ridiculous*, old boy!' like some Second World War Spitfire ace in the pub describing how he'd just stitched up a Messerschmitt.

We got onto the subject of drugs and I mentioned ice. He muttered, '*Bloody druggy!*' under his breath, but I thought I must have misheard.

Then a strange thing occurred.

David and I went for a drink in Wan Chai, ending up at Rick's Café, where we met two of his girlfriends. Dave introduced me to Tara and Chelsea, saying, 'This is my mate Chris. *He's* a drug addict.'

A touch embarrassing. I opted to gloss over the remark, but later I pulled him to one side. 'Dave, why are you saying *shit* like that?'

'It's true, mate,' he replied. 'You are a fucking addict.'

'I'm not!' I lied. '*Everyone's* taking pills and shit back home.'

'*Right*, old boy! Of *course* they are,' he said, with a get-real look.

For the life of me, I don't know why my associates were so freakin' weird. They were nuttier than squirrel shit. Fang was away with the fairies, Ron lived in the clouds and Antoine was always tutting about the amount of non-existent women's underwear lying around his flat.

I think Neil with his travelling menagerie and penchant for feathered hats was the most normal one of the lot – except for me. I had no issues, of course.

As if to prove my point, David asked, 'Have you got any *gear?*'

'*What!*' I couldn't believe it. '*Fuck me!* You do take liberties, Dave.'

'I know. It's just I used to do a bit in my university days.'

'…I've got some heroin.'

His eyes lit up.

'But you'll have to snort it.'

'That's fine.' He shot off to the gents, returning with a cat's got cream – mixed with Grade A opiate – look.

'What are you doing tomorrow?' he asked.

'No plans.'

'Do you fancy going to Lamma Island?'

'Yeah, why not!'

We met up at the ferry pier in Central District. With time to spare, I suggested we sit on a secluded dock that was swaying in the current and bumping against the sea wall so I could skin up a joint.

As I began to roll, so did David, into a conversation his lack of eye contact said was serious. 'Chris... you *know* I'm a bit hard on you... about the *drugs?*'

'Uh-huh.'

'It's because I lost two years of my life to heroin addiction... and I see you going the same way.'

Wow! Dave's chastisements began to make sense.

'I got addicted to the fucking stuff in Thailand. Came home and started dealing coke to traders on the Stock Exchange to support my habit. You should have seen how *desperate* they became, how fucking *unhealthy*. Some of them lost everything—'

'What happened?'

'I got pulled over and the police found gear in the car. Received a suspended sentence and a fucking big wake-up call.'

'How come you still do it?'

'I have a rule. Every few months, I indulge, but not for more than three days – to avoid the cold turkey.'

'And you think I'll go the same way?'

'I don't *think* so, mate. I *know* it. You're just like I was.'

Gary met us at the dock in Yung Shue Wan, leading us along a jungle trail to the three-storey maisonette he shared with a mate.

We spent a sweltering day inside, shirtless and sweating like stokers, smoking joints of hashish and watching a hilarious video compilation Gary's mate sent him from London.

When evening drew in, Damien, Gary's housemate, shoved a hundred ecstasy tablets into his underwear, saying he was off to a dance party on Hong Kong Island to 'knock 'em out.'

I thought 'Better him than me!' as the police had recently arrested a British lad in a nightclub raid for having *one* pill on him. The Chinese judge gave the guy *twelve* years!

I asked Damien if I could get one.

He said, 'Sure,' then tossed me an E and left for the night – or 4,380 nights in Ma Hang Prison if things didn't go to plan.

The rest of us hit one of the bars in Yung Shue Wan's relaxing boulevard. It was full of *gweilos* playing pool with locals to the sound of Goa trance. I broke the disco biscuit in half and shared it with Gary – David happy to stick with beer.

As Gary played killer with some mates, Dave said, 'Chris, tell me more about the Marines. Do you come from a military background?'

'Nah, I joined up for a bet.'

'Really?'

'Yeah. Me best mate's dad was a marine, a Falklands vet. Dan was always saying how the training was the toughest in the world and the blokes all drove Porsches.'

'Did they?'

'Nah.'

'So what happened?'

'We left school with hardly any qualifications. He joined up, then told me I didn't have what it takes.'

'And?'

'I reached for the telephone directory!'

'*Hah!* Bit of angry-young-man syndrome?'

'Yeah, you could say that. I ended up on the Potential Recruits Course at the Commando Training Centre.'

'Pretty fit, then?'

'Not *mega* fit. They're more interested to see if you've got the commando attributes, like cheerfulness under adversity.'

'Sounds like a race for the Pole!'

'Yeah! Means you can be ballbagged and dodgin' hand grenades, but keep a smile on your face and you're doin' alright.'

'So how was it?'

'Hard! Started with an hour-long swim in the pool, then they made us fall backwards off the high-diving board.'

'What if you couldn't do it?'

'You take the *Lympstone Express*.'

'Hah! Pack your bags?'

'And *fuck off*.'

My crappy anecdotes had Dave laughing. The ecstasy kicking in, I was happy to douse him in verbal.

I told him how I'd excelled in the gym tests, my dad having built me a climbing frame and rope swing for my fifth birthday, high as the house.

'You did alright then.' Dave sat back down after a trip to the bar.

'Until the last day, the commando crawl.'

'Crawling on the ground?'

'Along a twenty-five metre rope… stretched between two points ten metres off the ground… to simulate crossing a river. You lay your stomach onto it, pull yourself across and climb down a scramble net.'

'Bloody *Boy's Own*!'

'Cockleshell Heroes, mate!'

'You fell off, I take it?'

'My first attempt went well, but then I showed off by going too fast. Found myself dangling by my arms and embarrassment.'

'Failed?'

'I thought I had. We had this huge black Special Forces corporal in charge. He shouts, "Get him the safety rope!" But I thought, "*Fuck* that!" The scramble net was only a few metres away and—'

'*Only* a few?'

'Big climbing frame?'

'*Ah…!*'

'So I swung back and forward and then flew through the air like a monkey, grabbed the net and climbed down like it was normal.

'Only, this hard-as-nails SBS corporal calls me over. I thought I was done for…

'But instead of my marching orders, he asks, "What's your *name?*"

'"Thrall, Corporal."

'"*Thrall!* Is your family the Flying *Fuckin'* Fandangos?"'

On Saturday, we finished at midday at the Hong and could wear casuals into the office – but not fake Chinese headdresses. I went directly to Kai Tak Airport without stopping off to get changed.

For Sarah's sake, I wished it wasn't raining. Monsoon season had kicked in, soaking you every time you braved the great outdoors.

Most apartments being too small for tumble dryers, clothes hung in the humidity never get a chance to dry, so when people put them on the odour of mouldy dhobi filled the nostrils of all around.

But the rain and resultant whiff weren't the worst obstacles. It was the way locals brandished umbrellas – *bloody* dangerously! Walking at a snail's pace, the second an iota of H_2O fell they'd put them up in unison and swing them around, like Gene Kelly. Then the first gust of wind would blow them all inside out. You'd see loads of them littered along Nathan Road. It was a national disgrace and an umbrella disaster zone.

One time at work, all our pagers went off with the message: TROPICAL CYCLONE WARNING #7 IN EFFECT.

The pager beeped again, warning level eight. In an instant, everyone picked up their bags and shuffled towards the door.

Peter Liu told me a typhoon was on its way and level eight meant leave the workplace immediately. *Result!*

I tried to get home to make sure the rodents were alright, the wind making it a formidable task. Everything not tied down flew past me horizontally, along with the rain. One gust swept me off my feet, dumping my briefbag and self in the nearest puddle.

The Kee Lu On Trading Company obviously skimped on their shop sign, one of the chains snapping as I passed. The board swung down like a homecoming axe, cutting through my shirt and into my shoulder.

The situation was rapidly turning into a Hollywood movie, *The Day the World Blew Away*, forcing me to crash through the doors of the nearest McDonald's, fortunately still open, where I took refuge from storm and nutrition.

Sarah came out of the arrivals tunnel at Kai Tak wearing a smile and the yellow dress I'd bought her. I was a happy man. She'd flown halfway around the world to see me, *and* she was gorgeous.

I booked us into a guesthouse in Tsim Sha Tsui so we could have some privacy away from Vance's colleagues and Filipina friends *and* the roof life, which, having survived the exterminator's visit with only a few MIAs, I wasn't sure how to tell Sarah about.

We spent the afternoon catching up and life felt wonderful. When we'd bumped into each other in Plymouth that time, Sarah had just finished working as a holiday rep in Gran Canaria. Now, she had applied for a job as a flight attendant with British Airways, but didn't rate her chances. I hoped she landed the role, as she'd always dreamed of being the smile in the aisle, but I knew I would miss her if she did.

We met Vance and Lim for an extravagant dinner, which Vance insisted on billing to his credit card, and Sarah began looking for work in the morning.

The Park Hotel was selling off two-year-old beds, and I managed to bag an emperor-sized one for HK$100. I also had a phone line installed, hoping it would prevent Sarah getting homesick.

The following evening, I arrived home to hear she had been to an interview for a position selling water filtration systems in a department store in Causeway Bay.

She'd met Stephan de Fries, the Dutch director, at his Pier 6 office in Sham Shui Po, just north of Mong Kok. He'd advised her against taking the job as it was commission-based and she didn't speak Cantonese. But when she told him her boyfriend worked in a strange computer company, his ears pricked up and he asked to meet me.

I wondered what proposition Stephan de Fries had in store. With D-RAM selling like parachutes on the *Hindenburg*, I had a good idea.

The next Saturday Sarah was out job hunting when David Niven called to ask if I fancied buzzing about Tsim Sha Tsui for the afternoon.

After downing a glass of carrot juice blended with lime, bought from a street-side stall, David said, '*Wah!* You can just *feel* the goodness… Chris, have you got any gear?'

'No, mate, but we can make a trip.' It wasn't a suggestion – more a foregone conclusion and a plan of action rolled into one.

We headed for the little park in Mong Kok where my homeless friends hung out, and once again, I slipped a gram of China white into my gob – this time in the corner of a plastic bag, cut off, twisted and sealed with the heat of a cigarette lighter. I was all for going back to Hing Tak to smoke it right away, but Dave said, '*Bloody hell, mate!* If you're going to take this stuff, then you *have* to *inject* it!'

He insisted we find a chemist willing to sell a pack of one-millilitre syringes to a 'diabetic'. I stood outside the shop, not for the first time wondering what this crazy city had in store for me… and not for a moment considering it might just be the other way around.

Things didn't go smoothly for Sarah in the days that followed, and it wasn't just the furry intruders making her miserable.

For the newcomer, Hong Kong swings one of two ways. Either you fall in love with the vibrant, heaving intensity of the place or you don't. If you arrive in the Fragrant Harbour expecting a glamorous visitor-friendly hotspot like Paris, New York or… Plymouth, it can be quite a culture shock – one harder for women than men. Blokes don't have to deal with a constant barrage of stares, and gropes on the MTR. Some old Indian boy had flashed Sarah a chocolate surprise down by the harbour, and I could tell she didn't like the claustrophobia of Kowloon's crowded streets.

If you're not prepared to negotiate six lanes of traffic, vault over railings, cut through musty alleyways, cram yourself into the MTR carriage and wend your way through the crowds while thinking ten steps ahead, getting from A to B in Kowloon eats up patience and time.

Even the small things – people not standing aside on escalators as you rush for the tube – make life hard in the early days. No one seems aware of what being in a hurry is and your polite *'M'goy!'* can get you strange looks.

Idiosyncrasies aside, Hong Kong is an awesome city. Steeped in ancient culture and underpinned by a psychology different to your own, you have to turn its ways to your advantage – unless you're a high-flying executive living in the Mid-Levels, with Western neighbours, Filipino maid and chauffeur service, venturing to expat bars with expat friends for Western cuisine – or like the American consulate workers, having all your food flown in. It made you wonder if some of these cats ever meet a local during their time here – or see one.

What with getting my journey from Hing Tak over to Hong Kong Island – six stops on the MTR – down to twelve minutes, I thought I was making it work, but not Sarah. After two years in Gran Canaria, it was all so different. By her body language alone, I could tell she hated the place.

I hoped a trip to Lamma would cheer her up, what with the laid-back Spanish isle feel. We had a great day out, despite Hung Shing Yeh Beach's disconcerting shark nets and view of the island's power station.

After a drink and a bite to eat, we took the six o'clock ferry home –only Old Ron was on the boat, pissed as a friar. He opened the conversation with 'Hi, Sarah! You're looking really *fat!*'

'*Fuck off,* Ron!' she replied.

'Ron, you're a fucking knobhead at times!' I told him.

'Fine! I'll throw myself off the back of the ferry, then!'

Watching him disappear aft, I thought, 'This should be interesting,' but it wouldn't have been compensation enough for upsetting Sarah.

To make matters worse, her mother phoned while she was out. Sarah had an interview with British Airways, her mum hesitating before adding, 'Chris, you *do* know this is something she's always wanted?'

I did know, and I could see it was the right timing for Sarah too. My favourite girl wasn't going to last much longer in this place.

Back at Hing Tak, having seen her off at the airport, I sat on the corner of our huge bed, a lone fly on an abandoned sandwich, and as the memory of her face, her smile and her love washed over me, my head dropped into my hands…

Pier 6

LIFE AT THE HONG ALSO TOOK a downturn. As the storm clouds disappeared, so the *gweilos* dripped away – Ron and Sarah gone, and now David Niven. Following a move to Lamma, he'd got back into smoking weed and, feeling it was time to move on, announced he was off to Thailand with HK$2,000 (£200) to 'See what happens.'

Neil Diamond had a simpler exit strategy: he didn't bother getting out of bed for a week. With his usual simplicity, he said, 'It's great not having to come into the office. It's *really* boring.'

Gary left too. On my last visit to Lamma, he told me his Filipina girlfriend was pregnant. They married so the baby could be born in a UK hospital rather than a public Hong Kong one, which, according to Gary, was a much better option.

Antoine du Maurier, whose credentials on the Gung Wan Hong business card were actually genuine, moved to pastures greener *and* the continued task of having to hide all those pairs of pants his constant flow of carnally inclined ladyfriends left in their wake.

That left Pete, Emily and me… until *Kerry* turned up…

I met Stephan de Fries at his Pier 6 office in Sham Shui Po. He was a blond-haired-and-bearded, slightly overweight Dutch man in his late thirties, a sorted guy and the type to make things happen.

'So, Chris, I hear you work for this mysterious Gung Wan Hong. I heard about this place when I arrived in Hong Kong – you know, this advert about *thirty-eight lines*!'

I smiled.

'I even went there for an interview.'

'Hope you didn't fuck it up,' I thought.

'I met this crazy old guy wearing these weird sports clothes.'

We laughed.

He went on to say the D-RAM market was big business and as a sales rep surely I would be in a position to do a few deals, adding I could use his office and the Pier 6 trading name, registered in the Bahamas.

Ding-dong! My bell had rung.

'*Re-marks,* Chris!' said Ken Kwok, talking about central processing units (CPUs), not asking for my opinion.

A Dutch firm had contacted Stephan asking us to quote for three hundred personal computers. A nice little earner, we got Ken on the case right away. 'Re-marking' was a silicon swindle, one used to con half the PC owners in the world. Sitting behind their desks, congratulating themselves on the magnificent Pentium or 486 beast they had at their fingertips, little did they know such accolades didn't even figure in the equation. The dealers in Hong Kong would take a batch of CPUs, grind off the markings then reprint them with the Intel logo and a higher running speed. A 386 became a 486, and so forth. The benefit being – after a 'hotwire' job on the motherboard– the profit increased twenty percent.

Taking Ken's advice, we gained an additional US$45,000 margin. 'Everyone does it, Chris,' he said. 'You *won't* get the deal if you don't.'

The next day at work I looked up to see a beautiful Eurasian girl standing by the photocopier. After sitting a moment, captivated by the lustre of a cherry-brown skin and incredible legs holding up a faded denim miniskirt, I grabbed a piece of paperwork off the desk and made my way over.

'Oh! Jump in front of me,' she offered, in a well-to-do English accent, 'but *why* are you copying the instruction manual for a typewriter?'

'*Errh… you know…* in case of… spillage… *errm… coffee* spillage. You can never be *too* careful. But after you, *please.*'

'Thanks. What's your name?'

'Clit… *errh*, Chris.'

'So which is it, Clit or Chris?'

'It's definitely Chris,' I assured her, hoping I wasn't flushing.

'Well, *Definitely* Chris, I'm *definitely* Kerry!' She thrust out her hand.

'Good to meet you, Kerry,' I replied, with God's honest truth.

Kerry was half-English, half-Indian and lived on the Peak with her parents, her father being a high court judge.

We hit it off immediately, spending a good part of the day pretending to be on the telephone to buyers, yet in reality using the internal call function to talk to one another. Kerry infatuated me. Not in the sense of wanting to stalk her or anything like that – well, not yet – I just longed for her.

She was tall, voluptuous, with a beautifully structured face, green eyes and full lips I wanted to latch onto whenever they were in range. She was adorable and had the personality to match. I'd never felt this way before, only I didn't know how to tell her and reckoned just jumping on her probably wouldn't go down too well.

During our intercom sessions, she began to disclose vignettes of her past love life, going into so much detail it was a lot for a guy to take in. I was like a kid on sports day – I couldn't stop thinking about sacks and hopping.

Without realising it, I no longer thought about Sarah. Knowing she would never return to Hong Kong, my mind blanked her. It had to if I wanted to survive here – which I would. This place was my home and I had a fortune to secure.

As I perused their advert in the *South China Morning Post*, it seemed the LARGE COMPUTER OUTSOURCER: SORCECOMP US LTD weren't short of a buck or two. They sought an assistant operations manager, one with 'a foot in the Hong Kong computer market', to supervise their Asian launch.

I had a foot in the Hong Kong computer market. I had both feet – albeit smelly ones – in the Hong Kong computer market. I might not have sold a single microchip, but I wasn't going to tell their operations manager, William Daily, that at my interview, which took place on a burgundy leather sofa, over a glass of lager, to the sound of a talented piano player in a hotel in Central District.

I hadn't a clue what 'outsourcing' was, so I'd spent the afternoon flicking through the *Asia Computer Monthly* magazines lying around Fang's messy office.

'So what do you know about outsourcing, Chris?' asked William.

'*Well*, Will,' began the Fount of all Bullshit. 'An important part of Sorcecomp's strategy should be to get the *message* across to CEOs that *outsourcing* their *systems, software, networks, troubleshooting* and *advice* to a company like ours makes them *savings* in *time* and *money* and allows them to *focus* on their *core business*.

'I myself feel *extremely* secure in the knowledge that if I do decide to hop on board I'll be at the leading edge of an industry that's fast becoming a global phenomenon, while working for an organisation that's not only a market pioneer, understanding without parallel the needs of its consumers, but one with leading vision that with my input will become the benchmark our competitors aspire to.

'Just take the *North American* market – growing by *four hundred percent per annum*, for crying out loud! According to *Time Magazine*, outsourcing is the *fastest* growth business in *Europe, North America* and *Asia*. We're on to a *real* winner here, Will!'

'*Yes*, Chris! We *are* onto a winner!' said William, leaning towards me and rocking back and forth. 'And you might just be the man we're looking for. Will you be available tomorrow for a telephone interview with one of the managers stateside?'

'Well, I'm a *little* busy with a Dutch export deal. *What* sort of time were you thinking?'

'I can get them to call you at 8pm?'

'*8pm...*' I muttered, opening my briefbag to look in my non-existent diary. 'Yes! 8pm's fine, Will.'

The call came through from Dan Mayher, Sorcecomp's head of US operations, a young-sounding chap with a pleasant Yankee drawl. 'Say, Chris! How ya doin'? I heard you met Will! He's said great things about you!'

'Kind of you to say, Dan, but it's me that should be saying nice things about you. I've been keeping a track of outsourcing's *incredible* success story. It's got an *unbelievably* strong hold in the marketplace. I can't wait to come on board and make sparks fly this end!'

Dan concluded by asking me whether I minded moving to the
States for three months to undergo Sorcecomp's management training
programme. 'Sure!' I replied, after weighing up my other options...
which didn't weigh very much.

The next day Will phoned to say Dan was impressed and they had
narrowed down their choice to me and one other person. He said he
would let me know as soon as they made a decision.

On Saturday, Kerry invited me to her home on the Peak, saying – or
hinting – her parents were out. True to convention, but unable to score
ice, I made the trip to the tree-lined park in the afternoon. I took the
plastic wrap of contraband back to Hing Tak and smoked a load of it
up.

Feeling wildly high, in a sleazy sort of way, I took the MTR to Central,
a short walk from the Peak Tram, then walked through Chater Garden,
taking in its agreeable greenness and groups of Filipinas sat on picnic
blankets enjoying rice, fish and Coca-Cola fixes.

I crossed Queen's Road Central and made my way up Garden Road.
Nearing the Bank of China Tower, I stopped to gaze at the iridescent
display put on by a school of koi carp cruising around, seemingly oblivious
to their man-made pool and urban surrounds.

I passed St John's Cathedral and arrived at the terminus, sitting down
to wait for the funicular railway's quaint scarlet-red carriages.

As it trundled upwards, passing beneath bridges and through a corridor
of banyans and orchids, the whole of the territory came into view. I hoped
Kerry received my pager message and would be at the top to meet me –
which she was, looking as sexy as ever.

On the walk to her home, she pointed to a dilapidated garage, saying
it belonged to her family and sat on the island's most expensive piece of
land.

Obviously, I didn't tell Kerry that less than an hour ago I'd been
absorbing the world's most despised drug into my bloodstream through
the delicate tissues of my lungs. I hoped she wouldn't notice my eyes,
which whenever I took heroin turned from turquoise to a ghostly pale
blue.

She'd already been upset to find out I spent time in the Big Apple. I'd assumed it was criticism because the place had a reputation for being a drug haunt. But we'd got talking about River Phoenix's demise, Kerry saying she was a big fan and that after he'd dropped to the pavement outside the Viper Room in Los Angeles, never to return to this world, she'd locked herself in her room for two days.

Upon arrival at the colonial mansion, she offered me iced tea, gratefully received as I was sweating profusely, and then made an excuse about getting dressed into something more comfortable.

Just as I was thinking, '*Nah*, too much like a line from a film!' she returned, wearing a skimpy nightgown loosely buckled over black lingerie.

If there was ever a hint, this was probably it. If there was ever a guy who couldn't take a hint, that was probably me. I tried to make casual conversation but didn't know where to aim my drug-morphed eyes, which, with a mind of their own, gravitated towards a beautiful pair of tits.

At one point, she interrupted me: '*Oh!*'

'What's up?' I hoped her parents weren't back.

'Would you like to stroke my pussy?'

'*Uh?*' I wondered if it was my birthday.

'Would you like to stroke my pussy...' She indicated towards the window with her gorgeous eyes.

I looked over to see a black-and-white moggy clawing at the pane.

'*Oh...* sure!'

Kerry lifted the sash, and I stood up ready to pet her *pet*. But the cat let out a hissing snarl, leapt from her grasp and shot back through the opening.

'*Oh!*' she said, visibly upset and transfixed by the net curtains settling in the animal's wake. 'He's *never* done that before.'

As blood welled in the claw marks left behind on her previously flawless skin, I felt ashamed. I knew the reason for the creature's behaviour. It was time I left.

Back home, I smoked the rest of the heroin, not bothering to clean the silver foil with an alcohol swab to get rid of any impurities.

When I awoke the next morning, I knew I'd poisoned myself. I had a raging fever and thirst, and worse still my lungs were red raw. I threw on some clothes, staggered to the nearby 7-Eleven to buy five cartons of juice and spent the whole of Sunday in bed recovering.

On the Monday at the Hong, I slumped, suffering, behind my desk. Kerry hadn't arrived, so I paged her, my mood lifting when I read the first part of the message I got back.

MISS KERRY SAYS…

I hit the scroll arrow expecting to see… THANKS FOR SATURDAY. SORRY ABOUT THE CAT!

But the following text was far from fluffy.

…SHE ISN'T COMING BACK TO WORK. SHE IS MOVING TO LONDON. TAKE CARE.

'*No!*' She'd mentioned this, saying something about a job there as a presenter for MTV. I knew she'd had an interview but didn't think she'd be leaving so soon.

As if I wasn't pissed off enough at being a heartbroken emphysemic cat scarer, Dennis Chang asked me to accompany him to the boardroom to greet a customer from Thailand. Trying not to look as awful as I felt, I shook hands with Taksin Chanthachem, a managing director in his forties.

Like most bosses in the D-RAM business, he was friendly, debonair and spoke English well. It made me wonder what went wrong with Fang *San*, the twisted demon, who failed spectacularly on these fronts.

Having taken the order, Chang left the room to go and telephone one of our suppliers. Taksin said he had a while before his plane, so I did what Fang paid me for and rewarded him with some white face-time, dropping the hint I was involved in a company of my own and asking if he had any business to put my way. As I slid a Pier 6 business card discreetly across the table, his eyes lit up. 'Yeah, actually, Chris, there is something.'

In his possession were 400,000 Texas Instruments D-RAM modules damaged during production. Yet, he explained, they were perfectly okay for applications such as game consuls that unlike computers don't require chips with a fully functioning range. According to Taksin, a blueprint indicates the circuitry still functioning so manufacturers can redirect the delicate electrical current in the same way traffic gets rerouted around a closed-off road.

I asked for a buyer's price. He said a dollar US apiece but I would be able to sell them for a lot more. I knew just the person.

Steve Hammond owned a recycling company in the UK, Wrexham Reclamation. He bought outmoded computers from companies that had upgraded, stripping the motherboards of their gold and components for resale. I'd phoned him a few times attempting to shift surplus stock offers. He was a good bloke, sometimes just ringing to see how things were in Hong Kong and the market in general.

As Wrexham was eight hours behind, Steve wouldn't be in the office, so after agreeing a price with Stephan, I faxed the offer at US$6 each.

At just gone 5pm, I answered the phone to find an excited Steve on the line. He'd found a buyer for *all* of the chips *and* they wanted more.

I quickly did the maths: 400,000 chips at US$6 each came to US$2.4 million. Minus the US$400,000 cost would leave us with US$2 million – about £1.2 million, split two ways. 'Yeah, that'll do me!' I thought.

I stopped off at Pier 6 on my way home to let Stephan know Taksin was sending us the blueprints and samples for Steve's buyer.

We both felt a degree of surreal but measured excitement, but locking the door as he left the office, Stephan paused and asked, 'Do you believe this, Chris?'

'I will when the money's in the bank, mate.'

Back at Hing Tak, I realised I'd left my wallet somewhere or had it stolen. Knowing I might have to ask Fang for time off the next day to go to the police station, I asked Vance how I could explain this in Cantonese. With a broad grin, he taught me how to say, 'Mister Fang, sorry my Chinese not speaking well. Last night, one man pick my pocket. Is possible, not possible, I go to the police station?'

I learnt the phrase as best I could, until Vance laughed. 'You are so *smatt*! Sound *juss* like Chiniss!'

Now I felt prepared to meet Fangster in his own tongue for a bit of role-play, but before bed, one last matter needed attention.

For weeks now, I'd had a stabbing pain from an ingrown big toenail, so bad I had a problem sleeping. I pulled the skin back but the nail had burrowed in so deeply that blood began to fill the wound.

Rather than pay for hospital treatment, I took out my Swiss Army knife, sterilised the blade with Calvin Klein's Obsession and began sawing into the side of the nail. It was painful and bloody, but having embarked on the DIY surgery, I had to finish it. After cutting most of the way through, I switched to the small pincers. Gripping the offending appendage firmly, I shut my eyes, counted to three and yanked!

I couldn't believe it! Clenched between the jaws of the tool and dripping in blood was a dagger-shaped talon a *centimetre* in length. I put the *eau de toilette* to further use by spraying into the gash: 'Oooh… *oooh*… ouch… *AAAAHHHHH!*

'Fang San, doym'due, ngohge Jongman m'hai gongduk gai ho'a. Kahm maahn, yat go yan da ho bow'a. Duk'm'duk, ngoh tsut gai, m'goy, heui chaai gun'a?'

Fang looked up from behind his desk, attempting to appear nonchalant, yet as snakelike as ever. '*Hai bin do'a?* (Which police station?)'

I replied, '*Hai Wong Gok* (In Mong Kok).'

Fang couldn't help but flash a look of surprise at Dennis Chang, then nodded and said, '*Hai!*'

I felt chuffed. It was the longest exchange I'd conducted in Cantonese.

Figuring I should check at Pier 6 before going to the cop shop, I searched to no avail but eventually found it on the window ledge in the toilet. My panic over, I didn't give the issue another thought until I arrived at Gung Wan Hong the next morning.

Leaning against my keyboard was an envelope with my name on it. In view of Fang's paranoid nature, I knew what it was immediately – my dismissal notice… signed, not surprisingly, by Dennis Chang.

Fang *San*, the wily old dog, didn't want a *gweilo* in the office who could speak the language – even if it was only the impression I gave – as a Cantonese-speaking devil man might just try to steal his business.

Taksin, true to his word, forwarded the D-RAM samples and blueprints, and we Fedexed them to Steve Hammond.

Steve called to say his client had tested the chips to confirm the internal architecture and he would forward the payment by bank transfer. But as it didn't arrive the next day, or the day after, I gave Wrexham a call.

'Steve, it's Chris.'

'*Hi…* Chris.'

Something had gone wrong.

'Where's the money, mate?'

'You won't believe it, Chris.'

'I probably will, Steve.'

'The deal, it's split the company up. The directors fell out over *your* chips. One wants to buy, but the other doesn't. I'm *really* sorry, Chris.'

I told Steve not to worry about it. I wasn't bothered. We'd have been dumb as bubblegum to assume on a fortune before it was in the bank.

Two minutes later, the telephone rang: it was William Daily. I listened with fingers crossed as he told me Dan Mayher had been impressed with my interview… uncrossing them when he said they'd given the position to the other candidate.

With half a million pounds and an all-expenses-paid trip to the Land of the Brave no longer on the table, I settled for bean-fried sardines and quick noodles and headed for the kitchen to put the kettle on. Only I hesitated, thinking I should call Stephan.

'That's too bad, Chris,' he said, laidback as ever. 'I have other bad news. The Dutch company turned down our offer.'

'*Fuck!* Did you quote for re-marks, Steph?'

'Yes, I quoted for re-marks – like Ken said.'

'*Fuck… !*'

'Yes, *fuck – fuck - fuck*!' He sounded happy. 'Looks like this business is harder than we thought, Chris.'

'Yeah, it does, mate.'

It seemed a good time to swap a ridiculous bean-fish-and-noodle delusion for the reality of some Class A drugs.

Honest John

I TURNED UP AT HONEST JOHN's in Admiralty District off my face on meth. I smoked it the day our deal fell through and the next day as I perused the *South China Morning Post* job sheets. It seemed only logical to continue the drug fest on to the interview itself.

The business's *real* name was The East End Marketing Company. I called it Honest John's as John Bolt, the owner, wasn't *all* that honest.

He was an agreeable guy, though, in his fifties and built like a bear, with slicked-back white hair, a puffy face and a welcoming personality. He was actually from South London, but The South London Marketing Company would sound a bit dodgy to anyone who knows the place.

I got the position despite my body being in overdrive, the rivers of sweat running down my torso hidden by the suit I wore in the thick moist heat. Other than that, after three days without sleep, I felt on top of the game.

The job involved selling space in John's directory, *The Hong Kong Business Advertiser*. An impressive publication, it featured British Airways, AT&T, Jardine Matheson and a host of other enterprises, both large and small.

My task was to telephone companies, make an appointment with their managing director and then sell a space in the book – or renew their existing one. It sounded simple, but it wasn't. This was Hong Kong. If you wanted easy, you had to move to Sweden.

Edward Archibald-Henville, one of my two fellow salesmen, was an imposing yet exceptionally friendly character in his early thirties. A former captain in the Guards, he clad his portly build in an impressive double-breasted suit, red braces and purple tie. He had the same *bloody-hell-old-boy!* attitude as David Niven – *both* David Nivens, I should say.

'Taff' Jones was a dead nice chap from the Valleys. The same age as Edward, he was the opposite in manner, appearance and vernacular. In Caerphilly, he'd been a second-hand car salesman. With his simple black suit, gelled-back hair and gift of the gab, it was easy to imagine. He didn't suffer fools, which meant he was perfectly suited to this job.

As the FNG, I would be following up on all of the 'shit' leads – managing directors who refused to meet our sales reps, secretaries who proved difficult to get past on the phone, and firms that couldn't care less if all the staff at The East End Marketing Company died in a freak yachting accident as they were sick to death of being plagued by us.

What Ed and Taff said next blew my naïve mind apart. We were supposed to tell prospective clients, 'Not only does our publication get sent to all the businesses it features, but copies go to all the libraries, bookshops and newsstands in Hong Kong'. But it was a total fabrication. John only printed twenty copies and they were to decorate the office's shelves in case a client visited. Stranger still, he placed half the adverts himself.

'Uh?'

'It's like this,' said Edward. 'If we approach a company and they don't want an advert, John designs and prints them one anyway.'

'And the benefit?' I asked, baffled as a dog with an option.

'The benefit,' Taff cut in, 'is you approach 'em the next year and say, "You advertised with us last year, so how about renewin' your subscription?"'

'And do they *fall* for that?'

'I'm yet to meet one who didn't,' said Ed.

'Insist on meetin' the managin' director,' said Taff. '*They're* 'oldin' the purse strings. Don't waste time meetin' fuckin' minions.'

'And the beauty,' said Ed, 'is that managing directors are so busy they haven't got a clue if they've done business with us or not.'

'So how do you set up the meeting?' I asked, having had no luck.

'Easy,' said Ed. 'Phone up like you're an old school tie. Just sound confident and to the point.'

'What if the director refuses to sign the contract?'

'If they don't sign it,' Taff jumped in, 'I push the bloody pen into their 'and an' tell 'em to sign the fuckin' thing and stop wastin' my time coz I'm a fuckin' busy man!'

As John dropped a folder full of leads onto my desk, it all seemed straightforward, and despite coming down off the ice, I began to follow up. It was a lot harder than Ed and Taff made out, though, the secretaries knocking me back like Wimbledon champions every time. In the end, I resorted to lying my arse off.

'Oh *hi*, Jane!' my infiltration into British Telecom began. 'It's Chris here. Is the old boy around?'

'Simon's in, Chris, but does he *know* you?' his secretary replied.

'Yah, from the tennis club.'

'Oh, I'm sorry. I'll put you straight through.'

It had worked!

'Hi, Chris. *Simon*. Did you say the tennis club? It's just I stopped going there three years ago.'

'No, sorry, Simon, your secretary must have misheard. It's Chris *frrrom…* the *Hennessy* Hub. We're the advertising bods you ran with last year. You asked me to give you a buzz when it came to renewal.'

'Oh, *right*,' he replied. 'I've got a slot this morning. Eleven forty-five?'

'*Perfect!* I'll see you then, Simon.'

'Blimey, this is as easy as stealing biscuits!' I congratulated myself, chucking one of Honest John's glitzy sample publications into the fake Samsonite case I'd bought in the Wan Chai street market.

I took the MTR to Central, found Pacific Place and made my way to the mirrored skyscraper's thirteenth floor.

'*Hi*, Jane!' I smiled like a vicar at a garden party. 'Chris Thrall.'

'Simon's expecting you, Chris. This way.'

I followed her into an extravagant office to see my old chum 'Simon' at his desk. It felt like a scene from *Dallas*, as if I were Cliff Barnes paying a visit to Ewing Oil to see JR.

But I had to keep it real. Unlike poor old Clifford Barnes, I was the boss in this situation and the MD of BT was about to witness a corporate takeover and not even realise it.

'Simon! Long time no see, old chap. *Bloody* good view you've got here! Anyway, If I can just get your scrawl...' I pushed the contract across his desk.

'*Yah*... sure, but did you run this by Marketing?'

'*Marketing?* You mean... *J*... *J*... John—'

'*Keith!*'

'Keith, *of course!* I'm mixing him up with John at BA. They've gone for a full-page whizz-up. Damn happy they are too!'

'Oh! British Airways run with you guys, do they? *Bloody* good-oh!'

'They certainly do!' I whipped out the directory. 'They're right... *here!*' I showed him BA's glossy advert – one Honest John likely glossed over telling said airline about.

'Good stuff!' he said, so bamboozled he neglected to ask the obvious question: 'Which advert is ours?'

I was bloody glad too. All I needed was for him to summon 'Keith', who would soon realise that they'd never done business with us before.

Simon started to peruse the small print on the paperwork. So as gingerly as a tomcat sneaking up on his dinner, I took my pen and slipped it *slowwwly* into his hand. But as he was about to sign, he looked up.

'*Errh*... I thought you were from the Hennessy Hub?'

'*Yeaah*... '

'This contract is from The East End Marketing Company?'

'*Oh,* you know these *bloody* offshore accounts, Simon!'

'*Right! Gotcha!*' he replied, and made his mark.

It was time to say goodbye, bug out of Pacific Place and report to mission control.

I came through the door to find John, Ed and Taff hunched over a backgammon board. They looked up, welcoming me with a chorus of 'Whey-hey-hey!'

'How did you get on, old boy?' asked Ed.

'In the bag, mate,' preened ugly duckling turned mega-swan.

'Got any more lined up?' asked Taff.

'Yeah, I've got this Rainbow Publishing deal over in Causeway Bay.' I felt confident I was on for another hit.

'Well, go for it, mate,' said John, looking slightly surprised. These crappy leads were a tough old proving ground, one sorting out the liars from the other liars.

Leaving for my next engagement, I put on my best Captain Oates' impersonation, announcing with grave sincerity, 'Gentlemen, I'm going *outside*. I may be *some* time. *Errm*, see if you can get a good price for my skis, chaps, will you?'

Robin Swift was as unremarkable as the building he worked in, with none of the pretentiousness sometimes associated with the expat middle class. He listened to my cock-and-bull story, glanced at the glossy and said, 'Chris, that's not a Rainbow Publishing advert. We design them ourselves. Wait while I fetch last year's invoices.'

'Sure, Robin.'

As he walked off up a flight of stairs, I turned and fled, feeling wretched I'd lied to this humble man. Ignoring the lift, I took the stairs six at a time and then concealed myself in Causeway Bay's heaving masses.

It was late afternoon, so I took the MTR to Mong Kok, stopping at Hing Tak for a change into sports clothes and a brief chat with Vance. Then I left for a nearby weights gym.

Just as I was warming up, a tall, well-muscled black dude came over, introducing himself as Wilton in a South London accent. 'Mate, can you spot for us?' he asked.

'No problem, bud,' I replied, happy to meet a fellow Brit.

Wilton told me he'd given up his valeting business back in the Smoke to come out here for a change of scenery.

'What do you do for work, Wilt?'

'Doorman, mate. Joe's.'

'Joe's…?'

'Joe Bananas… *Wan Chai*.'

A plan formed. 'Are there any—'

An unexpected hush descended. Pumps and grunts ceased, weights lowered, machines fell silent. The Chinese bodybuilders stood like Easter Island statues staring across the sea to a far rising sun – only the star spellbinding these monoliths was on the gym's huge TV screen.

'Bruce Lee,' Wilton explained. 'They fuckin' love the guy 'ere.'

Never a truer statement, I sensed the pride these musclemen felt as their hero dispatched a disproportionate amount of bad guys – though with loyalty to triad societies asserted in Indian-inked dragons sprawling across torsos, these *were* the bad guys.

As the legend that is Bruce exercised the knowledge of the ancients with ease and perfection, I felt pangs of gratification myself. The gym's cross-cultural environment offered a sense of belonging, our subscription a metaphor for membership of the warrior tradition.

The clip ended and everyone resumed their workouts.

'Wilt, out of interest, are there any jobs going on the door?'

'Geordie's lookin' for people all the time, mate.'

I had an idea. I'd given my situation considerable thought.

I no longer wanted to lie my soul away and do deals with my conscience. Neither did I want to see my youth slipping away in a suit. I'd come to Hong Kong to make my fortune, and that spark still smouldered, but I was disillusioned with the business world. It was time to revert to what I knew best without rejoining the military.

Joe Bananas

I THUMBED THROUGH THE DIRECTORY and found Joe Bananas' number.

I didn't know much about the place – just that it was across from the Big Apple on Luard Road and a popular *gweilo* hangout. According to Wilton, it was under Scottish management, Geordie having worked his way up from doorman to become the only English one.

'Geordie, my name's Chris. Wilton said you're looking for security.'

'Awwh yeeah, meete, can ya pop doon tannite for'an intaview like, coz we're gettin' kind'a desprat, ya'knah? Have ya any experience, like?'

'Marines, mate. Seven years.'

'*Awwh.* Greet, man! I'll see yaz later, Chris, yeah?'

'Look forward to it, mate.'

I paged Neil and Old Ron, telling them about my interview and suggesting we meet in the Apple beforehand. They both beeped back in agreement.

Having descended into the depths, I bought a Corona at the bar and made my way to the rear of the club. Ron was sitting in an alcove, with Ghanaian Mark, drumming out a rhythm on the tabletop in time with the music.

'I used to be in a band, you know!' said Ron, half-cut, hyperactive and proud. 'Got to number seventy-two in the charts!'

'Fuck me!' A dark horse was Ron. 'What was your band called, mate?'

'Shambolic Scram! We only had one hit: "Don't Punch the Nun". I was the drummer!'

'You were the *drummer*, were you? I'd never have guessed, Ron! I thought by the way you're spanking the arse off that table like a Zulu on speed, you might have been lead vocals.'

'Nah, mate… drummer.'

I turned to Mark. 'How's the American kids?'

'My *friends* are fine,' he muttered.

'Still closer than your enemies,' I thought, but didn't say anything. 'Where's Neil?'

Ron laughed.

'What's funny?'

'*Heeeeeeeeeeh!*' Whatever it was sparked Mark's sub-Saharan shrill.

'*Neil's* what's funny, mate,' said Ron. 'Since he heard you go to the gym *and* are going for a door job, he wants to bulk himself up. He's gone to 7-Eleven to get more noodles!'

Now we all chuckled. It was typical of Neil's quirky personality to try to emulate what he aspired to in others, but God knows how he could eat anything with all the ice he smoked. Just as we stopped giggling, he appeared.

'Enjoy your noodles, mate?' I asked, as we suppressed smirks.

'*Oh!* I finished those ages ago. I've just been over to Joe Bananas to see if I could get the job you're going for.'

'*What…!*'

'Yeah, I went over, met this guy Geordie.'

'What did he say?' I tried not to flip chips.

'He said he had another guy to interview.'

'And…?'

'I told him that was my mate, Chris, and you weren't any bigger than me.'

'Neil, you're a *fucking* idiot, mate!' I said, not understanding his schizophrenia.

'Why should *you* get the job? You're no bigger than me!'

'Door work ain't about how *big* you are, Neil! It's about sortin' out disputes and making people welcome. Don't you think it's a bit rude, going for my job?'

'That's why I went first, to get it before you!' His smug grin told me he didn't get the point.

'Thanks for that, mate,' I said, getting up to leave.

I walked up Joe Bananas' marble steps and through smoked-glass doors with long bronze handles.

Ostentatious would be the word when describing the mass of mahogany-varnished pine and brass fixings – not to mention the American theme with its ye-olde advertising signs heralding the virtues of drinking Kentucky Bourbon and informing errant niblings that *UNCLE SAM NEEDS YOU!* And this was in addition to Old Glory hanging patriotically above the shelves of spirit.

The notice at the entrance – NO CAPS, NO SHORTS, NO SANDALS, NO SLEEVELESS, NO SERVICE PERSONNEL, NO DRUGS, NO FUR! – said it all, setting out the divide you needed to at least aspire to cross if you wanted to breathe this club's pretentious atmosphere.

I took a quick look around, noting garish photographs of Anglo-American favourites adorning plastic menus in the dining area, like the franchised pubs back home, then went up to the bar to ask for Geordie, who was as genuine in person as he sounded on the phone.

'So ya knah Wilt'n and yooz were in tha Mareens – good stuff, that is, like! Can ya start t'mara nite, like?'

Back in the Apple, I told the guys my good fortune.

'Oh, *bloody* hell! That's not fair!' said Neil, looking thoroughly unhappy, his demeanour switching like a five-year-old's to ask, 'Do you want a line of ice?'

Greatly appreciated, I snorted it off the table through a HK$100 note. It didn't half sting the sensitive tissue in my nose, but absorbing meth this way sent it directly to the brain. Plus, you didn't draw attention to yourself by smoking out toilet cubicles.

Within ten seconds, I was flying to the edge of the envelope. Mark, Neil and I got up to boogie, but Old Ron stayed seated, drumming on the table. 'An old back injury,' he explained.

After shaking our hooves for a minute or so, I was pleasantly surprised when a beautiful Thai girl cut across the dance floor.

You couldn't help notice her. A fantastic dancer, she wore a diamond-white miniskirt and crop-top, fingerless gloves and Yoko Ono wrap-arounds, all of which tripped fantastic in the club's ultraviolet light. She looked as though she was out to grab people's attention – she had. With so many goggle-eyed blokes in the place, it looked like an episode of *The Simpsons*. She was gorgeous *and* for some crazy misguided reason she wanted to dance with me.

Just as we were getting into the swing, I felt a tap on my shoulder. It was an English guy dressed in jeans and tracksuit top, both dirty and dated. He grabbed my shirt, then just stood there staring, menacingly, swaying back and forth and not saying a word. He didn't need to. The look in his eye said it all – 'Wan Chai Headbanger' – a cocktail of too much drugs and alcohol.

I stared through his worse-for-wear pupils, my meth-cranked eyes burning into the back of his skull.

'Would you take your hand off me, please, mate?'

'Or *what?*'

'Or, you don't want to find out *what*,' I told him, placid as an aunt.

I didn't want trouble, but I wasn't about to be intimidated either.

Fortunately, Mark walked over with his boxer-like bulk, curtailing the young thruster's ambition. He let go of my shirt, backed away with his eyes fixed on mine, then turned and walked over to his mates.

'Some guy here real asshole!' said my dancing partner, before joining her friends.

Mine got up to leave, so I thought it best to go with them.

I went over to my angry acquaintance and put forward the hand of friendship. 'See ya later, mate.'

'Ah… Sorry 'bout that earlier… I done *too* mush… *Know* what I mean?' His eyes flicked to Mark, as his buddies began proffering apologies on his behalf.

'No worries, bud. Look after yourself, yeah?'

Heading for the stairs, it struck me I didn't get the girl's name. I crossed back over the dance floor.

'Dream!' she replied, her accent a delight.

I thought, 'Yeah… of course!'

Mark got off the MTR at Tsim Sha Tsui, but Old Ron and Neil came back to mine. I wasn't upset with Neil over the interview fiasco. He just had no decorum to the point where you felt protective towards him, rather than angry.

We smoked the rest of his ice and chatted until the early hours, Ron giving us all this spiel about how he cut a mean groove and had wanted to join us on the dance floor, but following a car accident his injuries denied such pleasures.

'Yeah, right,' I thought, wondering if he genuinely believed people fell for such monkey bollocks.

With the time approaching 6am, Neil left for home, and as I had to go into work later to let Honest John know I was leaving the company, I told Ron to let himself out when he felt like it, then went to lie down. I wouldn't get any proper sleep, but I knew from experience it's a good idea to compose yourself before facing the music.

Lying there, heart pounding, it occurred to me Old Ron hadn't mentioned his landlady, her kids or anything to do with his lodgings for some days now. Worrying still, he hadn't shaved, his clothes were crumpled and there was a forlorn look in his bloodshot eyes.

When I lifted my head at 8.45, he was spark out on the floor, using his briefbag as a pillow. I felt hesitant to let him stay as I could imagine how Vance would feel if this alcohol-breathing eccentric engaged him in conversation.

When Ron was drunk, he assumed everyone else was on the same trip: the love boat to Goodtime City. He was also culturally inept, and it wasn't just the way he'd come into work wearing a stupid hat that proved he knew diddly-squat about Chinese etiquette. He thought it hilarious to know only two words of Cantonese – *cheesin gweilo*, 'crazy devil man' – and spout them to every Chinese person he met.

'Ron, you alright?' I gave him a prod.

'…Hurhh… Sorry, I crashed out there a while.' He began to get organised.

'No worries. You're always welcome to stay, but it's a good idea to give Vance some space in the morning.'

'…Of course, mate.'

I felt bad for him. Despite his idiosyncrasies, we'd grown close. I hadn't realised how much until now. Underneath the charade, he was a lovely person.

'Ron, mate…' I tried to be tactful. 'Is everything alright… like at home?'

'*Why* do you ask?'

'Well, don't take this the wrong way, but you look like you've had a fight with a hedge.'

'Yeah, I slept in a hedge yesterday… and a park the night before. It's not as bad as you'd think.'

'You serious, mate?' I asked, but I knew he was. He might tell the odd fib, but he wasn't one for leg pulling.

'After Gung Wan Hong, I couldn't get another job and had to leave the flat. My landlady's keeping hold of my stuff for the time being.'

He neglected to mention the small fortune he must have spent on booze.

It was a beautiful Saturday morning in Hong Kong. I walked along Tamar Street still buzzing on the ice, and with the sun on my face, it felt good to be alive.

Honest John's office door was ajar. I pushed it open to see him sat behind his computer. 'Alright, John. Okay to have a quick word?'

'*Sure*, mate. What's up?'

I didn't tell him everything – just that I needed to move on and wanted to thank him for all he, Ed and Taff had done for me.

John was fine about it and kind enough to pay me the HK$3,000 I'd made for the company, instead of just commission. He said although I'd only been there a few days, he was sad to see me go.

I took the MTR to Wan Chai to go to the street market, looking for a young triad I knew who fly-pitched knocked-off Marlboro. I'd come across him one day, pockets bulging, standing between a stall selling every kind of holdall imaginable and another, Chinese and Western cleaning products.

Having located the cigarette seller, I asked for '*Saam bow Manbolo, m'goy?*' but just as he handed me my three packs, two policemen appeared out of nowhere and began to patrol towards our black market transaction.

Instinctively, we peeled away. I shoved the unpaid-for smokes into the pockets of my jeans and pretended to peruse cleaning products, while he chatted to the women selling bags. When the coppers passed, we reunited and I gave him the cash.

It felt good to have the trust of a member of the Hong Kong underworld – even if it was only to buy ciggies.

After browsing a few clothes stalls, I found a black bomber jacket. I already had trousers and a couple of white shirts, and Wilton was lending me his spare dicky bow.

Making my way through the bustling market, I saw a crowd gathering around an old man. My curiosity kicking in, I eased to the front of the commotion. The little chap perched on one of five round cages that had 'things' writhing inside, whacking the steel mesh with a cane held in a thickly gloved hand while yammering in Cantonese.

I couldn't understand what was going on, until he threw open a latched door and pulled out the fattest and ugliest snake you ever did see. It was a drab greeny-brown and had an ugly toadish look. Grasped behind its head and held high, it looked a real brute.

I asked a fellow spectator what the old boy was telling us. It sounded as if he was giving the beast a real mouthful.

'*Errh*, the man say this *Fife-step* Snekk. If this snekk bite to you, you don' tekk more than *fife step* before you are dead!'

'Wonderful!' I replied, making a mental note only to take four steps if one of these bastards bit me.

The old boy took out a knife and with deft flicks began to gut all sorts of weird shit – kidneys, liver, heart, lungs – from the extended bowel of this highly dangerous yet unfortunate serpent while it was *still* alive!

'Wriggled in the wrong place at the wrong time,' I mused.

Having finished off this particular viper, thus preventing it giving anyone the five-step treatment again, the Snake Man opened another basket and pulled out a smaller yellowy-brown snake. He continued to rabbit away, stroking the little critter as he did. Then without warning, he thrust it at the only *gweilo* in the crowd.

Well, I wasn't having that! I grabbed the blighter the way handlers do on wildlife programmes, and as the crowd cheered, my translator leant over and said, 'Don' worry! This one *hamless*. Juss like to be stroke!'

'Who doesn't like that?' I thought.

Returning to Hing Tak, I smoked some ice picked up from Mark's, then changed into my bouncer's uniform, shoved some coins into my pocket and took a minibus over to the island. Meeting Wan Chai's big sounds and blinking brilliance seemed different to being here on a night out. As a doorman, I felt a sense of pride at being a cog in all the madness.

I walked up the steps to Joe's and met Wilton. He pulled the spare bow tie out of his pocket and said, 'Go and say hi to Sean, otherwise he'll think you're late.'

I probably was a couple of minutes late. 'But so what?' I thought, figuring this wasn't the military and the club was near empty.

'Hi, Sean,' I said to the Scot. 'I'm Chris, the new doorman.'

'You're suppose'ta be here at eight o'clock,' the little Hitler replied.

'Sorry, I was talking to Wilton.'

'Well, you should'ae come and reported to me first!'

'Sure, sorry,' I said, thinking, '*Shit*! Civilian life's stricter than the Forces!'

Even in the Marines, you can get away with being a little 'adrift' – not that you'd do that to your buddy standing guard in the Arctic Circle – but this jumped-up peon of a manager was hauling me over the coals for being two minutes late for work in his crappy theme pub. What a *wanker*!

It reminded me of my favourite Rambo film, *First Blood*, when the vagrant veteran, having reduced the Sheriff's Department *and* the National Guard to a bloody, screaming and pathetic mess, finally throws his teddy out of the pram for real and starts bawling about civilian life being nothing, that in the field there was a code of honour, that in the military he could fly gunships, but in civilian life '*...can't hold down a job PARKING CARS!*'

Not that I ever wiped out the local law enforcement agency or could pilot helicopters or had received a Purple Heart – other than the hormone tablet my mate had given me out of his mum's medicine cabinet to try and get high on that time. But my brother had owned a big survival knife as a kid, so I did feel Rambo and I probably had quite a bit in common.

Wan Chai's 'Crazy' Ones

BRIGHT LIGHTS BIG CITY and here was Wan Chai right in the centre. And bang smack in the heart of Wan Chai's intensity was I, and loving every second. What with the fluorescent eye-bombardment, the vibrant street scene and the soul-tuning beats wafting out of the clubs – not to mention the comfort of an unforbidding evening – it felt *exactly* the place to be, particularly working on the door of the most successful club in town.

At just gone 8pm, Joe Bananas received a trickle of punters – the odd tourists, and *gweilo* office workers still in business attire. Later on, however, with bloodshot eyes, shirts hanging out, ties half-mast and make-up not in the same place it was applied, this crew would present somewhat differently than they did to Mr Yakamoto from Tokyo earlier in the day.

Stood at the door tapping my foot to the disco funk, feeling agreeably high, I spotted my first challenge walking three abreast, over six feet tall, down Luard Road towards me.

'Man, you're a *fuckin'* racist!' said the biggest of the massive US Navy men, as I explained why I couldn't let them in.

'Sorry, guys. It's not prejudice. See the sign: "No service personnel".' I kept my eyes fixed on those of the alpha male.

'How d'ya know we're servicemen, mother*fucker*?'

'That's easy, bud. Other than Wilton here and another guy I know, I've never seen a black person in Hong Kong' – not far from the truth – 'let alone three walking side by side wearing Georgetown sweatshirts *and* with the muscles you dudes have got! Look at the *size* of those things! You work out, yeah?'

They broke out smiles and, reassured we weren't Klan members, wandered off to find another drinking hole.

Geordie appeared, saying I could order a meal and eat it in the staffroom. I wouldn't manage a morsel, the meth stealing my appetite, but went through the motions nonetheless.

I was further impressed when he handed me a bottle of Corona with a slice of lime wedged temptingly in its neck. What with feeling on top of the world already, it went down rather well – unlike the attitude of the next crazy.

Dressed in a black leather ankle-length coat, matching trousers, a shirt tied at the neck with one of those Texan drawstringed steer's heads and with long black hair greased back from a crusty chain-smoker's mug, he looked a cross between John Travolta in *Pulp Fiction* and Lord Vader. Breezing up the shiny steps, he waltzed right through the double doors, flashing a look of disgust when I said, 'Excuse me!'

'Don't worry about 'im, Chris,' said Wilton. 'That's Duane Jennings – a Kiwi. Owns the Karaoke Bar. Always 'igh on coke an' pissed. Thinks he can walk into any club in Wan Chai, and he fuckin' *'ates* doormen. Forget about 'im.'

I was prepared to take my partner's word, but like hell would I forget.

Stuart, the third doorman, approached, saying it was my turn to do a stint inside. Standing on the balcony, looking out over the punters, I experienced an immense sense of satisfaction. I don't know how it would have been without sucking up a load of crystal meth, but with the slamming tunes and my higher state of consciousness, it felt awesome.

If you plan to steal a drink in a two-tiered club, it's good advice to look *up* – not that I'm suggesting nicking stuff on a night out, but I knew the guy prowling across the dance floor like a hunting leopard was.

Early twenties, he wore a dress shirt and jeans, his innocent looks betrayed only by the way he moved, like a thief in the night, his eyes darting from side to side in surreptitious glances.

I watched him zero in on a glass of 'something' and coke. Oblivious to my presence above, he glanced all around and took a huge gulp.

'Any good, mate?' I shouted down.

Without losing a fraction of his composure, he looked up and said, '*Nah*... not enough *ice!*'

We started laughing, and for an instant, locking eyes, I think we both knew which 'ice' he meant.

Someone else caught my attention as he cut through the crowd. Tall, well built, with a shock of flowing yellow curls, he looked like one of my best friends back home. Only unlike my Simon, who shunned fashion, this dude wore a sharp tuxedo and looked the business.

Just as I was musing on the resemblance, a guy pushed his way to the balcony's rail, interrupting my view of the crowd. '*Oy, CUNT!*' he shouted in a Mancunian accent at the snappy dresser. 'What'a you think you *look* like?'

What was I supposed to do? It seemed this bloke was out to cause trouble, and preventing it was my job. 'Mate, do you know him?' I tendered.

The geezer, who wore a smart suit beneath blond gelled-back hair and narrow but handsome features, swung around. 'What the *fook's* it gotta do with you?' he spat, his face livid, his semi-dilated pupils telling me he was coked-up and going to make an issue out of this.

'No problem, mate.' I stared unblinkingly into his dots. 'It's just that shouting *cunt* might come across as rude.'

'*Oh!* Are *you* sayin' *I* don't *fookin'* know 'im?' His jab was an obvious attempt to wind me up.

Before I could reply, Sean stepped in, swiping a well-practised arm between us. 'Chris, dunn'ae worry about it.'

According to Sean, Lee Aimes was a regular customer – regular in the respect he came to the club every week, but not so regular he presented as a coke-dealing gangster with a chip on his shoulder.

I didn't think anything more about it, until the end of the night when Aimes made his exit.

'Goodnight, mate.' I smiled, attempting to de-escalate the situation.

'*YOU!*' he snarled, standing back and shaking his head, 'I've *'eard* about *you!* I know you're ex-military an' a black belt in taekwondo.'

'That's pretty astute,' I thought. *I* knew I was ex-military – because I was the one who'd left the Forces – but I didn't know I had a black belt in taekwondo. In fact, I thought I was pretty crap at it – Bruce Lee's budgie probably knew more about martial arts than I did.

'Look, I know you can kill a man with one punch, yeah?' he continued. 'But what you did up there on that balcony tonight, well, that took guts. But you wanna be careful you don't get yourself killed!'

'That's good advice,' I thought.

'Listen, if you ever need a job, or coke, *or* you wanna deal for me, just ask. I run things, *yeah*? All the coke in Wan Chai comes through me.'

Pleased to come through the first evening's shenanigans unscathed, I walked across the road and down the steps into the Big Apple. *'Lei ho?'* I asked the big Chinese guy on the door.

'Ho!'

'Lei giu mat ye meng'a? (You're called what name?)'

'Chan,' he replied, a big grin on a humble face and holding up a gentlemanly paw to usher me inside.

Easing through the 3am throng of drunken diversity, I bumped into Ray the manager.

'Hi, Chris!' he said. 'How's it going?'

'All good, mate. Just started working on the door of Joe's.'

'Nice one! Wanna drink?'

'Ah, mate! I left me wallet at home.'

'Nah, I mean on the house.'

'Oh, right! *Errh*, Corona, Ray, please.'

That took me aback! No one working in a bar had ever bought me a drink before, let alone the boss.

I thanked Ray and went to say hello to the DJ. He was chatting to an up-and-coming talent, Lee Burridge, who kindly bought me another drink. We discussed our passion for dance music, and then I settled back against the DJ booth to enjoy my beer and the tunes – not to mention the impending company of Lee Aimes, who was making his way through the crowd.

I knew what was on the cards. Instead of taking advantage of the fact our contretemps ended on a mutually high note and this unexpected meet provided an opportunity to move our relationship along – swapping photos of our kids, manfully slapping each other on the back, agreeing to meet at the top of the Eiffel Tower twenty years from now, not to mention promising to take a bullet for one another – no! Aimes would reinstate his position in the food chain by re-talking the cod shit he'd spewed over me earlier.

'You know, you were pushing it back there,' his psychobabble began. 'You seem like a good lad and you know 'ow to 'andle yourself. But I've gotta gun under me jacket, you know? Do you wanna see it?' His eyes menaced and drew closer together.

Seriously? Who tries to impress someone that's spent seven years in the Royal Marines, who's sick of seeing guns *and* cleaning and being responsible for the bloody things, by offering to show them another?

I ended up humouring the guy – 'Nah, mate, don't get that out in here' – as if I were a fellow hoodlum and violence a way of life.

Happy in his mind he was still Billy Big Balls, Aimes wandered off to gangsterise some other poor punter with the invisible gun story.

I felt a tap on the shoulder. It was the guy Aimes had been shouting abuse at earlier.

'You alright, mate? Lee giving you a hard time?'

'Well, he's putting me through my paces a bit.' I sensed he meant well.

'Don't worry. He likes to come across as top boy, but he's not a bad bloke when he's sober.'

'Is he ever sober?' I joked. 'What's your name? I'm Chris.'

'I'm Mal, Chris. I saw you working in Joe's earlier.'

Although only twenty-five, Mal worked for a top law firm in Hong Kong, and told me his passion was scuba-diving in the Philippines. The friend he introduced me to was equally as interesting. 'This is Kevin.' He indicated to the unassuming gent. 'Show Chris your card, mate.'

Almost everyone in Hong Kong carried a business card, but I'd never seen one this big. When I scanned through it, I could see why.

This quiet chap had won just about every contest in the martial arts field in pretty much every country holding such events: Korea's taekwondo champion, 1989, 1990, 1991, Thailand's Muay Thai boxing champion, 1990, 1993, Britain's middleweight boxing champion, 1993, 1994, and so it went on. Kevin told me he was head of security for the Excelsior

Hotel, but to look at him, he could easily have worked behind the meat counter in your local supermarket.

I was sufficiently impressed, and honoured when they invited me to do some training together. I didn't like to tell them that with the exception of some judo and the taekwondo lesson in the Marines I knew as much about the ancient fighting skills as a hamster does about yoga.

I clocked a guy at the bar who I'd seen sitting on the same stool every time I'd been in the Apple. He had a froggish face cloaked in long greasy hair and wore a motorcycle jacket, Black Sabbath T-shirt and ripped jeans.

'Alright, mate. I'm Chris.'

'Graham, pal,' he replied, a distant look in his eye.

As he spoke, Ray leant over to ask if I wanted another beer.

'Did you see that, Graham!'

'I'm a regular,' he said, unamazed. 'I never pay for drinks here.'

'Oh…!'

We talked for an hour, and I gathered he worked in screenprinting, but much of what Graham said came out garbled. I could tell he was tripping on acid, so I asked if he took drugs.

'Not me, mate.' He shook his head. 'I don't do any of that shit.'

It surprised me. In a club back home, I'm sure he would have said, 'Mate, I'm off my face!' but for some reason, he was holding back.

'Who's that grey-haired Chinese bloke?' I pointed to a distinguished gent in his sixties.

'That's Freddy,' said Graham. 'The owner. He's alright, but he's got this theory.'

'What's that?' I took advantage of his lucidity.

'He reckons people standing in the bar are all upstanding citizens because they tend to be office workers in suits.'

'Go on.' I had a hunch I knew what was coming.

'He reckons people who hang about in the back are all druggies.'

'*Really?*'

'Yeah.'

I wondered if this was why Graham said that he didn't take drugs. Perhaps it was some kind of cultural taboo in Hong Kong. But I felt like shaking a hoof, so I headed for my favourite stomping ground.

At the back of the club, something made me smile, especially in view of what Graham said. Sitting at a table in the semi-darkness with two other expats, a guy had racked up four lines of coke on the table. As they proceeded to snort a line, one of the Chinese barmen approached on his way around collecting glasses. He looked a friendly chap, with long hair, black-framed glasses and a permanent smile.

He neared their table, and one of the guys gave him the nod. With the speed of a striking cobra, still holding a tray full of empties above his head, he bent over, took the last line and then continued on his way.

'He seems a popular character!' I thought. Neither Dream nor Nicole were in the club, so I danced on my own, the meth making time fly. Later that morning, I noticed a guy reeling off tables as he staggered along, upsetting people and drinks.

I looked for Ray and Colin, but vaguely remembered seeing them escorting Lee Aimes out – if you can call carrying someone by their arms and legs 'escorting'. I hoped for their sakes he didn't regain consciousness or they'd have a bucketful of nonsense to deal with, especially if he began shooting up Wan Chai with his imaginary bullets.

I watched as the other misbehaver approached a table of girls, unbuttoned his fly and began to pull his trousers down, managing to intercept him with, 'You alright, mate? Had a few drinks?' before he did the full Monty.

'*Urrh?*' he slurred, through wonky facial features as he attempted to button his jeans. But it wasn't his lopsided face capturing my attention. It was his right ear – the one missing. Not for the first time that night, I found myself feeling for someone – not in a patronising way, but you have to empathise when a guy has the symmetry of a Toby jug in this media-led world. I wondered if this was the reason he felt the need to get so pissed and make an exhibition of himself.

'What's your name, mate?'

'*Shirley…*' he mumbled, unsteady as he tried to look me in the eye.

'Wow! A one-eared hard-drinking exhibitionist with a girl's name! This guy's got issues,' I reflected. 'Shirley, let's get you a cab, hey?'

'*Urrh…*' he replied, a look of gratitude slurring across his face.

Coming out of the Apple's dark and smoky beat-thumped atmosphere and into Luard Road at eight in the morning was a real awakener, akin to beaming out of the Starship *Enterprise* to find yourself in a crazy alien landscape. On this occasion, things had gone from regular madness to utterly surreal… and it felt *great!*

I checked Shirley had cash to pay the driver and hailed a cab. The cabbie pulled up, the look on his face saying he had a jerk in tow. The jerk got out and I bundled my girly-named friend in, then turned to assess the scene on the pavement, which could easily have passed for a patch of battlefield in a particularly horrific war zone.

In addition to the morning-after litter – hectic enough in itself – and evening-clad clients from the Apple, wide-eyed and excited as they discussed which after-party to go to, there was the boyish-faced drink stealer I'd seen earlier. He sat with a girl leaning against the 7-Eleven next to the club, pointing at six bottles of Smirnoff lined up on the pavement and singing, *'Eeny meany miny mo…'*

Their mate lay face down in the gutter, a big lad with a shock of dark curls, cradling a chubby stubbled mug. Along with cigarette butts and street filth, he wore grubby jeans and a T-shirt – a gap between the latter allowing his beer gut to breathe. He looked happy as Larry, like you would in your own bed. I thought it was a good time to say hello.

'Alright, mate?'

'*Heh-heyyyy!* 'Ere 'e is!' said the drink fiend, prodding his girlfriend – a blonde lass wearing T-shirt, jeans and skate shoes. 'I'm Clayton and this is Linz. We were *just* talking about you!'

'Where'd ya get the vodka, dude?'

'*Oh,* we just nicked it in there…' He pointed a casual thumb over his shoulder as if it's the norm to be sitting outside a shop displaying the goods you've just ripped off from it.

As he spoke, a police car screeched around the corner, siren blaring and blue lights flashing as it pulled to a stop at the kerb. I expected a degree of panic, perhaps a dash for freedom, but Clayton just shook his wear-worsened companion to let him know we had company.

Two Chinese coppers approached, and without warning, Clayton stood up and lurched towards the nearest one. Grabbing the radio mike attached to the officer's lapel, he proceeded to spew all sorts of crooked shit into it: 'Tango, bravo, come and 'elp coz we're *fuuucked uuuuuup!*'

The policemen were unamused, but also completely bewildered. They tried to fend Clayton off, but he lunged again and began to babble rampant kak into the mike once more.

Restored to life, but still looking the part of a tramp, their friend arose from the gutter, took three animated steps and dived through the open door of the police car. Then to the amusement of the crowd, he locked the doors and began a conversation of his own on the in-car radio. It was hilarious – so much so, I stood there, shaking my head in disbelief.

Meanwhile, Clayton and Linz gathered up their stolen booze and disappeared. One of the policemen unlocked the squad car and hauled Clayton's friend out, only they didn't know what to do. He hadn't exactly broken any law – at least not one they knew of.

They settled for thrusting the problem away from them, so I threw him a let's-go-this-way nod and we headed for the MTR entrance.

En route, he asked in a Northern Irish rasp if I knew Clayts and Linz.

'Just been speaking to them. They've headed off.'

'Aye, we'v'a pardy at arrs. Yurh comin,' he ordered.

'No worries. How ya feeling?'

'Ay'me fokked, so I am. What abowt yee?'

'I'm alright, mate,' I replied, feeling odds-on favourite.

'Yue bin in tha milidri.' He darted a knowing look. 'Bin in Norn Iron?'

'Belfast. Eighty-nine.'

'Ay'me from Derry. Aye fokkin hayt tha Bridish Milidri.'

'I bet, but I'm not in the military. You're still in the IRA, though, obviously, so what's your fuckin' excuse?'

'*Maye* fokkin excuse is tha' were in the Hong Kong. So bess pud'all tha' shite to one sayde?' He shrugged and gave me a quizzical look.

'I think we should, mate.' I smiled. 'I'm Chris.'

'Ay'me Derek, Chris. Less go take some drugs.'

The party was in Sheung Wan, not far from Gung Wan Hong, but approaching the turnstiles, I remembered I'd left my wallet with my MTR card in it at home.

'Yue don' need money in the Hong Kong, so you don't,' Derek assured me, hopping over the steel barrier, right in front of the guard. 'Compared ta back home, these folks never do fokk all.'

I followed suit, catching him up on the platform.

'What about the triads, Derek? Do you know much about them?'

'Oh... thass'a different story.' His demeanour turned serious. 'Yue don' mess with they savage fokkers, less yue wanna get fokked big time.'

Coming from the IRA, this seemed good advice.

Upon exiting the station, Derek nipped into a 7-Eleven, coming back out, jacket bulging, with cans of shoplifted gin and tonic. 'S'all abowt survival, Chrissy. Ay'me an uneducated fokkin druggy. Who da fokk is gonna look after me in this dog-eat-dog siddy?'

'Good Catholic then!' I smiled.

'Fokkin right!' He laughed. 'Ay'me off for a wee confession in a mennet, so Aye I am.'

Derek lived with Clayton, Linz and a host of other crazy bandits on the top floor of an ageing moss-mottled building. The place teemed with drugged-up expats, many I recognised from the Apple. We emerged onto the flat's roof garden to find a DJ playing the Doobie Brothers' classic, 'Long Train Running'.

'Crank it fokkin up!' screamed Derek, hurdling the deck-chaired drinkers as if he was an urban Olympian in a drug-soaked steeplechase. Then climbing up onto the terrace's guardrail, he began to dance crazy monkeyish to the pounding tunage, much to the astonishment of pedestrians in the street below.

Fellow partygoers scrambled up to join his primatological display, and as the rest of us funked around the rooftop, all tribal-like, some climbing onto chairs and tables, you wouldn't have wanted to be anywhere else on Earth at any other time in history.

Making my way back down into the flat, I spied the DJ from the Apple snorting cocaine off the kitchen table. 'Alright, mate?' I sat down opposite him. 'I'm Chris.'

'Alright, Chris,' he replied, a wary look in his eye. 'I'm Bob.'

'You alright, Bob? You're looking at me strange.'

'Yeah, I'm alright, mate...'

'But what?'

'*Well,* you're the guy from the club who always thanks me at the end of the night.'

'I'm not giving you a problem, am I? The tunes you bang out are great, Bob.'

'It's just that it touches my heart when someone thanks me. But I'm worried you might be a copper.'

'*Bob*! How many coppers do you know who take Class As and dance the night away in a pool of sweat?'

'Not many, I s'pose…'

'Look, I'm a doormen at Joe Bananas. I'm not a copper, but I was in the Marines.'

'The *Marines*? Do you know the Mucky Duck in Taunton?'

'You mean the one with a trophy cabinet where the local boys keep souvenirs from all the fights they've had with the lads from Forty Commando? The *Daily Telegraph* ran an article on it once.'

'Yeah!' Bob broke out a self-satisfied grin. 'Can you guess who used to be the DJ there?'

'My guess is that would be you, Bobby!'

'You'd guess right, mate. Fancy a line?'

'Don't mind if I do.'

The resultant elation almost made me forget I had to be back on the door of Joe's at three o'clock for the Sunday afternoon shift, a reminder this was my third day without sleep, I hadn't eaten so much as a glass noodle and had danced for longer than it took to run three marathons.

Burning the candle at both ends would be the euphemism to describe my Hong Kong experience to folks back home – but trussing said candle in dynamite, wrapping it in Semtex, soaking it for a month in a cocktail of rocket fuel and ether before hurling it into a flaming volcanic pit would be a slight more truthful. But international phone calls being the price they were and ignorance being blissful, the 'both ends' thing would be better for all concerned.

Fun and Games

I ARRIVED BACK AT VANCE'S at midday to find his place filled with the regular contingent of Bedlamites.

Jayne was in the kitchen with a friend, chatting excitedly in Tagalog as they cooked up bowlfuls of rice and fish. The other Filipinas and their Nepalese chums sipped Coca-Cola in the main room and bopped to the trashiness of Filipino rock, which sounded almost as bad as Cantopop.

Business colleagues including Benny and the shifty Mr Liu surrounded Vance in his office. With the exception of Liu *San*, they were all pleased to see me. We had grown close during my stay. Only, now I sensed a barrier forming between us.

My experience of Bedlam was veering from theirs. Working a regular job had lost its appeal. Pop music I couldn't stand. Food had long ceased to be important and fizzy caffeinated drinks didn't quite have the kick of crystal methamphetamine.

Vance kept hinting he was eating into his Army savings and looking for my support in the business arena, but I'd *been* there, *done* that, and needed a change.

I declined the offer of food and retired to my room, pulling the dictionary from a drawer while marvelling at how my whisker-faced tenants had managed to swap their trademark black pellets for the brand-new bar of soap I had in there. After brushing rat shit off the duvet, I lay down on the bed to brush up on my Cantonese.

Despite the language sounding arse-about-face, I thought I could use Chinese words with English grammar – not that I knew what grammar was, to be honest. Then there's the intonation. Getting this right is vital in *Gwongdungwa*. Some of my speech must have sounded as gibberish as a parrot on crack but I wasn't to know this, as I mostly practised on myself, and I thought I sounded alright.

Taking up a notepad, I turned my attention to writing a poem about my encounter on the dance floor with the beautiful Thai girl, Dream. I started scribbling:

> *I see you dancing under neon light*
> *I see you dancing in pure delight*
> *I see you dancing in diamond white*
> *Never has the night ever felt so right*
> *Dream. It's true*
> *Dream. It's you*
> *Lov—*

Rivalled only by the *ting-boppy-ting-ting* and the *whooshy whooshy why'ya* of the local pop artists, my lack of lyrical meter made me happy. I didn't finish it, though, as a frightening wave of tiredness wreaked tsunami-like through my torso.

'What the hell was *that?*'

The most unusual feeling ever, it was as if a massive electrified yawn had travelled up my spine, shuddering outwards in a violent jolting spasm.

It struck again – 'What the *fuuu…?*' – leaving me in a state of shock. Mother Nature was giving me a succinct reminder I was long overdue for sleep, so I rushed into the kitchen and built the strongest cup of coffee imaginable, gulping it down as if it was the elixir of life and evaporating fast, before jumping in the shower in a vain attempt to invigorate my overworked adrenal glands.

Polishing my Caterpillar boots and ironing a shirt, I worried I might not be able to perform my door duties. Afraid of losing another job, I knew there was a trip to make.

Standing outside Mark's room, I saw that the small brass padlock was missing from the wire latch on the yellowing doorframe.

Through the three-inch gap, I could see the situation inside was also very much ajar. An unknown profiteer had already removed the mattress from the bed, leaving its grey angle-iron frame and sagging mesh looking cold, crass and redundant.

I pushed open the door.

The pages of a newspaper spread in disarray upon the floor spoke volumes in themselves. Testament to the stark reality and ephemeral nature of the relationship between people, drugs and profit, they screamed out the grimmest of scenarios: *'Mark sold drugs to schoolkids and they took him away…'*

'Fuck it!' Mark's problems aside, I needed to score some ice.

I knocked on Alan's door, but he wasn't in.

I tried Kuku's, another friend of Neil's.

Kuku could only be a friend of Neil's – not wishing to sound cruel. It's just that Kuku was a walking advert for the reason why certain individuals should stay the fuck away from drugs.

In his fifties, but coming across as eighty-five, he'd been in a rock band back in the sixties. Following his five minutes of fame, years of busking for drugs along the Southeast Asian Hippy Trail had left him a pathetic shell. He looked like the mad scientist in *Back to the Future*, though with his filthy threadbare clothes, and brain cells held together with Rizla paper, he made Emmett Brown seem as sharp as a razor.

The three of us smoked ice in his room one time. I don't know what was worse: the foot of litter on the floor, the desperation in his eyes as he waited for a toot or his pitiful delusions about a fortune he would receive in royalties owed by a record company.

'I see myself as a musician-cum-street artist,' he'd said, but the only art I saw him perform was of the impressionist variety in Kowloon Park. With his guitar slung behind his back, he was doing a good impression of a beggar by running up to tourists and pleading for change.

Perhaps I should have questioned the point at which being up for anything and buying the T-shirt peters out and the reality of huddling in a drug den with a schizophrenic snake-obsessed meth addict and a has-been drug-addled beatnik kicks in – but I'm glad I didn't.

Kuku wasn't home either.

I stood there, trying to shake the heinous convulsions wracking my sleep-deprived self. I couldn't go to work in this state or I'd need the Red Cross for Christ's sake… and as if by magic, their emissary appeared.

'You looking for Makk?' asked the young Indian guy.

'Yeah, I was.'

'Police took Makk. Whad'is it you want?'

'…I wanted some *ice*?'

'Come with me,' was the reply the world wanted to hear.

He led me down a flight of stairs into a more upmarket corridor and then knocked on a door. After words exchanged in Hindi, the occupant went away and came back with a packet.

'Two hundred dollar,' said my Indian friend, short, sweet, perfect.

I cursed Mark – this was the biggest bag of crystal meth I'd ever seen at a quarter of his price.

Time was pressing, so I went up to the filthy bathroom and wiped a corner of the washbasin clean with a jacket cuff, crushing a few crystals onto it with my credit card and snorting them through a banknote. Running down the backstairs, I felt the chemical working its magic.

The look Stuart my fellow doorman gave me said it all. For good measure, he added, 'The Hong Kong Rugby Team's inside *misbehaving*. Good luck. I'm off!'

'Wonderful!' I peered through the glass. 'First shift on my own and I've got these Goliaths to deal with!'

Having learnt my lesson, I said hello to Sean, who glanced at the sports team, gave a better-*you*-than-*me* look and sent me back outside.

Awaiting the inevitable, I figured I would have to be as charming as possible with these middle-class hooligans. That way I might still have a job at the end of the night. I looked through the glass again just as the prop forward hopped his colossal arse up onto the bar and lay back, knocking drinks everywhere.

'Here goes nothing!' I brazened and pushed through the doors.

His shenanigans were causing a great deal of amusement, for his friends and the middle-aged expats enjoying Sunday lunch specials. They were lapping it up, and I didn't want my performance to let them down. So I stood there, arms folded, giving him an all-knowing look like an unimpressed headmistress, which caused further hysterics all round.

Having broken the ice, I grabbed the bloke's hand and hauled him off the counter to huge applause. I shot a look at my boss, who was chuckling to himself, and went back to my post.

No sooner had I stepped outside than another commotion erupted. One of his girlfriends was *dancing* on the bar! 'Here we go *again*…' I thought, although I was really starting to enjoy myself.

This time I played up my role as headmistress, holding an elbow and tapping a finger against the lips. *'You! Down!'* I ordered, as though *extremely* cross. The few people not creased up soon were when, with a cheeky grin, she launched herself at me and I had to catch her!

Just as I'd returned to the door, she did it *again*! Only, this time I made sure to stand well back as she clambered down from her trespass. Then she stood, hands clasped, head bowed, as if awaiting punishment.

'Throw her *out*!' shouted one of the guys, and the place erupted once more.

'Go like *this*!' I made a star shape with my body.

When she followed suit, shaking a puzzled head, I picked her up in a fireman's carry and plonked her down on the doormat outside. 'Stay there until you can behave!'

'What if I just walk in?' she tried her luck.

'I'll smack your bum!'

'Ooh!'

But whenever I turned my back, she'd try to sneak inside and her friends would scream, *'She's trying to get in! She's trying to get in!'*

Evening fell and Sean took over while I went on my break. Having ordered gammon and chips, I could only summon a slight feeling of hunger as I made my way to the staffroom. An English barman, Maff, was already in there. 'Mate, that's the *funniest* fucking thing I ever saw!' He chuckled. 'Even Sean cracked up. They'll like having you work here.'

I was glad Maff's break soon finished, as I didn't want him asking why I'd only eaten a few peas. I dumped the rest in the rubbish bin and then went to the toilet to snort a line before going back out.

Shortly after, a couple of women in their seventies left the club, having eaten. They looked like tourists and, with the exception of their full-on-and-funky rinsed hair, seemed pretty out of place in Wan Chai's red-light district.

'Excuse me!' said the purple bonce. 'You might like to know there's a strange *smell* in this place.'

'And, you *really* could do with some music,' added the blue-tinged beauty.

'I'm sorry about that,' I consoled them. 'It's just we've had a bit of a problem.'

'What problem?' asked Blue.

'Our poor old DJ died, Madam. There he was, mixing his heart out, playing the tunes he loved, and *BAM!* He popped his clogs!'

'I'm sorry to hear that,' she said. 'That *is* a bit of a problem, isn't it?'

'No, Madam, *that's* not the problem…' I shook my head at this terrible turn of events. 'The problem is he died three days ago and they still haven't moved him from the DJ box. *That's* what the bad smell is.'

'Oh, I *see*,' said Blue. 'How *terrible*.'

'*Awful*, Madam! You just can't get the staff these days.'

'*Can't* get the staff…' muttered Purple.

As they walked off down Luard Road, shaking their bingo bouffants, I wondered if I might not be all there.

The shift ended without further rumpus, the Hong Kong Rugby Team et al. each saying a big thank you, and even Sean expressing gratitude for my efforts.

Now I had to decide whether to go home and try to get some sleep or snort more drugs and dance in my favourite nightclub until morning.

Dancing in my favourite nightclub in the morning, having snorted more drugs, I saw the friendly Chinese barman on his way around collecting glasses.

'Having a good night?' I asked.

'Yeeah… actually, I'm having a good night,' he replied, thoughtfully.

'I'm Chris. How do you do?'

'I'm doing okay. My name is Jackson.' His voice had an endearing edge.

'Jackson, can I ask you something?'

'*Shoowah.*'

'Did you snort coke off the table last night?'

'*Yeeah!* An' you know tonight?'

'What about tonight?'

'Tonight I done my trip! *Ha-ha-ha!*'

'*What!* You took a trip, in *here*… while you're *working*?'

'Yeeah! One of the customer give it to me.'

'Any good?'

'Yeeah!' He grinned, his eyes squinting behind Buddy Holly specs.

Jackson wandered over to a table to gather the empties, exchanging words with a girl, an expat or tourist. He returned, looking confused. '*Errh,* Quiss'a?'

'What's up?'

'What's'it meaning when someone say, "Whadayooting"?'

'Who said that, mate?'

'That girl. I say, "Is this glass empty?" She say, "Whadayooting."'

'Jackson, she's being rude. She's got no right to talk like that.'

'No right'a?'

'No right. She'd never say that to someone in England.'

'But what's'it meaning?'

'It means, *what... do... you... think?* Like, is the glass *empty?*'

'...I see,' he said, but I could see he didn't. He looked so upset. How could I explain that some Brits feel they can go abroad and treat the locals like savages? Pride runs deep in the Chinese psyche. Putting someone down, even accidentally, is just about the worst faux pas a person can make – Westerner or local.

Just as I contemplated going home, Dream entered the club, strutting across the teak towards me with her arms raised like a zombie, which looked kind'a comical.

We danced until 5am, and just as I felt utterly drained, she disappeared. She didn't even say goodbye, which was a little dispiriting. I thought it best to leave.

I took the first MTR shuttle of the day, 5.30am, to Yau Ma Tei, one stop below Mong Kok on purpose. I loved being on Nathan Road in the wee hours. The pavements abandoned, bar newspaper vendors sorting the day's editions and the odd feline prowling around intent on catching and devouring one of the colony's fat rodents, the extra ten-minute walk always proved surreal.

Near deserted were the roads at this bewitching hour, save the infrequent red taxi carrying a lone fare along one of the six lanes of empty highway. With most of the neon signs extinguished by their electronic timers, a skeleton of hardliners remained stoic, the odd one flickering on and off, erratic and pathetic, into the vague moonlit surround.

This was *my* Hong Kong, *my* experience, *my* time – just me, the crystal meth coursing through my veins and the Kowloon Peninsula as my playground. I would hop up onto the railing beside the pavement to see how far I could walk along it. I'd always had a good sense of balance. With the added control meth gave, I cleared whole blocks, forced only to drop back down by side streets Pitt, Hamilton, Dundas, Soy, Shantung and Nelson, that cut across my route, interrupting my fun.

On this occasion, I paralleled the main road by ducking down a back alley. During the day, these odious cut-throughs provided refuge for young triads hawking copied CDs, who would retreat into the stale air, barrows atop with counterfeit pop, when a police patrol approached.

I edged my way along, slicing unafraid through the superstition and danger lurking in the pitch-black dank.

In my mind, I was a renegade doorman, a real maverick with a tragic secret history involving a woman, an unfortunate incident with a whoopee cushion and lots of people I'd had to kill. I represented a nightclub overseen by evil colonial masters, ones possessing utter contempt for local culture and ownership. The trip to my safe house in Mong Kok was a gauntlet I had to run. Being a true Zen master, having spent years chanting introspectively in a Tibetan monastery high in the Himalayas, I was completely at ease with both self and environment.

Of course, ordinarily, I shunned violence, but when a troop of triad combatants, armed to the teeth with an array of spiky and slicy weaponry, appeared out of a doorway and attempted to put an end to my harmonious existence, I was having none of it! With a *'Hurhh, hi-yah, uhh, uh-uh-urrhh!'* I nailed every single one of my assassins, with ancient and deadly – albeit made up on the spot – fighting skills.

Exiting the final alleyway, leaving piles of dead and dying tongs in my wake, I re-entered the real world, where three days without eating kicked in hard as the balance between raging on meth and the need to eat finally tipped.

There was an all-night McDonald's about four blocks down on the other side of Nathan Road. I jogged across the barren carriageway at a diagonal to shorten the distance.

Competing with Cantonese cuisine meant McDonald's was cheap in Hong Kong. I bought a breakfast of scrambled eggs and pancakes with maple syrup for fifteen bucks and swallowed it with hardly a chew, the feeling of intense hunger rivalled only by that of satiating it.

At Hing Tak, I woke the little Chinese guard with a whisper of *'M'goy!'* and threw in a *'Doy'm'due!'* apology. Even at this ungodly hour, rising from his equally-as-tired sunlounger, he grinned as if pleased to see me.

'Phwoaarurrhahh...' Lifting myself out of sleep and onto an elbow, I'd never felt so exhausted, despite sleeping ten hours. I checked the Rolex, reassured to see it was 6.30pm and I still had an hour and a half before work.

Lying back, shivering and yawning like a bad case of jetlag, I mulled over my next move. It should have been to call in sick and then go back to the pillow, rising only to grab more junk food as I was still famished. But I had another plan, one put into action before I'd opened my eyes.

I fumbled in my right boot, looking for the packet of ice I had stashed in the lining. If I was going to carry drugs around this city it had to be in a place no cop would look, and here they rested comfortably against my instep.

Having retrieved them, and the silver foil tray and toot from my briefcase, I heated up the most inviting crystal, running its liquid state along the shiny slide and inhaling the vapour until there was nothing left except a spot of residue on the foil and a thin veil of guilt lingering in the room.

The hunger and tiredness vanished, replaced by restlessness. I got my laundry together, pleased Vance's apartment was empty so I could get myself and my clothes washed in the shower without interruption.

But I had a problem. Along with feeling hyper came disorientation, a side effect of not enough sleep, meaning I got easily distracted. Although I *felt* I was flying high, all systems go, let's go disco, in reality the tiredness was clocking up and I was having trouble focussing.

I made it to Joe's with thirty seconds to spare, arriving out of breath and sweating like a Finn in a sauna.

Stuart was on the door with me, and as the club was almost empty, we both stood outside. 'What you been up to today, Stu?'

'Oh, I had lunch with Jean-Claude Van Damme at his restaurant, Planet Hollywood.'

'You serious?' I stood there, mouth agape.

'Yeah, he owns a share of it.'

'I know *that*. But I didn't know you went there with him!'

'Yeah, I'm a martial artist and an actor.'

I was fascinated.

'Have you seen *Lionheart*?'

'The one about the bare-knuckle fights?'

'Do you remember the Scotsman, fighting in a kilt in a car park?'

'Yeah, I do.'

'That was me. We trained together in Thailand before the film.'

'Good on yer, mate. Is there much extra work in Hong Kong?'

'A fair bit. But it helps if you can speak Cantonese and do some martial arts…' He took a step back and passed his foot over my head, explaining how the moves were exaggerated for the camera.

'I speak a *bit* of Cantonese.'

'You might think you can,' he said, laughing. 'But it's harder to learn than that.'

Stu went to check inside, just as a customer arrived. He was French, an antique dealer, and asked how I'd come to be working in a Hong Kong club. Pulling out a pack of Gauloises, he asked if I'd like one.

'No, I better not, my friend. I don't think I'm allowed, but I'll have a puff of yours before you stub it out, if you don't mind.'

'*Non!* Sure.' He smiled generously and offered the cigarette right away.

I took a sneaky draw, and as I did, one of the manager's cliquey friends swept up the steps.

'Didn't see that, love!' I joked, and continued to yap away. Five minutes later, Stu came back, saying Sean wanted me in the office.

'Everything alright, Sean?'

'No, Chris. I'm gunn'ae have to let you go.'

'Sorry?' I said, thinking he meant I could go home because we didn't have many customers.

'We got'ae no-smoking-on-the-door policy. If one'ae the owners saw you, I'd be up for the high jump. It's a pity. We've enjoyed having you here.'

'Well, I guess I'll be off, then.'

And that was that. I was.

Walking across to the Apple, I can't say I was all that dejected. I should have been. After all, Chris Thrall FC wasn't exactly having a good season:

HM Forces	10	'Mr' Thrall	10	(Penalty shootout)
Quorum Int'l	15	Chris Thrall	0	(Extra time. Rain stops play)
Girlfriend Sarah	0	Chris Thrall	0	(Match abandoned)
Beautiful Kerry	0	Chris Thrall	0	(Red card. Striker sent off)
Golden Triangle	7	Chris Thrall	0	(Match postponed)
Gung Wan Hong	0	Chris Thrall	0	(Red card. Striker sent off)
Crystal Meth	1	Chris Thrall	0	(Replay)
Furniture Deal	0	Chris Thrall	0	(Rain stop play)
Computer Deal	0	Chris Thrall	0	(Rain stop play)
D-RAM Deal	0	Chris Thrall	0	(Rain stop play)
Sorcecomp	0	Chris Thrall	0	(Lost on aggregate)
Crystal Meth	1	Chris Thrall	1	(Replay)
Joe Bananas	0	Chris Thrall	0	(Red card. Striker sent off)
Crystal Meth	1	Chris Thrall	0	(Injury time)

Ray was behind the bar. 'Hi, Chris!' he said with his usual cheer. 'How's things across the road?'

'I got sparked, mate! I smoked two puffs of a ciggy and the spineless fuckers fired me!'

'Yeah, they're pretty hot on that over there. Wanna drink?'

'Ah, mate, I'd love a Corona. I haven't got a clue what I'm gonna do now.'

'Try Rick's. They're always looking for doormen. I'd give you a job here, it's just we're fully staffed.'

'*Rick's Café?*' I queried. 'Who owns that?'

'Same Scottish mafia that owns Joe's, but the managers don't like each other.'

I thanked Ray and went to find Ron and Neil. Old Ron was drunk as a monkey and doing his little drummer boy act.

Neil sat staring hawk-like at a woman on the dance floor, his eyes piercing black dots due to way too much amphetamine. Chewing gum incessantly with his mouth wide open, he looked the part of a serial killer.

'Neil, you can stop that shit!'

'Stop what?'

'Stop staring like a fucking sex offender!'

'I *wasn't* staring!'

'You were, mate. Now pack it in! You're gonna get us all arrested and thrown in jail under the 1995 Nightclub Sex Pest Act.'

'*Is* there a Nightclub Sex Pest Act?' he asked.

Rick's Café

I PHONED RICK'S CAFÉ and spoke to a pleasant-sounding Scot called Reg. 'Come on down at seven,' he said. 'We'll have a chat.'

'Have a chat?' I pondered, wondering how to impress him with my limited experience and what qualities an employer looks for in a doorman. Surely, size was an issue, despite what I'd said to Neil.

I was a shadow of my former self, though. I'd weighed thirteen stone in the Forces, the result of training in the gym three times a week. Since my relationship with meth, I'd shed two of those stones. So when I went to meet Reg, I wore three T-shirts, a dress shirt and my bomber jacket. I felt like the Michelin Man and left home in plenty of time so I didn't end up doing my interview out of a bucket.

I arrived in Wan Chai with time to spare and went to the football ground on Luard to sort myself out. The last thing I wanted was Reg asking why I had so many shirts on – that would be embarrassing.

An amateur league team were having a kick-around, so I sat high up in the stand and pretended to watch. As there were no other spectators, I snorted a pile of ice off the corner of my credit card and readjusted my clothing. Just as I tucked the little packet into my boot, two coppers entered the ground and beckoned me down to the touchline.

Fucking muppets! It was typical of Hong Kong police mentality. 'Let's harass the *gweilo* because foreigners aren't supposed to watch football alone, so he must be up to no good!'

Well, I *was* up to no good, but they weren't to know that. I might have been doing a bit of choir practice while figuring out how to raise more money for the orphanage in Calcutta.

They took me into a toilet and searched me. Picking up my Marlboros, one of them asked, 'How mush you smokk?' as if heavy smoking is a sure sign of criminality.

'*Go!*' he said – annoyed they couldn't arrest me for smoking… or watching football.

Reg seemed a fair bloke. When I told him about my rapid exit from Joe's, he laughed and then gave me the job. It felt great to be back in work so soon.

Rick's Café was a nouveau-style cocktail bar on Jaffe Road, around the corner from the Big Apple and Joe Bananas. The managers were all Scottish, bar a Chinese man named Quan, the staff English expats or travellers. Apart from the name, it had none of the crappy theme nonsense of Joe's, although attracting a similar clientele.

In no time at all, I'd made friends with many of them. There was Erik, a huge German guy who ran an air-conditioning business. A Harley-Davidson fanatic, he owned two of them, he told me proudly. James, an executive with Peter Stuyvesant, always brought me a carton of Marlboro and took pride in introducing his colleagues, one of whom regularly gave me a hundred-dollar handshake.

Then there was Mr Chau.

I would give Rick's Café regulars the 'secret stamp' treatment to save them the HK$100 entrance fee and thank them for their business.

Mr Chau came in a lot. He arrived on his own and drank on his own, and the managers being too full of themselves never thought to make him feel welcome. I don't think they even recognised him.

The Hong Kong Chinese are a proud people, but it was a big thing for them to enter a venerable *gweilo* stronghold, a foray into the unknown and an attempt at gaining acceptance into the culture of the colonisers.

To give Mr Chau the secret stamp was the ultimate in giving face. So grateful, the kung fu master wouldn't stop saying thank you, insisting on giving me lessons at some time in the future.

The most touching aspect was that these guys spent as much time outside of the club, chatting to me, as they did inside. A bunch of US Marines invited me to a cocktail party thrown by their consul general. Erik asked me to a rooftop party at his, and the Peter Stuyvesant crowd to a do they were hosting. I'd never felt so popular.

Then payback time arrived. It was Saturday night and Quan and I were busy taking money when who should arrive but Duane Jennings – still leather-clad, longhaired and rude.

Breezing past the line, the Kiwi tried his favourite trick of walking straight in, only it was time for Duane to meet the Marines.

I shot my arm across the doorway.

'*Let me in!*' he barked.

'Queue's there, mate.'

'Don't cha knah who I am?'

'You're the owner of the Karaoke Bar and the queue's there, mate.'

He surged for the door, and again, I repelled his drunken state.

'Wha'ss up?' asked Quan.

'This guy thinks he can walk straight in.'

Duane the Pain made another bid for the entrance.

Now Quan put his arm out. 'Sir, we have queue tonight, you know?'

Jennings slapped Quan around the face and made another bid.

SMACK! I punched his sternum, sending him reeling backwards onto the pavement.

'What was *that* for?' he demanded, picking himself off the floor.

'That's for slapping my manager. Now, fuck off!'

'I'll be comin' back, and there'll be more of us, ya knah!'

'Yeah, an' I'll tell you *all* to fuck off!'

Problem sorted, I went back to helping Quan and welcoming people.

When the queue quietened, I looked inside. Drink flowed, music banged up and down, the customers happily in its thrall.

I spotted a Filipina knocking out a mean groove to the sound of 'Ain't No Mountain High Enough' with her four-foot-nothing physique. Taking advantage of the crowd, I dropped onto my knees, which brought me to her eye level, and had a boogie and a giggle.

Back at the entrance, I saw the queue had shrunk to nothing, so Quan left me to it. Just as I mused on how this section of Jaffe Road could be so deserted on a Saturday night yet, with the ambience given off by the club's neon sign and the sodium-yellow glow of the streetlights, appear so expectant, the expect*ed* appeared... in the form of Duane Jennings and the two bloody *big* bruisers accompanying him.

Once again, he glided up to the door, the dark overlord, restored to confidence by the stormtroopers abreast of him.

The guy to his right bruised sideways – a handsome yet meat-headed Maori. The one to his left bruised only in height. With a shock of curly brown hair, Romany skin and gold hoop earrings, he looked like the Mad Mental Pikey from Pakistan and not in my best interest.

'*Ere's* the one I told ya'bout!' said old Rockery Face, as excited as a child spotting the elephant enclosure at the zoo. 'I *told* ya I'd be comin' back! Now, let me in!'

'You're not coming in, mate,' the crystal meth told him straight to his bloodshot eyes, as I blocked the entrance, wishing I'd worn my three extra T-shirts to *really* scare the shit out of these clowns.

'I *am* comin' in, mate, and if you lay a *fuckin'* finger on me you'll 'ave *these* two to deal with!'

'*Really?*' I thought it best to check what 'these two' were doing here. I hoped they might just be scary-looking care workers.

'Fuckin' *really*!'

'*Hmmmh…*' I pondered, scanning the *Once Were Warriors* character up, down and sideways, and then the Dexy's Midnight Runner – just up and down, as side to side wasn't much of an option.

'I'll take that risk,' I said, jabbing him in the chest with a finger and making him step back.

Cor blimey! His head turned into a tomato on steroids.

He flicked a '*Well!* Whad'a'ya gonna do about this guy?' look at his henchmen, who stood like skittles yet to be hit, and then realising they didn't intend to fight for his honour, he carried himself off down the street the way the wind would a used fish-and-chips wrapper.

His boyos stood in silence, unsure what to do. Then having checked each other's reaction, they about-turned and disappeared up the road after him.

A couple of days later, I wandered into the Big Apple and who should I see grooving away with a group of girls but my Maori buddy with the extra-wide load and interesting choice of friends.

Putting on a looking-for-trouble face, I walked up to him.

His own face straightened like a junk's sail ripping in the wind.

'*You!*' I spat, adopting a floating-lotus stinging-buttercup pose.

'*You!*' he growled, circling me in likewise floral-danger, the other dancers backing away from our impending clash.

We must have gone around each other three times before bursting out laughing and the evil Silver Fern introduced himself as Mike.

'Mike, are you a bodyguard?' I wondered how he'd come to be escorting Duane the Pain on his troubled pathway through life.

'Nah, bro,' said the likeable Kiwi. 'I play rugby for the All Blacks. I'm in town for a friendly before the Sevens in March. That prat came up to me and Ryan in the Karaoke Bar, asking if we could help him with a bid'a business. We didn't have a clue what it was about, but we soon realised what a wanka he is, hey? Come and say hello to Ryan, he thinks you're class!'

Ryan was Irish, but more beatnik than pikey. He worked as a labourer on the new airport and was as nice a guy as Mike. He got quite excited and insisted on telling the girls he was with all about our encounter. 'Ya should'a *seen* diss goy's face!' he kept saying. 'Bejeezus! Ya should'a *seen* it!'

I made my way to the tables at the back to see if anyone had a joint on the go and found Hippy Pat, the Aussie, smoking a fat one. Hippy Pat came across as your ultimate misfit – unless you've ever been in Nimbin, New South Wales, where old Pat probably fitted in just nicely. With his baggy Goa-esque attire flapping around an ultra-skinny frame, and greasy lank locks hanging incestuous against a gaunt, John Lennon-specced face, he always looked a bit of a mess. God knows how he made a living, although I could hazard a guess.

I had a blow on Pat's spliff, musing on how I hardly smoked marijuana anymore, and as if reading my mind, Pat turned and said, 'Chris, you like ice, don't'cha?'

'Yeah, why?'

'Me mate Mack there sells shitloads of it.' He indicated to a guy on the dance floor wearing white jeans and a cycling shirt. 'He'll get'cha s'much as ya want.' He called Mack over. 'Mate, I told Chris you'll sord'im'out with a bid'a gear.'

'No worries,' replied Mack, also an Aussie, dropping into the booth. 'It's fucking medicine, hey?'

'Medicine?'

'*Medicine.* When I got off the plane from Sydney, I was shooting up two grams of heroin a day. After taking ice, I cut the smack out. I function bedda on it too.'

'You do?'

'Have to. I'm a manager for FEDL, the courier service. Nod'a job I'd wanna do straight, hey?'

'Right,' I replied, thinking how ice did seem a cure-all – boredom in the workplace a case in point. The list of positives for this wonder drug appeared endless.

Mack Zane was a warm guy. With his crew-cut brown hair, stocky build and smart attire, you would never guess he took ice, let alone sold it. He told me Japanese chemists first synthesised meth during the Second World War to boost troops' morale and endurance, adding that some legendary Grand Prix drivers injected themselves with it before races to increase focus.

My own supply had dwindled, so I asked if he would pop by Rick's Café at some point. Handing me a FEDL business card, he said, 'No worries, mate.'

Old Ron entered the club, dressed in his shirt and tie and looking pleased with himself. 'What's with the tie, Mister Dennison?'

'Got a job, mate!' he crowed. 'Italian restaurant.'

'Nice one, Ronster! You still sleepin' in the park?'

'…For the time being.' He looked down at his feet. 'I don't mind it, though. You meet a lot of nice people.'

We took up our usual spot in the corner and our routine of dancing and table slapping – only he would pause now and again, having seen me clock Dream. 'You fancy her! You *do*, don't you? *You do! You do!*'

'If you must know, Ron, I *do*. But can you shut up about it, please?'

He wasn't bugging me – something he excelled at – I just didn't like the reminder I felt out of her league.

We left the club past daybreak to go back to mine, but a teenage girl sitting on the pavement outside the 7-Eleven stopped us in our tracks. She was *off* her chops – jaw in spasm, eyes rolling back in their sockets, voice not making much sense. There was no way we could leave her.

She spoke with a North American accent, and from what we could gather her name was Shelley and she had a meeting with a drug dealer – as if she needed any more – over at Tsim Sha Tsui's MTR station at 8am. It was in ten minutes' time, so I whispered a plan to Old Ron.

As our train pulled up to the platform, Ron and I kept quiet, knowing Shelley was too far gone to realise. Then as the doors opened three stops later and we stepped out into Mong Kok, she said, *'Hey!'*

She wasn't happy, her hellfire fury coming across as gibberish as we walked along Argyle Street. Yet no sooner did we reach the sanctum of my room than she lay down on the bed, crashing out the moment her head touched the pillow. She was a pretty lass, who looked as though she hadn't slept for days. God only knows what she was doing in Hong Kong, especially in Wan Chai's Clubland in her state.

I awoke mid-afternoon. Ron had gone and Sleeping Beauty looked as if she had ninety-nine years left to snooze, so I headed for McDonald's.

By the time I got back, she was awake and sitting on the bed with her back to me. When I greeted her, 'Morning, Shelley!' she jumped a foot into the air and the generous chunk of ice she'd been about to smoke jumped even higher, before dropping onto the duvet in front of me.

I raised an eyebrow, picked up the glassy nugget and handed it back to her. 'I can't interest you in any breakfast, then?' I put the takeaway on the table.

'Guess I was pretty tired last night,' she said matter-of-factly. 'Who are you, anyway?' She looked down at the bed. 'Did we…?'

'I'm Chris, and *no*, we didn't!' I laughed. 'Do you want to tell me what you were doing off your nut in Wan Chai? In fact, what are you doing in Hong Kong?'

'I wasn't off my nut!' She tested her luck.

'Liar-liar, pants blew the fuck up!'

There was something about this girl.

Shelley's story was as complex as every other crazy maniac's in Clubland. Canadian, nineteen, her parents divorced, she had no contact with her father, which maybe explained her colourful behaviour and defiant attitude, and lived with her mother, a high-ranking official in the Canadian Consulate, in a penthouse apartment in the Mid-Levels.

She'd attended boarding school in Canada, but they'd expelled her for taking drugs. 'No surprise there!' I thought. After a year out, she'd enrolled in the American High School here in Hong Kong, earning another ejection.

Now she was waiting to go back to North America for her final year, her mother hoping Shelley would keep off the drugs and finish her education.

I tried to impart my twenty-six years of wisdom – with my recent record, undoubtedly questionable – but what with her blonde bob, blue eyes and cute figure, it didn't *quite* work out that way.

En route to Rick's Café that evening, having agreed to meet Shelley in the Apple later, I came across a guy pasting up flyers for a music event at the Hard Rock Café. 'How much do you get paid for that, mate?'

'Nothing, bud,' the Englishman replied. 'I'm a promoter and I'm flying these two DJs over from the UK. Do you like house music?'

'Love it!'

'Do you like Brandon Block and Alex P?'

'I've never heard of 'em, to be honest. No offence.'

'None taken, mate. They're the top two DJs in the world at the moment. You should get yourself down there Saturday.'

'Yeah, I will. Nice one!' I said, heading off to work.

It was a cool winter evening in Hong Kong and seeing English tourists walking around in shirtsleeves made me smile. Used to the climate, I was happy to be wearing my bomber jacket.

One of them approached the door with an expat friend who was showing him around Wan Chai. Mid-forties, they chatted a while before the visitor asked if he could get a pint inside. 'Sure, mate.' I held the door open.

Two minutes later, he burst back through it. *'You!'* he bellowed, glaring like the Spanish Inquisition.

His demeanour had changed so suddenly, I wondered if I owed him money or had walked his dog without permission.

'What's up, mate?'

'You!' He struck again, with more venom than the Five-step Snake. 'You told me I could get a *pint*, but they only serve *halves*!'

'Oh! I thought you meant a beer.'

'You *lied* to me to get me in here!' he levelled, taking what he'd read in the *Lonely Planet's* Dangers and Annoyances section too literally. Then he turned to walk back in.

I lunged for the doorway, catching his shoulder, and as he turned with a look of surprise, I said, 'Mate, can I speak to you, please?'

He stepped onto the pavement, looking the silly side of stupid after his outburst. I told him again, I thought he'd meant a beer and that I'd apologised.

'Sorry...' he muttered, staring down at his feet, and as he went to go back in, I shouted, 'Duncan, could you get my friend a drink on the house, please?' noting a look of humility replacing one of hurt.

An hour later, he apologised again on his way out. 'I thought I'd seen it all,' he stared at the ground, 'but it's taken a trip to Hong Kong and a guy like you to humble me.'

His friend chuckled. 'I've tried to explain that this isn't England and you have to be careful what you say to "people" around here.'

'People?' I asked, with a sneaking suspicion who he meant.

'*Triads*, pal.' He gave me a knowing look. 'They're the people that run Wan Chai. I've lived here long enough to know that.'

When I entered the Apple later, an excited Ray came out from behind the bar to meet me. 'Chris, mate, we've got a couple of your lot in here tonight!'

'*My* lot?'

'*Royal Marines!* One of them knocked a couple of blokes out earlier. Did me a favour actually coz they were upsetting the customers. He's in the corner.'

I made my way over, unable to believe that spotting me the moment I did him was Dave 'Dinger' Bell, a corporal I knew from Plymouth. '*Dinger*, what the fuckin' hell are you doing in Hong Kong?'

'Me and Knocker are on our way back from Brunei. Fuckin' Knocker only went and banged out a couple of civvies earlier!'

'Yeah, I heard.' I shook my head. 'Do I know Knocker?'

Dinger took me over and introduced us. They were both older and serving as NCOs with 40 Commando in Taunton. Dinger was a family man, whose dress and attitude could easily pass him off as a tourist, the sort of bloke who behaved with a degree of decorum.

Knocker, on the other hand, still lived the bootneck dream. At six foot four and 230 pounds, he had a crew cut, a ruddy complexion and wore the Marines' 'other' uniform of jeans, T-shirt and chukka boots. He'd served in the Falklands Conflict, completed four tours of Northern Ireland and had spent most of his career in 42 Commando, my former unit. On Fridays and Saturdays, he worked in Plymouth as a bouncer on Union Street. He lived, ate and breathed the Corps, and bloody hated and got paranoid around civilians, especially after drinking all day.

In the morning, Shelley invited us back to her place in the Mid-Levels, saying her mother was in Canada. I broke away to grab the boys, but Dinger had somehow managed to vanish with a girl he'd been chatting to – spousal fealty not being the Armed Forces' strongest point – leaving Knocker to jump in a cab with me.

Passing through the verdancy of suburban Hong Kong, up the winding Cotton Tree Drive, Knocker voiced his distrustful bent. 'So you was a bootneck, yeah?'

'Yeah, I was.' I knew the banal question to follow.

'What *unit* was you in?'

'Four-Two, mate.' I pandered to his cross-examination, making a mental note never to employ this guy as my barrister.

He continued to eye me with brooding suspicion, so I played my trump card: 'I'm a mate of J.O.D.'

John O'Donnell was a popular and long-serving corporal that I knew Knocker would know. John had served in 42 Commando a number of years and moonlighted on Union Street too.

'So *you* know *J.O.D.*?' he asked, with unnecessary amazement.

'Yeah, went on holiday with John last year. Skiing in Aviemore.'

'*Why didn't you say?*'

'Just did.'

'Yeah... right...'

It would have been laughable – except Knocker wasn't a person to laugh at – that knowing J.O.D. qualified me as a marine, not the seven years of service I seem to remember doing.

As Knocker and I entered the luxurious condominium, a uniformed porter stepped forward to usher us into a lift that spoke *more* better English than I did. We travelled up to the penthouse suite to find Shelley inside with an old school friend, Kirsty, and Hippy Pat and a traveller couple. Max, one of the Apple's Chinese barmen, was busy racking up lines of cocaine on the coffee table.

Shelley broke out the Moosehead, flown in from Canada, and I settled down to catch up on the goings-on in Plymouth with Knocker, who was still chuffed to bits I knew John O'Donnell.

Partway into our conversation, Max interrupted us by calling me over to do a line. When I rejoined Knocker, he asked, with a degree of unease, what it was we were doing.

'Bit of charlie, mate,' I told him.

'*Ah!*... bit of charlie... right.' He nodded vaguely. '*So*... what's that, then?'

'Coke, Knocker. You know what coke is, right?'

'*Yeah!* I know coke...' he said, looking even more confused, his eyes glued to the coffee table. 'I've seen *drugs* before...'

But the next thing I knew, he was grabbing my arm, the way a girlfriend might when you've just walked her into an alleyway full of thuggery.

'I'm talking *shit!*' he hissed. 'In all my years down Union Street, I ain't never *seen* drugs!'

'This ain't Union Street, mate. This is Hong Kong – although you'll find the same thing in Plymouth.'

'*Nah!*... If I ever found anyone taking that shit...' He bunched his big fists.

'Yeah! You'd have to fight a lot of people!'

'*Weeell*...' he said, not convinced. 'How can *you* be so calm?'

'You gotta be realistic. No point getting upset over a bit of white powder from a weed that grows in the dirt.'

He shook his head. 'No, I mean how can you be so *calm*? *Look* at you! You're not pissed or anything. It don't seem right.'

'It's been a while since getting bladdered, fighting, and puking over women was a good night out,' I told him. 'I'm not up for that any more.'

It was obvious Knocker felt way out of his comfort zone, and I could tell he was winding himself up for a violent act. Three two-inch lines of plant extract had frightened this huge commando, and if he couldn't bully people into his way of thinking, he was going to start punching.

I'd already made my mind up he wasn't going to unleash on this amiable crowd. I felt confident I could control him by guile, but if necessary, I would smash the coffee table over his head – lines an' all – then kick him in the bollocks.

In an attempt to calm Knocker down, I suggested we go onto the balcony and check out the world's most spectacular vista: Hong Kong and its vibrant harbour scene playing out in full.

There I was in out-and-out contentment, enjoying a sight like no other, but Knocker hadn't even registered its existence. The only thing concerning him was Hippy Pat – the blot on his landscape.

Pat, bless him, wasn't harming anyone, unless that anyone was overly concerned with fashion or hygiene. He stood chilling with his back against the balcony's rail, sunglasses on, soaking up the morning rays. His big toes had opted for a spot of sunbathing too. They were poking through his socks and creating an offence against Knocker's military standards.

'Better get a new pair of socks, mate, eh?' said Knocker, balling his hands and glaring to get Pat's attention – only Pat remained blissfully unaware and continued his Ra worship.

'*And* you better sort your *fuckin'* life out!' he taunted, waiting for one wrong word.

But just as I thought that it was time to step in, Pat's head tilted forward, he lifted his shades, looked this massive marine in the eye and, in his heavy antipodean twang, said, '*Yeaah...* yer *royt*, mate.'

'These people are weird,' said Knocker, eyeing Matty and Claire, the traveller couple, as we went back inside. 'I'm worried about you.'

'Worried! About *me?*' This was a different person to a few seconds ago.

'Yeah. I'm worried about leaving you in *'Ong Kong* with these freaks. Why don't you come back to Guz (Plymouth) and rejoin the Corps?'

'I'll be fine, mate,' I assured him. 'Just give my best to J.O.D.'

'Yeah, I'll do that. And give me your address. I wanna stay in touch. Check you're alright, sort of thing.'

Then he shook his head in disbelief and disgust and said, 'What the *fuck* am I talking about? I've never written a letter in my life! You just look after yourself, Chris, yeah?'

'I will do, mate. Have a good trip back to Blighty.' Despite his behaviour, I was grateful for the once-a-marine, always-a-marine loyalty for which the Corps is renowned.

And that was that. Knocker left the Fragrant Harbour, leaving two strangers nursing concussions and Hippy Pat staring down pensively at his poking-out digits, murmuring, '*Royt, mate…*Yer *royt*.'

Come late afternoon, it was only Shelley, Max and me left, chatting in the front room.

Max didn't look the way other Hong Kong Chinese did. With his high cheekbones, long face and eyes set at a slant, he seemed like he belonged in the Ming dynasty. He lived with Jackson, the other barman from the Apple, and told me they considered themselves more Western than Asian. 'We don't fit in here,' he said. 'We don't think like Chiniss do.' Then with a frown, he added, '*Errh*, Quiss'a. Why when I give you some line lass night, you say, "Max, you try to *kill* me?"'

'Ah! You were being so generous, I was joking you might be trying to overdose me! It was kind of you to share it with everyone.'

'*No* problem! I only have one gram. Is not enough for me, so I think better to share with everybody.'

'*Wha…?* One gram's not enough! I was *flying*, Max!'

'*No!* One gram nothing! Me an' Jackson snort two-metre line one time. We have photo – look like tennis court!' He grinned.

Max was a humble man. I didn't want to say goodbye to the two of them, but it was nearing 7pm.

Now that the festive inducement wore off, I felt tired and sketchy. The shuddering syndrome returned, sending waves jolting through my system. I was worried about having to stand on the door for five hours and glad Rick's Café shut at midnight on a Sunday. While I jumped in the shower, Shelley went to have a look in her mother's medicine cabinet for some Valium. With a cheeky smile, she handed me a double-strength blue one, saying, 'This'll sort you out!'

It did. As the cab dropped into Wan Chai, I began to mellow and the evening passed without incident, which is more than I can say of the week that followed…

Sacked... Again

I STOOD ON THE DOOR of Rick's Café with the yellow paisley-splashed tie tucked in my pocket. Old Ron had paged earlier, asking if I was up for a few beers. He finished work in the restaurant at midnight on a Monday, the same time I did. When out on the town, Ron had been wearing the tie for his waiting job, and I thought later, having ditched my dicky bow, I would join him. I'm not sure what I was thinking – a quasi-tribute to my old mate, perhaps? Despite spending his nights in the park, he always made an effort to look dapper.

Yawning incessantly, I prayed to any god available Mack Zane would turn up with the packet of 'livener' I'd requested. He said he would drop it off when he came over from the flat he and his Filipina girlfriend shared in Happy Valley, home to Hong Kong's magnificent racecourse.

Good to his word, Mack appeared out of the ether. Shaking my hand, he passed over a foil wrap containing veritable icebergs. In return, I tucked a folded HK$500 note into his shirt pocket.

We got chatting and I learnt he had met his girlfriend in Wan Chai when she'd been a working girl in one of the clubs. I thought it sincere of him to trust me with such information and kind that he invited me to his place anytime for a chat – or whenever I 'needed' something.

When Mack left, I tapped out a few crystals onto a window ledge, screened from the club by a blind, and put my flexible friend to good use. Taking a quick look up and down Jaffe Road, I pulled out a ready-rolled note.

'Jesus! This stuff hits you right away,' I thought, feeling fatigue rising from my body like an exorcised demon.

Being Monday, the club was quiet. I appreciated the company of a young Russian who introduced himself as Yuri in American-flavoured

English. Somewhat coyly, he asked if I could guess what had brought him
to Hong Kong.

'A tourist, Yuri?'

'Nope!'

After a few more of my stabs in the dark, he said, 'Watch this!'

He did the splits, then leant forward putting all his weight onto his
hands and lifting his legs a foot off the ground to turn his body into a
T-shape – and all right there on the pavement.

'Wow! Are you a ballet dancer?'

'Aha!' said Yuri, grinning modestly. 'I'm with the Bolshoi. We perform
in Hong Kong right now.'

'I'll have a go at that!' I told him, gymnastics one of my stronger points,
although I managed to go one further, lifting myself up into a handstand
and holding it several seconds before flipping back down.

'Hey! You are ballet dancer!'

'Nah, Yuri!' I laughed, my mind flicking to what Knocker would have
made of our campery and which one of us he would feel obliged to stave
in first.

'What do you do when you finish work?' Yuri asked.

'I'm off for a drink with a friend.'

'Oh, that's a shame… ' His face saddened. 'I have a bottle of vodka at
my hotel?'

Now, if I had a problem recognising when women were chatting me
up, I was even slower on the uptake with Yuri – or to realise that Yuri was
se fat gui, to use the local idiom. I thought he was just being friendly –
which he was.

Four smartly dressed middle-aged expats approached the door. As I held
it open, one of the two women hesitated and asked 'Are you Chris?' in a
Canadian accent.

'I am, and you must be Shelley's mum,' I replied, thanking Heaven she
hadn't returned from her trip the previous day, as she introduced herself
as Yvonne.

'I'm worried about Shelley,' she said, the stress clear on her face.

Despite feeling guilty about taking drugs and sleeping with this
woman's daughter, I reassured her everything would be alright, saying I

would speak with Shelley and talk her into going back to school – though knowing how headstrong this girl was, I had a job on my hands.

Later, during a quick tour of the bar, I heard *SMASH!* While practising his drink-mixing skills, Richard had dropped a bottle of rum, much to the amusement of the customers.

Reg raised his eyes.

'Aren't you supposed to get that in the glass, Rich?' I enquired.

He was a fun bloke and went out with Natalie, who also worked behind the bar.

'Rich, have you heard of this Brandon Block?'

'Yeah, man! *Top* DJ! Alex P too. Real wreckheads but mental with the vinyl. We're all off to see on Saturday, if you're up for it?'

'Yeah, I will be. Thanks.'

Duncan came out of the office. Knowing he wasn't as lenient as Reg, I cut the conversation short and was heading back outside when who should come through the door with a real stunner in tow but John Taylor, formerly of Gung Wan Hong.

'*Hello*, Chris! I didn't know you worked here.'

'Afraid so, mate. And who's this—?'

'Oh! This is Jennifer... from Taiwan... a friend of my wife.'

'How are you, Jennifer?' I asked his petite companion.

'I'm fine, thank you, Creese,' she replied, her accent divine.

Duncan gave me a look, so I said I'd speak to them later and returned to my post.

Looking down Jaffe Road, I saw one of the planet's most interesting mammals approaching. DJ Denzel was a Jamaican Rasta who shared his time between DJing in the Caribbean and here in Hong Kong.

He was a fine man, Denzel, and I think the feeling was mutual, as Rick's Café wasn't exactly his bag of grass but he'd pop down just to chat to me. From his bottom half, you could see he went to the Neil Diamond School of Fashion, though with his laces undone as a one-minute steak, he passed it off a lot better. Plus, you knew his top half wouldn't accost you with a python or try to force you out of the labour market.

I reckoned he might be lonely, because he was always by himself *and* he appreciated my jokes – his roaring a definite sign of too much time spent in solitude.

After yapping a while, I said, 'Hey, Denzel, watch this!' and then banged out the handstand routine I'd learnt from Yuri.

'*He-hey*, mon! Dat's sum tricky ting you got gowin'on'dare. Ornly you would do sumting li' dat!' Then bidding me, 'Irie, mon. A'll see you layta, al-right,' he went off up the street, stopping to turn and guffaw every few yards, shaking his dreadlocks as he did.

Shortly after, Dom turned up to say hi before hitting the Big Apple. He was a commercial diver who I'd met in there one night when we'd discovered he knew an ex-marine mate of mine from Plymouth and that they'd dived on a job here together.

'You been down today, Dom?'

'Mate, on the bottom of the harbour at seven this morning, *E'ing* off my face! I didn't leave the club til five-thirty.'

'*Wha*? You been diving on ecstasy?'

'Mate, it was great! I was dancing on the sea floor!'

'You're a *nutter*!'

'*Yeaah*,' he suddenly looked serious, 'and so are you, from what I've been hearing. What's all this shit you've been taking ice?'

'What's wrong with ice?'

'What's *wrong*, mate, is that stuff seriously *fucks* people up! There's a queue of *gweilos* a mile long at the airport messed up on that shit and having to get the fuck out of Hong Kong. Do you wanna be next?'

'Don't worry, mate, I'll be alright.' I said, appreciating that here was a guy looking out for a fellow Brit he hardly knew. But if Mack Zane could take this stuff every day and still function okay, then why couldn't I?

The club slowly filled. Erik, the biker, stopped out front for a chinwag. Mr Chau, the kung fu master, came in promising profusely to give me lessons soon. And James, from Peter Stuyvesant, kindly brought me a carton of Marlboro, which I shared amongst the staff.

And just as I was wondering why only blokes stood outside talking to me, Jennifer, John's Taiwanese friend, popped her face around the door. '*Creese!*' She came outside to grab my arm. 'Come and dance with me!'

Slightly pissed, she must have been, because there's no way a typically reserved Asian girl would ask a doorman – one she'd just met – for a dance. I felt chuffed, as she was adorable… or sexy… or whichever is the greater.

'Jennifer, I'd love to. It's just my manager wouldn't be too happy.' I was thinking of stroppy-Jock Duncan. I didn't think Reg would mind. Without another word, she slipped back inside.

The next thing I knew, the door flew open, Duncan shouting, 'Chris! You're on'ae dance floor, pal!'

'*Yes!* El *Nice-O!*' I congratulated myself, making my way onto the varnish to meet her.

As we began to trip and whirl, kicking up a storm to the Weather Girls' 'It's Raining Men', the DJ got on the microphone: 'Let's hear it for the *dancing* doorman, ladies and gentlemen!' the crowd clapping and cheering.

Later, as she left the club with John, Jennifer dug in her handbag and pulled out a business card with the name of a Taiwanese cosmetics company on it. She scribbled a Hong Kong pager number on the back, handed it to me and asked for mine so she could contact me next time she was in town.

Walking towards the Big Apple to meet Old Ron, I reflected on what an eventful night it had been – and that it was still young.

A tourist from Tyneside stopped me, asking for directions to Club Nemo. I told him the way and asked if he wanted to see a trick. 'Why not, meete!' he replied.

I dropped into the splits, palms flat on the pavement, pushing up into the perfect handstand and holding it for twenty seconds.

'What do you reckon, mate?'

'Aye, that's'a cannae trick, that is like!' he replied, looking slightly surprised. 'That's bloody good, that is like!'

Neil Diamond came out of the 7-Eleven, shovelling quick-noodles into his mouth with a plastic fork.

'Alright, Neil!' I surprised him. 'How many of them have you scoffed?'

'Oh, *hi*, Chris!' he said, putting a massive emphasis on the 'hi' and sounding like a theatrical lovey. 'This is my *fourth* bowl!'

'Any bigger?'

'I don't know… it's *really* hard to tell.' He looked sad now that the Mr Olympia title looked doubtful.

'Well, keep trying! There's a door job going begging at Joe's.'

'*Yeah…* I heard you got *fireeed.*'

He made such wide eyes and dragged the word 'fired' out so long, I changed the subject. 'Did you hear about Mark?'

'*Yeaah!*' he said, drama still in his voice. 'He's been *arrested.*'

'Do you know what prison he's in?'

'No! But I spoke to Kuku, and he's going to use the compensation from his court case with the record company to get him a solicitor.'

'Oh, he's fucked then!' I almost laughed aloud at the thought of the conversations Neil must have with Kuku as they flew over the cuckoo's nest together. 'Is Kuku gonna pay for some pigs to have flying lessons, as well?'

'What do you mean?'

'Never mind.' I pulled the tie out of my pocket. 'Let's go and find Old Ron.'

We found Ron in a cage at the back of Wan Chai Police Station. My pager had gone off with a request to bail him out.

He looked out of sorts, what with the unsavoury characters banged up with him, sticking out even more as the only *gweilo*, but his serene smile let us know the dark horse was taking it in his stride.

'Been buggered yet, mate?' I asked through the bars.

'Not yet, Marine Boy, but I'm still hoping. Nice tie by the way!'

'Yeah, I put it on for our night out… Didn't know we'd be spending it in here, though. I feel a bit *overdressed.*'

Shit! This was great! Life doesn't get any better than seeing your best mate stuck in a cell with serial rapists!

'So do you need money or shall we just bust you out with dynamite like the good old days?' I reached in my pocket for my wallet.

'No need, Chris,' said Ron, as a jangling policeman appeared to unlock the door. 'I got a hold of my boss, in case you couldn't make it. He's paid my bail.'

'Good move, mate,' I said, skegging the shithole of a place. 'What are you in for, anyway?'

'Ice cream…'

'I *like* ice cream!' said Neil.

'*Ice cream?*… The stuff you eat?'

'Yeah,' he shrugged, the picture of innocence.

'You're a real rotten bastard! Do you know that, Dennison?'

'I know,' said Ron, looking anything but guilty.

As we walked away from the cop shop, down Jaffe Road towards Clubland, Ron revealed all. He'd been delivering ice cream when he first moved to Hong Kong. On the day he was due to leave the job, he crashed his boss's van. The guy had no insurance so he told the police Ron stole it, saying he left the company a day earlier. The police stopped Ron this evening for a routine search and discovered there was a warrant out for his arrest.

We made for Delaney's on Luard Road – an upmarket Irish pub that sold an impressive collection of malt whiskies and rugby shirts from a rather jazzy, mahogany, brass and glass-shelved bar area. En route, I noticed more flyers advertising the mysterious Brandon Block and partner and their Hard Rock Café gig. Everyone I'd spoken to assured me of the same thing: '*Best* DJs in the world!' I was looking forward to Saturday.

Being early on Tuesday morning, Delaney's was almost empty. We bought drinks and sat at a table in the corner. It must have been four seconds before Neil asked if I had any ice, which thanks to Mack I did. Only, I didn't have tinfoil. 'Don't worry,' said Ron. 'I'll ask behind the bar.'

'*Wha…?*' I blurted, but it was too late.

What the hell did he think he was doing? What do three misfitting blokes in a pub in Wan Chai require tinfoil for… other than the *bleedin'* obvious! I hoped the girl serving would simply lean under the counter and produce a roll conveniently tucked away for some strange purpose – but no!

She shouted to her manager, '*BOSS!* Do we have any *TINFOIL?*'
'*Wha?*'
'*TINFOIL, BOSS!* Have we got any *TINFOIL?*'
'*TINFOIL?* I don't know if we've got any *TINFOIL.* I'll ask in the kitchen. How much *TINFOIL* do they want?'
'How much *TINFOIL* do you want?' she asked Ron, her voice reverberating around the bar with such volume, I worried she'd get us arrested and shatter every window on the island.

'*Oh…* about that much,' said Ron, holding his fingers apart like a reminiscing angler and indicating a piece just big enough to take drugs.

I wondered if now was the right time to start searching for a hole to crawl into or maybe just smash my face into the table so hard they'd have to consult my dental records to find out who I was. You could even hear the word '*TINFOIL*' bandied in abundance out in the kitchen.

I was all for leaving the pub immediately, but Ron told me I was being 'paranoid' and to go to the toilet and get on with it.

He was using that word a lot lately. It was starting to get annoying.

I locked myself in a cubicle, but just as I had it all sorted and was taking a first inhale of the sweet-tasting fumes, I realised I wasn't alone.

I could hear footsteps…

There was a knock on the door…

My heart stopped…

'Let us in!' whispered Laurel.

'*Jaldi! Jaldi!*' whispered Hardy.

'You *freakin'* idiots!' I hissed. '*Why* couldn't you just *wait?*'

With Dumb and Dumber squeezed in beside me, I got the illicit activity underway, again, only to hear someone else enter the gents.

I put my finger to my lips: '*Sssh!*'

We stood in silence, waiting an inordinate amount of time, and just as we heard a running tap and the washing of hands, Neil shouted out, '*EXCUSE ME! WOULD YOU MIND FUCKING OFF, COZ WE'RE TRYING TO TAKE DRUGS IN HERE!*' and despite the possibility of fifteen years sweating our proverbials off in a cockroach-infested slammer, Old Ron and I creased up.

By 10am, a good few bars later, it was only me left – Neil taking leave earlier along with a few chunks of ice, likely to go and charm his pet earthworm, race some snails or dissect an anaconda. Ron lasted until nine, disappearing at Lee Aimes' invitation to go to his place and smoke weed. Lee, as I was finding out, was a real nice guy when sober.

Feeling like staying out, I'd made my way to Carnegie's, a popular *gweilo* haunt, and sat by a table of drunken expats who'd been in the Apple all night and a bloke on his own drinking shorts.

One of the girls leaned over. '*Excuse me!* Why you *wearin'* a tie?'

'Sorry?'

'I said, why you *wearin'* a tie?'

'I've been out with my mate,' I told her, feebly, feeling unsure of the reason myself.

'Well, you look *fuckin'* ridiculous! Do you think you're better than us?'

'No...' I mumbled, and feeling angry and stupid, went back to my Corona.

'*Mate!*' The shout came from the lone drinker, a Cockney, who extended the hand of friendship. '*Any time* you wanna wear a tie, you wear a fuckin' tie, *yeah?*'

It was a diamond thing to say, my mood uplifting immediately. I shook his welcomed paw. 'Sorry, mate. I saw you out last night, but I don't know your name. I'm Chris.'

'*Noyce* one, Chrissy,' said the solid character. 'I'm *Brandon*, mate. *Brandon Block*.'

'FUCKIN' *HONG KONG! HONG* FUCKIN' *KONG!*' screamed Brandon on the microphone to the Hard Rock Café's massive crowd, as a remixed 'Earth Song' blared around the club.

'*HONG KONG!*' we roared like Spartans on the battlefield.

It had been a night to remember, and Brandon and Alex P certainly lived up to their reputation as world-class DJs.

Brandon had introduced me to 'P' in the Apple. '*P! P!* Meet Chris. Chris is coming to the gaff were playin' Saturday. Fuckin'... *errh...*'

'Hard Rock *Café?*' Alex P suggested.

'*Yeah*, that's it!'

I laughed.

On the Friday night before the gig, they'd staggered arm in arm past Rick's Café, both drunk as skunks. 'We're looking for a *titty* bar, Chris!' P informed me, eyes as excited as a chocoholic who's just discovered that certain nightclubs are built out of Fruit and Nut.

'Sorry, we haven't got any tits, P – well, other than Duncan, our manager – but come in free of charge and have a drink on the house.'

They accepted my offer with enthusiasm, and as I introduced them to Duncan's girlfriend, who sat stamping hands, Brandon said, 'How ya doin', love?' and planted one on her.

I asked Duncan to treat them to drinks, only he came outside five minutes later with a look of disdain. 'Chris! Who are *those* fucking guys? They're causing a fucking *rrriot* inside!'

'*Those* two, Duncan…' I swelled with pride, 'are the *best* DJs in the world!'

I had a feeling I wouldn't be in that job much longer.

The set the boys played 'back to back' was superb, the music banging so hard it wouldn't have surprised me if Hong Kong Island had sunk a few feet into the harbour.

At my request, Brandon and Alex had come to the door, letting the Rick's Café staff in as VIPs. We all had a great night.

It'd started out as a laugh too. After we'd packed up the chairs on the patio garden, wiped the bar down and locked up, Reg bought us beers on the house. Someone brought up the subject of the zodiac, and I said I could guess people's star signs. Rich challenged me to try.

'*Virgo*, mate! *Easy!*' I replied, knowing intuitively I was right.

'*Fuck me*, Chris! How did you guess that?' He chuckled.

'Don't know, mate. Just can.' I tried to look nonchalant.

'What about me?' asked Reg.

'Sagittarius!'

'*Whoa-ho-ho!*' Everyone joined his amazement.

'And me?' Rich's girlfriend, Natalie, jumped in.

'*Errm…* Leo?'

'*Nope!*' she said smugly.

'I'm joking. It's *Capricorn!*'

'No *way*! How do you do that?'

'I don't know,' I replied, tongue in cheek, and certainly not volunteering that meth seemed to take you to a higher state of consciousness... or that it might just be coincidence.

After the Hard Rock Café, and with the first rays of sunlight starting to sparkle life into the sleeping harbour, we took a tramcar to Wan Chai.

Travelling the narrow-gauge line along Des Voeux Road Central, sitting on the upper deck of this delightful mode of transport with the drug and alcohol combos keeping our morale high, an extremely pissed Rich decided it was time for a blazing row.

'You *uuuugly old cow*!' he slurred across the aisle at Natalie.

'*Faaarck yooooou*, you *blind bastard!*' she shot back, the inhibition of a gin queen.

Rich stood up and raised his voice. 'I wish I WAS blind rather than have to look at *you... you... MINGER*!'

Nat stood up and raised hers even higher. '*MINGER?* That's CHARMING considering the girlfriends YOU'VE 'AD... you... PLEB!'

'*Errh... errh... errh...*'

As Rich attempted a retort in equal pitch and voracity, his grasping for insults had us in stitches, Nat fighting to suppress a smile.

Fortunately, for the driver, Wan Chai arrived, sending us all into purgatory in the guise of the Big Apple – a cruel twist of fate giving us the least opportunity to absolve ourselves of our sinful behaviour.

Now if leaving the Apple in the morning was an experience to tell the grandkids, so was going back in at this enchanting hour. Making our way down the mirror-lined stairway's creaking wood, the dull thuds coming out of the club's smoky atmosphere rose up to meet us – meekly at first, yet as we descended they smothered the sound of the awakening metropolis.

Being below street level, the Apple had no windows. This lack of natural light together with a wonky crowd synced to the beat and still buying drinks made it feel as though you'd entered a time warp – a scene no different to 11pm the previous evening.

It seemed wonderfully inappropriate and far better than scrambled eggs. With meth coursing through my veins, it felt great to return to this timeless environment and satiate the restlessness with uplifting tunes and a slide on the boards.

I looked around for Shelley, to no avail – her absence a sure sign of delinquency taking place elsewhere in the colony. I missed Dream and Nicole's presence too. So as the last of the crusaders from Rick's Café took leave or comforted up on the sofas, I resigned to dance heaven on my own and Josh Wink's 'Higher State of Consciousness', which seemed entirely appropriate.

'CD decks? Waste of time, Chris!' one of the DJs in the Apple had said to me during a discussion about the merits of the incoming digital era's mixing equipment. 'It always comes out on vinyl first,' he'd concluded – a touch arrogantly, as it happened, because here I was in DJ Denzel's apartment, listening to the most impressive set I'd ever heard.

I'd bumped into my Rasta friend when leaving the Apple. I'm not sure which of us was higher or who'd had the better night, but neither of us wanted it to end. I welcomed the invitation to go back to his flat to smoke some weed. As I skinned up, he got on his decks – the likes of which I didn't know existed. Denzel extolled the virtues of digital sound while showing off the machine's functions, the music speaking for itself.

I soon found myself lost in remixed reggae, whirling dervish on his flat's shiny floor. Denzel was a digital DJing genius and he appreciated, more than anyone, the way lightning dances across a statically-charged sky. At one point, I looked up to see him with his camera, cackling demonic at the show he was capturing on video.

The downside to our festivity was that, coming down off the drugs, poor old Denzel got all upset. 'What's wrong, mate?'

'Nobaddy like me, mon.'

A tear rolled down his cheek.

'*Nah*! That ain't true! You're a *super* geezer! Not everyone walks down Jaffe Road to chat to me on the door!'

It seemed to cheer him up.

The upside was, whenever I met him in the future, he'd always remind me of the video, saying he'd shown it to all his friends – so he must have had some.

It was kind of Lee Aimes to invite me to his thirtieth-birthday bash, at the Excelsior – a lavish hotel enjoying a staggering harbour view from Causeway Bay's waterfront.

Our relationship didn't exactly have the best of starts, what with the imaginary gun episode. I'd have preferred an invisible box of chocolates or non-existent tickets to the football. Yet here I was in the supermarket wondering how to cement our blossoming amity with a real bottle of HK$400 champagne… without the real money to pay for it.

In the end, I resorted to something I hadn't done since I was a kid – I shoplifted it. I took a quick look around, put it under my jacket and walked out.

I can't say I felt particularly good, especially as it was a present, but I can't say that under the circumstances I felt that bad. As the Irishman had said, in this neck of the woods it was sink, swim or get the fuck out of the pool. I was in survival mode, and as with killing the fluffy white bunny on exercise in the Marines, I put the moralising on hold.

Back at Vance's, I found some wrapping paper and a gift-tag. I wrote: *LA, Best Respect, CJ*, and then made my way to the Excelsior.

Sitting in the exquisite setting of the saloon bar, in his usual attire of suit and open-neck shirt, Lee appeared touched by my gesture. He only had three other guests: his father, an uncle and a chap named Gonzales, who looked something of a rogue.

I went to the bar to get a round in and, lo and behold, who should be serving behind it but Shirley, my one-eared friend with the drink and striptease problem, who I'd poured into a taxi on several occasions.

'Hello, Shirley! I didn't know you worked here!'

'Yeah, I'm head barman.' He smiled, and then, with a degree of bemusement, asked, '*Erm*…why you calling me *Shirley?*'

'That's your name.'

'Is it?'

'Yeah – well, that's what you told me.'

'*Did* I?'

'You did!'

'*Really?*'

'Honest!'

'Ooh *fuck*!'

It was the 'Ooh *fuck*!' of someone who's long since resigned the events of a night out to other people's memories, like trying to recall a film you watched when stoned.

'I put you in a cab.'

'*Did* you?'

'A few times now.'

'*Awwh*, mate! Thanks a lot... *errh*—'

'Chris.'

'What you 'aving, Chris? On the house, mate... *Oh*! And my name's Alex.'

After a couple of hours, Gonzales suggested we go to the Apple and meet Lee there later. He was an interesting character, dressing nouveau gangster-style like Lee. With his shaved head, goatee beard, gold hooped earrings and Mediterranean swarthiness, I think he might have been a pirate – one more likeable than rogue.

'There's nothing like taking a shit in your own home!' he informed me on the MTR, and then asked if I minded a detour to his flat.

Having evacuated his chocolate hostage, he showed me a load of hooky gear, the sale of which supported his stay in Hong Kong.

'You don't work, then?'

'*Hah!* I don't *work*, mate!' He grinned. 'Hardest work I ever did was chasing Pakis up the street as a kid!'

I wondered what his résumé looked like:

Gonzales.

Current Occupation: Buccaneer.

Qualifications: Chasing Pakistanis.

Experience: Same.

Strengths: Same.

Hobbies: Same.

'He must know the right people in this city,' I thought, not knowing how I'd survive without a job.

He poured a packet of cocaine into the bowl of an aluminium ladle, added some bicarbonate of soda and a little water and then held it over the gas ring on the cooker. 'Do you like freebase, Chris?' he asked, with a piratical glint.

'*Freebase?*'

'*Crack!* Do you wanna smoke some?' He stopped heating the spoon and hung it by its hook on a cooling fan.

'I'll have a go!' I said, happy at the bonus this excursion had thrown into the mix.

After a couple of minutes, Gonzales began scooping out pasty lumps with a kitchen knife and filling a small, heavily tarnished bulbed-glass pipe, which he stuck in my mouth and held a lighter to. As I sucked, the bulb filled with smoke like a miniature crystal ball.

'*Fill the ball, Chris!*' he urged.

As I did, he took his finger off a hole in the pipe's side, releasing the precious chemical on the final part of its journey from South America.

'How do you feel?'

'*Huht… Huht…*' I raised a finger, fighting to keep the smoke in. Then finding a space on his living room floor amongst some knocked-off leather jackets, I pulled a forty-five second handstand.

'*Wow!* Pretty *good*, I take it!' he mused.

'Pretty *fucking* good!' I told him, and then had another blow.

Shelley was in the Big Apple, so I took the opportunity to talk to her about school. Despite spending a fair bit of time together, I didn't know much about the girl – the estranged relationship with her father, her aspirations, even basic things such as which part of Canada she was from.

I was aware, however, we'd grown fond of each other and that our mutuality stemmed from a similar experience of life and the meth to which it had led us.

Although enjoying Shelley's company, I hadn't made a move on her again. She was a lost young woman who needed guidance in this mad existence, not someone taking advantage.

Who was I to be dishing out advice, though? I needed some myself, and even when I got it, I couldn't take it. The time wasn't right.

The manager of a hostess bar in Tsim Sha Tsui had offered her a job 'talking' to his customers, rich businessmen away from their wives. I soon put her straight on that one.

After an hour, having convinced her that this wasn't another lecture, she said, 'Okay, I'll go back.'

'Go back?'

'Yeah, I'll go back… to *Canada*… to school.'

Lee came into the club to the sound of Juno's 'Bee in my Bonnet', and as he made a beeline for me, I could tell he had one in his. In the three hours since Gonzales and I left him, he'd managed to get way past wasted, *again*, and had fallen foul of security at the Excelsior's nightclub.

Kevin headed the team over there – the martial arts expert I'd met through Mal the lawyer. Knowing how placid Kevin was, I reckoned these guys had done nothing to provoke Lee, who always proved adept at winding himself up. The Excelsior's doormen prided themselves on being a professional and accredited crew, taking their work somewhat more seriously than their counterparts in Wan Chai. I knew this because I'd eavesdropped on a conversation one of them was having outside the Apple one morning as I sat on the curb waiting for a cab.

As the guy stood telling his mate how he'd undergone a six-day course in bodyguarding techniques, I couldn't help but smile. Not only is six days not long enough to learn how to look after a guinea pig, but this guy was eighteen stones of flab – he looked better off protecting a pizza.

With his shaved head and goatee beard, he was a definite candidate for the guy that always dies first in a Schwarzenegger film. To make matters funnier, he began to practise the drills he'd learnt, right there on the pavement.

'*Right!* Pretend you're pointing an Uzi at me,' he said – his friend doing just that, only to find himself disarmed of the make-believe weapon.

I reckon that despite its reputation as the Heart of Darkness, Wan Chai must be the safest place on Earth, what with half the population armed with fictitious firearms.

'*Right*! Pretend you're pointing an M-Sixteen at me…' and so it went on, as I sat cringing at the soldier of fortune's performance, wondering where he'd parked his white van and hoping he'd left a window ajar for the Rottweiler.

Suddenly, he stopped in the middle of executing a 180-degree turnaround on his imaginary assassin's invisible Beretta. 'Do you wanna know who knows a lot about weapons?' he asked his friend.

'Who?' replied the non-existent Ninja.

'That guy there…' said the bodyguard, pointing at me.

'How do you know that?' Kato asked, looking lost.

'Because he's sat listening to *everything* we've been saying and he's not said a word…'

The Ardoyne, Belfast, 1989. Four-Two Commando Royal Marines had just arrived in the province for a five-month tour of duty.

On patrol, there were four in our 'brick', and being election night, tension in the city was high. Everyone knew the IRA would do all it could to interrupt the voting process.

Patrolling in single file, SA-80s held at the ready, thirty rounds of 5.56mm ammo in the magazine, we came across a small park with a tarmac footpath running along one side. 'We won't go up here,' shouted 'Tulley' Tull, our corporal. 'It's renowned for booby traps. Break into diamond formation and we'll cut across the grass.'

Just as 'Jock' Campbell, our tail-end Charlie, stepped backwards onto the neatly mown lawn, we heard *BANG-BANG… BANG, BANG-BANG-BANG, BANG!* A sniper armed with a Kalashnikov had opened up from the window of a nearby house, its occupants taken hostage earlier in the day.

As tufts of grass flicked up at my feet, I heard Tulley holler, '*Take fucking cover!*' and the sound of our firing-mechanisms slamming home and echoing off walls.

We sprinted across the open space, making for a lone hut and almost diving on top of one another behind it in our attempt to avoid the incoming fire. When I glanced back, hoping to locate the gunman and return a few rounds, I saw Jock lying sparked out on his front, thirty metres away. I scrambled up to run over and drag him into cover.

'Get the *fuck* down!' screamed Tulley.

'How the *fuck* can I do that?' I thought, deciding to ignore him.

But before I'd taken five steps, Jock lifted his head and began looking around in a daze. Then in an instant, he gathered his wits, rifle and equipment – the latter items flung from his body – and came running over to collapse next to us.

'*I'm hit! I'm hit! I'm hit!*' he shrieked, as I ripped open his combat and flak jacket, searching for an entry and exit wound, and Tully got on the radio to inform HQ we'd been contacted and had a casualty.

'Jock, you're *not* fuckin' hit, mate!' I yelled. 'I can't find any *holes*!'

'*I am! I am!* I'm *fuckin'* hit!' he screamed, desperate I believe him.

It wasn't until we returned to base – Jock having the tenacity to refuse an ambulance and patrol in with us – that the truth prevailed.

One round of 7.62mm had sliced the antenna off the electronic-countermeasure unit he'd been carrying, another passing through his weapon sling and smashing into his chest. Having knocked Jock to the ground, spinning him around and throwing off his gear, it ended up in the top pocket of his combat jacket. Being a 'short' round, fired from a distance of sixty metres, it had a lesser impact – enough for Jocky to live and fight another day. As I was but five metres from Jock at the time, and with greeny-brown geysers kicking up around me, it wasn't difficult to work out who the shooter had set his sights on next.

Did I know a lot about weapons? I knew enough to know they're very dangerous.

'*Right*... gonna go... back *fookin'* Excelsior,' slurred Lee. 'Gotta *teach*...'

'Teach *what*?' I asked the inebriated reprobate.

'*Cunts*... lesson.' His rambling was so incoherent he shouldn't have been considering teaching anyone anything.

From what I gathered, as he was leaving the hotel one of the security team said something that wound him up – though knowing how Lee looked for trouble when drunk, misconstruing situations to cause aggro, I doubted the guy had acted maliciously.

I tried to rationalise with him. 'Lee, man! I know the head of security at the Excelsior. He runs a professional team. They wouldn't give you shit for no reason. Besides, they're all frickin' kung fu ninjas! They'll beat the shit out of us!'

'*Don'* care… *Ooh ooh*… they *fink* they are?'

'*Well…* they probably think they're a highly trained outfit who work for one of the best hotels in the world. They'll let you rabbit on like a pissed-up teenager, while trying not to laugh, and then wrap your legs around your neck, stick your head up your arse and send you home in a cab.'

But Lee wasn't having it. There was no reasoning with him in this state. He was hell-bent on making a fool of himself and getting hurt in the process.

I was starting to get annoyed at the hackneyed hardman routine. 'Alright, if you wanna fight, let's go and beat the shit out of 'em together!' I led the way out of the Apple with Lee bouncing off the walls. As we passed Chan, he just smiled. It was history repeating itself in Wan Chai.

At the end of Luard, a footbridge crossed over Gloucester Road's busy six-lane highway. Lee followed me up the steps, and without saying a word, I hopped up onto the two-inch-wide handrail.

'*W-w-wha?*' he stammered, as I walked along it, twenty feet above the traffic whizzing by below.

Sobering immediately, he screamed, '*What are you doing!*' then rushed over, grabbed my jacket and pulled me down.

'*Hmmh?*' I reflected. 'Maybe he's not such a death-wishing psychopath after all?' It was touching that, despite his fighting talk, he didn't want to see me get hurt.

'Lee, if you don't get up and walk the rail, dude, you're in no fit state to start beating people up. Besides, you gotta be careful in this city. You don't wanna upset the wrong people.'

'What do you mean?' Lee shot me a sideways look.

'*Triads*, mate! You try this shit with them and you'll end up going home in little boxes.'

'You think I'm scared of *fookin'* triads!' He looked furious at the very suggestion. 'I'll introduce you to some *fookin'* triads! I'll introduce you to the *bosses*! Come on, we're going to Club Nemo—'

Despite a developing fascination with this secret brotherhood and the way they operated in the underground, in flagrant violation of the 'rules' yet with concealment and discretion, Lee's pointless bravado was boring me. I was about to say, 'Don't bother, Lee,' but instead, I turned and walked off, leaving him ranting at the cars flashing by.

The sensible thing would have been to go home and get some of the sleep I'd deprived myself of for five days, but I hooked up with Shelley and we went to an all-night dance party in a hotel basement in Admiralty.

We left the place at 8am, ghosts in a big city, and ended up sitting on the steps of a pedestrian overpass, vague and out of focus, a plan of action no longer a factor in this lifetime.

I could hear a young girl's voice muttering, 'Der-der-dum-dum-dum der-der-dum-dum-dum-der-der,' trance-like, repeatedly. I wondered who it was and why there was something familiar about it. After an hour, I looked to my left to see Shelley sat beside me, humming the base line of the track playing when we left the gig.

Although there was something decadent about the scenario, I was happy to sit there with commuters weaving around us. If I'd removed myself from the situation, it would cease to be. I'd have been stealing from myself, denying place and time and meddling with a reasoned existence.

I tried to awake from a thousand sleeps, the hands on my watch telling me I had twenty minutes to get to work – *'Shit!'*

I could have sorted myself out and made it over there, perhaps a little late, if only I had some ice. The packet now empty, exhaustion told me I had no chance.

I telephoned the bar and spoke to Rich. 'Can you tell them I'm ill, mate?' I said – not necessarily a lie – and then went back to the pillow.

When I arrived at the junction of Jaffe and Luard the next evening, there was a guy standing outside Rick's Café wearing a bow tie and bomber, talking to Duncan. As I approached, the boss said, 'Chris, what'ae *you* doing here? I've had to get someone to replace you, pal!'

I wouldn't have minded if this was about missing a night off sick, albeit the only one since working there, but a comment Reg made earlier in the week – 'Chris, look at the *weight* you've lost!' – told me this was about the drugs and that's why I'd been sacked… *again.*

China DJ

'DUK'M'DUK, NGOH TSUT GAI LEEDO'A, M'GOY?' I asked the cab driver back at Victory Avenue, having seen Shelley off at the airport.

I was delighted that the phrase, 'Possible, not possible, I get out here, please?' impressed one of the Big Apple's DJs when we'd shared a taxi a few days ago. Now, fighting back tears, I didn't feel so delighted. Getting out of the car, I bumped into Vance.

'Jou san!' he greeted me, as always a huge smile, then seeing I was far from sporting the same, he asked what was wrong.

I didn't know what was wrong *or* how to explain I'd lost another job and that my little companion had flown away and I missed her terribly.

I just shrugged.

'Errh, Quiss'a...' he began, his hesitancy an indication of the question to follow, 'do you take the drug?'

Trusting Vance and feeling I had nothing to lose, I looked down at the pavement and nodded.

'Oh, *Quiss*! This *very* bad!' His frown spoke more than he did. 'You know, in Hong Kong culture, taking the drug before you make your fortune is *very* bad. When you make your fortune, is *fine*, but before, peepall think you are *loser*! Please...' – he held my arm – *'don'* do the drug!'

It was good advice. Moreover, a request from a friend to whom I owed a great deal. Only it wasn't a life choice I could make. In the same way a window cleaner doesn't just get up one day and decide to become a barrister, although entirely feasible, I just couldn't see it as an option.

Back in my room, I decided to try to cheer myself up by ringing Mr Chau to arrange those kung fu lessons he'd promised.

'Quiss'a! Why you *no'* working a' Rick's Café?'

'Mister Chau, they gave me the sack. Anyway, I was phoning to ask—'

'*Sack!* Li' you go' *fired?*'

'Yeah, I got sick and—'

'Quiss'a, listen. How abou' you call when you ge' another job?'

'But, Mister—' The line went dead.

Hell! I had no idea what that was all about, but whatever it was, I felt more dejected than ever. It seemed a good time to reach for the wrap of crystals I'd bought off Mack the previous day.

I clung to the rust-blotched pipework in the ferry's toilet cubicle with one hand, chopping up a line of ice on the rim of the steel washbasin with the other.

On the ageing tub's three-hour journey to Taiping, the choppy waters of the channel buffeted it incessantly, the frothy crests picked off the waves by the wind slamming into the bulkhead – a reminder that the other passengers knew nothing of my secretive act but Mother Nature damn well did and she wasn't about to let me forget.

It was hard to believe I was wending my way towards an upcoming meet with the managers of the biggest nightclub in Southern China. In fact, it was hard to believe what had happened, full stop.

> DJ Required to Work in CHINA!
> English or European. Must have knowledge of Western pop music and speak Cantonese.
> Telephone: (852) 335 1212 for an interview.

Having rung the number in the *Post* on the off chance, I arrived at an office in Kowloon Tong for an interview. The only person in the room, a Chinese woman, showed me a fifteen-minute promotional video featuring highlights from the world's most magnificent nightclub.

A huge construction, it was set out on three tiers, a balcony on the top one occupied by fifty or so Chinese girls in their teens, all dressed in yellow crop-tops and matching miniskirts – their part in the proceedings slow to register in my mind.

The second level entertained businessmen and their friends in private function rooms, all with leather suites, waiting service and karaoke TV.

A huge dance floor featured a spectacular light and laser show, fireworks and a ballet-cum-dance troop in eye-catching pink silk pyjamas.

To top it off, as the camera panned in to the DJ arena, the Western DJ was cueing up a record on a set of *Technics decks!* The owners of this mega-palace hadn't skimped on a single yuan.

As the film ended, the secretary asked, 'Wha' you think?'

'I think it's great!' I replied, despite the fact I would have told Ronald McDonald the exact same thing.

'Can you go to China, day after tomorrow, meet the managers?'

'Sure!' I couldn't believe my luck. 'But how come you're asking me? What about the other interviewees?'

'*Hah!* Nobody else come for interview. You're the *only* one!'

I'm not sure what I was thinking, applying for a job as a DJ. The last time I used a record player was when they came in a small canvas-covered box, the kind with an arm you pulled over to play a stack of forty-fives.

In preparation for my adventure, I called Ray at his home. 'Mate, do you mind if I go to the Apple and write down the names of some tracks?'

Ever the good-natured friend, 'Sure, Chris. No problem,' he replied.

I got to the Apple at 6pm, when a Filipino band played cover tunes for an hour before one of the club's DJs took over. Just as I'd scribbled down a number of popular dance hits, the band finished their version of 'Pretty Woman' and the lead guitarist approached the DJ booth. 'We finish now,' he said. 'Over to you.'

My watch said 7pm, the time a DJ should have been there with a track cued up to play. As no such person materialised, I flicked the power switches on the decks and amplifier, took up the headphones – covering only one ear as I'd seen DJs do – then slapped Corona's 'Rhythm of the Night' on the right turntable and Kym Mazelle's 'Love Me the Right Way' on the left. It wasn't quite the house music I was passionate about, but funky dance tunes nonetheless, ones that would go down well with the Chinese clientele.

Feeling good to go, I hit the start button on the right deck and gently eased the stylus into the vinyl's opening grooves. As the foxy voice of the Italian band's female lead floated the opening lines out of the club's speakers, the crowd of drinkers supping anonymously at the bar came to life with *'Whoop-whoops!'* and began to hop, skip and windmill their way onto the dance floor.

I felt full-on phenomenal! I knew, there and then, I loved this job.

The first challenge of my not-yet career came when the track ended. Matching Kym Mazelle's beats entering one ear with those of her Latina counterpart in the other, I spied Craig, one of DJs, coming through the door. After I'd eased the slider over, the tracks in perfect synchrony, Craig gave a thumbs-up and came to stand at my side.

'You better take over,' I ventured.

'*Nah*, mate! You carry on!' He gave me a rewarding smile.

I managed to mix in the next disc okay, but the third sounded like a herd of three-legged mustangs running up a flight of stairs pissed. Craig frantically chop-chop-chopped a hand against his throat, so I whacked the slider over to La Bouche's 'Be My Lover' to salvage my career.

When I stepped onto the dock in Taiping, a middle-aged gent wearing gold-rimmed spectacles, grey slacks and a cream sports jacket held up a piece of cardboard with 'Kwis' written awkwardly on it in blue marker pen.

I guessed it was Mr Lee, the only Hong Kong-born and English-speaking manager at the club. After a handshake, we made our way through the mass of disembarking passengers and into a yellow Mercedes with two guys occupying the front seats. Mr Lee engaged me in friendly chat but held me at a distance, the way a potential employer does when they might have to break the bad news to you later.

Driving into the sticks, I noted how barren the place looked compared to the bustling city I'd come from. Every so often, we passed a construction site in the scrubland along the roadside, reminding me of the new developments you see springing up in the Spanish countryside. The buildings with their white walls and terracotta roof tiles looked to be Mediterranean in style too.

As the car sped towards the nightclub – a majestic structure looming out of the desert like a mirage – I questioned Mr Lee on the investment behind the project. He said that enterprise in New China involved a triumvirate of government, corporate and special-interest groups.

I took it that 'special' meant our old friends, the Brothers of the Marsh, were alive and kicking in the Middle Kingdom, albeit with their allegiances rooted in the peasantry becoming somewhat skewed in recent years. Mr Lee let out a chuckle, gave a subtle wink and pulled out a 9mm automatic. 'China is very dangerous place, Quiss!' he said.

With a further flash of bad boy in his eyes, he lifted the jacket of the front passenger to reveal the gunmetal finish on a snub-nosed Magnum. 'This Mister Liang,' he announced, as the athletic-looking man in his twenties turned with fist in palm and bowed several times.

'Mister Liang is China bock-sing champion. In China we call kung fu "bock-sing". You know that?'

'Yeah.' I smiled, liking kung fu, 'bock-sing' and my new company.

'If we, the manager, give you the job, Mister Liang will be your bodyguard. Is *okay?*'

'*Errh…* 'I replied, wondering how to explain that former Royal Marines don't need wet-nursing.

'*No!* Here *many* criminal! Chiniss criminal kill you first, then see if you have money. Unnerstan' me?'

'Uh-huh.' I nodded.

'Here *not* like Hong Kong. Here peepall *very* poor.'

Ego aside, I knew it was true. I'd read that the Chinese government executed 18,000 offenders a year in an effort to stem the spiralling crime rate. A teacher I'd met had been on a train in Guangzhou when the police boarded, dragged off a *suspected* pickpocket and shot him in the head on the platform.

'Do you ever have trouble at the club?' I asked.

'*Yeah!*' Mr Lee replied, sounding pleased. 'One time, we have table of customer who don' pay the bill an' get in their car an' try an' drive away. When we stop them, they pull out *two* guns. We pull out *seventeen!*' He grinned. 'Then Mister Liang, here, kick driver in head through window, knock him unconscious. Then they pay the bill!'

A few hundred yards before the nightclub, the driver pulled into the courtyard of a magnificent villa.

'If you get the job, here is your apattment,' said Mr Lee.

'*Apartment?*' I queried. 'How much will I have to pay?'

'No money! Apattment is *free*!'

Lucky me! I was starting to feel like a celebrity, but I noticed Mr Lee always placed an emphasis on '*if* you get the job'.

'Wai' here now,' he said, and turned to acknowledge a local woman. 'This Miss Wu, the housekeepa. *Errh*, you like Chiniss food?'

'Love it!'

'Okay, Miss Wu make you Chiniss food. But Miss Wu not speaking Cantonese, only speaking Mandarin. Is okay?'

'No problem,' I replied, happier than a ferret up a rabbit hole and not caring a squashed gnat if Miss Wu spoke in tongues, Esperanto or Outer Mongolian in sign language with a postmodern twist.

'*So*, Mister Liang, he come an' get you seven o'clock, go to the club, meet other managers. Yeah?'

'Yeah!'

By 7.10pm, Mr Liang had yet to materialise, so I thought, 'Ah! I'll take a walk over there.'

I left the security of the compound and jogged along the deserted highway in near-total darkness. In the far distance, I could see a humongous flashing sign announcing 'OK Nightclub', the building itself lit up like a Vegas casino on the plain's otherwise empty skyline. As I came up over a small rise, I met with the big grin and bows of China's kung fu champion, the humble Mr Liang, coming in the other direction.

Walking up the red-carpeted boulevard, a bodyguard was the last thing on my mind, for thirty stunning hostesses in figure-hugging *cheongsams* lined either side, shimmering in ruby like the scales of a koi carp. A slow wave of curtsies and alluring smiles squeezed us towards the main door, two soldiers snapping to attention as we entered the spacious lobby.

Mr Liang led me along a marble concourse with red, gold and cream décor and into the main arena. We crossed the vast dance floor to the sound of Canto-romantic pop and made our way towards a table in the shadows to the side.

Mr Lee sat with four other gents, who might well have been the original protagonists in the Cultural Revolution. Austere in both dress and manner, I couldn't help thinking, 'What do these relics know about running a nightclub?' but not speaking a word of English, they kept a measured distance.

Mr Lee proved to be the consummate host, though, supplying me with drinks and enquiring into my past and family background. The only thing he didn't ask me about was my DJing experience – or the lack of it.

I also got the distinct impression I was being given a lesson in the art of war, 'Tactical Disposition', because when it came to discussing the post every question came with the precondition 'If...' – '*If* we like you...' '*If* you get the job...'

'*If* we like you, what salary do you want?' was the next one.

I hadn't even thought about it.

'*Ten* thousand Hong Kong?' I replied, pitching below the wages I'd previously earned.

'*Hmmh?*' Mr Lee mused. 'We think abou' that... *if* you get the job.'

Ceremonious music interrupted our banter, the ballet troupe appearing out of nowhere to fall into formation on the dance floor.

The performance evolved from a subtle display of unblemished romanticism into one of passion and danger, all fuelled by thrilling acrobatics, fireworks timed to perfection and the flowing crêpe streamers waved wildly by the players, who looked sensational in their colourful tasselled raiment.

The show came to a decisive finale, a clash of cymbals signalling the dancers to drop as one, remaining motionless as a dozen flash-bangs sent streams of bright white sparks arcing high into the air before floating down to meet their prostrate pose. Symbolic, I thought, of homage truly earned. With the lightshow dimmed and a fog of dry ice swirling across the stage, it had been magic to watch.

As a young lad in the DJ pit gave volume to The Original's 'I Love You Baby' and the troupe made their exit, Mr Lee asked, 'Quiss'a, *if* you get the job, would you join in the dancing?'

'*Whoa!* Mister Lee...' I wasn't sure if he was serious. 'Why would they want the DJ in the ballet troupe?' I wondered. I didn't think I was sufficiently in touch with my feminine side or had anywhere near the coordination needed to do the other performers justice. I would have looked like a contestant on the *Generation Game*. Besides, what would I tell Knocker the next time I saw him? 'Took your advice, mate. Gave up the demon drugs, left Hong Kong and rejoined the Corps... the *Dance Corps*. Now I'm a ballerina in China!'

A few of the customers got up to boogie, and my feet began to itch. As Mr Lee still hadn't broached the subject of my DJing skills, and conversation with the Red Guard hadn't made the great leap forward Mao envisioned, I asked if it was okay to go and meet them. *'Yeah-yeah!'* he effused, which told me I'd pushed the right button and now was my time to shine.

I walked across the dance floor and shook hands with the DJ, who grinned big teeth, then made my way over to the club's massive stage. In time with a crescendo in the music, I placed my hands flat on the platform's waist-high edge, pushed slowly up into a handstand and walked my upside-down self across to the middle, flicking back down into a flamboyant groove like a closet disco king granted five minutes of fame.

A surge of clubsters rushed to grab a piece of this *gweilo's* mad act. I spurred them on with overhead claps, wolf whistles and a stupid face – a stupid-*er* one – rewarded by a sea of smiles, and limbs and torsos displaying varied ability and musical interpretation.

Two young guys pointed at their chests and mimicked handstands, looking like Muslims in prayer. I invited them on stage and drew an imaginary halfway line. Then I backed up, flipped up and walked two-thirds of the way towards it, turning to see one collapse after three steps yet the other able to walk the length of the stage and back!

The crowd roared, loving seeing the foreigner beaten at his own game and on their turf.

I made my way through a blaze of smiles, handshakes and thumbs-ups into the centre, hoping Mr Lee and the Gang of Four were making a note of it.

The customers were delightful. Many had formed circles into which they thrust promising hopefuls. The crazier the funk, the better the response it received. I went from group to group like the ambassador in the After Eight Mint advert, before collapsing in my chair for a well-needed sip of Chinese beer.

Before the glass touched my lips, Mr Lee leant over, '*Errh*, Quiss'a! *When* you come here, *work* for us, we pay you *eighteen* thousand Hong Kong a month, not *ten* thousand. *Is okay?*'

Back in Hong Kong, Vance kicked my newfound happiness into touch. His positive exterior had developed visible cracks – savings *and* wife gone, the new business venture not the success he'd hoped for and our recent chat about my drug use not helping matters.

'Errh, Quiss'a, you know you costing me a lot of money'a?'

'*Vance!* How was I to know the business would fail?'

'*No*! I not talking abou' the bissniss.' He looked agitated. 'I mean to stay here. The room? An' I take you out for food many time. I pay abou' seven thousand for you.'

I suddenly felt cheap and stupid.

'Vance, I'm sorry I didn't pay more for the food. But the room? You said just pay the aircon.'

'Pay the aircon is fine, but the apattment still cost money.'

'Sorry, Vance. I'm gonna pay you back.'

'*No* need. I juss saying friends muss support each other. Unnerstan' me?'

'Yeah, sure.' I said, knowing what I would do with the first $7,000 of my salary.

On a happier note, my pager beeped, telling me a certain Taiwanese lady was in Hong Kong and looking forward to seeing me. Delighted when we met in a department store in Yau Ma Tei, I gave Jennifer a peck on the cheek. '*No!*' She pulled away. 'In my culture, we don't do like that!'

Well, didn't I feel foolish! I figured here was a girl living the jet-set lifestyle and it would be an appropriate greeting. There was always so much to learn about Asian culture.

We made our way to a bar in Wan Chai, tripping the light fantastic for a couple of hours with an elderly Japanese businessman who was blind-drunk banzai and sweating Asahi into his suit.

Following our exertion, we took up seats at a *dai pai dong* and ordered beers. Jennifer and I didn't have all that much in common. In addition, I felt slightly intimidated by her beauty and virtuousness, knowing as every second ticked by it clashed with my known-only-to-me wretchedness.

A homeless person walked by in the gutter. Passing our table, he gave us a long stare, his pupils coming across as void and evil.

'Why's he looking at us?' my date asked.

'He doesn't mean any harm,' I assured her.

'I think he take the drug...'

'Why's that?' I asked, a wave of discomfort sweeping over me.

'Because he have crasie eyes,' she replied. 'Juss like you.'

Humping my bergen up the steps to Mong Kok's railway station, daypack front centre, briefbag and case weighing a ton in each hand, I paid a heavy price. Physically and mentally exhausted and dripping perspiration, I felt anxiety flitting around in my stomach like bats in a cave.

I'd spent all night in the Big Apple saying goodbye to friends – all of whom wished me luck, some promising to visit. Neil Diamond wasn't there, though. He'd managed to avoid me for a couple of weeks, having sold me a packet of 'ice' knowing it was some dreadful plastic shit. When I asked Ron where Neil was, I was surprised to learn he'd left Hong Kong, his parents sending him to a rehab unit in the UK.

Approaching me on the platform, the look in Mr Lee's eyes only served to increase my panic. 'Why you bring so mush stuff?' he asked angrily. Then he said something in Mandarin to his lackey, a mainlander, who glanced sideways and shook his head like Genghis Khan on a bad day.

I told him I didn't have anywhere to leave it. Why would I want to? I didn't plan to return to Hong Kong, at least not in the near future. Flustered, he suggested dropping some of it off at the office in Kowloon Tong, one stop on the route. From there, Mr Lee explained, Genghis and I would complete the journey without him as he had business to attend to in Hong Kong.

Transferring gear between bags, I flapped harder than a superglued sparrow. Not having slept for days, I just couldn't focus. My heart raced, my hands trembled and sweat poured out of me like a burst water main. The faster I tried to pack to keep Mr Lee and his pet gorilla happy, the bigger hash I made of it and the more I felt their eyes burning into me.

Flunky *San* only interacted once during our journey – as we left Immigration in Shenzhen to find a cab. Swamped by a horde of vagabonds, I stopped to give a couple of bucks to an elderly gent who thrust a convincing stump. But Flunky *San* interrupted my gesture, grabbed my arm and, with a look of disgust, dragged me away. I was starting to dislike the guy and happy when the cabbie dropped me at my villa.

That night I didn't sleep well – and not because I would be DJing in the biggest nightclub in Southern China the next day. There was a rectangular gap in the brickwork of the recently built property, high up on the wall in my bedroom where they'd yet to install an air conditioner. I'd dreamt a bizarre dream in which a contingent from Guangdong's gazillion-strong mosquito population set out on a search-and-destroy mission. Alighting on my face, they'd dabbed their proboscises into my head, stocked up on the good stuff and flown off.

Unfortunately, I awoke to find thirteen of the tiny swine *had* landed on my face... and tried to eat it.

I looked like the Elephant Man – although that's doing John Merrick an injustice. I looked worse. I had an ugly cliff jutting out of my forehead, the eye below it closed over from a bite on the eyelid itself. The one on my nose only added to my alien look.

I smoked the last of the ice, trying not to think about my distorted grid, and then made my way to the club. As I walked towards it, the place looked less conspicuous than at night, but an impressive venue all the same.

A soldier with the onerous task of letting kids into sweet shops sprung to attention, saluted and pulled the door open. Crossing the dance floor, heading for the sound pit, it was hard to believe this HK$30,000,000 pleasure dome was all mine to enjoy. *I* was the house DJ, and the smiles of the staff stocking up the bar let me know just that.

I spent a good few minutes admiring the technology – a sound mixer twice the size of the Big Apple's, a CD player adding infinite possibilities to a set, and the top-of-the-range decks themselves. Taking out the list I'd made in Wan Chai, I began thumbing through the record collection. I found an abundance of mainstream dance-pop hits but none of the classic anthems I'd hoped for – 'Let Me Show You' by K-Klass, 'Perfect Motion' by Sunshine – sort of to be expected but disappointing nonetheless.

Now it was time to start putting a set together, one that would take the crowd on an emotional rollercoaster. Strike's 'U Sure Do' would surely do when it came to complementing the exiting ballet troupe, so I whacked it on one of the decks and cranked up the volume. Having got to grips with the turntable's speed controls, I brought in Corona's 'Try Me Out', followed by Alison Limerick's 'Where Love Lives'.

Feeling I had the hang of things, I experimented with the CD player, chuffed to bits I could take a sample of the famous line – 'Houston, we have a problem' – from the *Apollo 13* soundtrack and mix it into the set at any given point.

The young Chinese DJ made his way across the dance floor, smiling, and nodding his head to the music. His name was Wen, and with his over-large parka, baggy jeans and enormous skate shoes, he looked like a doll from a children's television programme. Our partnership kicked off in a mix of simple Cantonese and even simpler English.

Perusing the records I'd lined up, he said, *'Gei ho!'* then pulled out Jive Bunny and the Master Mixers with an enquiring look.

'No!' I put him straight. This wasn't Butlins, and I wasn't a freakin' Redcoat.

As the record slid back, Wen looked at the top of my head, kicking with his own. He wanted to see the sunglasses I had resting there – only a cheap pair bought in a night market, but their rectangular blue lenses and chrome frame made them look as smart as paint.

After trying the shades on, he pointed them skyward in a direction that for all I knew could have been Tibet. 'You, ness time, Heung Gong. Me giff you munnee?'

I laughed. Hong Kong seemed a long way off now.

'Keep them,' I told Wen. 'They're for you.'

'No *munnee?*'

'No money!'

His face lit up.

After some more practice, he took me outside and into a large open-sided food tent. Inside were enough soldiers to stage a coup and so many red and gold stars on green it looked like a Christmas tree convention. We found a space on one of the wooden benches and began using our chopsticks to wave the squadrons of bluebottles away from the food.

'How many nightclubs feed their entire staff three times a day?' I mused. It must be old Confucius again: workers do their jobs and, in return, boss provides delicious rice and omelette.

That evening I was champing at the bit and ready to do more damage than a psycho at a sleepover. The effect of the ice still strong, it was an amazing feeling to walk the red carpet and take up position behind the decks. The club had filled to near capacity, and as I brought in the vocals of Strike's Victoria Newton, I swear to God I was God – even forgetting the ugly swellings on my face, which no one seemed to notice. The floor filled immediately, Wen and I estimating four hundred people – not bad for a first effort.

After I'd played for an hour, one of the managers came over and started interfering like a football club chairman. He kept pointing at Wen and then at the decks, gesturing he should take over from my open-shirted and sweat-drenched self.

My heart sunk – even more so as Wen went on to play the tracks I'd carefully selected, the *coup de grâce* being when a certain big-eared, carrot-crunching bastard grabbed the limelight instead of me.

I knew a couple of my mixes had gone tits-up, but I hadn't done *too* badly. Wen kept trying to explain something, but his English wasn't good enough and neither was my Cantonese. There was only one other guy here that spoke my language – a barman – but he wasn't around, besides, '*Happy-happy-happy!*' wouldn't exactly give me the answers I needed.

The same thing happened every night for a week. By the end of it, I'd had enough. The next time the old boy approached the DJ arena, I felt myself getting angry. 'Tell him I *don't* understand!' I said to Wen.

All he could translate in return was, 'You *don'* control crowd.'

Copying what he heard, the Jurassic dictator jumped in. 'Yoo *don'* contwol cwow!'

'What are they babbling on about?' I wondered, wracking my brain to work out what I was doing wrong. How could I not be controlling the crowd? I was doing what I'd seen every DJ do, taking the music up and down with the clients in tow. What could a seventy-year-old Chinese bloke know about DJing anyway?

Up until now, I thought I'd come down off a five-day ice bender rather well. Only, I began to feel irritable. I walked over to where the stegosaurus sat glaring like a jealous lover. 'What do you mean, I don't control the crowd?'

He threw his arms out. '*Contwol* cwow!'

It was the final straw.

I booted one of the chairs at his table halfway across the dance floor and went back to the apartment.

It was an especially stupid thing to do. Making a seventy-year-old Chinese man lose face in front of a club full of people wouldn't resolve anything. But, unbeknown to me, there was nothing to resolve…

When I entered the club the next evening, I saw the DJ from the promotional video standing at the bar. 'Hello, mate,' I said, putting out my hand. 'Guess I've lost my job, then!'

'Afraid so, mate,' he replied, his accent familiar. 'Haven't they told you?'

'They can't. Mr Lee hasn't been here and no one else speaks English.'

'Bad luck. The secretary in Hong Kong called me in England four days ago begging me to come back, said they'd pay my flight and double the salary. I even brought my wife and my mountain bike… and our ironing board!'

'What's your name, bud?'

'Rob.'

'I'm Chris, Rob. Where you from in the UK?'

'Oh, you wouldn't know it.'

'I might.'

'Place called Beliver.'

'As in Beliver in Plymouth?'

'That's right! How do you know that?'

'I live in Whitleigh, mate – two minutes up the road!'

After a heated exchange with the bar manager, Rob came away with a crate of beer to take back to the villa. It was only then, after playing a tape recording of my set and receiving compliments from Rob, that the truth unravelled.

'*Ahh*! Control the crowd,' he said. 'They don't mean like a DJ does back home. They mean get up on the stage. You know, like a Butlins Redcoat – make a few jokes, play silly games.'

'Why the fuck did they advertise for a DJ, then?' I asked, understanding now why my handstand spectacular impressed them so much.

'They're Chinese, Chris. They don't understand the difference between a DJ, an MC or MT *bloody* V!'

It all fell into place. *That's* why they hadn't asked me to DJ at the interview. *That's* why Mr Lee asked me if I would join the ballet troupe – I'd dismissed that with a laugh.

Shit! I'd even phoned my dad to tell him I was DJing in China. He was over the moon.

The next day Mr Lee turned up and he was *furious* – not with me but with the 'stoopid ol' bastards' as he kept referring to them.

'I *tell* to them, Quiss! I *tell* to them, don' do anything until I get back. But *stoopid Chiniss bastards*! Don' listen to anyone! Go telephone to other DJ. He okay but he *nothing* good like you. You know, Chiniss peepall *not* used to the Westerner, sometime *very* afraid. But Chiniss peepall *not* afraid of you. I tell *stoopid* Chiniss bastards.... You know what I tell to them?'

'No. What did you tell them, Mister Lee?'

He pulled his face closer. 'I *tell* to them... you are *ginyuss!* You know *why?*'

'Why's that, Mister Lee?'

'Because you are, Quiss. You are *ginyuss!*'

I thought back to Vance's words: 'Quiss, I feel you can do anything...'

I wished I felt the same.

Voices at Vance's

'HELLO, VANCE!' I GREETED HIM upon arrival back at Hing Tak.

'*Hey*, Quiss! How you doin', mayte?' He gave me a welcoming smile. 'So the China job not go so well'a?'

'Not so good, mate. How's things with you?'

'Well, the bissniss not go so well here either. But I muss keep trying.'

'Oh, shame to hear that, Vance.' I pulled out HK$7,000 of my 'payoff'. 'Sorry it's a bit late, you know?'

'Ah, *no problem*!' He looked the happiest I'd seen him in months. He was a humble gent, my brother Vance.

When I dumped my bags in the back room, it all looked so different. The massive bed, empty of linen, struck me as strangely desolate, putting it to me straight: 'You don't belong here anymore...'

I took the MTR to Wan Chai, a short walk from Mack's place in Happy Valley. A week without meth, there was only one thing on my mind.

As Mack fished around in a cupboard looking for his stash, his wife, Clara, appeared in the doorway of their bedroom dressed in her underwear. I thought she would shut the door in embarrassment, but she didn't. She just stood there staring, and as I turned to talk to her chap, she disappeared.

After a smoke with Mack, I went to see Old Ron at his 'new' flat on Johnston Road in Wan Chai, my China experience as distant a memory as an English cup of tea.

'Nice place, mate! How can you afford this all of a sudden?' I gave the spacious but dated apartment the once-over.

'Oh, *you* know...' he replied cagily. 'Borrowed some money from my sister in London.'

Something didn't seem right, but I let it drop.

Vance had gone out, so I relaxed smoking meth in my room, only someone entered the apartment, talking in overly loud Cantonese. I left it a while and then peeked around the kitchen door to see Liu *San* with three younger men. He was giving them some sort of business presentation, writing on Vance's huge whiteboard to make his point.

All of a sudden, I felt uneasy...

Mr Liu was using the word *bing* with a heavy emphasis in *every* sentence – 'Blah blah *bing*, this... blah blah *bing*, that...' and 'Bing *San* (Mister Bing)' – and written all over the board at least twenty times in turquoise marker pen, in *English*, was the word *bing*.

I knew many Hong Kong Chinese didn't believe a *gweilo* could understand their language. I knew that they had an amusing yet often dark sense of humour. I also knew what the word *bing* meant when spoken in a mid-level tone. *Bing* was Cantonese for ice. *Vance had told him!*

I was angry this snake was in my friend's home thinking he could get one over on me. But something bothered me more. Mr Liu and his boys didn't present the way Vance's other business acquaintances did. Liu dressed like a spiv, wearing a tight-fitting silver suit, white socks and winkle-pickers. With his gelled, curly hair, he looked like a reptile in a crap wig.

The guys he was with all wore jeans, tracksuit tops and training shoes... *just like the lads at Chungking I bought weed from...*

It all fell into place.

Mr Liu and his cronies were fucking triads!

It took me aback when Dream asked me in the Apple that evening if I had any ice. I didn't know she smoked it – although I suppose someone with the stamina to dance all night long has to get their energy from somewhere.

I was amazed too, when she bought a chocolate bar in the 7-Eleven so we could use the foil to smoke it in a discreet corner of the park. Most surprising of all was that upon my suggestion we go back to my place, the beautiful Thai said, 'Yes.'

There had been an interesting turn of events already – another near fight-night in the Big Apple. I'd been standing near the bar, chatting to

Mal and his training partner, Kevin, who were in the club with a few mates.

'Can I get you and your friends some drinks, guys?' I asked.

'Nice one, Chris,' said Mal, reeling off a list longer than the Great Wall.

I went up to order, over the moon when Ray passed the heavily laden tray over without charge. When I rejoined the boys, Mal said, 'Chris, do you mind if I ask you something?'

'Sure, go for it.'

'Do you take drugs?'

'Why do you ask?'

'It's just you see our mate there…' he nodded to a short, flabby guy with a shock of curly brown hair who was dancing with gusto, drenched in sweat, in the middle of the bar area. 'How come he's so fucked and you're not?'

'I don't know the answer to that, mate.' I laughed. 'I guess I like to keep a bit of control. Hey, watch this!'

From the splits position, I pushed up into a handstand and held it on the spot for a minute while clapping my feet to the beat, much to his amazement – and old Mr Lu's, who clapped wildly and chuckled like a cartoon dog.

I asked Mal to excuse me while I went for a dance with Dream.

Interrupting our boogie, I leant over to where I had a cigarette burning in the ashtray, but this massive blond dude, who looked as though he should be in a boxing ring with Sylvester Stallone, saw me reaching for it and stubbed it out. The way his eyes kept flicking across to Dream said he was pissed up and pissed off.

'Smoke bothering you, mate?' I asked.

'Ged bahk an' dance vid hur!' the Hamburg Headbanger ordered, tensing his arms and torso, his face going red like a contestant in the World's Strongest Man.

'No worries, friend. Are you gonna join us?'

Not getting the rise out of me he'd hoped for, he picked up the ashtray and held it above his head.

'Mate, you don't wanna hit me with that!'

'Vhy not?'

'Coz it'll hurt!'

Exasperated, he clenched it in his bratwursts and then smashed it on the floor.

Typical! When I told Mal and the world's hardest man, Kevin, what had happened, they hadn't seen it. 'Just say the word, Chris, and I'll knock him out,' said the lawyer, the two of them moving to stand next to Dream.

'Well, this is alright!' I thought. 'Drinks on the house, bodyguarded by two bloody nice blokes and a date with the most beautiful women in Asia!' Putting the piss-taking gangsters in my home to one side, what could possibly go wrong?

I was forgetting this was Hong Kong, not Helsingborg. When I returned to Hing Tak with an angel on my arm, the devil on my back would no doubt have his say.

The first time came in the middle of having sex. I'm *sure* she whispered, '*Oh*! My *boyfriend* not this good!' But I put it out of my mind, thinking she was either talking past tense or might be mental.

Undoubtedly, it had been the best part of the magical mystery tour so far. She was *so, so* sexy! What a memorable night, and the first of many we'd spend together.

In the morning, Dream went out, returning with McDonald's breakfasts and a few small sachets of mineral salts from a chemist that, she assured me, were good for mind and body after a heavy night.

I soon needed them, having returned from the shower to find her chatting on the telephone.

'Who was that?' I asked, as she put the handset down.

'My boyfriend in England,' she replied casually.

'*WHAT!*' I thought to myself. '*NO!*' Not only had any ideas about a future together just been smashed like crockery at a Greek wedding, but *I* didn't even use that phone to call abroad any more. That was really taking a liberty!

After she left, I spent the day in my room. No one else was home and I happened to have the television tuned into the CCTV channel the building's management provided.

Just as I was setting up the tinfoil, Mr Liu's three young thugs appeared on the screen, only instead of going to Vance's front door, they stood whispering in conspiratorial tones beneath his office window.

My heartbeat stepped up.

'What the fuck are they doing?' I wondered. 'Why don't they knock?'

Then it hit me like a cold plunge! 'They must be checking to see if I'm home before calling the police to tell them about my drug use!'

By fuck did the sandwiches fall out of my picnic! I ran into the kitchen, grabbed the pepper pot and went around the apartment sprinkling it over the floor – that fucked the sniffer dogs. Then taking up the biggest kitchen knife and shoving it down the back of my jeans, I ran up the stairs and onto the roof.

I leant over the parapet just in time to see them leave the building and begin weaving their way through the pedestrians on Victory Avenue *in single file*!

'*Triad foot soldiers!*'

I don't know if it was visceral military intuition or because I'd read about this method the young hoods used to cut through crowds – either way, who walks in single file when they're with mates, for Christ's sake?

I ran down to the front entrance with the knife sticking out of my waistband and tried to tell the security guard in Cantonese – the one I felt didn't like *gweilos* – that if these guys wanted to get clever, I would mess them up big time.

He rattled off a reply, throwing his arms out like a chick leaving the nest.

At that moment, Benny Tsang walked up the front steps, muttering, 'Bread is the body of Qwyste. Wine is the blood of Qwyste.' When he saw me, he said, 'Hey, Quiss! How you doin'?'

'Not good, Benny.' We went into the flat. 'I've got a problem with *fucking* triads, mate!'

'*Twiad?*' he asked, looking bemused. 'You mean like the gangsta?'

'*Yeah*! I mean like the *fucking* gangster, Benny!' I slammed the knife back into the drawer.

'Oh!' he said, viewing the cutlery compartment with suspicion.

The next day, despite feeling edgy from having no sleep, what had happened took flight from my shoulders. An occasional nagging thought questioned whether I might have overreacted, at the same time reminding me there was *some* kind of problem and it was frickin' *bizarre*…

Walking the streets of Lan Kwai Fong, feeling lonely and discarded, searching for any sign outside a club offering work, I had other things to worry about.

Back at Hing Tak that evening, I was reaching for the tinfoil when I heard voices coming down the main stairs. I didn't think too much of it at first, but they wouldn't let up.

'Ham ga chan!' someone kept shouting, the fortress-shaped walls adding a hollow echo as it reverberated around the courtyard.

'Hahm-sap lo!' fired off the other, as if to complement the first.

And so it continued, on and off throughout the evening, so strange and so haunting. I had no idea what they were saying, but I knew it was to do with me and it made me shudder.

I flicked through my English-Cantonese dictionary. *Ham ga chan* I couldn't work out, but *hahm-sap lo*, I could. It meant 'salty-wet man'.

'*Salty-wet man?* Do they mean sweaty?' I wondered. 'Like a freakin' delinquent? Have I committed a no-no by bringing women back here? Is it something to do with Mack Zane's girlfriend appearing in front of me the way she did? How could they know about that?' It was so baffling. I decided to ask Vance about it when I saw him.

For the time being, I had to get out of there. I needed to find someone who could explain all this to me, so I went to the Apple to see if Max or Jackson were around.

'Jackson got fired, Chris,' said Ray. 'He was late too many times, and Max hasn't turned up for three evenings.'

'You shouldn't have sacked Jackson, Ray! The customers loved him.'

'Sorry, Chris, had to, mate.'

I could see I was overstepping the mark, so I shut up, accepted a beer and told him about China.

Graham, the heavy metal fan, was sitting in his usual spot, as permanent a fixture at the bar as his greaser's attire was on him. 'Where's that girl you're normally with?' he asked.

'Shelley? She's gone back to Canada, mate.'

'Anyone else on the go?'

'*Well...* not exactly on the go, but I did spend an enjoyable evening with a Thai lady you might know.'

I neglected to mention the small issue of the boyfriend.

'You mean *Dream*! Good for getting the McDonald's in after a night in the sack. Did she give you some of those little Alka-Seltzer things?'

'How do you know that?' I asked, stunned and not sure if I wanted to hear the answer from this spotty metal-head who never changed his clothes.

'Been there, mate!' he replied smugly. 'So has every Tom, Dick and Harry in here!'

'Fuck me!' I thought. 'Don't you know a bloke's got feelings?'

I spotted Nicole on the dance floor. Miserable or not, there was always time to get lost in the Music, which we did for a couple of hours. Although attractive, Nicole didn't quite have the sex appeal Dream had, but she was always so pleased to see me that it meant a lot more. She was a lighthouse in the dark, impervious to the sea storming all around me. We never spoke in depth. Our smiles said it all. We were supposed to meet on the floor, in the Music, and enjoy a moment in time.

I guess my relationship with meth was a similar deal – get high, live now, forget. Only these nasty waves of anxiety and panic had suddenly entered, uninvited, into the mix and put a biscuit in the breadbin.

Old Ron came into the Apple. I was happy to have someone to talk all this craziness through with, someone who'd lend a sympathetic ear.

'You're *paaaranoid*, mate!' he said, with his irksome smirk.

'Fuck off, Ron! You haven't been in the Forces. You don't notice it.' I wasn't in the mood for his Doubting Thomas act.

'Notice *what*?'

'Okay, it's like this. When we were in Northern Ireland, yeah? One of the lads noticed that the players we searched on the street – the paramilitaries, I mean – well, they all wore a certain type of clothing. You know, so they could recognise each other. It made sense coz we did the same – jeans, chukka boots and T-shirts. These triads all seem to wear jeans, white trainers and shell-suit tops.'

'*Nah!*' said Ron.

I wondered if he was just naïve and oblivious to it all, or whether there was something he was holding back. It was as if he wanted to protect these guys. I knew I wasn't being paranoid. If I despised the term before, I fucking hated it now.

'And another thing, Ron, you don't speak any Cantonese. How could you know what's going on?'

'*What!* And *you* do?' he mocked. '*Gweilos* don't speak Chinese, mate. Come on, let's get a cab back to mine.'

The sun came up and we flagged a taxi down. As soon as we got in, and as if to prove his own dick-brained point, Old Ron initiated the *cheesin gweilo* routine.

'Leave him alone, Ron.' I cringed.

'*Why?*' Ron shot back.

'Because they get that shit from every drunken *gweilo* getting in the cab. If you wanna talk to the man, learn some Cantonese.'

'Too hard, mate.'

'Really?'

'Yeah!'

I leant forward through the gap in the front seats. '*Erh, m'goy?*'

'*Hai!*' the driver replied, looking in the rear-view mirror.

'*Lei ho ma?*'

'*Ho!* (Good!)' He smiled.

'*Lei sik'm'sik gong Yingman?* (You know, not know, how to speak English?)'

'*M'sik gong* (Not know how to speak).' He shook his head.

'*Ngoh sik gong Gwongdungwa ho siu* (I speak Cantonese a little). *Ngoh hai Yinggwok yan* (I'm an Englishman). *Ngoh jyuh hai Heung Gong yat nin'a* (I've lived in Hong Kong one year). *Ngoh jungyee Heung Gong. Ngoh jungyee Heung Gong yan* (I like Hong Kong. I like Hong Kong people).'

'*Ho ho!*' He smiled again.

'*Sik jo faan may'a?* (Eaten rice, not yet?)'

'*May'a* (Not yet). *Hai Yinggwok, jo mat ye?* (In England, you did what?)'

'*Hai Yinggwok, ngoh hai gwanyan* (In England, I was a soldier).'

'*Oh! Pee-yow pee-yow!*' he said, holding up another of Wan Chai's invisible guns. '*Lei sik gong Gwongdungwa gai ho!* (You speak Cantonese very well!)'

'*Dojeh* (Thank you very much).'

'*M'sai!* (No need!) *Lei hohk Gwongdungwa hai bin do'a?* (You learnt Cantonese in which place?)'

'*Ngohge pungyau gaau ngoh* (My friend taught me).'

'*Ho!*'

'*Jun jaw, m'goy* (Turn left, please). *Dukm'duk, ngohdeih tsut gai leedo'a, m'goy?* (Possible, not possible, we go out here, please?)'

'*Hai!*'

'*M'goy sai. Jeurk lei ho wun* (Thank you. Appoint you good luck).'

'That's a conversation, Ron,' I said, as we got out of the cab. It might not have been spot on, but at least I was making an effort.

'*Hah!* That *shit* you said there? You were just saying the same thing over and over again!'

Then for good measure, he caught the driver's attention, pointed at me and said, '*Cheesin gweilo'a!*'

You couldn't win with Ron.

His flat was more spacious than I remembered. It had a huge front room with three bedrooms coming off it and an open kitchen at one end.

'Who's in the other rooms, Ron?'

'No one at the moment. Tom was in that one, but the landlord kicked him out for not paying his rent.'

'What, DJ Tom?'

'Yeah, Snooker Ball Tom.'

'Where's he living now?'

'On a sofa at a mate's place. He was round here earlier.'

'And, what are the hooks for, Ron? It looks like a butcher's shop!'

There were ugly black crooks, spread equidistant across the ceiling.

'Snuff…' Ron replied casually.

'*Snuff!*'

'Yeah, you know, hard-core porn films where people are tortured to death. The landlord said they used to film them here before he bought the place.'

'*Shit!* It's a strange island this one, Ron.' A Chinese proverb, 'Life is meat', came into my head as I began to imagine the awful things that must have gone on in this place.

Ron showed me his room, and we sat down on the bed's flowery-pattern duvet. Ron had drunk a lot. His eyes were bloodshot, his hair thinner than ever. With his sole shirt hanging loosely on his skinny frame, he looked as dishevelled as when he'd slept in the park.

I wasn't in too good a state myself. I'd used up the last of my stash and the convulsions plagued me once more.

'You alright, Chris?' asked Ron. 'You haven't got any ice, have you?'

'Nah, mate,' I replied, thinking he was being scornful.

He stood up, felt around the doorframe and – *hallelujah!* – pulled out a score bag containing a few crystals, their unexpected appearance seeing them sparkle more than usual.

'There you go.' He threw them across the bed.

'What about you?'

'I need a beer, mate. That's what I need.'

As I was smoothing out the tinfoil Ron fetched from the kitchen, he asked, 'Can you change traffic lights with your mind?'

'*Urrh*...? You think I'm crazy?'

'Not at all. It's just I went through a phase once... thinking I could make traffic lights change.'

'I'm not crazy, Ron. I ain't Neil, you know.'

'I never said you were. I was living in America at the time, for a year on a student exchange.'

'And?'

'One night the family I stayed with told me to come down to the basement, about midnight, and lying on the floor was a rolled-up carpet. I knew they were going to kill me, wrap me in it and dispose of my body.'

'What happened?'

'I ran out of the house in my pyjamas! I ran to the nearest police station and they called the British Embassy to arrange my repatriation. When I got to Heathrow, I was still in my nightclothes.'

'*Fuck!* Do you think you might have imagined it?'

'Not sure…' He shrugged. 'To this day, I'm not sure…'

As I took a hit of ice, the cigarette I had burning rolled off the ashtray and singed the bedcover. '*Shit*! Sorry, Ron! I've blimed the duvet, mate.'

'*WHAT!*' he shouted – a little over the top. 'Why don't you say *sorry*, Chris!'

'I *said* I'm sorry, Ron. Don't you think you're overreacting?'

'What do you *mean*, overreacting?' He was fuming.

'Ron, I'm really sorry. It's just, you spend some time in the military and you get to see a lot more serious shit than a hole in a fucking duvet!'

'You don't get it, Chris?'

'Get what?'

'I haven't spent time in the military and I don't *fucking* care what happens in it.'

'Careful, Ron… I lost a few friends in there.'

'Chris, I grew up in India. Both my parents were killed in a robbery when I was eight. *You* say it's only a small hole in a duvet, but it's *my* duvet! *I* bought it… there's no one else that's gonna look after me.'

'Ron, I'm so sorry, mate. I had no idea.' I felt ashamed.

'*No one's* got any idea! What it's like to grow up without parents, to go through life a failure, to be a complete *fuck-up* whose business collapsed so he came out here for a new start…' Then he muttered, 'No one knows what it's like to be an *alcoholic*.…'

My preconceptions falling down around my ears, my ego smashing like a shot plate and landing in pathetic shards by my feet, it all fell into place: Ron's drinking, his low self-esteem, his misogynistic outbursts when pissed, his sniping comments about my military career, his drumming on the table instead of dancing *and* his closeted admiration for me. *Shit!* Poor Old Ron was a broken man and, too wrapped up in my own problems, I hadn't even seen it.

Rather than go back to the uncertainty at home, I took the MTR five stops to Quarry Bay, some distance to the east of Hong Kong Island, where Jackson and Max shared a tiny loft flat.

They were pleased to see me, and walking up their rough wooden stairway I hoped they'd shed some light on the situation. Sharing Ron's ice, I asked why I didn't understand Hong Kong people.

Jackson looked up and exhaled a plume of vapour. '*No*, Quiss! Not *you* don' unnerstan' Hong Kong *peepall*. Hong Kong *peepall* don' unnerstan' *you*.'

In a crazy way, it was what I needed to hear.

Jackson was behaving strangely, as if something agitated him. Shortly after, he made an excuse and left. 'Is Jackson alright, Max?'

'Don't worry. Jackson always get funny when he take ice.'

'And how's your nose, Max?'

While going out for sushi back along, he'd told me he had nose cancer and was on a waiting list for an operation. I'd read about there being a high rate of the disease in Hong Kong, supposedly linked to the population's intake of salt fish.

'Oh...' he sighed. 'Haven't got the money for operation now.' Max went on to explain he was going out with a girl still in high school and that she was pregnant. The money he had saved would pay for an abortion.

I liked Max a lot. He understood me, even more so than Vance did, and I could be open about my drug use. When I spoke Cantonese, he would say, '*Shoowah!* Unnerstan' you, *no* problem!' I could tell our cross-cultural friendship meant as much to him as it did to me.

'Here, Max, take this.' I gave him my Rolex.

'*No!*'

It was a HK$30,000 watch, three grand in sterling, and enough second-hand value to sort his problems out.

He made a telephone call to a friend in the jewellery business, but the guy must have got this Sea Dweller model mixed up with the cheaper Submariner version because he told Max it was worth a lot less. I didn't push the issue, saying it was there if he needed it, as I worried I was making Max lose face.

'*Heui chaai gun'a!* (Go police station!)' shouted an interfering and anonymous voice down the stairs as I entered Hing Tak.

'*Pok gai!*' I sent back, and went inside the apartment.

Vance was in the office, talking in whispers with Benny, so I went to my room. A moment later, Benny stuck his head around the door. '*Errh,* is everything okay, Quiss'a?'

'Depends on what you mean by okay, Benny,' I replied, wondering what they had been discussing.

'Depen' on *what* mean okay,' he mimicked, contemplatively. 'Is there a problem?'

'These people shouting, Benny. That's a bit of a problem.'

'Shoutin'?' he asked gently.

'Out there.' I pointed to the back door. 'Saying not very nice things about me.'

'*No!* They don' talk abou' *you.* You know, Cantonese is very difficult language.'

'No? Then what does *heui chaai gun'a* mean?'

'Is meaning, go to the poliss station.'

'*Exactly!* Why are they shouting that?'

'*Errh...* mebee, they lose their pet dog an' they say, "We muss go to the poliss station an' find it?"'

'Benny! Nobody in this building owns a fucking dog! They certainly don't go to police station looking for 'em when they go missing!'

'*Ahh...* don' go poliss station'a?'

'No, they don't. Listen, Benny, I'm not upset with you. I just need to know why they shout that.'

Benny took a conspiratorial glance all around before continuing in almost a whisper. 'You know, Quiss, when I was'a young boy, juss finish school, juss statted working, I live in a village. Sma' village, not like Hong Kong.'

'Uh-huh.'

'One day, I get sick... with the fever... from the fish?'

'*Hepatitis?*'

'*Yeah-yeah! Hepatitis.* Well, I cannot even to get out of bed. A'm so sick, my mother have to wash me, feed me, for three month'a?'

'Uh-huh.'

'The peepall in my village, some I known *all* my life... Well, they stat shoutin' when they come pass my home.'

'Shouting what, Benny?'

'Oh, shoutin' like, "Hey you, *bad man*! You *don't* go to work! *Death* to your family!"'

'*Ham ga chan?*'

'*Yeah!* This the one. You know it'a?'

'Yeah, I know it.' I had it imprinted on my brain. 'Thanks, Benny.'

I felt sure one of the voices belonged to the security guard – the white-haired guy who didn't like me – and, despite Benny's advice to the contrary, I was determined to have it out with him.

When I got to the guard booth he wasn't there, though. Instead, it was my always-smiling friend. That this old chap could be part of the conspiracy was a spear through the heart. I'd grown fond of him. I thought he was my *pungyau*. Whenever we met, I would greet him with, '*Sik jo faan may'a?*' and he would reply, '*May'a!*' with his huge grin, and then ask me, '*Lei heui bin do'a?* (You go which place?)' I would reply, '*Faan gung* (Going to work),' or '*Wahnging* (Gym).'

Now, as I approached, I felt emotional and choked up. I couldn't bear the thought he might be taking the piss along with all the other haters.

'Benny, ask him why he doesn't like me. What have I ever done to him?'

As Benny spoke, I stared at the ground, gutted, as a wave of rejection swept me back to my youth, and for the first time in years, tears began to well.

Interpreting the old man's words, Benny said, '*No*, Quiss! He say he like you very mush. He say you always buy him drink. He say you *kind* man, always tekk time to talk to him.'

Hearing the way I hoped I came across to Hong Kong people nearly sent me over the edge. I had to go back inside and have a word with myself.

'Where did it all go so wrong?' I didn't know if the guard was telling the truth – maybe I'd just put him on the spot – but I'd definitely done something to upset the owners of those voices.

'*Ham ga chan*. This mean very bad thing,' said Vance.

'What do you mean, *very* bad?'

'It mean like something abou' your family, like they gonna kill them or want them dead.'

'And *hahm-sap lo*, Vance. *Salty-wet man*. What's that all about?'

'Why you ask me?' he replied, suddenly looking uncomfortable.

'Because I've been hearing it for two days, mate. It's like everyone's talking about me, all around Hing Tak!'

'*No!* They *don'* talk abou' you!' he said, the most aggressive I'd ever seen him.

'How do you know, Vance? It means like a bad person, right?'

'*Yeah*. It mean like a very bad man. But they don' talk abou' *you!*'

He looked away, the nervous quivering in his eyes and lips telling me there was something I wasn't getting.

In desperation of needing to hear what he was avoiding telling me, I grabbed his arm. '*Vance!* For *fuck's* sake, man! I've been hearing it for *two* days now! They're shouting it about *me!*'

'*No!*' Vance looked me dead in the eye. 'They shouting it abou' *me!*'

'Huh? What are you talking about?'

'You know, Quiss. I don' tell you, but since the Quorum bissniss fail… you know, you told to me it would work?'

'Uh-huh.'

'Well, since then, what with my other bissniss not doing so well, I haven't been able to pay the rent for three month. Not pay the rent in Hong Kong culture is *very* bad. Mean like you are *loser!*'

'Vance, if those voices were about you, why am I hearing them now?'

We were supposed to be settling down to sleep amongst the massage beds in his shop in Tsim Sha Tsui's Ocean Centre shopping plaza. I don't know for what reason, but Vance insisted we stay there tonight. He said we *absolutely* could not remain at Hing Tak.

In the sanctuary of his showroom, as I watched him trying to get to sleep fully clothed on the floor, having given me the sole put-you-up bed he used when working late, I felt ashamed and confused. Ashamed I'd involved him in the Quorum debacle and that I hadn't been able to stop taking drugs, but confused about all that nonsense at Hing Tak.

Now, to add to the uncertainty, I was still hearing those denouncing taunts – this time rising up from the food court directly below. 'Go sleep,' Vance urged, although it was only 9pm.

'I can't, Vance.' I got up off the camp bed. 'I have to work out what they're saying.'

I stood on the first-floor balcony listening to the same jeering insults of *'Ham ga chan!'* and *'Heui chaai gun'a!'* floating upwards, ghostlike and ephemeral, like the souls of slain Vikings having one last slash of the battle axe as Valkyries carried them skyward to Valhalla.

It was literally the stuff of nightmares. *Everyone* seemed to be talking about me. 'What have I done to upset them?'

Vance appeared at my side and I tried to explain what I could hear.

'*No!* They talking, but is restaurant.'

I wasn't convinced.

'*Errh…* Quiss'a?' He rested his hand on my arm.

'What, Vance?'

'Do you want to go to the hospital?'

'*Hospital!* Why do you say that?' I was offended and upset.

'Because I think you are not very well, Quiss,' he replied.

While Vance slept, I left the shopping centre to spend a lonely hour wandering the backstreets of Tsim Sha Tsui, thoroughly dejected, anxious and lost.

I went over to Old Ron's place. Not only had he found the money for his rent and deposit, but he'd also given up his job at the restaurant. For the life of me, I couldn't fathom his newfound wealth. I had trouble believing a benevolent sister lent it to him.

I'd only been there two minutes and was just beginning to explain what had happened at Ocean Centre when Ron interrupted me. 'You can't stay here,' he said. 'You know my tenancy agreement won't allow it.'

It annoyed me, because I *hadn't* asked to stay. And besides, it was extremely shallow of my so-called 'mate' not to offer me a sofa in my time of need. In the early hours, upon one final hint of 'You can't stay here,' I said goodbye and left.

I went to an all-night McDonald's and sat amongst the homeless people sprawled across the plastic seating. At 8am, I made my way back to Vance's. I had some crazy mad hope that everything would have calmed down, that Vance would say, '*Hey,* mayte! The *bissniss…*' and we could all go back to living the dream.

It was far from it.

The moment I entered the apartment, Vance confronted me: 'You cannot stay here! You muss *go* from this place!' I tried to reason with him, but it was too late.

I knew underneath all this Vance thought a lot of me, but on the surface our relationship had become impossible to endure. Once again, I found myself packing my belongings, this time leaving all the unnecessary items behind.

What should I do? My money had all but run out. I had no drugs left and no idea where I could go. I left my bags outside his door, then as an afterthought went back and tied them to a water pipe with a flimsy length of string. It was a token effort, but Hong Kong people were honest enough, so I wasn't worried.

I walked to a nearby park to give myself space to think. In the middle of the grass was a circular piece of tarmac with a series of benches around it and an ivy-clad trellis overhead to shade off the hottest part of the day. I sat down, put my head in my hands and once again tried to get to grips with harsh reality. Having thought about it, I walked into the centre of the feature and pulled a handstand – a *forty*-seconder! '*Fuck 'em!*'

Sitting back down, I whipped a Max*Tech* Group business card out of my wallet. On the back I'd written in miniature the names and phone numbers of all the people I knew. One name stood out: Antoine du Maurier. Even though I hadn't seen him since Gung Wan Hong, we'd always got on well. I headed to the nearest 7-Eleven to make the call.

'*Sure!*' he said. 'But my parents are coming over from France in a couple of days. Can you be out by then?'

Two days was fine by me, so I went to pick up my gear, but when I got to Vance's door, the string I'd tied my bags up with was still smoking. Someone had burnt through it with a cigarette lighter and made off with my small daypack.

'*Fuck it!*'

It wasn't having a bag stolen that bothered me, despite losing an expensive camera, my smart but stinking Next loafers, Swiss Army knife and a Take That tape that, *errhum*, Sarah gave me. I was upset because it hadn't occurred to me Hong Kong people could be like this, especially neighbours in the block I'd lived in for months.

I ran up the stairs to see if I could catch the culprit, to no avail, so I went back to Vance's and knocked. I wanted to say sorry for all the trouble I'd caused, as well as thank you and goodbye. Only I didn't quite get the reception I'd hoped for.

Vance began to get angry, making it clear that I wasn't welcome. 'British *cunt!*' he levelled, his lip wavering like a little boy who's just sworn in front of his parents for the first time.

I laughed. 'Fuck off, Vance! You don't mean that.' Inside his newly adopted exterior, I knew he didn't.

I took a cab to Antoine's upmarket gaff, a modern maisonette with its own dock in a picturesque settlement on the banks of an inlet in the New Territories.

It should have felt great to be in the calm after the storm. Instead, I spent the two days physically exhausted and ravenously hungry. While Antoine was at work, all I could do was lie on the floor and sleep, rising only to raid his food cupboards of the few tinned delicacies: mussels in white wine, foie gras, anchovies – even a jar of capers went gratefully down the hatch.

All too quickly, the respite ended. I'd hardly seen Antoine. The longest conversation we'd had was when he said sorry I had to leave but as his parents were arriving soon he needed time to clean up his place – adding that he wanted to make sure there were no female undergarments lurking around ready to expose his sex, drugs and pancake-roll lifestyle.

Sitting on my backpack in Tsim Sha Tsui's sunshine, its life-giving rays weren't working. On the pavement alongside Nathan Road, I wasn't far from Chungking Mansions, the place I'd always thought of as a wannabe craphouse. Now I wished I lived there, that I had one of those tiny curry-scented rooms to call my own.

The anxiety I'd experienced had long since taken its leave. As the effect of the ice wore off, it too fled, like rats from a sinking ship. In the sober light of Kowloon's midday, what had happened at Vance's and the shopping centre no longer registered as more pressing issues occupied my drug-zapped mind.

I watched car after car drive down Nathan Road – BMW, Mercedes, Rolls-Royce – dreaming that one of the stinking-rich businessmen would pull over and say, 'Hey, son! You look like someone who deserves a break. How about starting as a junior exec in my company?' I felt that if I could just get a *chance*, like a gambler desperate to recoup their losses, I could make life good again.

With regular exhaustion, a good three-hour nap can see you feeling back on top and rigid as a rickshaw, but not with ice. After days of sleep deprivation and excessive energy expenditure, you end up owing Mother Nature big time. If it wasn't for the worry of having another bag stolen, I would have curled up on the pavement and sought solace in oblivion.

As it was, I bought a third ham-and-cheese pastry from a street vendor, retired to a rubble-strewn park around the back of Chungking and lay down on a bench. With an arm through the straps of my pack, my briefbag and case tied onto it, I attempted to sleep off a few more degrees of wretchedness.

I awoke to see a couple of girls laughing at me, but I was too tired to care. I gathered my belongings and took a walk, unsure where I was heading in both body and metaphor, until it suddenly became clear. I found myself staring up at three brass balls and a sign that read *Pawn Shop*.

'Ten thousand dollar,' said the elderly Chinese gent behind the grille, removing the jeweller's loupe from his eye, having looked at my Rolex for no more than a second. He knew his game, as well as another travel-story tragedy.

'You *bloody* good man!' I thought, having lost only £350 of my original investment.

In an ideal world, I wouldn't have wanted to hock my watch, but this was no time to get sentimental. My back was against the wall. Plus, as my dad would say: 'It's only a rusting piece of metal, son!' – although in truth, he was referring to motor cars, which unlike Swiss watches tend to go down in value.

With more money in my pocket than at any other time during my stay in Hong Kong, it was time to go over to Mack Zane's place and invest some of it on *two* grams of those enthralling little crystals. If I didn't,

I might end up living a normal life, a happy-ever-after story, and how *awful* might that be?

Having secured drugs, I had to do likewise with accommodation. On a whim, I called Stephan de Fries, and when he invited me to stay with him and his Indonesian wife in their *house* in Sha Tin, an expensive borough in the New Territories, it felt as though things were picking up.

Our first evening together, I managed to force down some of the delicious pasta Cathy cooked, making polite conversation as I did so.

In the newspaper the next day, a café bar in Soho District advertised for staff. I arranged an interview for 3pm, but as usual my drugged-up timekeeping proved abysmal and I had to run all the way up the Mid-Levels Outdoor Escalator – which, fortunately, is only the longest of its kind in the world and not the universe.

I offered a sweaty hand to the owner of the Soho Shake on Elgin Street and went through the entire meeting hyperventilating and so full of anxiety I could hardly get my words out.

To make matters worse, one of the interviewees came into the Big Apple occasionally. Perish the thought, he approach the next time and ask what the fuck was up with me that day. I began to run through the scenario in my head: '*Well*... it's *glandular*... a *heart* condition... *Well*, glands *and* heart... a birth defect, you can say. And the *heat, phew!* Doesn't bloody help matters, does it?'

Although being high usually created a buffer that fended off negative thoughts, a few crept in now. Wandering around Lan Kwai Fong, I knew I had to find work, but underneath the cushion, I could sense I'd burnt all the bridges available to a *gweilo*.

With a feeling of desolation, I gave Edward Archibald-Henville a call. '*Chris*, dear boy! *Bloody* wonderful to hear from you! In fact, I was just telling someone the other day what a *bloody* good bloke you are!'

'I need a job, Ed.'

'*Oh*... I *don't* think John—'

'No, mate, that's not why I'm phoning. *Anyone* you know?'

'*Weell*... there *is* this marketing chappy.'

'Thanks, Ed,' I said, resolving to call the guy the next day.

After roaming the streets a few more hours, job-hunting to no avail, there was one last person I thought I should try. I made my way over to Wan Chai to see Glenn, a likeable Cockney who worked the door in Club Nemo. As a *gweilo* in Clubland, I hoped he might know of any bars taking on staff.

I didn't know much about feng shui, but enough to understand this metaphysical system is a fundamental tenet of Chinese culture. Literally meaning 'wind-water', the ancient art involves the designing and situating of buildings in line with the yin-and-yang philosophy of harmony with nature, the organisation of the décor also a key factor.

Feng shui follows certain principles such as having mountains behind for security, water in front to ward off evil – or a fish tank set strategically on the premises – as well as mirrors positioned in places to deflect unwanted visitors from the spirit world.

As I climbed down the steep staircase into Club Nemo, it was immediately evident this was a Chinese investment. With Hong Kong's heights to the rear, the harbour to the front and a mirror-lined entranceway, it was an experience to see feng shui in practice.

At the bottom, there was a fair-sized stairwell with a lectern for taking the entrance fee and cigarette posters on the walls. Around the corner, you entered the club, which stretched off to the right towards a long U-shaped bar with low tables and comfortable chairs set around it.

Above the bar was an ornamental surround with hanging drinks glasses and an air freshener and huge television mounted to the side. I looked up to see an old Chinese film on the screen, the kind where kung fu fighters fly with ease through air laden with ghouls and intrigue.

Beyond this, to the far right, was a dance floor with booth seating in the semi-darkness at the back. There was no DJ box, so I figured they must pipe the music from the bar.

With the exception of a Filipina waitress, the staff were all locals. Still early, there were only a handful of customers, all middle-aged Chinese men sat at the bar enjoying an after-work tipple to the sound of 2 Unlimited's 'Tribal Dance' thudding at half-volume in the background.

I couldn't see Glenn so I went up to the bar. A young Chinese chap, small and wearing round silver-rimmed spectacles, shook his head and pointed to a guy I'd just walked past.

He was short, even for a local, and looked late forties, though I reckon his face belied at least ten years. His hair, parted down the middle and brushed back into wings, showed not a speck of grey and he was dressed in a modest suit, white shirt and black tie.

When I said hello, he just nodded, cold, the way of the old school. The kind of acknowledgement that told you *gweilos* were not of major concern to him but their money no doubt was. He might not have come across as such a shifty character if it wasn't for his eyes. One looked northeast and the other one didn't. However, there was one thing immediately likeable about 'Paul' Eng. It was his typically Chinese straightforward way of doing business. He simply said, 'Glenn gone Thailan'. You wan' job? You can do doorman job?'

'Yeah, I wanna job! I can do door work!'

'Okay. Statt heeya eigh' o'clo' tomorrow nigh'.'

I revelled in my good fortune. This feng shui business really worked!

Club Nemo

I RETURNED TO STEPHAN AND CATHY'S beautiful home in the North. Sha Tin had grown from a small market town into a highly modern urban district encompassing other settlements along the banks of the Shing Mun River. It was set apart from the peninsula's growing conurbation by a green-topped mountain range, the Kowloon Hills. The house, situated in a small terraced row on the edge of the jungle, enjoyed a tropical laid-back atmosphere.

Unfortunately, the mood inside was not so relaxed. I found Cathy by herself and as I attempted to initiate conversation her body language told me something troubled her. I had a feeling our lifestyles clashed too much for comfort.

Here was I dressed in a T-shirt, black body warmer, grey jeans, black Caterpillar boots and Casio G-Shock diving watch – albeit all new and bought with the money from the sale of my Rolex – and here was she in pure wool Christian Dior and silk neck scarf, with a Cartier timepiece and matching jewellery.

I spent most of my time high on drugs, working in nightclubs, dancing in them or being fired from them, and she as an executive with Garuda Indonesian Airways, who had probably never seen a drug, or the inside of a Wan Chai nightclub. Stephan swam in a different stream, though, and always showed a warm side.

The next day I was in Wan Chai when he paged, asking me to meet him at a skyscraper on Hennessy Road where he did consultancy work.

I'd been there once before, but this time, having smoked a load of ice on top of two nights without sleep, I got all confused and set off in the wrong direction.

The pager went off twice more, much to my annoyance. It made me realise how much my life had changed since the business days when I would make sure to be in the right place at the right time, and often to conform to other people's so-important schedules.

'Fuck you, Stephan!' I thought. 'Why don't you come and find me?'

When I eventually located the premises, the girl at reception asked me if I would like a glass of water. It was kind of her to offer, but left me wondering if it was obvious I was a drugged-up mess.

Stephan appeared in the lobby carrying my bags. 'Come,' he said, leading me outside to sit down on the building's ornamental front wall. With my nervous system fraying like an overstretched rope, I fought to compose myself.

'Chris, I have to ask you to leave the house.'

'Is it your wife, Stephan? She doesn't like having guests?'

'She likes having guests, Chris, but she doesn't like you. She doesn't *trust* you.'

My heart plummeted, like a skydiver's when their chute won't open. It broke me and, not for the first time during my stay in the Fragrant Harbour, tears began to well. I didn't know what was wrong with me. I never cried, but now I seemed to bubble like a drinking fountain during a heatwave.

As my face started to leak, Stephan asked, 'What's *happened* to you, Chris?'

I picked up my bags, a pastime that was getting boring, and said, 'I'm a drug addict, Stephan. *That's* what's happened to me,' and then I walked off.

I went to Ron's apartment to ask if I could leave my things there. Tom was with him, still wearing the miniature red snooker ball on a leather thong.

He'd been there a lot lately. He and Ron seemed to be becoming the best of friends. I found them huddled in front of one of those new laptop gizmos, Ron saying he'd bought it with the money from his sister.

Only, it didn't add up. If someone was on the bones of their backside, you could understand a kindly relative giving them the money for a deposit – but not enough to pay for food, rent, outgoings *and* expensive and unnecessary toys, especially when the recipient had given up their job to swan around Hong Kong doing a good impression of bugger all. Besides, Ron had no one to look after him in this world. He told me that himself.

'How is it, Tom? I thought you got kicked out?'

'He's only stayed once,' said Ron.

'Yeah, I owed too much rent.' Tom shrugged, not looking at all bothered.

'But he's not staying anymore,' said Ron, who deemed it necessary to keep interrupting. 'You know, don't want problems with the landlord.'

'Of course not.'

'You can't stay here either, Chris,' he continued, his words adding to my growing sense of alienation.

'Ron, I'm not asking to. I've got to work this evening, anyway. Club Nemo.'

'Club *Nemo*, eh?' He gave me the disbelieving look.

'*Yeah*, Club Nemo. Anyway, got a paper? I need to find a flat.'

'A *flat!*'

'Yeah, I sold my Rolex.'

'Hah! *Right…*'

In the *Post*, I came across an advert for a place in Wan Chai, HK$4000 a month plus deposit. After calling the landlord, I set out with Tom to have a look at it.

We met Gabriel outside the apartment block. In his fifties and originally from Bombay, he was a short, portly gent with neat-cropped pomaded-back hair and small brown eyes that flitted around in a constant state of suspicion. He wore a charcoal-grey ankle-length shirt and seemed friendly enough.

We were on Jaffe Road, about a quarter-mile east and ten minutes' walk from Clubland. Yet this part of town was distinctly different to the modern sector where the discos were. This was old Hong Kong, a rundown part of Wan Chai where decades of sun and typhoons saw buildings crumbling, where faded signs hung on rusting hinges above modest outlets. There was none of Hong Kong's trademark flashing neon, nor any record-breaking skyscrapers or Japanese department stores. The nearest 7-Eleven was streets away. Stray cats and dogs flouted stereotype, curling up in harmony on the pavement to enjoy the sunshine, while proprietors of small businesses sat side by side on the steps of their premises, shovelling in rice and putting the world – or at least this part of it – to rights. Elderly Chinese dressed in traditional garb trotted past pushing barrows toppling with various enterprising arrangements – rubbish bags, defunct television sets, and sacks of foodstuff to supply restaurants. Overall, this ageing and unpretentious part of town buzzed with authentic activity. A setting, I'm sure, for many a Hong Kong gangster movie.

The building was a similar decaying weathered beast to those adjoining it. We entered its gaping grey mouth and took a faithful lift all twenty floors to come out into a small hallway with an apartment either side. With peeling white paintwork, a beige stone-tiled floor and decorative but rusting ironwork in place of glass in the windows, it was a relic from a bygone era. My hook, line and sinker had fallen and we hadn't even seen the flat.

The view at eye level from the hallway's north-facing window was of the buildings across the street, but above them Causeway Bay's mirrored-glass towers edged into view. Through a gap created by an intersecting street, you got a rewarding snippet of the dazzling harbour scene. A corridor led to a door out onto the balcony, a huge storage recess full of junk and the entrance to the emergency stairway.

Inside the apartment was a living area, empty of furniture, with a worn dark-wood parquet floor, sickly pastel yellow paint and room to swing half a cat *if* you sucked your stomach in. The suicide-pink kitchen had a single-ring cooker and space for two people at a squeeze; the bathroom, tiled in seventies swimming-pool blue, a toilet and stainless steel washbasin.

The bedroom with the northerly view Gabriel used as an office and storage for his henna export business – a little disappointing, but by the sound of it, he didn't use it that often. The room to the south would be mine – a small pale-green-glossed affair with a heavily stained concrete floor. It too was empty, less a dirty air conditioner high up on the wall.

The view from the window – this one having panes in it – took in the rear of the high-rises on Lockhart Road, though rising above them in the far distance was the majestic Peak.

I opened a window and looked way down to see small courtyards to the rear of businesses lining the alleyway below, protected from the elements and the litter raining down by makeshift roofs constructed from plywood sheeting and tarpaulins. Every so often, you glimpsed the rain covers' colourful striping through a mountain of plastic bags, cans, bottles, cartons, condoms, tampons, nappies and other rubbish thrown down from windows such as this.

While Tom made embarrassing comments, such as how with a telescope you'd be able to see in through other people's windows, I made a decision. Even though most Westerners would turn up their nose and run a mile from this dump, I loved the place. I told Gabriel I would take it and arranged to pay him the rent and deposit and pick up a key in the morning.

It was a Thursday evening in Club Nemo. It might well have been Thursday in Hong Kong and a host of other countries too, but that was of no concern to me. I lived one drug-fuelled moment at a time, although some, I'm sure, would dispute my definition of living. Grand schemes of creating wealth had gone out the window. Careers, pensions, partners, kids, second car, hobbies, pets, compost heaps, and bonfires on a Sunday – if I'd ever planned such luxuries – had followed suit.

No longer was I in touch with folks in the UK – even Ben, my kid brother, I'd not spoken to for weeks, maybe months. Nor had I sent any money back to cover the mortgage or checked to see if my tenant still lived there. I only bought food on the hoof and certainly didn't intend to go stocking any refrigerators. My place didn't even have one... or anything else.

My sole concern was staying high above these problems, as coming back down to meet them, along with the torture that went with it, wasn't an experience I wanted to put myself through again – not if I could help it.

I'd put on my best shirt, washed and ironed at Ron's, but Paul Eng, the last person I would have expected to help me get dressed, shook his head and led me into a storeroom. Standing on a crate of Schweppes Light, he reached into a nest of sweatshirts hanging like ducks on a butcher's rail

– or flamingos, to be more precise, as he handed down two brand new white ones with Club Nemo printed on them in pink lettering.

Then Paul introduced me to the two other doormen. About the same age as me, Chee Chu was short and on the chubby side of stocky. He had a surprisingly cherubic face and hair cut in a wavy bob.

Dai Su, slightly older, was a giant of a man, especially for a Chinese. With a face like a horse, he must have stood at least eighteen hands and wore his mane without rosettes, opting instead for a curly bouffant in the eighties' New Romantic-pop style.

Both wore shell-suit tops, jeans and white trainers, together with gold bracelets and necklaces as wide as the boys on whom they hung. Chee Chu had a matching dress watch, but Dai Su a simple plastic digital, which clashed with his jewellery and looked like a swimming pool locker band on his huge wrist.

Chee Chu was more adept in English, but both were far from comfortable speaking it. They seemed amicable enough and I looked forward to cracking on with them, as you do with your workmates. They pretty much kept their distance that first night, though.

Instead, I gleaned my knowledge from a 'middle' man drinking shorts at the bar. A middle-aged, middle-class, middle-management expat, he had an accent that was Middle England too. He told me he worked on the airport construction project and was a regular at Nemo's. I didn't get his name, but he seemed to know who I was and took it upon himself to give me an impromptu rundown on the staff profile.

'You know they're all triads,' he said.

My ears pricked up.

'They belong to the 14-K society. The 14-K runs Wan Chai. You haven't met David yet, have you?'

'Who's David?'

'Nice chap, the owner – but he's not mafia. He has to pay these guys to run the place, though.

'Paul there, he's *Dai Lo* – Big Brother, the gang leader. He's small fish in the grand scheme of things, but he's a fucking shark in here and an important man in Wan Chai. He may look like Ratso Rizzo, but you *don't* want to upset him. Not if you like your fingers and toes.'

As we spoke, the short barman with the round glasses refreshed the guy's drink. I expected him to say thank you and pay, but he did neither.

'See your man, Chee Chu, over there?'

'Uh-huh.'

'He's *maa jai* – a runner or errand boy, bottom of the food chain. But don't be fooled, he's a street fighter through and through. He's tough and he'll pick up anything in a scrap if he can smash an enemy over the head with it.'

'Are there many scraps in Wan Chai?'

'Now and again there are.'

'Who with?'

'It might be a dispute between families. Sometimes they come onto another's territory without permission. There was a showdown between the Wo Hop To and the Sun Yee On over on Lockhart a few years back over protection rights to a restaurant. Three hundred people clashed heads.'

'*Three hundred!* How do they know who's who?'

'They have their ways.'

'How?'

'It could be something they're wearing, or a matchstick between the lips… something subtle. On top of that, each society uses their own set of hand signs and gestures and slang.'

'What about this guy Dai Su?'

'He's *hong sao.*'

'Meaning?'

'Literally, it means "violent hand" – an assassin. Every so often he disappears for a few days, gets smuggled into China to do a hit on someone.'

'What sort of someone?'

'Anyone he's told. He wouldn't question it.'

'So is *everyone* here triad?'

'Depends on what you mean by triad.'

'How come?'

'There's *triad* and there's *triad.*'

'I don't follow…'

'Never mind. Catalina, the waitress, *she's* not, nor is Jason, the tall bloke behind the bar. Sidney and Michael, the other two, are what you might call up and coming—'

'*Maa jais?*'

'Yeah, "little horses" in Cantonese. But they don't just let anyone in. Background's important. Then there's a certain proving ground... initiation ceremonies and so forth.'

'Background?'

'Yeah, background. Triads will work with anyone, even *gweilos*, if they can make a buck out of it. But it's only pure-blooded locals allowed into the true brotherhood. That's why Jason has a hard time.'

'Why's that?' I said, snatching a glance at the handsome and unassuming Eurasian-looking dude.

'He's educated abroad. He wants to become triad, but he's *dzum gwoh hahm seui.*'

'Something about *salt water?*'

'It means soaked in salt water, someone who's been overseas. They don't trust them. Jason studied in the States, I think.'

'How do you know all this?'

'If you're interested, you'll find out. Take your man Glenn–'

'Yeah, I know Glenn.'

'He was here six months, didn't understand a thing... had his tourist head on the whole time. Shame.' The middleman shook his own head.

'Why's that?'

'Think about it, Chris. How often do you get a chance to experience a culture that turns all your accepted understanding on its head, one whose ancient mandate hasn't changed for a thousand years and embraces a completely different set of moral codes and beliefs? You've got yourself a job working for the world's oldest, secretive and most ruthless criminal fraternity. *Triads*, mate, who rely on their own language and cunning. Do you know what I'm saying?'

I nodded.

'Why would you want to come all the way to Hong Kong just to let it fly over your head? You may as well get a job at Burger King.'

'...I see. I kind'a think that way myself. I've been trying hard with the language. So you speak Cantonese, I take it?'

'The basics. But you don't need Cantonese to get by in Wan Chai.'

'How's that?'

'It's all in the *eyes*, Chris. If you really want to know what's going on, watch the eyes.'

As he threw back his head and laughed, I knew I was going to love it there.

Leaving the club that morning in March, a diamond sparkled against a backdrop of blue. The anticipated inclemency holding off – for the time being, at least – it made for one hell of a day in the Fragrant Harbour.

Gabriel's flat was on Thomson Road, not far from Club Nemo. His teenage son answered the door. When I said, 'Chris,' he said, 'Anil,' then went to fetch his dad. I had a quick butchers inside – quite spacious, with the expected Asian kitsch.

With the key to the flat in my hand, deposit and rent paid, I was just turning to go when Gabriel said, '*Oh*! Mister Creese. One more t'ing.'

'What's that, Gabriel?'

'In this apartment, there is no taking drug!'

Walking towards Ron's, I saw Tom leave the building, so I expected my friend to be awake. But when he finally opened the door, his eyes were still asleep.

'*Wakey-wakey!* Sun's shining, mate.'

'*Urrh*… come in,' said the living dead.

'What did Tom want?'

'*Tom?*'

'Yeah.'

'Tom hasn't been here.'

'I just saw him leave.'

'No, he didn't, mate,' said Ron.

I had no idea what these two were playing at, so I shut up.

'Ron, I need somewhere to crash for a couple of hours?'

'You can't stay here *again*, mate!'

'Ron, I *haven't* stayed here!' I wondered why he thought I had. He must have remembered turfing me out that time. 'I've got my own flat –

it just it doesn't have a bed or fuck all. Not until I get my pay from the club.'

'Club?'

'*Nemo's.* I told you.'

'Oh, you work in *Nemo's*, do you?' he sneered. 'You can crash, Chris, but just this once. That room there. Pete and Em are moving into the other one.'

'Pete and Emily *Sax*? Gung Wan Hong?'

'Yeah, they're still working there, but they've had to leave their place in Tsim Sha Tsui.'

After snatching a few hours' sleep before the drug in my system woke me up, I dressed, snorted some ice off the dressing table and went into the front room.

Ron had gone out. Tom sat rolling a spliff and talking to Pete and Emily. It was good to see the two of them and strange to hear news from the Hong.

Partway into the conversation, Tom piped up to ask if I wanted a flatmate.

'Sure, if you don't mind a squeeze.'

'Nah, not me, mate. Friend of mine called Apple... Filipina.'

'Oh, yeah. What does she do?'

'Ha! I *think* you can guess. She's alright, though. Do you want her pager?'

'But I haven't got a bed... or anything else.'

'You can have the bed in our room,' said Pete. 'We're buying a new one.'

I paged Apple, asking her to call me. Although a touch stressed, she sounded pleasant on the telephone, saying she would come right over.

An hour later, she still hadn't arrived, so I paged again. When she called back this time, I could tell something was wrong. She said she couldn't find Ron's flat and would I meet her in Wan Chai Market.

I found our agreed spot, but she wasn't there. After fifteen minutes, I started to feel panicky and confused – *again.*

My pager went off: MISS APPLE OUTSIDE MR RONALD.

'Is she serious?' I wondered. 'Is this a joke?'

I ran back at a jog, only she wasn't there either. I knocked on Ron's door, but they'd all gone out, so I sat down in the stairwell, leaking like a trawler's net and trying to get a handle on the situation.

Discombobulated would be the word. Life had turned into one big acid trip with the monkey controlling the organ grinder. My pager beeped: MISS APPLE IN MARKET NOW.

'*What!*'

I resolved to run back there.

As my feet slammed down on Tai Yuen Street, they beat out a rhythm: '*No*-way!–*No*-way!–*No*-way!' Their negative vibe reiterating what I already knew: she *wouldn't* be there because she *couldn't* be there. It wasn't how the game worked. That would be like trying to control the outcome of a dream. Every time you think you have it in the bag, someone slaps you with a sideshow that convolutes the carnival.

Of course, she wasn't there! *Too* logical, at a time when nothing was. My stress level rose above me. My heart no longer pumped blood, just amphetamine-laced confusion. The more my pulse raced, the more my head spun one way and the marketplace the other, leaving me out of body and out of mind.

Clinging to a food counter on the mad merry-go-round, I used their courtesy phone to call her pager service, leaving a message to get back to me on this number. It rang immediately. '*Apple!* I'm in the market.'

'You weren't there!' She sounded as though she would burst into tears. 'I'm in the MTR station now.'

For the life of me, I couldn't work out why she didn't just meet me in the place we'd agreed. I told her to wait at the A1 exit and not to move until I got there.

When we finally met, it was like a reunion of two holocaust survivors, a wave of relief sweeping over us as we rushed for a lifetime's worth of hug. The problem soon became apparent. The drugs had spun her out even more than they had me.

She was a pretty, skinny little thing. Walking towards the flat, having collected my bags from Ron's, I felt a sense of companionship and a degree of paternalism towards her. She was as lost as I was in this unforgiving metropolis, but at least I didn't have to sell my body to survive here.

'*Fuck!*'

'What's wrong?' asked Apple.

'The key won't go in the lock!' I tried it again.

'Why not?'

'Don't know!'

And then it hit me: '*Tom!*'

'What about Tom?'

'Tom's been staying at Ron's… without Ron knowing. I reckon he's kept his old key. Ron must have thought it was me and gone through my pockets while I was asleep and swapped what he thought was one of his apartment's spare keys for this shitty one, so I wouldn't realise.'

'Why he didn't just take it back?'

'Ron's got this stupid envy thing going on. This is his way of having a smug snipe at me.'

Gabriel brought round a replacement, but he was far from pleased – unhappier still to see Apple with me. What with his comments about drugs and now this, we weren't getting off to a good start.

I dumped my gear in the empty bedroom, turning to see Apple shivering with exhaustion. 'You need to sleep, babe, don't you?'

'Uh-huh.' She nodded desperately.

I whipped off the bomber jacket and wrapped it around her, then made a bed on the bare concrete with my spare clothes. 'Right, I'm off out to buy a blanket. Get some sleep.'

On Hennessy Road, I came across a shop selling general household items, rewarded to find a stack of grey blankets in its open frontage. Bingo!

I picked one up. Sewn onto a corner was a tiny label. I flipped it over looking for a price tag – but what I saw instead…

'*URRH!*… what the *FUCK!*'

'*Infected!*… *tuberculosis!*… *Red Indians!*'

I couldn't believe what these sick people were selling! The label had the word WASTE printed on it in small red letters. I *knew* what these blankets were. The same as the ones infected with disease that North American settlers gave to the Native Americans, purposely decimating the indigenous population so the Europeans could lay claim to the continent. Finding them, *here in Wan Chai*, shook me to the core.

I felt a chilling Cantophobia descend on Hennessy Road, swirling through me and opening my mind to a parallel reality I'd been oblivious to before.

I stood frozen to the spot. 'How the *fuck* could it be…?'

Had the world I lived in for almost a year been a smokescreen to keep me in the dark? Was this the true reality of Hong Kong life? How had I been blind to it all this time?

If I were Alice, it seemed I'd found the rabbit hole.

'Lady in the shop knows… guy on the corner knows… now you know.'

I could sense a grotesque subterranean agenda – one communicated through subliminal methods such as the label on this blanket. *Surely*, it was allegorical, a coded signpost understood only by those privileged with the cipher.

'Is this linked to the triads….?' I wondered. 'Benny Tsang communicates with his brother without saying a word… is that something to do with this?'

'Guy in the club… said it was all in the eyes.'

Whatever was going on, I had to buy one. Apple was about to crash and if I looked elsewhere, it might take ages, what with the confusion I felt.

Back at the flat, I found she'd gone out. I missed her immediately. It was lonely in that bare space on my own. I used the opportunity to snort a line of ice to get me through the long night ahead.

An hour later, she returned, saying she'd been out for supplies. As she unloaded her pockets, I didn't need to ask how she'd acquired them, but mused over the random selection: a few processed food snacks sealed in foil bags with Japanese writing on them, a comb and a shitload of unnecessary toiletries.

Leaving her curled up on the floor, while I washed in cold water and polished my boots, I wondered if she was having a problem dealing with reality.

Being early on a Friday night, Club Nemo was empty, less the regular contingent around the bar. Chee Chu and I sat on barstools behind the lectern. Feeling fidgety, I took the Cantonese dictionary out of my leather bum bag and began to copy some of its pictograms on a scrap piece of paper.

Chee Chu took no notice, until I asked how he wrote his name. Then he shook his head and walked off, leaving me wondering if it was a taboo for a *gweilo* to learn the language, the thought occurring he might think I was a cop.

A large guy dressed in filthy clothes made his way down the stairs. He paused at the lectern, staring into my eyes as the acrid stench of cigarette butts wafted out of his pockets. Then he muttered, 'Han'some…' smiled cagily and made his way inside. Stopping in front of Paul Eng, he bowed his head as if waiting for some kind of dispensation.

Paul stared dead ahead – as dead ahead as he could with his affliction – right through the bloke, then nodded, purposefully, as if uncomfortable with whatever arrangement they had made but knowing it was a matter of 'face'.

The man walked once around the drinkers at the bar, his eyes bulging black globes edged with paranoia but his head held high and projecting the vestiges of a battered self-respect to his silent but reproachful audience. He paused by Paul, nodded with his head low, and then walked back towards me.

In the semi-privacy of the stairwell, he stopped and placed his hand on the lectern. His sleeve rolled up, it looked as though his arm was dotted with injection sites, although in hindsight these unsightly welts may well have been infected mosquito bites from sleeping rough.

He leant his shoulder against mine, doing what Americans call 'invading my space', and as the smell of the street eclipsed all others, he said, 'Me no speaking goo' English.'

'You sound alright to me.'

'*No!* Me nutting… No have job… no have house… no have money. In Hong Kong, me nutting… Me down *heeya*!'

From my conversations about drugs, fortunes and rent paying with Vance, I guessed the point he alluded to must be way below the floor.

'I think you're alright, mate,' I told him.

'*No!* You *no* unnerstan' me.' Agitated, he started up the stairs. 'Me no speaking goo' English. Me nee' computer. If have computer, you unnerstan' wha' I try to tell you…'

He may have been rambling, but I had the drift of it – computer or not. 'What's your name?' I asked.

'Johnny,' he said, gazing into one of the mirrors like a man banished to the far fringe of wretchedness by stones of contempt. 'You kno' wha' I see?'

'What do you see, Johnny?'

'I see *nutting*…' He went to walk up the final few steps.

'Johnny!' I stopped him. 'Do you know what I see?'

'Wha'?' Fearful curiosity replaced the dejection on his face.

'Brother Johnny.'

As a look of comprehension replaced one of unease, Chee Chu returned and Johnny made a quick exit.

I whipped out the dictionary and found the Cantonese for 'taking drugs'. 'Chee Chu? This guy *pok duk*?'

'*Wha*…?' he replied, scowling. '*Pok duk*?'

'Take drugs?' I clarified.

Chee Chu shook his head in disgust and walked off.

'Christ, I can be so dumb!' I kicked myself.

I hadn't been trying to get my new friend into trouble and I wasn't being a hypocrite. I'd simply wanted to show Chee Chu that as a doorman I knew how to recognise such things and I could be a valid member of the team that had accepted me into their midst.

By 10pm, the club had begun to fill, mainly Chinese businessmen, a splash of expats and a few 'numbered' Filipinas looking to be bought drinks.

I went to take a leak, and as I washed my hands, Shirley – or Alex – my one-eared barman friend came through the door. Since learning I'd put him in a taxi on several occasions, he was always delighted to see me, so I thought he would be the ideal person to ask to borrow HK$100.

'Sure, Chris! No problem,' he said, diving into his wallet with the enthusiasm of a lottery winner and handing over a note with a smile.

As he did, Tommy Lau, a worker from another club, walked in. A chubby, bespectacled chap, he came across as nerdy and not exactly the brightest button in the jar. He seemed an unlikely candidate for a triad, but working in Wan Chai and dressed by Puma, he must have been at least low-level or wannabe. I'd chatted to him the previous evening, mainly about my flat and how many square feet it was. Because of the cramped living conditions in Hong Kong and how the size of a home relates to status, it was an often-asked question. He'd seemed friendly enough.

Only now I saw a different side. I clocked his furtive glance and a look of uncontrollable disapproval. What I'd done wrong, I wasn't *quite* sure, but that face was familiar.

Paul Eng joined me at the front of the club. English wasn't his major, but he knew enough to ask where my apartment was. I added, for conversation's sake, it was currently empty of furniture.

Without another word, he slid Dalek-like to where Jason stood at the till and came back with HK$4,000.

'Thanks very much, Paul!' I said, reflecting on how in my own culture I would have had to provide a birth certificate and three years' worth of bank statements, sign over my mortgage, agree to work overtime, make sure my National Insurance contributions were up to date *and* leave a bodily organ as a deposit to curry this sort of favour in the workplace. Once again, I admired this straightforward approach and Confucian ethic. If boss looked after worker, then worker would work hard and respect boss.

I felt certain the guy sat at the bar was Martin Chen – one of the Triad Police I'd met while working at Gung Wan Hong.

Despite the guy being kind enough to buy me dinner and tell me about his work in the Hong Kong underworld, none of that mattered now. I'd tried to live that life only to see it dump me on the floor and kick me in the teeth while I was down. Now the goalposts had shifted and allegiance to my 'new' family was at stake.

If this was the same bloke, he'd likely suffer a nasty death if caught working undercover in a triad hangout. I didn't know what to do, so I decided to speak to Jason. With his Western education and understanding, he was easier to approach than the others and less abrupt towards me too.

'Jason, do you know that guy?' I asked discreetly.

'Mister Ng. He's a businessman.'

'Are you sure?'

'Yeah, he's been coming here for years. Why, wass wrong?'

'Oh, nothing. I thought I recognised him, that's all.'

Deep inside, I was drawn to this place, as if I owed it something. Compared to sitting on my backpack on Nathan Road, a near-broken man, it was a much better deal. I felt at home, a sense of acceptance and pride at being the only *gweilo* working for the Chinese in Wan Chai. Some might say the scene was sucking me in, the way of opiate into a bloodstained syringe, but that wasn't an issue in my mind…

Triads

HEADING EAST ALONG JAFFE ROAD towards my flat the next morning, I knew someone was following me. You don't survive a tour of Northern Ireland intact without being able to sense when something's going down on the street – unless you're a chef. With all the weird shit going on in Club Nemo, it was obvious these guys would want to know more about me.

Pretending to do up my bootlace, I saw Tommy Lau check himself and hop into a doorway. It was another bizarre event to add to last night's tally…

At closing time, I'd accompanied Dai Su around the club as he checked the dance floor with a torch searching for any drugs or valuables the customers had dropped.

He found a pack of cigarettes and gave them to me. I picked up a smart silver pen and tried to return the favour, but, as usual with my attempts at giving gifts in the Fragrant Harbour, he'd declined it. Putting his violent hand aside, I liked the guy. He was easier to get on with than Chee Chu and appreciated my jokes – thus proving the age-old adage about laughter being the best medicine when it comes to dealing with murdering sociopaths.

At 11pm, Chee Chu had said, 'You tekk break now,' so I popped over to the Apple. Mr Lu, my elderly friend 'The Butterfly', was sitting in his regular spot, talking to the abundance of women who flocked around his kind persona. When I told him I'd taken a job in Club Nemo, he stopped smiling, his wrinkles dropping from fun into serious mode. 'Be *careful!*' he said. 'Paul Eng is *bad* man! *Very* bad man!'

I arrived back at the apartment to find Apple gone, so I decided to fetch the bed Pete promised – the mattress, at least – thinking it would be a nice surprise for her when she returned.

After changing into my sandals to give my long-suffering feet a break, I pinned a note to the door and took the lift back down to check out the handbarrow I'd spotted on the ground floor.

I didn't think anyone would miss it for an hour, so I aimed it in the direction of Ron's, deciding not to mention anything to him about the incident with the key. I wanted to see his face when he realised I really did have a flat.

When I crossed Hennessy and Johnston Roads' busy nine-lane junction, bumping the cart over the tramlines, a busload of school kids waved and laughed. I guess with my sandals on and jeans turned up to keep them out of the dirt I looked like a local deliveryman. I felt like one. I can't imagine many *gweilos* ever pushed a handcart across Hennessy.

Old Ron was in the front room, talking to a Filipina named Rose. I'd seen them out in Wan Chai a couple of times. It surprised me as he didn't seem to do the women thing that well. During our last heart-to-heart, he'd let slip a green banana, saying he'd paid prostitutes in the past but hadn't been able to do the business and ended up chatting to them.

I couldn't get a handle on him these days, anyway – not in a job, his own flat (*avec* meat hooks) and now a bargirl on his arm. He was turning into a right old bad boy.

Rose was pretty, petite and chatty, but came across as devious – as did many of the girls working in Wan Chai. It went with the territory.

Ron asked if I had any ice, so I set up the gear. But when Rose's eyes widened and she said, 'I never try this one!' I told her find someone else to get her addicted to the stuff. She whispered something to Ron and they looked at me and laughed.

Feeling instantly more alive *and* fidgety, I went to the window to check out Johnston Road. The usual bustling Hong Kong street scene played out with people buzzing in all directions, but one guy caught my eye. Dressed in a yellow shell-suit top, jeans and trainers, he passed by three times in five minutes, stopping on the corner each time.

I felt sure this shifty-looking geezer was watching Ron's flat. People in Hong Kong didn't loiter aimlessly. People in this hectic trap went directly from A to B, usually with a work related item. Did the colour of the tracksuit tops worn by the little horses, the *runners*, represent affiliation to a particular triad society, I wondered?

As Rose got up to leave, Pete arrived home, so I put my underground uniform theory to him, and Ron once more. The lover boy scoffed, but Pete said it could well be the case.

'What were you and Rose laughing at, Ron?'

'Oh, *that*? She said you look like Jesus.'

'*What?*' I'd let my hair grow since leaving the Forces and sprouted a slight beard, but I'd seen *Life of Brian* enough times to know it's not a good idea to get mistaken for the Messiah – I had enough on my plate. I decided to find a barber later for a short back and sides.

When Pete gave me a hand outside with the mattress, I said, 'Pete, I'm not mad, you know.'

'Nah, mate.' He gave me a pat on the back. 'I know you're not.'

Arriving back at the apartment building, I saw the elderly owner of the pushcart standing in Jaffe Road, scanning up and down for a culprit. Seeing me approach, he launched into a tirade of rapid-fire Cantonese.

Rather than accept I'd done wrong and apologise, I launched into one myself and we had a flaming row in the street.

'*Ngohge pungyau fangaau dung deiha yanwaih ngohdeih mou yau chohng!*' I said, explaining that my friend was sleeping on a cold floor because we had no bed and this surely justified the short-term loan. Then I dragged the mattress towards the lift, leaving him standing there, jabbering to the crowd that had built up.

As soon as I got the bloody thing into the flat and calmed down, I felt terrible – my language skills might be improving, but my people ones weren't. I made up my mind to apologise to the gentleman, which in Cantonese culture meant I would have to buy a cake.

By 4.30pm, Apple hadn't come back. I had a feeling she'd found a better option – if there is a better option than living with a drugged-up Jesus impersonator who hijacks handcarts.

I went out and found a barber for my crop, returning to the flat to shave before work, only there was no hot water – or a mirror.

I remembered seeing one in the junk room out the back. As with the cart, perhaps I should have enquired who owned all this clutter, but it did look like a dumping ground, so I figured no one would miss an old mirror.

The amphetamine making me curious, I looked forward to coming back later to see what else was around. It may well have been rubbishy items at a glance, but it was all so neatly stacked I couldn't help thinking there was more to this hoard than folded-up newspapers, plastic bags full of plastic bags, and others, rubber bands and paperclips.

The hot water wasn't hard to sort out either. As there were no pans in the Barbie-pink kitchen, I took the cooker and gas cylinder into the bubonic-blue bathroom and set the ring up on a stool beneath the steel sink. There was no pipe underneath to worry about melting as all the waste water poured straight down onto the sloping floor and ran out through a drain at the far end.

I turned on the tap and began to fill my Heath Robinson contraption, but the water suddenly stopped.

Coldness came over me…

I sensed foul play…

'Is someone having a laugh?… Did someone wait for the exact moment I needed water then turn it off at the mains?' I worried it might be something to do with borrowing the handcart or because I'd taken drugs in the place when I said I wouldn't. It all seemed so very peculiar.

When I got to the club I was out of breath and panicky, having run the last few blocks. Descending the stairs, I wondered what Saturday night in Club Nemo had in store.

Jason and Chee Chu stood in the stairwell, having a heated exchange. Jason looked up with a wary smile – 'Hi, Chris' – but Chee Chu just grunted, which didn't do anything to calm my anxiety.

I went inside to say hi to Paul, who stood talking to Dai Su and Catalina. Sidney and Michael were busy serving drinks, and Chen *San*, the club's elderly cleaner, sat at the far side, mop in hand, waiting to clean up any spillages. After saying hellos, I went back to the bottom door, but not wishing to intrude upon Jason and Chee Chu's dispute, I moved a little way up the stairs.

I couldn't help overhearing them, though. Somebody had done something to upset Chee Chu because he kept raising his voice. Then to my surprise, he pointed at *me*. 'What's up?' I asked.

'It's nothing, Chris,' said Jason, looking embarrassed. Only Chee Chu kept stressing *'Yat baak man!'* and *'Sei chin man!'* repeatedly, and when I looked again, he was still jabbing his finger towards me.

I knew what it meant: $100 and $4,000. Tommy Lau must have told him I'd borrowed money from Alex and he'd somehow found out about my loan from Paul. When Chee Chu left, I asked Jason what I'd done wrong. 'No, he's got no beef with you, man,' he said, but I felt far from convinced.

Paul came and stood behind the lectern. As he and Jason knew which punters to charge or give VIP treatment to, I left them to it and sat on a stool inside the door.

Chee Chu walked up to me, gawked a while, then smiled and said, 'Very *goo*! Mush more han'some!' I realised he was talking about my newly shorn appearance. He had such a sincere look on his face – like a child when they tell their best friend something in innocence – that I felt touched… only it didn't last long.

Two seconds later, he said something to Catalina, who let out a sycophantic giggle, and then reached up and took the refill out of the air-freshening machine and began spraying it all around *my* barstool. He kept up a flow of Cantonese witticism, to which she kept reacting.

From my experience with Vance and Lim, I knew he was taking the piss out of my stinking Caterpillar boots – or the owner of the feet inside them. But something was becoming apparent. I didn't think they smelt *that* bad – certainly none of my *gweilo* friends ever mentioned them – it was that the Chinese appeared to have a highly developed sense of smell.

I wondered how Chee Chu could be so blatant, especially after complimenting me on my haircut. Living in the Not-So-Fragrant Harbour really spun your melon at times.

By 10.30pm, the club had about twenty-five drinkers, almost all Chinese men sat around the horseshoe-shaped bar, and a couple of Filipina bargirls slumped in the comfortable chairs. Paul was on the next table over with

David, the owner, drinking shorts with two Thai girls sent over from another club to 'entertain' them.

I could only see one Westerner – a white guy, likely a tourist – stood drinking at the far end of the bar. The music pounded, but the dance floor was empty.

Paul had introduced me to David, a retiring man in his late fifties, who was dressed in a grey suit, white shirt and modest tie. Unlike the *Dai Lo* he drank with, there was nothing suspicious about him.

As I sat on the barstool, thankfully over the anxiety of earlier, an Indian chap came into the club. Slightly older than me, he introduced himself as Raj. Unlike the other Indians around town, he didn't wear traditional clothing, opting instead for the white shell-suit top, jeans and trainers of the Wan Chai doormen – the little horses.

With pride, Raj told me he worked at the Pink Panther, over on Jaffe Road. He was a friendly bloke, and I felt comfortable talking to him. What with both of us being foreigners working as doormen in Wan Chai, he seemed a guy I could trust.

It surprised me that a Chinese-run club employed him. Both Chee Chu and Dai Su *hated* Indians, but they cracked on with Raj as if he were an old friend.

From my stool at the front of the club, I watched as Paul and David's Thai acquaintances made their way to the bar. Without warning, one of them fell to the floor. Her friend dropped down astride and began shaking her – a touch *too* violently for horseplay?

I assumed they were showing off in front of their important dates, but when I looked again, the face of the girl on the floor had turned grey.

Truth dawned…

This wasn't frivolity…

One of them had collapsed!

I jumped off the stool and ran over. By now, the friend was hysterical, slapping her palms against a lifeless chest. I pushed her aside, bent down and placed my open mouth above the unconscious girl's, rewarded to sense a slight breath on my tongue.

Checking her pulse at the wrist, I couldn't feel anything, so I swapped to her neck and discovered a faint beat. I timed the barely detectable palpitations to find – '*Shit!*' – her pulse raced at a hundred-and-sixty beats per minute – *amphetamine overdose!*

Two pairs of legs approached. I looked up to see Paul and David. Paul looked down with callous eyes and without any emotion in his voice said, 'Throw her in the alleyway.'

'Did I just hear that?' I asked myself, stealing a look around the bar.

The scene I took in deadened me. It was frightening.

Everyone had put their drinks down and stood rooted to the spot, all staring trancelike, their angry black eyes fixed on me. The music thumped away, but the place felt silent, the atmosphere tight and ugly.

Paul's instructions went straight through me, like a dud coin in a vending machine. Ignoring him, I looked to David, the more human of the two, and said, 'She needs an ambulance or she's gonna die.'

He hesitated, his eyes flicking from side to side seeking guidance, and then knowing he was going against the *Dai Lo*'s order, his speech wavering, he said, '*Okay!* Everyone *l-l-listen* to him! He know *w-w-what* he doing!'

As relief washed over me, the Westerner approached, an English guy. 'Do you want a hand, bud?' he asked, crouching beside me.

'Yeah, mate,' I whispered. 'Go over to the 7-Eleven and call an ambulance.'

'Right!' he scoffed, thinking, 'Surely *someone's* done that already.'

But his thinking was in England; that if this happened in a bar back home people would be falling over themselves to offer assistance.

'Take a look,' I urged quietly.

When he stole the same glance I had earlier, shock crept across his face. 'Yeah…' he whispered. 'See what you mean, bud. I'm onto it.'

Melting off into the stairwell, he gave a discreet nod and disappeared.

A young Filipina got up from her chair and went to leave. She wore an orange parka with fur around the hood. 'Give me your jacket, love?' I asked, expecting her to whip it off and hand it to me. Instead, she burst into tears and ran out, leaving me wondering if things could get any weirder.

Dai Su hovered over me, and as he was no stranger to death, I asked him to get me a blanket, *anything*, from the backroom. He returned with a bunch of dirty rags and – '*Urrh!*' – threw them down.

I went to check in her handbag to see what drugs she'd been taking, so I could tell the paramedics and improve her chances.

The other Thai grunted like a cornered animal, lunged and wrenched the bag back. What Vance had said about drugs being taboo here must have been true. It seemed this girl would risk her friend dying rather than face exposure.

My English friend did us proud, and it wasn't long before the disco's beams bounced off the reflector stripes on the ambulance crew's fluorescent jackets. Choosing life over Hong Kong's taboos, and sure that this little angel's parents in Chiang Mai would do likewise, I told the lead paramedic her pulse rate and what had likely happened. He nodded in agreement and they stretchered her out.

Everything went back to normal – whatever normal was in this fucked-up fish tank. It was as if we were all actors in a movie slowed down to frame-by-frame advance then speeded up once more.

Catalina the waitress came over. 'What happened there?'

'I think she overdosed,' I replied. 'Least the ambulance guy seemed to think so.'

I didn't think anything of it, but no sooner had the words left my mouth than she walked over to Paul Eng, and judging by the way they kept glancing over, I reckon she told him word for word what I'd said. The look in their eyes said it all: 'You *fucked up...*'

In the morning, Jason invited me to breakfast with the staff. I felt honoured they were treating me as a member of the 'family'. Despite ignoring Paul's order to throw the girl out with the rubbish, I think not to have asked me would see me lose face.

Tommy Lau accompanied us to the restaurant, a plush one on in the centre of Wan Chai. I resisted the temptation of asking him if he had a newspaper with eyeholes cut out of it or had considered a career with MI5.

Walking along like the cast of *Reservoir Dogs*, the crowds of commuters parting out of our way, no one talked to me, and all kept a discreet distance.

Tommy walked with a tough old Chinese bint, Lin Mai, the sort to have left many a sailor slumbering drugged-up and wallet-less in a backstreet B&B. Every other word Tommy used was *gweilo*. It wasn't hard to work out his topic of conversation.

I sidled up to the *Dai Lo*. 'Paul… you know… the girl?'

He nodded, his eyes fixed ahead as always.

'I did the wrong thing, eh?'

He nodded again, the way a triad boss does when he's pissed off.

'Right,' I said, knowing nothing more needed saying.

I sat next to Jason for the meal, the exquisite surroundings belying an atmosphere fraught with contempt. Leaning over the table, I asked, 'Paul, can I pay something towards the food?'

He shook his head.

'Do you fink Pau' don' have *munnee*?' asked Sidney, the little barman, looking incredulous at my audacity.

I picked up the pot of jasmine green tea and – determined to get something right – poured for the two people either side of me, filling their fragile egg-sized cups but making sure not to overfill them.

Lin Mai said something to Tommy. I heard the words *yau lai*, 'manners', which pleased me.

Only Tommy replied with, '*Gweilo blah blah blah…*' and a derogatory laugh, returned by all at the table – except Jason, who let out a token 'Hah'.

Tommy wouldn't give it up, much to everyone's amusement, but he wouldn't make eye contact with me either. I looked to see Jason staring at the table. I felt as much for him as I reckon he did me. Having been educated in the States meant he could see the situation from both sides, yet fitted in to neither. He'd been defending me in front of Chee Chu the night before because he understood borrowing money in Western culture is no big deal.

Jason also knew that what I did for the Thai girl was what any European would have done and that I couldn't have known otherwise. But we weren't in Europe: we were in the Wan Chai gangland, where the *Dai Lo's* rule is law, pride is everything and life means nothing. He didn't want the boss to lose face; he didn't want me to lose face. Caught in the middle, he was in danger of losing face himself.

He also knew that every expat knows what the word *gweilo* means. But it wasn't until Tommy said, 'Hah-hah! *Pok gai, Gweilo!*' that I thought, '*Nah!*' I stopped the cup midway to my lips and looked directly at him. His eyes darted around, nervous as bees, and if it's possible for a Chinese person to go red, then the fucker did.

I turned to Jason and quietly asked if I could leave: *'Duk'm'duk, ngoh tsut gai, m'goy?'*

The table froze… *Gweilos* didn't speak Cantonese.

Jason, still focussing on the tablecloth, nodded slowly.

I got up and walked out.

Back at the flat, chaos met me at the door. Water seeped over the threshold, flowing across the hall and into the lift shaft, the place itself an ankle-deep aquarium. I had no idea why the water supply had stopped – just that it had come back on and I hadn't turned off the tap.

I stepped into the flood, exasperated and confused. Why didn't Hong Kong ever go the way I wanted it to? I was the real-life Frank Spencer – only this time the cat had done more than a little 'whoopsie' on the carpet.

I soon found a part of the problem: the drain hole in the bathroom was blocked. Using a dustpan, I began scooping up the water and pouring it out of the window and down onto the litter-covered roofs of the courtyards below, mopping up the hard-to-reach areas with some old clothing from the junk room.

I'd almost finished when someone knocked on the door. I answered it to find a cute Chinese girl, only about eight, standing on the doorstep. 'My fadder wan' to know, will there be any more wotter?'

I felt awful. Sending up his English-speaking daughter meant he must know it was a *gweilo* living there and causing problems.

'Tell your father I'm very sorry,' I said, wishing I could do more, and then went back to clearing up the remaining puddles.

Pete's mattress was sopping wet. But as Apple was unlikely to return, it took up too much of the precious space anyway.

High up at the back of my room was a two-foot-by-three-foot recess, and lying in it was a bed-sized sheet of plywood. Together with some lengths of bamboo in the junk area, it gave me an idea.

Having dragged the mattress out to the mysterious backroom, I rooted around in some of the plastic bags until I found one containing neatly coiled cordage. I selected a few lengths of nylon rope and picked up some of the poles, musing that the person hoarding this stuff must have whipped them from a construction site because in Hong Kong they use bamboo scaffolding instead of steel.

I set about lashing them together to create a sturdy five-foot-high framework to support the plywood. After a couple of hours' work – *hey presto!* – I had a bunk bed with space underneath to hang my clothes. All it needed was a lightweight mattress to make it the perfect place to sleep – for someone who did sleep.

Being Sunday, I had the night off work and could relax for the day. Happy with my achievement, I went back and forth into Wan Chai, buying bits and pieces for my place... *and* a cake.

I approached the old man as he was loading up his cart with bales of old newspapers. I didn't look him directly in the eye – that seemed rude – I just placed the cake on top of one of the bundles and whispered, '*Doy̆m'due* (Sorry).'

He nodded a silent acknowledgement, the smile in his eyes telling me we were alright.

The blue-and-yellow-flowered Hawaiian-pattern mattress had probably been as close to Oahu as I had, but it was a bargain in that shop on Lockhart Road. I threw it onto my homemade bedframe and, using the window ledge as a step, hopped up to join it. It was a *spot-on* fit and comfortable too.

My next task was to buy some of the colourful tatami floor mats I'd seen in the market. In red-and-straw and green-and-straw, they would set the place off perfectly. But before doing so, I had to smoke some crystal methamphetamine – I didn't want to rush things.

Wandering the marketplace, conscious of speeding my face off, I happened across an ornate black-lacquered box. About the size of a small coffee table, its shape was that of a flat-topped pagoda.

At first glance, it appeared to have an idyllic cultural scene inlaid in mother-of-pearl on its lid – the kind you see decorating Chinese teapots. On a second look, the picture was actually of an elderly man taking his wife rather surreptitiously from behind on the balcony of their picturesque home. Their bodies contorted in such a way that they were able to smile and wave nonchalantly at a couple passing by on the footpath below.

It represented the Chinese sense of humour to a tee. Thinking it would look great in my place, I bartered with the bric-a-brac stall's owner, delighted when he accepted HK$200.

'Fuck it!' As I went to open the door to the apartment, I realised I'd left my key inside. I couldn't bother Gabriel again, not after the last fiasco.

To help dry the place out I'd left the windows open. It seemed an appropriate time to go and explore the roof.

After hiding my antique box and matting in the junk room, I tried the door onto the balcony. It wouldn't open, so I climbed the back stairway instead. Halfway up it angled right into total darkness. It was creepy, *solitary*. I felt the way a grave robber must do inside a crypt. Curiosity getting the better of me, along with the need to get into my flat, I edged upwards into the gloom.

At the top, I could feel a steel door. I groped around until I found a handle, but it wouldn't turn. I increased the pressure until it gave with a loud clank, jarring me to the core.

As I eased the door open, its rusting hinges screeched and the tiny pinpricks of light penetrating the frame morphed into brilliant rays of sunshine and a spectacular panorama – a view right out over the rooftops and across the aquamarine harbour to Kowloon.

I stepped out of the exit's brickwork housing to see an equally impressive vista to the rear. Rising with awe-inspiring dignity above the tower blocks were huge rolling mountains clad in a carpet of green shades like crumpled crushed velvet. Gazing at the prominent ridges it was easy to see why the locals believed them to be sleeping dragons.

The roof setting itself was something to behold, shaped like a first-second-and-third-place podium at a sporting event for giants. I'd come out on the top level, raised to accommodate the stairway exit and the lift shaft's massive motors. When I looked north towards Kowloon's waterfront, the level down to the right was the roof of my apartment, the one to the left over the storage room and the emergency stairs.

Almost as fascinating as the scenery was the amount of disused television aerials littering the concrete. There were hundreds of them, mostly bent or flattened. Years of storms had seen them weave together, their cables interlacing like creeping vines to give the impression of fern fronds on a futuristic forest floor.

Another intriguing thing was that someone *lived* up here, on the level to the west. This city had its own shantytown like any other, only with space a premium in Hong Kong it was high up in the air and fragmented across the tops of the buildings. When the summer typhoons smashed through the colony many of its inhabitants paid a heavy price for living rent-free on these perilous perches.

Now I had an idea why the door out onto the balcony wouldn't open. Whoever resided up here had wedged it shut with a length of wood. That way they ensured themselves the privacy of both the vantage point and the whole of the west lower tier.

Privacy or not, it didn't stop me from having a good skeg below. A white BMX bike, likely salvaged off the street, leant against the parapet. A fanatic throughout my teenage years, I felt a little envious of the owner. I wished it were mine so I could bomb down the road to work, pulling wheelies and three-sixty-degree spins. The triads would have something to talk about then…

'The *gweilo* borrows money *and* he stinks!'

'Yeah! And I saw him *riding* on the *pavement!*'

From a metal ring bolted to the parapet, seventy metres above ground, a fifty-foot wire cable spanned to the building on the opposite side of Jaffe Road. Tagged at foot-long intervals with plastic ties was a see-through nylon hosepipe supplying water to the other rooftop. There was something *vaguely* familiar about the set-up…

Through the frosted glass of a window directly across, I could see the silhouette of a large lady. She was brushing her hair in the mirror, but the hairbrush's outline gave the impression she was singing into a microphone. But the strangest thing of all had to be the clear plastic bag nailed to the bottom of the bolstered-shut door.

'What the *fuck* is in *that?*'

It was full of *weird* shit. I'd never seen anything remotely like it. It looked like dog faeces or fish guts or meat in a bolognaise sauce. Whatever it was, it was a real spinner… pure mojo.

A noise caught my attention. Someone else was moving about on this crazy, lost world plateau. Keen to catch a glimpse, I crept on my hands and knees to the side of the roof overlooking their makeshift camp. Peering over the lip, I could see the sky-dweller had really made a home up there. There was a fair-sized shack constructed out of scrap wood, packing crates and tarpaulin. The oil drum, presumably, was to collect rainwater.

Of most interest was not my neighbour himself – a man in his thirties with long, ragged hair like a troll, filthy bare feet, dirt-blackened jeans and a T-shirt with holes in it – but *what* he was doing.

Crouched directly below me, he was burning pieces of folded-up paper in some sort of ritual.

Not wishing to disturb him, I pulled away from the edge and went back to my own mission.

I dropped the five feet down onto the roof of my apartment and, clearing a path through the television aerials with my boot, made my way to the three-foot-high stone-capped parapet to the rear. If my geography was correct, my window should be open a few feet below.

Over the edge lay an awesome sight. It was *so, so* high up, insanity even to consider what I had planned. But insanity didn't bother me: fear of the unknown condemned good humans to a life of soap operas and nine-to-five grind. Besides – a former commando, a big climbing frame and mind-altering drugs – where did fear factor in this equation?

As the wind rustled fresh-tasting air around me, it gave the illusion the building swayed gently with it, bringing the absurdity of my extraterrestrial location closer to home. You didn't get a breeze at street level at this time of year.

Nor were there any of the smells Hong Kong is noted for – meat and fish frying alongside vegetables, mushrooms, garlic and ginger, splashed in soy sauce and vinegar and carried in warm blasts of air out of the side doors of restaurants. Also absent, the unique aromas of the herb and dried fish wholesalers and street vendors heating up pungent-smelling treats in well-used peanut oil.

Fortunately, the human odours – raw sewage, badly dried clothing and unwashed armpits – didn't make their way up there either.

I took one last glance down to see staff out the back of the businesses below appearing antlike and surreal. Then grabbing the parapet, I vaulted over it, launching myself into the void, rewarded to feel the soles of my boots scudding down the crumbling masonry as they brought me to a precarious stop.

From here, I transferred my toes across to one of the brackets securing our building's rusting waste pipe to the wall. After checking to see if it would take my weight and pausing to suck in the breathtaking scene all around, I wrapped my arms around the iron tube one at a time, as though it were an urban palm tree, and shinned the few feet to my open window.

As with all the old buildings there was a rectangular metal frame, for hanging laundry out to dry, bolted just below the casement. I stretched a foot over to it, gripped the open window for support and pulled myself into the room.

During my dramatic re-entry, something hanging off the apartment block opposite caught my eye. Through a semi-tilted blind, I could make out the head and shoulders of an elderly balding man as he moved unhurriedly, almost *eerily*, around the room. But what interested me more was the piece of broken mirror dangling on a piece of string and spinning in the wind outside his window.

It was a real attention-getter to see feng shui taken so seriously – even more so to realise that as well as the strange rooftop man there were the ghosts of dead ancestors and God knows what other ghouls and demons from the spirit world milling around up here. In my naïvety, I thought I had the place to myself.

Making sure I had my key, I went to collect the straw matting and antique box from the junk room. While there, I couldn't resist having another rummage through the heaped miscellany.

I opened a shoebox to find it full of *used* MTR cards. 'I wonder… ahhh!' Now I *knew* what this stuff was! Not the load of old rubbish it appeared but a hoard of curios and antiquities – anything that could possibly be lost or dumped on a Hong Kong street.

There were handbags and wallets, reading glasses and sunglasses, umbrellas and items of electrical equipment, in addition to carrier-bags containing rubber bands, paperclips, string, and other carrier-bags.

I came across a large fake-leather holdall. As with everything else, it stunk with the musky odour you'd expect from items of lost property hoarded for years in a dark airless room. I slid the zip open to find a veritable library inside – books of all sizes and kinds.

One of the titles was *Culture Shock! Hong Kong*.

A shiver ran down my spine.

'Not a tourist book… it's a guidebook… to guide you.'

I felt sure this publication was for people like me – the ones who'd come to realise there was something strange going on in this colony. It had been put there *especially* for me and I wondered by *whom*.

With the uneasy feeling I wasn't alone, I stole back out to the corridor, to find it empty, my gaze drawn to the shadowy entrance of the back stairway, my curiosity to what might lie in its murky depths.

Before I set foot on the steps, I found my answer.

In the dimness on the first half-landing sat a camp bed with ragged blankets and a filthy pillow. Tucked underneath was a bag, presumably containing the squatter's possessions, its grimy shade of white and faded blue Pan Am globe an indication that the bag had seen better days… as had its owner… as had the airline that supplied it.

My senses alive, it fascinated me to think what part this person might play in the craziness. *Everything* about this has-been Hilton seemed spooky, eccentric… and *wonderfully* intriguing.

I went back and picked up my furnishings, grabbing the *Culture Shock!* book and a few newspapers for good measure.

Having arranged the coloured matting as best I could, it didn't look as good as I'd hoped – slapdash came to mind – as the mats overlapped and I had to fold them back from the wall.

The antique box looked great, though, placed in a corner. I was pleased with that. Not only was I on my way to becoming cultured, I was doing it in the culture of the city I loved.

As I settled down on my new floor and reached for *Culture Shock! Hong Kong*, a convulsion wracked my body, followed by a deep yawn – reminders that the drug's effect wore dangerously thin. I considered making the trip to Mack Zane's but caught up in the moment I opened the book, by chance on page 10, my attention riveted by a paragraph headed: *THIS BOOK IS WRITTEN FOR YOU.*

'*Written for you…*'

Fascinated, I read on and learnt that this book was for people 'who want a deeper understanding of what makes Hong Kong tick…'

'Yes!… yes!'

I knew from the subliminal messages contained in the wording of this 'guide' book I'd found a key to understanding the secret double world I'd discovered.

The next page that appeared to open of its own accord had the heading: *THE TRIADS.*

Transfixed, I learnt that these secret anti-establishment brotherhoods, made popular by novels such as *Shuihuzuan – All Men are Brothers* or *Water Margin* – had been a part of life in the lower strata of Chinese society for a thousand years. United in the underground as rebels fighting against the impoverishment levied on the peasantry by oppressive ruling dynasties, in recent years these societies had altered course somewhat from their original philanthropic intentions – the longest surviving being the Three Dots, hence the English nomenclature of triad.

According to the book, the triads now controlled extortion rings, drug manufacture and distribution, pornography, counterfeiting, robbery and vice, and were replacing chopping blades with guns and grenades and smuggling their members in from Guangdong to conduct robberies on banks and jewellery stores.

My *reason* for being here all began to make sense! I'd been caught up in one of those heists on my first trip to Hong Kong!

'I was *meant* to be in the territory then… *wow!*'

'*…and meant to be receiving these cleverly concealed instructions now.*'

I looked up to find it dark outside. So engrossed in my reading, I'd been doing it by the light of a gibbous moon, its beams adding mystical allure to my enlightenment.

Another vicious wave of tiredness shuddered through me. I decided to get up off the floor I'd been on for five hours and see if this place had any light. It did, but in a city famed for its illumination, I had enough to fill a matchbox.

Leaving the flickering bulb on with two gnats buzzing in its draw, I let myself out of the apartment and tiptoed down the hall. It was time to meet my neighbour who lived on the stairs.

I sat on the top step for a while to allow my eyes time to adjust to the darkness, hearing gentle snores rising to meet me. Then creeping downwards slower than a cat burglar on Prozac, I began to make out the fuzzy thinning hair and monkey-like features of the old man whose head poked out from the sea of blankets.

After crouching there watching him for a moment, feeling sad he was all alone with few possessions and no family or home of his own, I stole back up to the flat, rummaging around in my bergen to find the half-bottle of brandy I had in there. For the life of me, I couldn't remember where, when or why I'd bought it. I might be living with spirits, but I hardly ever drank them. Sneaking back down, I placed it on the floor by his pillow.

Lying back on the tatami, head propped on one arm, I flicked through one of the newspapers until an article caught my eye. It was about a journalist in Shek Kip Mei who had written one word too many about our triad friends, subsequently opening the door of his office one afternoon to greet a chopping blade slicing through the air towards him. An eyewitness reported seeing a van...

What's Going On?

I FELT SURE THE WORLD I fell asleep in was a good deal more mysterious than the one I woke up to now.

My fluttering companions had long since abandoned the fifteen-watt bulb, no doubt opting to explore the real deal pouring in through the window, along with the barking of a canine, an occasional car horn, twitters of the feathered variety and the jet wash of a 747 passing high above my anonymous loft as it came in to land at Kai Tak.

A desperate need to kill raging thirst and hunger raised me off the floor and out of my stupor of apathy and exhaustion.

I took a drink from the tap in the kitchen and, yawning incessantly, rode the lift down and headed for the 7-Eleven on Hennessy Road.

Every molecule within screamed, *'Raisin Bread and Condensed Milk!'* and it was all I could do not to rip open the packet and try to bite through the tin right there in the shop.

Back at my pad, unable to stop the cavernous yawns, I grabbed the only utensil in the kitchen drawer, a screwdriver, and smacked it twice through the lid of the can. After taking a slug, I laid out the ready-sliced loaf and blew into one of the holes, forcing the milky nectar out in a slow-flowing spill over the bread *and* my new matting. Then I crammed the sickly lifesavers into my mouth as fast as possible, feeling the ravenousness of a starving beast and waves of rushing gratification.

I can't describe that feeling in mere words, except to say, if I had been in the room with a timber wolf and a sirloin steak, the result would have been 2:0... and not to the animal kingdom.

I awoke on my bamboo bunk at 6.30pm – plenty of time to get myself up, washed and boots polished, like a good marine. But there was no way on God's green Earth I would turn up at Nemo's in this state. When I'd opened my eyes, it had taken me quite some time to remember who I was – not to mention what I was doing in this strange room, five feet above a floor scattered with old newspaper, a leaking milk tin, an empty bread bag and a garish-covered guidebook.

I must have slept for another six hours, but still felt near death. Shivering, yawning and famished, I felt the way a grizzly bear must do when coming out of hibernation – although a grizzly bear's first priority isn't a trip to Mack Zane's place.

I brushed my teeth, took a cold splash bath and put on the second of my Club Nemo sweatshirts, wishing I had clean socks – maybe Mack could lend me a pair.

When I approached the fruit-and-veg stall on the corner to use their courtesy telephone, who should be standing there but my little friend with the camp bed. He smiled and asked, *'Lei ho?'*

'Ho ho,' I replied, feeling as far from *ho* as possible.

'Lei yiu?' he enquired, pointing at the goods on display – I guess as a gesture of reciprocation, having sussed where the brandy came from.

'Oh, errh… *m'hai, m'goy.'* Although grateful for his offer, fruit and veg was the last thing on my mind.

The phone rang for an age. Just as I was about to put the receiver down, Mack answered. 'Sorry about that, Chris, in the middle of the road over here.'

Remembering Clara, his saucy girlfriend, I understood the euphemism.

'Is the "corner shop" open?' I asked.

'Come on over, mate,' its proprietor replied.

Mack was an easy-going guy, who didn't have a fucked-up agenda unlike many of the people in Wan Chai. Whenever I went to Happy Valley, he always had a silver chute laid out with a generous offering of his own crystal tapped onto it. He smoked it through a water pipe, to filter out impurities, which added to the ceremony.

Only on this occasion, in an attempt to rectify my messed-up self, I smoked too much, and after borrowing a pair of clean socks, I left for work in overdose mode.

When I stepped out of the building, the floodlit racecourse in front of me appeared spectacular – *I* didn't. My heart raced like a Grand Prix car slipping gear, the occasional fibrillation serving to rescind the adrenalin and leave a tide of anxiety and panic riding high in its place.

Walking along Wong Nai Chung Road, contemplating taking a cab but feeling too removed from the population to do so, I bumped into Jason on his way to the club. It was a surprise. For some reason I'd assumed he lived in Wan Chai.

'Hi, Chris!' he said, a big smile, and then doing a double take asked, 'Are you alright?'

'*Errh,* no, mate, I'm f-f-f-feeling a bit ill.'

'Oh! Take the night off,' he said, reassuringly, as if it was his decision to make. 'I'll tell Paul you're sick. Don't worry.'

'F-f-f-fanks, Jase,' I replied, breathing a sigh of relief. It didn't *sound* as though I would get into trouble.

I flagged a cab but got out a few blocks from my place to keep the fare down. Walking past a table of customers at a *dai pai dong* on Lockhart Road, I heard, '*Chris!*'

I looked over to see Adrian, a Hong Kong-Vietnamese lad who'd worked at Gung Wan Hong for a couple of weeks. He was a chirpy, fun kid who always put on an American accent. Educated abroad, he lived with his parents in the Mid-Levels. But as he approached me, saying, 'Hey, Chris! How's it going?' I couldn't answer, because every time I tried to speak anxiety fluttered up, leaving me stammering like a shell-shock victim. 'H... w-w-whaaa... *erhhh,*' which increased my panic attack.

'You alright, buddy?' He patted me on the shoulder.

'Yeaahh*ooorr... amin... m-m-m*wight.' I gestured to my collapsed mandible as if this would make it clear what was wrong.

'Do ya wanna eat?' He pointed to his table.

'Ah*uh... ehuh...*' I replied, throwing my arms out and sloping off sideways like the town drunk, feeling seven shades of idiot and leaving him speechless.

EATING SMOKE

I arrived at Nemo's the next evening only to find another Westerner on the door, wearing a Club Nemo sweatshirt.

'Well, *whoopee-do*!' This scenario was nothing new. I was starting to feel like Bill Murray in *Groundhog Day* and wondering if Asia was in danger of running out of replacement *gweilos*. I'd had enough surprises on the walk here alone…

A plastic tunnel had been set up along a block of Jaffe Road to protect the public while builders on the bamboo scaffolding above carried out maintenance work. As I walked towards it, I noticed none of the locals went underneath, all opting to walk on the street and take their chances with the traffic and falling objects. Just as I began to wonder why, it hit me! Surely, this was another example of the superstition surrounding spirits in dark places *and* further confirmation of the duplicitous nature of this mysterious underground cult I'd unearthed.

Approaching Clubland, I'd spotted a crowd on the corner of Luard and Jaffe and had gone to check it out. The atmosphere I walked into was apocalyptic. It felt as though the end of the world was imminent and everyone stood motionless, awaiting their fate. The traffic had come to a standstill, the air had a tense, electrified edge and even the usually booming music appeared to have reined itself in.

For walking down the centre of the road, strategically distanced ten metres apart, was a gang of Nepali boys dressed in ragged attire – some barefoot – carrying weapons ranging from bamboo fighting canes to hammers, axes and chains. The swarthy, saturnine look on their faces matched that of their movement. Someone had pissed them off and they were out for blood.

It must have been a member of another immigrant gang because there was no way it could be a soldier from the 14-K. If that had been the case, the first little horse to spot them would broadcast a code word over his mobile and within a minute fifty other telephones and pagers would go off in clubs, restaurants and apartments and these tough men from the hills would be running for their lives in fear of having their own weapons used against them.

But no sooner had they appeared than they disappeared, and, once again, the playing speed of the movie *Wan Chai* went back to normal as if nothing had happened.

I knew it had happened, though, and that there was more to this than a migrant mob looking to rumble. It was another snapshot through to the dark side. I could tell from their dull, deadened eyes that these boys well understood the secrets of this camouflaged and iniquitous 'other' world.

'You must be Chris?'

'Yeah, and you are?'

'I'm Drik,' said the short skinny guy with frizzy blond hair tied in a ponytail and a pasty complexion. He spoke with a slight South African accent, only it had a clipped, aggressive edge to it.

'Drik?'

'Hendrik. I work at the Pink Panther but Paul's asked me to come over here for a few shifts.'

I was surprised to hear that another *gweilo* worked for the Chinese in Wan Chai. 'You're South African, Drik, I take it?'

'Ja, Durbs. But I lived in England most of my life.'

'And what are you doing coming here... to Nemo's?'

'Oh, you *know*...'

I didn't know, but thought I could guess.

'Paul asked me to help you out for a few nights.'

'Me or the club?'

'...You.'

'Because of what happened with the girl? I made Paul lose face?'

'Ja, you did—'

'And what the *fuck* was I supposed to do? I couldn't let her die!'

'You should'a put her over your shoulder and thrown her in a cab.'

'*Ah...*' I hadn't thought of that. 'So is that the reason you're here?' I felt sure it wasn't – you didn't need a babysitter to tell you how to put someone in a taxi.

'*Weeell—*'

'Well, *what?*'

'They think you're a cop.'

Inside, I apologised to the *Dai Lo* for not coming to work the night before. 'Is okay,' he said, and I knew to say no more.

I said hello to the staff, wary of Catalina's slyness as I did.

Chee Chu surprised me, though. He seemed remarkably upbeat, pleased to see me and concerned for my welfare. He said, 'You sick? You bedda now? *Goo*!'

I didn't think anyone seriously believed I might be a cop. If the 14-K did suspect such a thing, I'd be the last person to hear about it, receiving the news in the form of a 'steel' telegram like the Essex boy and the journalist. Plus, anyone with a genuine interest in my background only had to enquire around the clubs in Wan Chai to find out I'd worked in three of them, or visit the shabby apartment block I lived in – which Hong Kong's answer to Columbo already had.

The club was almost empty, a few regulars around the bar ignoring 2 Unlimited's advice to 'Get Ready for This', but as I sat on a stool inside the door, tapping my foot to the tune, musical chairs turned into happy families – or *family*, I should say – as the 14-K arrived.

One by one they filed in, twenty tough-looking Chinese aged from twenty to sixty, wearing smart slacks, collared shirts with V-neck sweaters or fashionable suede jackets, and expensive shoes.

My interest jumped to astonishment when Raj, the Indian bouncer from the Pink Panther, came through the door, ignored my hello and joined them at the bar. He looked nervous, *twitchy*, the way Jason did at times. 'Why was he, a foreigner, hanging around with these pure-blooded, hard men?' I pondered.

Like the rest, he carried a small leather holdall with a zip along one edge. His was light tan in colour, others brown or black. When he laid it on the bar, I eyed it with curiosity. If I had to guess what was inside, it would be like playing I-spy in a butcher's shop. Some*thing*… begin*ning* with… *C*… *B*.

In the morning, I popped into the Big Apple for a chat with Ray and a carve-up on the dance floor – Michael Jackson spins and handstands my mood to a tee.

Walking back to my apartment, through glorious sunshine and bustle, I felt full of the joys of the Hong Kong spring – despite Drik's presence at the club. I was pleased my Hong Kong adventure was at last going smoothly, proud of my job and of building up my *guanxi*, my 'network', in Wan Chai.

I got on well with everyone in the Apple. Chan always let me in free of charge, Ray would never accept money for a round, and Chung, a new waiter, delighted in teaching me kung fu moves. I'd grown fond of Mr Lu the Butterfly Man and my friend Max. Lee Aimes and I got on better than ever and Old Ron was always a mate, despite the nonsense with the key and the secret he was keeping from me. Nicole, my dancing partner, was a charm, but I hadn't seen Dream since our fling and wondered if she'd left Hong Kong. Alex and Kevin, from the Excelsior, always took time to chat, as did Mal the lawyer when he wasn't in the Philippines on one of his diving trips.

And I had my neighbours, Mr Wheel Cart and Mr Camp Bed, both of whom must have been delighted to have a wreckhead *gweilo* on the books.

Now I said hello to my newest friend, the dry-cleaning man, who stood behind the counter in his open-fronted shop, a block from my home. He reciprocated with a beam and a 'How are you?'

Yeah! Everything was going well.

'Whad'is happening with the water?' asked a furious Gabriel as he and Anil mopped up in their office, the sopping wet bags of dye dragged out into the main room.

'You ruined the bloody henna and whad'are you doing with the cooker in the bathroom?'

I thought both answers were obvious, but as the sunshine glinted in his beady eyes, highlighting the silver intruders in his hair, I humoured him anyway. After what he said next, I wished I hadn't bothered.

'You know we are moving in here.'

'Moving in here?'

'We are running out of money and leaving our flat.'

'Well, you can't move in here – that was never part of the deal.'

It was no good. My continued protestation met a blanket disregard for how I felt. As far as the obstinate bastard was concerned, this was his place and he deemed it fine to have three grown blokes living in the space of a microwave. He wouldn't even agree to a reduction in rent.

I shuddered to contemplate the amount of piss Chee Chu would rip out of me when he found out I lived with two *Yando yans*. He'd have a field day and get through a few cans of air freshener while he was at it.

'Foowah *you*,' said Chee Chu, thrusting two soft-packs of contraband Marlboro across the lectern.

'*Thanks*, Chee Chu!' I felt chuffed to bits.

Then ripping off two American tourists for HK$100 each, he checked Paul wasn't around and handed me a banknote. '*Tekk it! Tekk it!*'

'Are you sure?' I wondered if this was some kind of loyalty trap.

'*Mou* problem!' He squinted and shook his head. I didn't want to steal off the club but there was *mou* way I could make him lose face by not accepting it.

I liked this guy. I understood him better than I did myself. He was a hard-as-nails street fighter, a runner, whose home would always be the lawless streets of Wan Chai. His creed, allegiance to those who were prepared to fight next to him – even if they were a hard-to-read devil man. My loyalty was no longer in question, proven to this man during a scrap we'd mucked into together...

A young Cockney had walked in without paying the entrance fee. I put my arm up – 'Excuse me, bud!' – only he barged through to join his friends. I got up to go after him, but the *Dai Lo* raised *his* arm, signalling with his eyes that this idiot wasn't worth it.

On his way out, the gobby little muppet said, 'See ya later, mate,' then slapped me round the face. By fuck, I was off that barstool quicker than a whippet out the trap, launching myself at the knobhead to pan his face in. In the ensuing scuffle, his mates hustled him towards the exit, saying, '*Sorry, mate! We'll* sort it!' just as Chee Chu arrived and laid one on him.

Amazingly, the *instant* it'd kicked off, Jason, Sidney and Michael vaulted over the bar, knocking customers and drinks out of the way to come to my defence, picking up an ashtray, a beer bottle and a set of ice tongs as they did.

It shed new light on things: that despite my cock-ups I was a part of the family, and *no one* fucks with the family, not the 14-K in Wan Chai.

I was so *'Arrrhhh!'* fuming that Jason took me into the back room to cool down.

Two minutes later, Chee Chu burst through the door, even angrier and so flustered he could hardly get his words out. 'He don' do dat to *you*!' roared the chubby, cherubic-looking hardman, grimacing. 'You kno', if he come *back*, I make *wun* phoncall. *Effrywun* in Wan Chai come heeya, *kiwll him*!'

'Thanks, Chee Chu,' I said, feeling at home at last.

Something changed – something inside. I lived in Wan Chai's filthy backstreets. I got a kick out of being one of the few *gweilos* working in this environment with toughnut Hong Kong workmates surrounding me. I loved the richness of this culture, its people, customs, etiquette, superstition and pride, their ancient fighting skills and cuisine. I was more adept than any Chinese I challenged to a peanut-picking duel with the chopsticks. I knew enough of the language to get by and, bizarrely, found myself *thinking* in Cantonese. During my breaks, I stopped going to the Apple, finding a secluded spot in the park instead to practise Shaolin kung fu, learnt from a book I'd found in the junk room.

But strangest of all, I started to dislike the foreign devils – not my friends but the ones gallivanting around the territory, flying arrogant attitudes as if they owned the place.

It pained me to stand in the 7-Eleven queue and hear a six-foot-six hairy-arsed Rugby Sevens fan screaming, 'What's *wrong*? Don't you *understand* English?' at a four-foot-nothing elderly woman who'd never ventured further than Sham Shui Po in her life.

As I walked back to my place – or 'our' place – I was still smouldering from the incident with the Cockney and the thought of going back to an invasion of privacy only rekindled my anger.

I banged on the door of their room. 'Right you *fuckers*!'

Gabriel answered, eyes puffed from sleeping. Anil lay on the mattress they shared on the floor.

'Whad'is up?' he asked, looking bemused.

'What is *up* is we're going to play a game called flying flatmates. If you two aren't out of here by the time I get back, you're both going out that *fuckin'* window!'

It didn't do any good. They were still there when I returned. It just served to remind me how far my life and self had slipped from that of the happy-go-lucky bloke who'd arrived in the territory less than a year ago *and* confirmed this was their apartment and they weren't going anywhere.

In the following week, I took out my frustration on a few more people. The first time, Jason had said, 'Chris, there's a problem with one of the *gweilos*.'

An English bloke stood smashing glasses against the bar. I told him the score, but as I returned to the door, he did it again. I gave him another caution and when he ignored me a second time, I asked him to leave. He braced up with the *you*-can't-tell-*me*-what-to-do! routine.

Flipping out, I pushed him full force in the chest, then picked him up with his arm pinned behind his back and ran him out of the club.

The next occasion, a colossal African-American sailor had been walking through the crowded bar, drinking a beer bought in the 7-Eleven. I told him he couldn't bring his own drink in only to see him doing it again half an hour later.

When he tried to enter the next evening, I told him to go and find another club. He wasn't happy, reappearing in the dark rectangle of the top doorway with a taller, angrier shipmate whose black shaved head glimmered in the moonlight.

'Come on out, *motherfucker*!' hollered one.

'We gonna *kick* your *fuckin'* ass!' the other.

A tense scene to put it mildly, as these guys weren't pansies making idle threats as the expats did: these dudes were the real deal from the real hood – one no doubt equally if not more drenched in gun-toting, drug-soaked violence. To make it more unnerving, all I could really see against the blackened backdrop was the white of their eyes and teeth and the colour of their sports shorts and vests as they continued to hurl abuse.

'*Fuck me!* I've gotta fight it out with the Harlem Globetrotters,' I thought, making up my mind to have a damn good go.

Paul Eng stood with his back to them, counting out the takings onto the lectern. Yet again, he raised a meaningful arm – all three times I went to climb the stairs – while continuing to look down at his task.

But it wasn't just me with a violent streak. One night, Chee Chu and I stood in the stairwell – Drik thankfully putting in fewer appearances at Nemo's. Dai Su, the giant executioner, came charging towards us *carrying* a Chinese bloke over his shoulder. The guy wore a shabby suit and together with a weasely mug looked to be a seedy underhanded rat. Chee Chu hadn't noticed, but when Dai Su let out his feral grunt, throwing the guy on the floor in front of me, it soon caught his attention.

I knew this was 'Chinese' business, so I hopped out of the way and watched as the two of them, utter hatred in their eyes, set about kicking the man in the head as hard as they could, like a pair of Millwall hooligans catching a West Ham fan out of sight of the CCTV cameras.

After twenty-odd blows had rained on this chap's swede, he somehow managed to force his way between them, bounding up the stairs like a terrified rabbit with Cantonese insult chasing at his heels.

These two didn't see the scrap of paper drop from his grasp and flutter onto the steps. I waited until they'd gone then had a look. It was a list of racehorses – hooky ones, I guessed, as the intrigue deepened.

When Drik was working the door, it proved a double-edged sword. On one hand, I learnt a lot about the triads and the way they operated – although 'triad' was never a word he used, preferring to say 'them' or 'they'. The downside was that he viewed me as an outsider, as someone who didn't understand Wan Chai or its people. When he revealed how he'd come to be working in one of 'their' clubs, his loyalty, although bigoted, began to make sense.

His wife had divorced him and he'd come out here for a fresh start, but as with many fresh starters in Hong Kong, he'd brought excess baggage – in his case, a problem with alcohol.

'By the time "they" found me, I was sleeping in McDonald's.'

'And?'

'They said if I'd run a few errands for them, I'd be taken care of… you know, a place to stay and a job—'

'What kind of errands?'

'Running a few things here and there.'

'Things? Where?'

'Diamonds to Japan, gold through Nepal.'

'Drugs? Did you ever smuggle drugs?'

'No!' He looked serious. 'Drug smuggling is the only thing you can't lie your way out of. It's a fool's game... *You* can do it if you want.'

'Me? Why would I do that after what you just said?' I gave him a sideways look, thinking he was being his usual flippant self.

'Not drugs – *gems, gold*. Paul will sort you out.' His ever-suspicious eyes flicked to the *Dai Lo*.

'Oh...'

I liked the feeling of coming to belong in this place, but I remembered the Butterfly's warning: 'Paul Eng is *bad* man! *Very* bad man!' I wasn't desperate enough to subjugate my soul to his dark and dubious command.

Plenty of people in Wan Chai were under the *Dai Lo*'s control, though. The next night a load of them piled in, all doormen from the area, all wearing white shell-suit tops, jeans and trainers and waxing exuberant about a scrap they'd just had with a load of US sailors.

Looking at these guys, I mused on what a tough bunch of Han they were, especially the one who waved his bloody skinned knuckles in my face, laughed and said, '*Ha!* We juss *kiwll* da *gweilo!*'

A few stood out from the rest, having darker skin, broader facial features and a shorter, stockier stature. I wondered if these genetics had found their way here from the North. You could just imagine their progenitors lugging huge blocks of stone up to the Great Wall or steering horses with one-handed dexterity while slashing away at Mongol insurgents with a Dao fighting sword. Whatever their histories, these guys looked hard... *fucking* hard.

And talking of hardmen, Old Ron appeared. It was good to see him. I didn't often get the chance these days, what with working most nights. Standing there leaning our backs against the club's front wall, it felt reassuring to have a friendly face to talk to. With Ron being almost ten years older, he always felt a bit of a father figure to me – except when he jumped in with his mickey-taking shit over my interest in the Wan Chai underworld.

'So, Chris, are you still being followed by *triiiads?*'

He was referring to an incident that took place the previous week. I wished I hadn't mentioned it to the moron…

I'd gone for my 11pm break. No sooner had I left Nemo's, I noticed a guy tailing me. Slightly older than most street-level triads, he dressed in the same attire, only his shell-suit top was a gaudy mauve and green as opposed to the usual white. Not only did he look a nasty piece of work, but I'd also seen him in the club talking to Paul one night.

I walked off around the corner and down Hennessy Road, keeping an eye on his reflection in the windows opposite. Just to be sure, I ducked into a *cha chaan teng*, a small restaurant, purposely sitting in full view of the window and open door. As the thug passed, he happened to glance inside and, after a double take worthy of a Morecambe & Wise sketch, carried on by as if he hadn't seen me.

I started counting and before I got to six he came through the doorway and sat down, trying to appear innocuous, a few seats away. It was pure comedy but left me wondering why these guys took such an interest in me. Maybe they did think I was a copper… or perhaps it was something to do with the drugs.

A couple of nights later, two little horses followed me to the park as I went to practise kung fu. I'd scooted ahead and climbed up onto a fifteen-foot-high modern-art feature, a pile of huge granite slabs, and waited for them to come past. They'd paused right below me, looking all around, astonished I'd vanished. Good job I hadn't told Dennison the Doubtful about that.

'Are they still wearing *tracksuits*?' Ron continued, with what appeared to be faked amusement. But when I said, 'Ron, take a look over there,' indicating to a group of twelve shell-suited hard nuts, his face took on a noticeably different, somewhat guilty, look.

Later I sat at the bar, talking to Jason. A little while into our conversation, he stopped mid-sentence, his eyes locked towards the door. I turned to see the Sun Yee On Triad piling through it – fifteen of the boys who ran Tsim Sha Tsui – with their *gweilo* doorman, another Chris, a mate of mine.

It had to be the defining moment of my time so far at Club Nemo. The place, packed to the doors, now had *two* troops of *maa jai* foot soldiers from rival gangs boosting the numbers. As with Jason, the guys from the 14-K clammed up while not moving an inch. But only their verbal conversation ceased – the communication continued with their *eyes*. They were still *talking* to each other.

I'd never seen a situation like it with my own pair. They weren't just conversing in this covert manner, but they were also telling their uninvited guests to get the fuck out of our club while you still can. It turned into a Mexican standoff, the expats and tourists remaining oblivious to the atmosphere, the intensity of which you could slice with a knife – or a chopping blade.

'Alright, Chris?' I asked my counterpart from across the water. 'What are you guys doing this side?'

'*I…*' he took in the same vibe, '*think* we're about to leave, mate.' As he spoke, one of their mob must have given a discreet signal, his guys turning as one and slipping in a snake out of the club.

I'd gone over to the booth at the back to check if the young Filipina was okay – the one being pushed back and forward by a group of triads – only I'd forgotten to adhere to the rule that Chinese business is Chinese business, letting my heartstrings think for me. As I leant over the table and asked, 'Is everything alright?' I soon got my answer.

'*I* tell you,' began the unassuming triad in his early twenties as though he'd known me all my life, 'an' *my* father tell you, an' *his* father before him…'

I stood transfixed by his unblinking eyes and unwavering delivery.

'*Nothing* will happen to this girl. You can leave us now.'

I spun around and walked away, feeling foolish I'd interfered. But I wasn't afraid to challenge the Chinese if I thought they were feeding me a line. One night a distinguished-looking gent got up off his barstool and went to leave the club. Nearing the door, he stopped and asked where I was from.

'*Ah!* The *English…* Soon we will be rid of you from our land.'

He referred to the next year, 1997, when the British would hand over control to the Chinese government, returning Hong Kong to its rightful ownership – only I knew it wasn't that simple.

There was massive uncertainty about what would happen when the motherland received the prodigal son back into the fold. Colonialism and capitalism had intertwined with the culture here to a point where there was no going back for the indigenous population. Western-cum-Hong Kong tradition defined the place and was omnipresent throughout.

Despite the fifty-year buffer period acknowledged in the Sino-British Joint Declaration – the One Country, Two Systems principle – the people were understandably worried that forcible changes would take place the moment the colonialists relinquished power.

I didn't want to take this guy's facile dig without reply, so I asked him if his mother spoke Mandarin and did he want to hand control of his business over to the incoming government and become a part of the new machine? Being an astute and educated man who could tell I'd done my homework, he stopped playing and said, '*Very good!* I see you understand Hong Kong people.'

I sensed double-speak; that in truth he referred to an evil cult that communicated through labels on blankets, telepathic eyes and subliminally scripted guidebooks. 'I know that there's something going on here most foreigners don't see,' I replied.

He looked into my eyes, and as I returned the gaze, his pupils dilated and began to swirl with a mystical fog – crystal balls that I knew held answers… ones I desperately needed. Then he snatched a look at the bar, flapped his jacket open a touch and pulled a book halfway out of the inside pocket. 'You need to read this…' he whispered.

The book's title was *Understanding the Chinese Mind*. I *knew* it! I *knew* I was on to something!

I Start to See It

HOW THE ANTS WERE GETTING into the kitchen didn't interest me. What did was the *way* they were moving – in from the right in an endless line along the sealant where the sink met the wall. Midway along the traverse, they marched upwards onto the splashback's white tiles, their line forming a perfect crucifix, about three inches long, before travelling back down and exiting stage left. It was an apparition of such miraculous proportions that a call to the Vatican would surely have seen a line of pilgrims stretching from my door to Rome.

'*Evangelistic ants… letting you know you've wandered from the flock.*'

I stared for an age, trying to work out if Gabriel had something to do with it as he'd been in here, preparing a chicken. These trained ants posed a real conundrum.

'*There's method in the madness… the writing's on the wall.*'

'I know the writing's on the wall… I can see it… well… I can see a cross… is that writing?… is that where that expression comes from?'

Gabriel had left a packet of *ghee* out on the side. I picked it up, feeling sure it could give me an answer.

Ghee is an important addition to many dishes, particularly for those connoisseurs who wish to truly capture and appreciate the authentic flavour of the region.

'*Hmmh… ?*' I pondered. I wanted to *appreciate* the *authentic* flavour of the region. I desperately wanted to understand what in God's name was going on in Wan Chai. 'These Samalan Atchi people that make the *ghee*... are they in on it?... is it a global conspiracy?... are my flatmates involved?'

'*All of the above... think about it... makes perfect sense.*'

I remembered what I'd originally gone into the kitchen for: sugar and water. Drik told me it would stave off hunger because I had no money to buy food. I'd sneaked into the kitchen to steal some off the Indians – the sugar, that is. Even they wouldn't begrudge me water, so long as I kept it off the floor.

Before work, I'd been going over to Tsim Sha Tsui to smoke Apple's drugs. She had a job in one of the hostess bars there, and now a tiny bedsit. I'd never asked her why she hadn't taken me up on my offer of a place to stay. There was something about the furious look Gabriel had given her that time, and the fear in her own eyes, that told me they both knew more about this cult than they were letting on.

I think she fancied me. The previous evening, she lay back on her bed and pulled up her top to expose her perky little breasts. 'You *want*?'

I'd smiled. All these games people played were so *confusing*...

On my way to work from her place, I stopped to chat to Raj on the door of the Pink Panther, noting several little horses standing spread out along the pavement, trying to look innocuous.

'Raj, can I ask you something?'

'Sure, Chris?' he replied, his eyes fixed on the road.

'How long have you lived in Hong Kong?'

'Nine years.'

Leaning closer, I whispered, 'And how long did it take you to *see it*?'

'About *four* years,' he hissed under his breath without hesitation, confirming my suspicions that in Wan Chai's clandestine culture it's more about what goes unsaid than said, the covert than the overt, the subtle than the obvious, and, most crucially, it was all in the *eyes*.

'Raj, I've only been here eleven months... but I can *see* it now.'

As I spoke, a cream Mercedes with tinted windows pulled up at the kerb. One of the *maa jais* walked over and opened the door. Out stepped evil – a slick, yet ruthless-looking tong with snake eyes and a smart beige suit. From his demeanour, he looked to be high up in the hierarchy – a 'dragon', perhaps.

'Talk of the Devil,' I murmured to Raj.

'*Sssh!*' was his terse reply. '*You go now!*'

In the club that night, I went into the storeroom to get some ink for the entry stamp. Determined to explore this crooked world, I had a nosey around.

Tucked in next to the electricity cables on the conduit overhead were two sawn-off iron bars – about three inches long and perfect for holding in your fists to add to the punch you'd give an unwelcome guest. I found a length of metal rod on top of the air-conditioning unit, a heavy chain behind the refrigerator and a rusty meat cleaver underneath it.

'Wow! It's like something from a Bruce Lee film!'

The discovery of the weapons served as a reminder of the culture of violence surrounding me. Now I understood why the 14-K employed a *gweilo* on the door. I had to make sure the foreigners didn't do anything stupid, defusing volatile situations to protect Nemo's licence and the drunken members of the *Do-You-Know-Who-I-Am?* Club. Being hacked to bits by thugs with butcher's knives would scar you for life – the additional battering with barstools, ashtrays, beer glasses and the other items secreted around would be an added bonus.

I could see that my role was to act as go-between, a mediator, to stop Eastern face kicking the shit out of Western ignorance – not that every Westerner was ignorant. Many got on remarkably well with the Chinese. *So* well, it was hard to work out…

My pager went off, telling me Miss Jennifer was in town. We arranged to meet at seven in the morning, agreeing she would come to the club.

Just as the last customer left, she arrived, looking as pretty and well turned out as ever – only behind the stony eyes of my pokerfaced workmates lay minds scowling with contempt. I could only assume it was because I had a date with one of their 'own'. I felt angry – it was none of their business and she wasn't even from Hong Kong.

It was good to get out of there and go over to the Big Apple for a beer – a better option than sugar-water now I had my pay. After our drink, we headed into Wan Chai to find a *cha chaan teng*.

With polite conversation and delicious food, everything was going smoothly, when – *SMASH!* – a little boy carrying a stack of plates dropped them in front of everybody.

Everything – chatter, clinking crockery, movement – froze.

The other diners sat stock-still and silent, chopsticks literally halfway to mouths, with the exact same look of cold passivity in their eyes that I'd seen in the club the night the girl collapsed.

I had a horrible premonition.

In what seemed slow motion *and* split second, the proprietor pulled a bamboo cane from beneath the counter.

I saw the fear in the kid's eyes.

As the man began to whip him, the way one might a dog that had savaged an infant, I *knew* that little boy…

'*M'goy!*' I stood up, interrupting the beating. 'Come on. We're out of here,' I said to Jennifer, as anger coursed through me. '*Ngoh m'jungyee lei faan* (I don't like your food),' I told the bloke, who stood, looking puzzled.

Not a *gweilo* walking these shores loved Hong Kong the way I did, but *this*? This was unadulterated inhuman *depravity*. What the fuck was going on?

How come when I'd lived with Vance he'd been a legend, his wife a dream, Benny Tsang a dear man and Larry Kong a caring uncle, yet all along I'd been surrounded by this dark agenda – backstabbing neighbours who stole my things and this bizarre, unspoken and *ugly* understanding people seemed to have – and I hadn't even noticed?

The haunting shouts, the blankets, the Thai girl, the eyes, the strange guidebook, the mirrors and spirits in dark places, the guy with the psychology text and now *this*? It was all starting to feel science fiction, like the television series *V* or the frickin' *Twilight Zone*.

What should I have done in there? I didn't want to make the guy lose face. I didn't want to alienate myself from a culture I was struggling to come to terms with, but there was no way I could watch him hit the boy.

Back out on the pavement, I turned my fury on Jennifer. 'What the fuck is wrong? How can everyone just sit there and watch that shit?'

'I *know*, Creese,' she said, the quaver in her voice telling me there was something I was missing. 'I *hate* it myself. Every time I come to Hong

Kong, even juss to arrive at the airport, I *hate* the people here because they are like this. It's *always* like this!'

'When I see the guy hit the kid, I wanna stand up and say *stop* that! But I'm afraid, you know? That he's gonna turn that stick on me.'

'Don't lie to me, Jennifer! You weren't afraid he would hit you, you're just like everyone else. You're afraid of what people think, afraid to do the right thing.'

'I don't know what you mean,' she said, and I knew it was bullshit.

She'd had the same void look on her face in the *cha chaan teng* that the staff at Gung Wan Hong had when Fang *San* started tearing the place up, like Ken Kwok when he'd been dismissed and Jason in the restaurant that morning. From her nervousness, I could tell she felt compromised. I just wanted her to be straight with me – as Vance would have been. He was always upfront and unabashed when it came to explaining the Sino-Western difference, yet others felt the need to convince you our cultures aligned and God bless Coca-Cola.

But it *wasn't* the same. We weren't talking France and Belgium or Trinidad and freakin' Tobago. Jennifer expecting me to believe she'd considered intervening was akin to saying Goering often turned around to Hitler and said, 'Actually, I think you're a bit of a *cunt*!'

'You know exactly what I mean,' I said.

As we spoke, her eyes flicked nervously over my shoulder.

'No... I don't–'

'I mean *THAT!*' I spun on my heel, catching a passing Chinese man giving her look of hatred – I assumed for daring to be seen with a *gweilo*.

'*Oh....*' She stared at the pavement. 'Creese, I don't think this is gonna work. Your life so different. You work in the night-time, drink beer in the daytime... My life not like that.'

I knew it was true. I didn't think our relationship stood an ice cream in Hell's chance of progressing. I was a drugged-up doorman who lived in a shithole, had a growing penchant for violence and now thought of a Filofax in terms of how useful it would be if you had to smack someone over the head with it – not to plan your career schedule or a meet with Alicia and her pretentiousness for a cappu-fuckin'-ccino.

When I said goodbye to this beautiful angel – the one I felt honoured to be with, the one who paged *me* when she got into Hong Kong, the one who wanted to dance with *me* the *doorman* in the club as opposed to the other fifty blokes in there – I knew it would be for the last time.

My next date didn't go too well either. I went to the Big Apple after work for a beer with Sidney and Jason, who suggested we go on to McDonald's for breakfast.

As we were leaving, Mack Zane came over for a 'quiet' word. 'Chris, can you help out one of yer countrymen?'

'Sure, Mack. What's up?'

'His name's Les. He just got off the plane and he's *clucking*, mate. Do you know where he can get some number four?'

I told Sid and Jase to go and wait for me in the restaurant. I knew a few homeless guys who sat outside it, selling straws of heroin.

One of the down-and-out Chinese spotted my approach. I nodded discreetly at Les and peeled off into the fast-food joint to find my workmates sitting by the window.

'What was that about, Chris?' asked Jason. 'Why'dat guy just shove something in his mouth?'

'*Oh*! He was just asking me where the MTR was,' I replied, wondering if these guys ever missed a trick.

Queuing for pancakes and maple syrup, I watched a heinous old letch chomping open-mouthed while staring at a table of schoolgirls. He looked like a cat busy devouring one mouse but with his sights fixed on the next, oblivious to his packed surroundings. My thoughts flicked to the hideous hooks festooning Ron's ceiling, shuddering at the vile imagery that came to mind and the element of depravity that seemed to pervade the darker layers of this society.

'*Ching chau!*' Jason blurted out.

'*Ching chau!*' Sidney too, for the whole place to hear.

I ignored it, but from the way they smirked, I knew they were referring to me and I had an idea why.

My poor size sevens continued to sweat their way through Hong Kong life, especially now that the spring warmth swirled around us. I washed them at every opportunity and wore my sandals when I could, but after a night standing in the club, combined with the crystal meth escaping my body, they obviously *hummed* – at least to the locals' keen sense of smell.

I finished my food and said goodbye. Then walking off into Wan Chai, I pulled my dictionary out. *Meih gok*, 'smell', and *geuk*, 'feet', didn't fit the bill, but with a niggling suspicion, I looked up 'odour'. Upon finding it, I was rooted to the spot. It read *chau*, and in brackets, *ching chau:* a malodorous man.

Back at the flat, having bid *'Jou san!'* to my friend in the dry-cleaners and asking if he wanted anything from the 7-Eleven, which with a grin and a shake of the head he'd declined, I crashed out for a few hours.

I awoke feeling a groggy and went into the kitchen to get a glass of water. Remembering the ant parade, I looked to see if they were still marching around in crucifix formation on the sink splashback's tiles. But they were gone – every single one of them disappeared.

I spotted a dried-up smudge of blood, the realisation dawning that they hadn't been making a random geometric pattern at all. They'd been following the outline of the cross-shaped thumb smear Gabriel must have left when preparing the chicken. It was hard to believe it could be that simple.

Thankfully, the Indians were out. After a smoke from my new stash, I set about cleaning up my room. I remembered seeing a mini vacuum cleaner in the junk room. Figuring someone may as well put it to use I fetched it. Only, it didn't work, so I set about fixing it using Gabriel's kitchen knives and screwdriver, getting myself into a hypnotic trance.

Over-concentrating, I forgot I was supposed to be tidying the place up. Before long, it looked as if a dirty bomb had gone off. There were bits of electric motor and plastic casing everywhere, the machine itself way beyond repair. Too tired and hallucinating, I couldn't have put it back together if my life depended on it.

In addition, lying all over my askew tatami were crumpled newspapers, books, empty bread bags and condensed milk tins – the latter still leaking, much to the pleasure of the ants, who'd trekked all the way from the kitchen for a feast.

Being Sunday, my night off, I went to the Big Apple and spent a good few hours on the dance floor with Nicole and an Aussie named Troy. After Nicole left, Troy invited a few of us back to the apartment he shared in Sheung Wan. A nice bloke, mid-thirties with balding long hair, he was a graphic designer and a good friend of Mack Zane.

In the cab, he introduced me to Cameron, a successful lawyer who lived with his wife in the Mid-Levels. With his chubby figure, squinty eyes, glasses and mop of curly hair, he looked like an adult Billy Bunter. What he was doing hanging around Wan Chai's scuzzy fleapits was a spinner to say the least, as were his actions at the party.

'Cameron, don't think me rude,' I said, as Troy tipped a healthy amount of crystal onto a tinfoil slide. 'But you do know that stuff's pretty addictive? Have you smoked it before?'

'*Nope!*' he replied with an air of invincibility.

'Are you sure you want to? You'll be craving it within a week.'

'I'll be alright,' he said – and I thought, 'No, you won't…'

I got talking to Troy's attractive Chinese flatmate, Su Lin, and later, as I said my goodbyes, she stood up and whispered, 'Let's go to your place.'

Talk about *gutted!* She was sexy times twenty and I would love to have shown her my jigsaw puzzle collection but I was too ashamed of my room. It wouldn't have been so bad if it was in a bit of a mess, like the one I was in now, but my place was in the seediest part of Hong Kong's most dubious district, in a building you wouldn't find a foreign devil breathing in, let alone living in, with a bamboo bunk that wouldn't have looked so strange if it weren't for the delicate shades of shit, crap and buggery I'd carefully selected to decorate the floor beneath it.

During the week, the feminine element continued to confuse me.

The most stunning of all the lookers coming into Club Nemo was a voluptuous Thai named Danni – only Danni had history just like every other double-sided maniac in Wan Chai.

Danni's portfolio included the not-so-obvious fact that she used to be a bloke… and she was *beautiful.* Unlike the ladyboys I'd seen in Thailand, she had none of the telltale signs you associate with women who used to be men.

Danni liked me and was always up for a laugh. She'd plonked herself on my lap one night as I sat in my usual place at the front of the club. I'd felt a little uncomfortable as the triads had a thing about anyone different to the norm – *their* norm – and I had enough on my plate without inviting further piss-taking. But technically she was or at least wanted to be a woman and not wanting to upset her and act all trite, I'd let her sit on me a while.

The conundrum I now faced was her walking into the club holding hands with none other than my young mate Antoine du Maurier.

I thought, '*Fuck me!* Does he know she's a he? Or *used* to be a he? Or still is a he? Or is a he-she?' Plus, I didn't know if Antoine was gay or straight, or whether he knew she was a kathoey or had no idea, or some other combination my head whirred too much to work out.

Did he know she was on the game and that no amount of drinks he bought her would guarantee a lay, and if he wanted to take it further it would cost him a shitload more again? It even bamboozled me, so I kept quiet. Besides, working out sexuality, gender or which bit fitted into where would all be good character-building stuff for the young buck.

The next shift, it was my turn to do some figuring out. It was the morning after a busy night, the usual mix of customers enjoying the club's underground ambience.

Mack and Troy had been in, having come over from the Apple for a boogie. Lee Aimes and Gonzales the Pirate stopped by for a chat and a JD and coke before bugging out again, likely to search for buried treasure or to watch someone walk the plank.

Now Old Ron appeared, sporting the smug look he had been a lot lately. Partway into our chat, he said, 'You do know people call this place *Aliens?*'

It didn't occur to me to ask what he meant, my mind going into overdrive wondering *which* 'people' he was talking about and whether 'Aliens' was a reference to the Chinese, the triads, the foreigners or *me*.

After Ron left, the shivering-tiredness syndrome kicked in, sending a spasm of unrest through my overstretched self. It was happening a lot lately, particularly at this early hour as the effects of the meth wore off. I helped myself to a pint of black coffee from the pot stewing behind the bar and went back to my task of helping to collect glasses.

'*Errh*, Quiss'a!'

I looked up to see a Chinese girl hovering near me, one of the few locals that 'worked' in the bar and whose name I didn't know.

'You can tekk me home and fuck me,' she said, as if it were a done deal.

'Sorry?'

'Paul Eng say, I go home with you tonigh'. You can do wha' you want.'

'Right…' I said, ignoring her. '*Head* games…' I tutted silently. 'Always fucking *head* games.'

Things went from spinning to spinnier the night after. First off, Johnny the homeless guy came down to the lectern – something he did a lot now. The only problem was that I could never quite understand him. He always spoke simple English in double Dutch. As my nostrils battled the cigarette butt stench rising from his pockets and the smell of the street permeating his clothes, I fought to grasp the meaning behind the mumbo-jumbo coming out of his mouth. I didn't want to be short with him as I felt I was probably one of his few friends, but it was hard trying to concentrate on the door while listening to his blather.

On this occasion, he began to go on about his role in life – or, from what I could gather, the things the triads got him to do for them. 'My job to ge' da girl… Bring da girl to da man.' He indicated inside the club, leading me to believe he meant bringing homeless girls for the *Dai Lo* to pimp out.

'You kno', I can ge' you da wun. Da wun dat make you *urrh*!' His head flopped around.

I guessed it was a reference to heroin.

'Also, can ge' you da wun giff you *goo' hosspower*… No nee' *sleeping*.'

'That rings a bell,' I thought.

'*Many hosspower.*' He pointed up at the air conditioner and began to waffle off random power ratings, writing them on the top of the lectern using his nicotine-stained finger as an imaginary pen – 7200, 3400, 2400.

It meant absolute custard to me, but from this point forward, I came to think of him as my friend Johnny *Horsepower*.

Later that evening, I stood on the dance floor watching a chubby expat doing his party trick – swinging a full glass of beer around in an overhead arc while keeping the wet part on the inside. Everything was going glamorously to the tune of Cappella's 'Tell Me the Way' until I looked over to the entrance and saw Apple stumble through it – *off her face*!

She'd smoked far too much ice to the point where, even from a distance, I could see she was babbling incoherently to Dai Su and unsteady on her feet. I knew her reason for coming to Nemo's was to see me. It must have been, because girls who worked Kowloon Side weren't exactly welcome in this bar. It wasn't as if she'd just popped by to sip a vodka and coke.

Dai Su had been chatting to a group of fellow doormen, and the reception they now gave Apple seemed to confirm this. They were pushing her around like a plaything, taking it in turns to both mock and interrogate her. My heart went out to the young Filipina – a long way from home, limited prospects in Hong Kong, and used and abused by a circus load of freaks. But stirring again – and why, I sensed, she'd taken so much meth to pluck up the courage to come here – was a piece of that little girl's heart had attached itself to me.

I didn't go over – it would only make things worse, Chinese business being Chinese business. I just stood there thinking what a shitty deal it is to be a working girl in Clubland with these misogynous brutes treating you as subhuman and dictating your every move.

The meeting I had a few days later was a lot less complicated.

Jemma was an English expat in her early twenties. She started chatting to me in the small hours and continued to do so until closing time. Although laced on the straight side, it was good to talk to a girl without the sociocultural quagmire and mind games presented by the Asian ones of late.

She told me she worked in an office doing something, somewhere, and had come to the club with a friend. I can't say I paid too much attention, perhaps not polite, because as our conversation continued

I found my mind wandering to the age-old question. I hoped so. She had a well-rounded figure, collar-length blonde hair, blue eyes, and lips designed like a docking bay for pleasure craft.

After work, we had a drink in the Apple, and it wasn't long before we were walking up Wan Chai Road, hand in hand, heading for the Half-Day Hotel – its nickname a clue as to the clientele frequenting it. It wasn't such a bad deal, though, and certainly a step up from the sleaziness of Chungking Mansions, which cost double the HK$100 I handed to the elderly Chinese couple at the front desk.

The walls of the room were pale blue, the same as the curtain over the tiny window. A simple wooden table sat on bare floorboards, but most importantly, the bed had clean linen – even if the faded yellow spread could have passed for a mainsail at the Battle of Trafalgar.

I'd love to be able to say the sex we had was out of this world, maybe go all Mills & Boon and divulge a manly chest, supple breasts and a masterful performance… only I'd forgotten a minute detail. I hadn't slept for nine days.

I remember getting down to it, and that's all – until the police woke me up. They entered the room with the hotel's anxious owners hot on their heels, all flabbergasted I'd paid for half a day but had slept an *hour* into the rest of it!

Poor Jemma! What she thought when she couldn't wake me from my dead-to-the-world slumber, I'd worry about later. My priority lay with the two goons who continued to prod me like a sack of bad spuds.

'Wass your *nem*?' one of them demanded.

'Errh… errh… *Chris*…' I replied, hoping they wouldn't push for a surname as I couldn't remember what mine was.

'Where you work?' Kojak continued – making sure to leave no stone unturned.

'*Errh*… I'm a DJ… in China.' I told him the only thing that came into my head.

'You pay the munnee, *now!*' he said, and with that they went to leave the room. But just as I was cursing the freakin' absurdity of Cantonese mentality at times – the dumb couple calling the police out over a measly HK$100 – he turned back, scowling. '*Don' do the drug!*'

'Yeah, right,' I replied, looking around for my clothes.

Back at my flat, I had another surprise – one that knocked on the door.

Apple stood there and, despite the growing squalor, I invited her in. Only now that I knew the 14-K had their hooks into the girl, I grew suspicious. After the scene in the club, I bet they'd sent her there to spy.

She asked a load of questions but seemed on edge, probably because of the drugs or shyness because she had a crush on me. But I reckoned there was more to this than a casual visit and that it had something to do with the dark agenda I'd uncovered.

It all began to blur. I couldn't focus on what she was asking me or comprehend why she felt the need to ask it. I tried to remain aloof, my words ambiguous, adopting a manner that told her I knew all about her little game and the people she worked for. And although she tried to give me the bemused-smile routine a few times, I felt sure *she* knew that *I* knew, and didn't give her much of a welcome.

When she left, I got angry. It wasn't right for Apple to be keeping tabs on me for them. I'd never done anything to hurt her. I took the lift down and rushed into the street, scanning up and down to see if I could catch her meeting an accomplice, but she'd vanished. It was time for what Old Ron would call a symbolic gesture of defiance… although I had no intention of swimming over to the mainland.

Instead, I went to the fruit stall on the corner, bought a big red apple and said to the owner, 'Do you know what we do with the *bad* apple?' Then I threw it high into the air and right over the flyover at the end of the street.

He looked *so* surprised, it made me stop and think, 'Maybe he doesn't know all about this massive underground conspiracy that she's a part of?' But I'm sure he did. Everyone seemed know about it, certainly a lot more than me.

Eating Smoke

'SIK YIN! YAT GUN HO LOK!' came that bizarre shout down the stairs of the club, *again*, as I sat behind the lectern enjoying a busy evening.

I'd been hearing it for days in both English and Chinese accents. I knew what it meant. I just couldn't see from the stairwell who kept shouting it from the street above.

Sik yin, literally translated, means 'eating smoke' – 'smoking', as in cigarettes, to use Western vernacular. *Yat gun ho lok* means 'a can of coke'. But why people were shouting it at me, I had no idea. It was another of Wan Chai's anomalies, so I put it out of my head.

'*Errhum!*' someone coughed over my shoulder.

I'd been staring up at a vintage kung fu film playing on the club's television screen.

'*Crazy old fat bald man!* Do you think that's a *respectful* way to address an ageing Chinese gentleman?' the cough's owner continued.

I turned to see it was Cameron, Troy's lawyer friend, with the sense of humour.

'Bloody disrespectful if you ask me, old boy!' I said, shaking hands and joining him in laughter.

'How's it going, Cameron? You remember me, yeah?'

'I remember you, Chris. I also remember you saying if I smoked that drug I would be craving it within a week.'

'*And?*'

'I've smoked it *every day* since!'

He sounded so pleased with himself that I wasn't sure if he was thanking me for the warning or telling me to fuck off with the lectures, so I tried to change the subject – only Cameron had other ideas.

'Chris, you work here most nights?'

'Yes, mate. Why?'

'You *recognise* the customers… and know what their, *errhum… needs* are?'

'Sort of…' I said, clocking telltale beads of sweat on his brow.

'Well, Paul there,' he nodded to the *Dai Lo*. 'You know he runs things around here and can sort you out with any, *errhum… supplies*, you might need. When you're greeting the customers, I mean?'

'Cameron, are you suggesting I sell drugs on the door?'

'That's *exactly* what I'm suggesting.' He gave an exaggerated nod. Then leaving me astounded, he wandered over to chat to the guy he'd mentioned.

Sitting back behind the lectern, I took what he said with a pinch of salt. With my own track record, I wasn't about to sell the world's most addictive drug to anyone, not to feather my own nest and certainly not to relative strangers. But after a while, I got to thinking, 'What's the story with this guy? A top city lawyer hanging around a squalid mafia joint, friends with the *Dai Lo*, trying to get me to sell shit he's addicted to himself to other poor souls? Surely he knows the 14-K doesn't need *gweilos* to peddle drugs for them?'

I'd been reading up on drug rings in Hong Kong in a book I found in the junk room. At some point during its estranged life, it had lost its front cover, so I didn't know its title but poring over the information was fascinating nonetheless.

I learnt that drugs would often be smuggled inside consignments of trade goods, and packages in the mail. It said that because of their anti-establishment roots the triads had always been a target for persecution by China's ruling elite so in advance of the 1997 handover many senior triads had emigrated to Commonwealth countries and now ran their empires from abroad.

A photograph showed a gang of *maa jais* operating a drug racket on one of Wan Chai's backstreets, the caption explaining that by running a comb through his hair one of the little horses was signalling to his accomplices to warn them of an approaching police patrol. In triad slang, this person was a 'singer'. I found the suggestion that these guys communicated through hand signs and gestures acutely intriguing.

A picture on the next page featured a couple of ageing heroin addicts from the colony's homeless population. Moreover, the massive infected wounds around their injection sites. I thought of poor old Johnny Horsepower.

A couple of days later, I'd popped over to Old Ron's before work. I found him larking on the sofa with Rose.

Talk about preoccupied! I wish I hadn't bothered. There can't be anything more torturous than being in a room with all that in-your-face I-just-found-true-love crap, the sort that restates itself with slobbering sentiment every three seconds in case anyone has missed the relationship of the century and not yet stuck a knife into their own head.

Contemplating the best place to puke – in the bathroom, on the floor, all over them or all over myself – the latter purge having the added bonus I might drown – I saw them whispering, *again*.

Old Ron looked over. 'Are you a *singer*?'

'Say *what*?'

'Rose and I want to know, are you a *singer*?' They giggled like fuckers.

'Do you mean a *singer* singer, or a singer like a normal singer?'

'Oh, just a singer…' They both sniggered, so I ignored them.

Someone hurled another shout of '*Sik yin! Yat gun ho lok!*' down the stairway, this time in a Chinese accent.

Curious as to why I kept hearing it, I looked up to see Craig, my DJ friend from the Big Apple, appearing in silhouette against the moonlight.

'*Errhum!*' he coughed, giving me a feeling of *déjà vu*.

'Got a cold, mate?' I joked.

'Errh… *no*,' he replied, indignation in his voice and scowling as if I'd just asked the dumbest of questions.

'What brings you over from the Apple, Craig?'

His eyes widened, conspiratorial fashion. 'I've come to sell some *bags*, mate!' he said, then chuckled as he went inside.

'*Bags?*' I pondered. What was he doing selling drugs in here?

As my head whizzed faster than a Black & Decker during a power surge a few things fell into place. Hadn't Lee Aimes said all the cocaine in Wan Chai came through him? And Cameron suggesting I sell drugs for the *Dai Lo*, and now Craig openly announcing it.

Then there was the conversation with Drik about smuggling gold and gemstones for the boss, and the one with Gonzales at his place. '*Hah*! I don't *work*, mate!' he'd said. I knew he sold stolen gear to support himself, likely a good deal of drugs too, but how did he have the contacts to do that in Wan Chai?

And what about Old Ron's resurgence from homelessness, his new flat, his bargirl 'friend', his gentleman-of-leisure persona *and* his expensive laptop? Didn't Drik say the triads recruited people who were down and out, like Johnny Horsepower said about the girls he brought to the *Dai Lo*?

I thought back to my conversation with the middleman. '*Triads will work with anyone, even gweilos, if they can make a buck.*' Perhaps Old Ron's financial acumen had received a second chance and he was now reaping black rewards by laundering money for the 14-K.

And what was the deal with little Apple coming to my place and asking all sorts of strange questions? I was sure she'd been doing it on behalf of *them*.

It all suddenly seemed to make sense. If the 14-K wanted to control the expat drug market – a big chunk of the pie – they would need *gweilo* gophers to be able to do it.

I found myself deliberating over the whole triad issue more and more. But it was *so* confusing. I couldn't differentiate this agenda from the other conspiracy that seemed to pervade the streets of Wan Chai and emanate to the four corners of the globe.

'Is it true whad my friend in Lundun is delling me – dat if I go to Englund and I don't wanna work den the government will pay me money?' Anil looked baffled.

I liked him. He was a good lad and it wasn't his decision to move in here.

Born in Hong Kong, he didn't dress in traditional clothing like his father, opting instead for the urban fashion of Cantonese youth. With his short-cropped hair and unblemished face, he appeared younger than his seventeen years and was a handsome kid. Gabriel had said he'd taken Anil to Mumbai last year and he'd been shocked by the poverty he saw.

I chuckled now, imagining in my own mind what his friend's explanation of the UK's social security system had conjured up in his.

While we chatted, I couldn't help glancing over his shoulder, wondering what Gabriel was doing on the landing outside our door.

'Suspicious… packages… drug packages.'

He was decanting henna from a hessian sack into small bags, wrapping these up in brown paper and sticking airmail stickers on them.

'Gabriel… lived in Wan Chai twenty years… must be a part of the conspiracy… not going back to Mumbai… not to poverty.'

'Hmmh…?' From what I read in the triad book, I reckoned he was putting more than henna into those *packages* he was sending to *India… a part of the Commonwealth*!

The following evening I got talking to a recently arrived Brit named Darren. Tall, with blond hair, he told me he lived with his cousin, Julian, a Club Nemo regular who had been in Hong Kong some time.

While Julian chatted to the *Dai Lo*, I asked Darren if he'd noticed anything unusual during his stay. 'What do you mean?' he asked with a hint of reservation.

'This whole triad thing, mate,' I continued, taking in a group of little horses stood drinking not far from us. 'Most people don't even notice… but look at those guys…' I pointed with my eyes. 'Can you see they all wear the same clothing? Jeans, shell-suit tops and white trainers.'

'Oh *yeah*…' he replied, with a degree of unease.

Later, as I stood yapping to Rose outside the 7-Eleven, Julian walked down Luard Road towards us. 'Hi Chris,' he said, shoving out his hand and giving me this Masonic-like handshake, wiggling his middle finger in the palm of my hand. 'How's it going in the club?'

'Fine, mate,' I replied, wondering if he'd simply assumed I was a member of this underground cult. I worried I may have divulged too much information to Darren.

Drik was back on the door the next night, our relationship fractious at best. He'd say things like, 'So, do you see it yet, Chris?' like Durban's answer to Rolf Harris.

'Errh... I...' I'd reply, digging deep to grasp that elusive cipher.

'Keep trying!' he'd continue, cutting me off with contempt and leaving me floundering in frustration.

I looked to him as the guy with the answers, the ones needed to gain admission into this secretive domain where *gweilos* worked hand in hand with triads. A world where people on the bones of their arse, isolated and desperate, could gain acceptance and respect from a new set of peers and find a home both metaphorically and, in Old Ron and Drik's cases, literally.

But I knew it wouldn't be easy. If this thing had been going on around me throughout my time here, perhaps my whole life – which considering the global angle, it likely had – then no one would simply throw the door open and say, 'Hi, Chris! Come and join the party!'

If that was the case there would be no need for a hidden agenda communicated through instructions on food packets, labels on blankets, double-speak in travel books, 'singers', and combs run through hair.

No, it was up to me to put the jigsaw puzzle together and when the last piece fell into place I would see this thing as clear as day and earn a place of respect in the underworld collaboration.

With Drik sent here to act as the old dog to guide my progress, I felt like the new kid on the block, as if he was the wizened kung fu master to a wayward young fighter, one flashing the occasional glimpse of genius. But just like the cantankerous Mr Miyagi in *Karate Kid*, he wasn't about to feed me too much information. He would damn well make me paint the fence and polish the car. He would drip-feed me until the drips became a puddle, the puddle a lake, the lake an ocean – the force of which he would hold back with the omnipotence of a modern-day Moses, allowing this Israelite entry into the Promised Land, before withdrawing his staff of infinite authority and letting the waves crash down on any fool who dared follow.

It wouldn't be an easy induction by any means, but I wasn't about to let him see me sweat, both figuratively and literally, which proved nigh on impossible as I always rushed to the club so as not to be late.

I spent the first half-hour of every shift trying to calm myself down, willing the beads of moisture on my forehead not to turn into rivers and praying for the anxiety to evaporate so as not to make it obvious I was higher than the choir.

Following that came waves of confusion, fuelled by sleep deprivation, leaving me struggling to interpret the situation as a whole and the allegory behind its constituent parts. I found myself hanging on Drik's every word, desperate to make sense of the subliminal instruction his speaking in tongues contained in an attempt to please our hidden masters and access this select group.

Drik asked, 'What did you do today?'

I thought for a moment, 'Oh, *you* know… just sort'a putting the puzzle together,' hoping this was the correct answer, or at least one that would appease the right people.

'I played cards,' he said with disinterest.

I wondered if this was a metaphor for jewel-smuggling because a pack of cards has diamonds in it.

'Drik, should I… *you know*… be playing cards?'

'Ja! You can make a lot of money and it sure beats working.'

I imagined Drik slipping through airport customs, a leather holdall under his arm and a lie at the ready.

'Do you read much, Chris?' he asked.

'Do you mean… do I read the *signs?*'

'*You* can read the signs,' he replied, pulling open the lectern drawer, 'but I prefer this.'

He took out a fantasy-fiction novel and handed it to me. Its title, *The Craft*, let me know I was on to something, an instruction manual to decipher Wan Chai life. The back cover said it all.

> Chezek Smit isn't who he appears to be. Handpicked from the Order's Military Guard, his remit as Special Operative is to infiltrate the Alliance's rebel command…

'Whoa! Handpicked from the Military…'

'*Special Operative…*'

'The Alliance… is that the Wan Chai alliance?' I wondered.
It all seemed to make sense.

It was Pippen Yen who taught him the Craft…

'Is that supposed to be Apple… because apples have "pips"?'
'Apples are poisonous… be careful.'
'Yeah…' I hadn't thought of that.'
I knew she had a lot to do with this. She'd tried to get clever with me
in the flat that time – the flying apple let everyone know I was onto her
little game.
'You sussed her little game…'
'Yeah… I sussed her little game.'

The Alliance's foremost agent, Malik Asah, isn't convinced. But not
even his alien intelligence can predict what is about to take place…

'Is Drik this alien being…?' I wondered. But that would be science
fiction and this thing, whatever it was, was real – although people did
call this place *Aliens.*
'Whoa…!'
This situation was so bewildering. So much so, I continued to pore
over the book for an hour, at the expense of the club and the customers
coming into it.
To make it more difficult, whenever I asked Drik a question – never a
direct one. I knew the game better than that – something loose such as,
'How should I be doing *this*?' or 'Is it good to wear trainers… you know,
like… *white* ones?' his reply would be curt and indifferent: 'Maybe', 'If
you like' or 'Whatever', which made me feel I was on the right lines but
never actually got me anywhere.
Yet, despite the bones Drik threw to me, I could tell he still objected
to my presence… and then the crunch came.
'You know, *everyone* knows you take drugs, Chris,' he said, as I stood
by the door, trying not to look as though I took drugs.
'And?' I threw back at him, thinking, 'Is that your *best* shot?'
'…*I* like a drink, Chris,' he continued. 'But *not* before work.'
'Right…' I replied, wishing it were that easy with crystal meth.

The following day I left work in melancholy mode. It was all starting to get too much. So I took drugs. *Whoopee-flipping-do!* Half the planet did in one form or another. There must be a reason behind it. I didn't wake up one day and think, '*Ah!* *That's* what I'll do! I'll leave a good career in the Armed Forces, go out to Hong Kong and get messed up! *In fact*, I'll piss off the nicest Chinese bloke I ever met, lose fifty frickin' jobs and girlfriends and ruin my health – *result!*'

No, it was me against the world – which could only mean one thing. It was time to go to Wan Chai Park and do some handstands on top of the kids' climbing frame – much to the amusement of the Tai Chi practitioners who had the choice of my display or the slightly more accomplished one of a local woman, her two fighting swords whirling spectacular and flashing lethality in the morning sunlight.

It normally sorted my head out, this and some kung fu practice. Other times I would look for a nightclub still open where I didn't know anyone and could dance in a quiet corner, away from all the chaos.

The last time I'd wandered through a door at random, twenty Filipinas in bikinis jumped up and rushed towards me, shouting, '*Creese!*'

'*Crikey!*' That'd spun me out. I'd been seeking solitude, not a gang-bang.

But my trip to the park didn't quite do it for me this time. I could no longer enjoy anonymity – hardly surprising when tracksuit-topped thugs observe your every move and you're at the centre of a massive conspiracy that everyone seems to be in on except you. Leaving for home, I got to wondering where my life was going… or had gone.

Walking down Lockhart Road, I opened my wallet and took out my bank and credit cards, recalling the days when I used them to book plush function rooms for business presentations. Why I still carried them, I had no idea. They were no good to anyone unless their favourite pastime was being heavily in debt. As much use as an invisible stop sign or a chocolate fire engine, I dropped them on the pavement. '*Hah!*' A symbolic gesture to the conspirators that I really didn't give a fuck any more.

It should have been a perfect velvet morning in the beautiful enclave I loved, but as the sun's warmth beat down, reminding me I wasn't all that bad, I fought back tears.

I walked right past my friend in the dry-cleaners, knowing he must be in on this and ridiculing me as well.

Further humiliating, I'd noticed that every time a local buzzed the lift in my building and the door slid open to reveal me inside, they'd get all flustered and refuse to get in.

Now, as I stood waiting to go up to my apartment, a Chinese woman stepped up, unafraid, beside me.

I looked at her and she smiled.

I burst out crying.

I awoke that afternoon, having climbed down the waste pipe so I didn't have to face Gabriel. When I went to get a glass of water, he was standing in the front room, waiting to pounce. '*Mister* Creese! Why you throwing away your creditcadds in the street?'

'How do you know about that?' I asked, though not at all surprised.

'*WE'RE* knowing *EVERYT'ING! EVERYT'ING* you *DO!*' He gave me several overstated bobs of the head. I think he meant to look like a man in the 'know', but instead he looked like one of those nodding dogs the owner of the car in front bought in case you hadn't seen one before.

An image of him discussing me with the members of his drinking club came to mind. He spent a good part of each day there.

'Yes, *WE!*' he continued. 'Do you know whad I am *meaning* when I am saying, *WE?*'

The slow realisation of what I'd suspected all along dawned, so I kept quiet.

'This is *Wan Chai*. There's nothing you are doing in *Wan Chai* thad I don't get to hear about!'

'I bet there's not,' I thought. 'I bet you're in this thing up to your onion bhajees, deeper than a pothole in Delhi, along with every other person around here.'

'You know, Creese…' his tone softened, 'thad I am having a problem.'

He came closer. I'm not sure if he wanted me to smell the alcohol on his breath, but that's what I smelt.

'You know I am liking to have a liddle drink.'

'Lecture sounds familiar,' I thought.

'Bud in my religion it is forbidden. So I am keeping it quiet, you *know?* Do you *understand* whad I am telling you?'

'Yeah, I think so, Gabriel... thanks.'

From this point on, I kept my mouth shut about the whole triad, *gweilo*, global thing. Instead, I kept my eyes and ears open, determined at least to find out what was behind the *Sik yin! Yat gun ho lok!* shout people kept floating down the stairs of the club.

'Have you got it yet?' asked Drik. 'It's not *that* difficult, Chris.'

'What's not *that* difficult, Drik?' I replied, thinking I must be close to cracking this thing.

'...Nothing.' He looked the other way.

I began to scrutinise his every interaction with the punters, looking for any sign of secretive communication – the kind the triads used.

Then, BINGO, *BLOODY* BINGO! I had my breakthrough! It was all in the *cough*! How could I have not seen it – or *heard* it – before?

When a customer approached – a regular customer – they raised a hand to their mouth and let out a small but distinct cough. Drik then reciprocated the gesture.

'What a *damn* clever way to communicate!' I mused.

It was so simple, so discreet, yet so effective. It must have been why DJ Craig looked at me sideways when I'd asked if he had a cold the other day.

It reminded me of being on the parade ground performing weapons drill in the Marines. The spectators would wonder how in Heaven's name we could throw our rifles around, fire off blanks and change formation in synchrony without the Drill Instructor issuing a command. The reason was that one of the guys would be the designated 'Hissing Sid'. His job was to hiss, 'Tsst-tsst, tsst-tsst,' so we could hear, and keep in time, but the crowd couldn't.

I kept my newfound understanding a secret from Drik, kicking myself for not noticing it earlier.

When Drik went into the bar, I decided to put my knowledge to the test. The next guy down the stairs was a young Chinese. Short, scrawny and dark-skinned, he dressed as a *maa jai*. As he drew near, *'Errhum!'* out it came.

'Errhum!' I responded, smiling as I did.

He put his wild eyes up close to mine, grinned and said, 'Very *goo*!'

Then he went to go inside – only he stopped in the doorway, turned and whispered, *'Sik yin! Yat gun ho lok!'* and laughed.

A Day at the Races

THAT WAS IT! I was determined to figure out the symbolism behind 'eating smoke' and 'a can of coke'. It was time to go into military mode; time to watch and observe.

'*Watch and observe…*'

'Yeah…'

'So, have you figured it out yet?' asked Drik.

I felt for the man. This was his whole life – a former down-and-out, no longer drinking himself into oblivion and sleeping in McDonald's but the frontman of a Wan Chai nightclub, one fiercely loyal to his 'new' family of 'funny coughers'.

I'm not saying I wasn't lapping up the thrill of working in a bar full of headcases, or looking to belong but my main reason for wanting to understand this closed-off community was that most of the people I knew appeared to be *in* it *and* prospering from it.

And another difference between Drik and me was that I had other experiences under my belt, such as wearing the coveted green beret in an elite band of brothers, which was far more rewarding than working in a Hong Kong nightclub and way beyond this poisoned dwarf's comprehension.

'It's not *that* difficult,' Drik continued.

'*Smug bastard… ask him why you can't just kill somebody… surely the 14-K must have enemies that need knocking off… beats playing stupid games… test the big mouth's mettle… cut through this initiation shit… get to the proving ground.*'

'Drik, why can't I just kill some—?'

Before I could finish, a shout of *'Sik yin! Yat gun ho lok!'* interrupted us, this time in an English voice coming from something of a commotion above.

A large group of expats funnelled through the top door, only from the way these cats were dressed they didn't seem your typical English abroad – more a band of wandering minstrels, somewhat inebriated and having a whale of a time.

A surge of pinstripes, chequers, polka dots and flowers, adorning an equally diverse range of clothing, made its way down the stairs. There were suits and dresses of all styles and eras, some seeming as though they'd roared out of the twenties, others like they'd come back from the future. One guy wore a white tuxedo jacket with a pair of boardshorts, flip-flops and wrap-arounds. There were hats to write home about, cravats and silk scarves, loud ties and buttonholed sprays, an arsenal of umbrellas and the odd walking stick for good measure.

I looked across to Drik.

'Race day,' he informed me, but I remained none the wiser. '*Horse* racing. *Macau*,' he added.

'Ah, right!' I remembered it was May 1st, Labour Day, a public holiday in Hong Kong.

It was a strange sight. Weirder still they *all* seemed to know me. The guy with the *Miami-Vice*-at-the-beach look slapped me on the back and said, 'Don't think about it *too* hard, mate!'

Another, 'Have you *still* not got it yet?'

And a Chinese girl placed her hands on my knees and looking into my eyes said, 'Honey. It's no' *dat* difficult!'

I thought, 'Where have I heard that before?'

'Sik yin? Yat gun ho lok?' I pondered, forming my hands the way you would if you were holding a cigarette and a can of coke.

Then for the second time in an evening, it hit me like an overweight elephant!

I *kicked* myself for being so blind!

They were *hand signs*!

The next couple of racegoers were a guy and a girl. Upon seeing Drik and me, they adopted a ring shape with one hand and two pointing fingers the other.

A glance at Drik confirmed he returned the gesture, before raising a hand and giving a discreet cough.

They replied in kind.

'You *clever bastards!*' I mused. 'How *simple* and how *discreet!*'

Yet again, someone who thought he knew a bit about life just found out he knew enough to write a pamphlet. I might have been out of the umbra but I was still light years away from working it all out.

As the flow of customers eased, Drik went inside, leaving me to marvel at my new discovery, unable to believe it had been staring me in the face all along... *as had the cigarette poster on the wall, the one rooting me to the spot and sending a shiver down my spine.*

'No *fucking* way!'

The advert was for a Chinese brand and featured 'Mr Popular' in polo shirt and chinos, smiling at the camera, happy with his choice of smoke clasped between *two fingers on one hand... while holding a can of coke in the other!*

My existence blurred. I turned to check out two similar promotions on the opposite wall.

Sure enough, there smiling *deliberately* at me had been a young Eurasian woman sitting by a tennis court *taking a reassuring drag of nicotine with her right hand and encircling the grip of her racquet with the left!*

The one below that was the boy next door, sitting in a group of too-happy-to-be-true friends at a beach party, puffing away proudly *with a two-fingered cigarette-holding salute while making the okay circle!*

'Unbe-fucking-lievable!... what a *clever* way to let members of this *weird...* triad... expat... cult know they're on *home* ground!' How could I have missed it – the club didn't even *sell* frickin' cigarettes!

As a fog of intrigue washed over me, I heard *'Ha-ha!'* from above.

I looked up to see Gonzales the Pirate bounding down the stairs the way granddads do at weddings when they get too pissed and forget they're not twenty-one anymore. Boy, he was in a good mood and cutting a dash in pinstripes and a white-banded trilby with a red flower tucked into it. With his dangly gold earrings setting off a scoundrel's grin, he looked to have had a good day at the races and had probably stopped off at his place for a little cook-up session.

Nonchalant as can be, I made the ring and two fingers sign. I felt like a secret agent proffering, 'The moon shines bright over Prague this night,' and further excitement when Gonzales returned the encrypted greeting as if I truly were a spy coming in from the cold – although a hostage returning from a three-year relationship with a Lebanese radiator would be nearer the mark. Then slapping me on my hand-signed thighs and pulling a comical look, he said, *'Wake up and smell the roses!'*

Finally, I was on the right lines and gaining the trust of the clandestine clique's members. 'How have all these expats got involved?' I wondered. 'They *seem* to appreciate I'm trying.'

My complacency didn't last long, though. I soon found myself knocked off my plateau of appreciation and saturated once again with others' contempt. Something *awful* happened…

I took a look inside to see the flamboyantly-dressed funsters crowding the horseshoe-shaped bar as though it were a miniature racecourse and they were up for a punt on the ashtrays and glasses speeding around it. When I returned to the stairwell another racegoer descended the stairs *and my world stopped dead–*

'*Found out… cheapskate… bubbly.*' For dressed in top hat and tails the guy brandished a bottle of champagne… *the exact same one I'd shoplifted for Lee Aimes' birthday!*

'*WE'RE knowing EVERYT'ING!… there's nothing you are doing in Wan Chai thad I don't get to hear about!*'

Recalling Gabriel's warning, the realisation the Cult knew my every move hit home hard. My pulse rocketed, sweat poured; there seemed no escape.

'Can I stick this bottle behind there, mate?' Fred Astaire asked, his eyes glinting… *accusingly.*

'S-s-su*ure*,' I stammered, muddled with adrenalin-fuelled angst, feeling disgraced now my dishonest deed was out in the open.

As I sat there, downtrodden and depressed, Lee came into the club with a worried look. 'CJ, you alright, brother?'

I stared down at the floor.

He put his arm around my shoulder. 'Look, you gotta look after yourself, our kid.'

'Why?' I replied, sounding as miserable as I felt.

'Well, people are saying you're not yourself anymore.'

'Yeah! Apparently I'm out the loop.'

'Nah, mate! You're not out the loop. Someone ooh buys me a bottle of champagne for my birthday's not out the loop.'

I wondered if this was the Cult testing me, trying to see if I would take credit for a gift I hadn't paid for.

'I nicked it, Lee...'

'Oh...' He seemed a little surprised. 'Well... *ooh* gives a shit! You just gotta get a grip, mate. You gotta go easy on that stuff, yeah?'

'Uh-huh.'

'You afta take care of yourself, CJ, yeah?'

'Thanks, Lee.'

'Ron, I need you to help me,' I asked, as we walked towards Wan Chai Park during my evening break for a 'private' chat.

'Why's that, mate?' he replied.

As he spoke, two *maa jais* exited the park. One of the triad's eyes flicked warily at me and then fixed knowingly on Ron, and, '*Errhum!*' out it came.

'There goes the privacy,' I thought.

'*Errhum!*' Ron coughed back.

'*That's* why, mate!' I said. 'That's *exactly* why.'

I knew I had him! It was time he started acting like a friend and gave me some answers.

'What do you mean?' he bluffed, turning his head away.

'*Ron!* You know *exactly* what I mean. Don't *fucking* tell me that guy didn't just cough and you didn't cough back. You always treat me like this, Ron... like I'm some sort of frickin' *alien*.'

Still looking away, he muttered, 'I think the world of you, Chris.'

I adjusted my tone. 'Look, Ron. I'm not trying to cadge in on your fun, but I need to know. I'm asking you as a friend... *help* me... *please?*'

'How can I help you, Chris?'

By fuck, the poor bloke looked stretched, in danger of compromising his newfound status with guys you shouldn't dare compromise.

'Ron, just tell me, is it good to do this with your hands?' I made the smoking-a-cigarette and holding-a-can-of-coke signs.

He glanced down, paused, and said, '...At least they'll see you're trying.'

Back at my place the next morning, I wanted to dive into the *Culture Shock! Hong Kong* guidebook, determined to work this whole thing out. But first I had a job to do – crystal meth taking priority over getting to grips with the finer points of international criminal fraternities.

I cleared a space on the floor and, using scissors swiped from the kitchen, set about making a water pipe with the Yakult yoghurt containers and drinking straws I'd bought in the 7-Eleven.

I carefully poked two straw-sized holes in the Yakult's foil lid, and then drank the sweet fruity liquid and washed the pot out in the bathroom, making sure to leave an inch of water in it.

The concertina-type straws were ideal. Having cut one in half, I edged the straight part into one of the holes and bent the second piece into an upside down U-shape and slid it into the other. To stop the cigarette lighter melting the latter, I rolled a banknote-sized piece of foil into a gently tapering toot and popped it in the end. It was perfect!... the only problem being it didn't work – I'd made the holes too big.

I repeated the process, not once but four times, ending up with a result to make *Blue Peter* viewers proud. When I sucked the top straw the apparatus *pup-pup-pupped* away like a miniature steam engine. Only, in my tired state, it had taken *five* hours to complete and now the floor was covered in drinks containers, tinfoil and drinking straws. The place looked like a crack den.

Having tested my creation, I picked up the *Culture Shock!* book, flicking it open at: *THE JOB DESCRIPTION.*

> ...staff derive a sense of security from having their duties defined in black and white.

'*Hmmh*, is that a reference to this underground clique…?' I pondered.
'Are their duties written in black and white in this guidebook…?'

'This conspiracy is black and white… you either see it or you don't.'

'Ah…!'

I thumbed to the section headed: *THE TRIADS*.

Bank and jewellery shop robbers in Hong Kong used to wield the chopping knife. Today, triad members threaten their victims with handguns and grenades.

I sat up straight, *stunned* in disbelief!

'What shape do your hands make when you're holding a gun and grenade…?'

'Sik yin!… yat gun ho lok!… smoking a cigarette!… holding a can of coke!'

The answer had been there all along, right in front of my eyes!

'You see it now… don't you?'

In the club that evening, I sat thinking through it all. There was still so much that didn't make sense. Rather than kick back and relax with the ground I'd gained, it served to wind up my curiosity and fill me with a sense of unease. As for the incident with the champagne – surely that was some kind of dark warning.

For that reason, before I left for work I'd tucked something into my bum bag for insurance purposes. I had Gabriel's screwdriver.

I'd done my best to learn about the culture, both above and below ground. I'd tried to respect everybody I'd met, a few bloopers excepted. But *fuck* 'em! If they weren't going to respect me and my life was in danger I would duly protect myself – by whatever means.

But without thinking, I'd shoved my bum bag in the draw of the lectern. Returning from a circuit of the bar, I found Drik and Chee Chu with it open and knew how desperate it must have seemed.

'*Diu lei lo mo!* (Fuck your mother!)' came the primal scream from inside the club.

I looked up to see a young *maa jai* chase another frantic-looking other towards the door.

Judging by the vengeance-fuelled pace and red-misted eyes of the chaser, something had taken place and serious face had been lost.

The first guy entered the bottleneck of the stairwell and lunged for the stairs, but the second grabbed his shirt and wrenched him out of mid-air. As they smashed into each other, I hopped out the way, spread-eagled against the wall. Screaming Hell's fury and using their mobile telephones as clubs, they began beating down on one another.

Eventually the chased leapt for the stairs again, but the attacker grabbed his clothing once more. With the adrenalin of an injured rhino, the guy surged forward, a sudden rip leaving his shirt a dangling rag in the other guy's hand. The young *maa jai* looked at it in disbelief, yelled, '*Diu lei lo mo!*' then ran up the stairs after him.

Although brief, it was the most brutal fight I'd ever seen. Only, now there was blood all over the floor and I had a strange premonition the law might turn up.

Dashing into the back room, I grabbed a mop, but I was forgetting this was Chinese culture and an anxious Mr Chen, the club's cleaner, snatched it from me.

And lo and behold, just as Chen *San* finished his-and-his-alone's task, who should put in an appearance but two of Wan Chai's finest.

'Do you see figh' in here tonigh'?' one of them asked.

'*Fight?*' I replied, dumb as a bear on *Mastermind.*

'Someone report figh' in here, tonigh'?'

'No fight in here, Officer.' I shook my head at the utterly ridiculous suggestion that there had been a *fight… in here… tonight.*

They seemed satisfied – as did Paul Eng, who sat at the bar watching the scene unfold.

But as they bugged out, something *bugged* me…

I took a closer look.

It was a cellulose capsule, a *fake blood capsule*, lying broken where Mr Chen had unknowingly swept it to the edge of the stairwell.

'Why would anyone have fake blood in a nightclub… unless they wanted to stage a *fake* incident… or a *fake fight!*'

'Was that a set-up?' I wondered.

Perhaps it was an attempt to lure the interfering *gweilo* into intervening in a Chinese matter, giving the young *maa jais* an excuse to unleash Hell-by-mobile-phone on me. The violence seemed so real, though – hard to fake that level of ferocity. As for the coppers, who called them?

This was a bar run and frequented by gangsters, who took care of their own affairs. Anyone going to the police would end up looking like they'd tried to wet shave using a Samurai sword on a rollercoaster.

From the incident with the Thai, I knew Paul Eng wouldn't risk the club getting a bad rep and him losing face, and from the reaction of the Chinese customers when the girl had collapsed it was clear they couldn't give a shit about calling the emergency services when someone was *dying*, let alone getting a sissy-slap courtesy of Motorola.

And the foreigners? Why would anyone call the Old Bill over a couple of guys running *out* of a club to fight? Besides, tourists didn't carry phones and all the expats used pagers.

The coppers seemed genuine but the way they'd arrived, right on cue, was as if they were trying to get me to spill the beans to expose me as a grass. The newspapers *did* bang on about a worrying number of officers with triad affiliations.

'Hey, Chris! I thought I'd stop by and say hello.'

Hell! Stephan de Fries was the last person I expected to see in Club Nemo.

'Paul! Can I take my break now?'

The *Dai Lo* nodded.

Sipping beer at a street-side restaurant, it was good to see Stephan, his friendship acting as a buffer from the Cult's prying eyes.

'So how are you *really*?' Stephan asked.

'Oh, you know…'

'No, Chris. I don't.'

'Stephan… in Wan Chai…'

'Yes, Chris. I *know* Wan Chai.'

'*Knows Wan Chai…!*'

I brought my voice down to a whisper. 'Well… *there's something going on here…*'

'*Yeees…*' said Stephan, his manner turning grave.

'*He knows…!*'

'Like in the club… There's *something* weird going on… with the triads.'

'*Yes*, Chris…'

Our exchange darkened, unexpectedly, like hearing a rumble of thunder and looking up to see an overcast sky.

'*Eyes… eyes.*'

His eyes now regarded me with enmity, exuding the dull menace I'd come to associate with the cult.

'And do you know what *happens* to people who *interfere* with triad business?' he continued.

I had a feeling the point was about to be reiterated.

'They end up *DEAD*!'

When I arrived home, Gabriel confronted me. 'You know the police have been here.'

'Police?' I replied, with indifference.

'*Yes*! I am showing them whad you have done to your room!'

I stared at the Fat Controller, and unable to work out if this was Cult doublespeak, I ignored him.

I hadn't *meant* to let my room get this messy, and felt sure I could rectify it. But this particular day, it wasn't going to happen. I'd smoked way too much ice and now felt as sideways as a shopping trolley. I was deeply anxious the Indians might come into my room again while I was at work. Plus, I had no way of locking it.

In the end, I grabbed a length of bamboo from the junk room and wedged it between the wall and the door. It meant I had to climb out of the window, shin up the waste pipe and go out across the roof, but that was fine by me.

The first person to arrive at the club after I did was Johnny Horsepower. He initiated the me-*nutting* me-no-*munnee* routine, and my heart went out. I felt kinship with him: we were both desperados.

I told him I would meet him in the park at seven in the morning. His eyes lit up and he looked at me cow-like for several seconds, then off he went.

'Chris! What about the *Indians?*' asked Drik.

It was a bad time to be bringing up the subject. I was having enough struggle dealing with the here and now, feeling spun-out worse than washing, let alone worrying about what the Indians were doing–

'Back at the flat...!'

'Oh *shit...!*'

'What about the Indians, Drik?' I replied, wishing I could be as nonchalant as an omelette, but inside, the panic and terror grew.

'They're breaking into your room,' the personality-disordered plankton replied, oh-so casually.

'Fine upstanding Citizen Bamboo Cane... broken... snapped!'

'Shit!' I kicked myself, imagining Gabriel standing in my room, tutting at the mangled bamboo pole in his hand.

I didn't bother asking Drik how he knew. Everybody – Gabriel, Old Ron, Gonzales, the Dalai Lama, Pope John Paul the Second *and* the Queen of Sheba – knew my every move. Gabriel recently had a telephone line installed and I reckoned he must have called the bar to conspire with this low-life.

'Are you saying I should get *back* there?'

'Would if I were you,' Drik replied, deadpan.

My heartbeat rose to industrial proportions, a sound more fitted to stamping out car body panels – *or licence plates!* The terror had me in its grip, *its massive, ugly, frightening grip.*

I just knew I had to get back there, like *yesterday!*

Sure that I was being watched by the triads – which, considering I was in a club run by them, probably wasn't far from the truth – I picked an empty cardboard box off a stack of rubbish by the fire exit, then went out the door as if I was chucking it in the skip out back.

When I got outside, chuck it I did – but not in the skip. I couldn't give a backflip in Beijing where that thing ended up. All I had in my mind was sprinting down the alley, which cut through all the blocks and would eventually get me home.

'They're waiting for you…'

I checked myself.

The pitch-black was a real contrast to the dazzling disco lights of a moment ago, the sounds of booming beats and rapturous vocals fused with fever-pitched conversation a distant memory. I expected to see a chopping blade glint in the moonlight at any moment.

I felt afraid… *extremely* afraid. I knew *they* were waiting for me.

Looking through the darkness, I could see the street lighting on the intersecting road. I don't know what filled me with the most dread: that bladed thugs might be hiding along this macabre gauntlet, or them picking up my trail if someone spotted me crossing over that street.

'Remember the drills… Marine… standard operating procedures… vary your route… keep these bastards guessing.'

I quickly put a plan together. Rather than continuing along the cut-through or breaking left to proceed down Lockhart or Jaffe – what they'd be expecting – no, I would take the alley two blocks and make a right onto Hennessy. I'd be past all the clubs and if I got a shift on, I might make it home unnoticed.

By fuck, I was scared… absolutely fucking terrified.

Once there, I would enter my apartment block from the far end of Jaffe – they wouldn't anticipate that.

If I got that far in one piece, I'd take the lift to two floors below mine and then the backstairs up to the roof – outmanoeuvring any lookout. I could shin down the waste pipe and peer through my window to see how many were lying in ambush.

Gabriel and Anil I didn't reckon to be a problem. A quick butt in the face would put an end to their Bollywood dream – not that I wanted to hurt either of them, especially the boy.

'Fuck him… he ain't gonna do you any favours.'

But if he was going to get involved in adult business and try to get all clever with me to impress his dad, then he wasn't about to do me any favours and there was no way I would go down without a fight.

I wished I had Gabriel's screwdriver. After Drik and Chee Chu's snooping, I'd left it at home, replacing it with something more tactful – a Mini Maglite attached to a foot-and-a-half of chain. No one could criticise me for carrying this. It was simply a smaller version of the torch

Dai Su always carried in the club, and we all knew its true purpose – no Edison in that equation.

I reckoned I could take out a *maa jai* or two as well, if it came down to it. What I would do then, though, God only knows. Grab my gear and head for the airport? Telephone the embassy and tell them to get me the fuck out of Dodge?

I began placing one step in front of another, rolling the edges of my feet, commando-style, inching forward into the terror and flinching worse than Scooby-Doo at every noise shooting out of the ether.

Was that the sound of a scurrying rat or a triad moving position under the cover of darkness? Cats wailing or *maa jais* signalling my approach?

The conversation I could hear in the window above had to be members of the Cult angrily discussing my escape from the club, barking orders down the telephone, telling the tongs to spread out, to keep their eyes peeled and death-by-a-thousand-cuts when they caught me.

I was shaking, my heart pounding a mass of drug-and-fear-induced adrenalin through my veins to send me up to a place I'd never been before… *a place where I looked down from above the rooftops to see a young man I felt strangely akin to… threading his way through a tunnel laden with suffocating menace… violent killers… laired mutants… bonded by a web of horror and permeated by the terror…* and it wasn't until nearing the end of the second alleyway that I came back down, yet as frantic as ever.

'*Vary your route…*'

Instinct told me to cut right onto Hennessy. As I quickened along it, everything seemed normal – the usual taxis buzzing by, no hectic neon, just a subtle ambience created by streetlights and restaurant windows. It felt somewhat reassuring, but not enough to counterbalance the fear.

I stuck to my plan and was soon inching down the waste pipe towards my window, high above a grisly demise outside the building yet only in trepidation of the possible one within and *just* wondering if that bastard, Drik, might be playing with me.

I peered around the frame – 'You *bastard*! You *fucking bastard*!' – to find the scene exactly as I'd left it.

There were no Indians or triads lying in wait for a bloody massacre, only a length of bamboo, standing proud and doing the job I intended it to do – wedging the door of my room shut. The Indians, like Elvis, had left the fucking building.

The Murder

WHEN I ARRIVED AT WORK the next evening, no one mentioned my disappearing act. I suppose it should have struck me as strange.

I didn't ask Drik what the fuck he was playing at. I wouldn't give him the satisfaction. He had no idea about me – about who I *really* was. I wouldn't play his misanthropic games anymore, a slave to his sad existence, cliquey riddles and wild goose chases.

The club was filling, mainly with Chinese. Being Saturday, it would be full of the usual suspects by midnight. As it was, the techno-pop blared through the bar regardless with the disco lights in tow.

Dai Su had the night off. Paul Eng was over at the Pink Panther and wouldn't be in until later, and 'Roy', a Chinese manager who only worked on Saturdays, stood at the bar, chatting with Chee Chu and an attractive local girl. Although I didn't know her, something told me she was as devious as anthrax and not the sort you'd introduce to your parents… unless you hated them.

Roy was a tall, clean-cut dude in his forties. He spoke English well, and I felt we got on okay. They seemed to sense me watching them as I noticed a couple of surreptitious glances in my direction.

A moment later, the girl approached, making a 'play' of fussing in her handbag for her mobile phone, pretending she wasn't looking where she was going before lurching *two* steps into me.

'Pok gai, Gweilo!' she spat.

'*Sorry*, love!' I replied. 'I'm afraid I don't speak Chinese.'

Oooph! She rushed back over to her compatriots, initiating a frantic discussion and lots of pointing.

Before I knew it, Roy and Chee Chu bounded over, looking like hounds arriving at a crossroads desperate to pick up the fox's scent – in this blooding, the one in play so obviously me. Standing closer than perverts on the tube, they continued their frenzied discourse and then whipped out their mobiles and began stabbing at the keypads.

As they began barking orders down the line, my imagination simmered in concern, my senses stewing in trepidation. The pantomime of glancing expectantly up the stairs told me to expect the Family – and I don't mean Mrs Chee Chu and the kids.

'I make wun phoncall… effrywun in Wan Chai come heeya… kiwll him!'

I didn't know if this was this was a piss-take, or perhaps I really had fucked up, so I retired to the stairwell, my heart thumping in my chest.

Within a minute, I looked up to see two mean-arsed tongs taking the stairs sideways, three steps at a time, giving me the distinct impression this wasn't the right time to be playing around with hand signs.

'Fuck you, *Gweilo!'* the first one levelled, the insinuation more in his hate-filled eyes, the second mumbling something in Chinese as they went inside.

The near-same scenario played out again… again… and again, until the bar had filled with the hardest men Hong Kong had to offer, all leering at me as if I was a done deal. The nervous glances of David, the owner, told me something was going down in the *Dai Lo's* absence and he felt far from comfortable about it.

I had to face reality… I was going to die this night. Judgement Day had arrived, and once again, adrenalin rushed terror around my body, my heartbeat crashing like Wagner's cymbals.

I looked up at the familiar rectangle of the top doorway. Someone stood smoking a cigarette just out of sight to the right-hand side, the smoke wafting across the blackened backdrop with dramatic effect, telling me straight: *sik yin* ruled the day in Wan Chai… and I fucking didn't.

SMASH! A beer bottle whizzed down the stairs, past my ear, and shattered against the wall, the shards landing like hailstones around my feet.

I didn't flinch. A beer bottle wasn't my problem tonight. It was the agenda behind it. It felt as though the whole of the nightclub district was out for payback and the next visitor only served to confirm this. It was Darren – the guy who lived with his cousin, Julian, the friend of the *Dai Lo*.

'Alright, *mate*!' He blew the words into my face, his voice saturated with sarcasm. 'Do you remember you told me all the triads wear white tracksuit tops and trainers?' He stood there, three steps up, gloating like a fucker. 'Well, *looky here*!'

A quick skeg sent my panic crashing full force into the stark reality that *he too* wore the signature get-up.

How *stupid* was I to trust him with my observations? He must have listened as though I were Little Red Riding Hood blabbing all to Grandmother – only the wolf was in his true clothing and in this thing as deep as the *Titanic*'s keel.

'Could it *really* be that I'm about to die?' I wondered. 'It's been a good life. It's got to end sometime. And if that's tonight, it'll be with dignity and a *fucking* big smile!'

My thinking helped. The fishing boat, smashed down and temporarily submerged, had righted itself but still lay dead in the water awaiting the final black curtain. Its captain, although scared, wasn't about to jump ship, wasn't afraid to die... only of acting like a coward.

'You're going to get it now,' said Drik, as he joined me in the stairwell.

'What's that, Drik?' I was pissed off with this jumped-up little prick.

'I said you're going to get it tonight, Chris,' he replied, calm but slimy.

'What the *fuck* are you talking about?'

'Do you remember borrowing a hundred bucks off Alex and not bothering to pay it back? *Oooh*.' He added a headshake to his attempt at a reprimand.

'Drik, you know *fuck* all! I paid it back the next day out of the advance Paul gave me. Alex is a mate – that's why he lent it to me.'

'What about the time you told Chee Chu that Johnny takes drugs?'

Shit! That caught me off guard.

'I… didn't *tell* him he takes drugs… I *asked* him if he did… trying to get a feel for the customers, like a doorman's *supposed* to.'

I found myself in an awful moment of clarity. I could see now *what* all this was over, *where* it was heading… *and that the girl had been the bait!*

The four-minute warning had sounded. The beast was on its way, the hellhounds straining at the leash, but I wasn't about to let Drik or any of these thugs see the panic balling inside me.

More expats and Chinese flooded into the club, loathing in their stares and poison in their comments. 'Payback time, mate!' suggested one, '*Gweilo* gonna die!' another, and this was in addition to the abuse wafted down from above by ghosts I couldn't see.

But the next thing that Drik pulled me up on put the final nail in my coffin: 'And *who* were you supposed to meet in the park this morning?'

As he looked at me, contempt radiating from his narrow eyes, the finality of my situation slammed home: *Johnny Horsepower!* In my bid to escape the club last night, I'd forgotten all about him!

'You fucking *idiot*, Thrall!' I was so angry. *Gutted* to think of the poor bloke sat waiting for his mate Chris to come along, as promised. But – *'Fuck it!'* – at least I had arranged to meet Johnny. How many times had Drik or any of these other bastards done that?

He left me alone, a condemned man marinating in eleventh-hour fear. The disco beats thumped away with indifference, far detached from my microcosm of horror, like in-flight entertainment on a jumbo jet spiralling towards the ocean. It had come down to the wire. Chris Thrall, the clothes I stood up in, a hovel of a room and a drug-sapped existence, against the wrath of Wan Chai. Yet, despite my meth-soaked mind in hyperdrive, I came up with a few conclusions…

The first being that these idiots were *fucking* day-trippers – white jeans and unsuitable heels, disposable barbecues and personalities on a fraudulent foray to Fantasy Fucking Island. *Spectators* that needed to belong to a lousy gang and play pathetic games to feel they had a life and too parochial to realise they were messing with a Royal Marine – a Royal Marine *fucking* Commando – one who'd stared down the barrel of a gun on more than one occasion and laughed his arse off when he did. One who viewed death as an occupational hazard when your occupation is leading a full-on-and-mental life.

What were they expecting me to do? Make a mad dash for freedom and bury myself in Mother's apron? They were deluded if they did.

It was time to fight, and the next chancer to look at me sideways would be wearing a fucking lectern, the one after that achieving lifelong VIP status in Club Crappy Nemo when I sunk the entry stamp an inch into his forehead.

Also, this might be the Hong Kong underground where people operated below the radar of the law – even the law operated below the radar of the law – but the club still had a number of tourists inside. They weren't going to sit around writing postcards and drinking iced tea the next day, having witnessed a doorman's untimely demise.

Nor would the people around Wan Chai keep schtum after seeing me turned into a jigsaw puzzle – not *all* of them. What did they plan on saying to Interpol? 'Oh *yes*, Officer. I saw him taking a crate of empties into the back room and I think he *errm... spontaneously combusted... or was abducted* by *aliens*.'

Nah! I could see it now. These vile reprobates were messing with me. This entire thing – from the moment the girl fell into me, the exaggerated phone calls, Drik's snipes, the triads and the expats chipping in their ten cents' worth, the flying beer bottle – had been a set-up. Degenerate pack animals dying to see me flash yellow and wrap myself around the nearest copper so they could all have a laugh.

Only, the schoolyard bullies had underestimated me. So now, it was my turn to enter the game – what with face being a two-way thing.

I was about to enter the bar when a movement caught my eye. I looked up to see Nicole making her way hesitantly down the stairs with the look of a frightened fawn. I had a hunch what she was about to say.

'*Creese*, they're *fucking* with you!' she whispered. '*Please*, don't say I told you! *Please*, they'll kill me!'

The poor girl was terrified. Fear hissed in her delivery. She'd risked it all... *for me!* The life of a Filipina in Wan Chai was nothing, worth less than a discarded cigarette butt. What a brave kid she was, a true friend amongst phonies.

I *freakin'* knew it! *Fucking Day Tickets!* So now it was my turn to have some fun.

Drik came back out. 'So, are you *scaaared*?' he asked, his mockery pitiful, his delusion as laughable as a shrimp taking on a killer whale.

'*Scared*, Drik?' I replied, summoning a look of bafflement to make Oliver Hardy proud. 'Have I *missed* something? Don't worry, I'll take care of you if you're *scaaared*.'

Then slapping his pint-sized head, I walked into the bar area, impervious to the thirty sets of eyes throwing daggers at me.

I stood there, gazing around and *laughing* at them – at least on the inside – frickin' gangsters with their slavish expat cronies and ridiculous bloody coughs. Then giving them a grin to take to the bank, I did a Michael Jackson spin in time with the music… and then danced the jig of my life.

Come 4am, the punters had thinned out, the thugs and their *gweilo* bedfellows too. I stood at the bar, talking to a couple of English blokes who worked in construction on the new airport. 'I've not long left the Royal Marines,' said the younger of the two.

'Oh, I did a bit of time myself.'

'*Yeeaah?*' He eyed me warily.

I counted in my head, 'One, two, thr—'

'What *unit* were you in?'

Fuck me! A graduate of the Knocker School of Paranoia, or what! What was it with these marines? That no one else could *possibly* be cool enough to be in their club? It wasn't *that* good. I'd much rather have been an astronaut, a dolphin trainer or the Milky Bar Kid.

'*Forty*-two Commando,' I replied.

No bootneck would ever refer to the unit as that. It was always Four-Two, and only civilians and imitators called it Forty-Two. But the guy was as dumb as a doorstop and couldn't see I was lampooning him. He threw a '*T'huh!*' to his mate and talked down to me for the rest of that short conversation.

Paul Eng came over to say that as the club had emptied I could go home. Walking along Jaffe, I noticed a sleek black Mercedes pull away from the kerb and begin stalking me through the morning-after litter.

As the terror rose up inside me, rekindling a fire not long put out, I decided to give them the slip by scooting up a back alleyway…

I awoke late after my ordeal. Something bothered me. It wasn't that a check of the G-shock told me I should have been back at work, or that the drugs had once again reduced me to a shivering, starving and confused wreck. Something awful happened last night – and not just the shit that went down in the club.

I hopped down from my bamboo bunk, landing unsteady on my feet, filled with nervous uncertainty and fearful anticipation. Lighting a smoke, I noticed a photo on the page of an old newspaper on the floor.

'No…!'

'*Mercedes… chopping blades… woman… baby.*'

A massive wave of *déjà vu* sent me sinking to the floor.

'*Surely* not…!'

'*Alleyway… backstairs… ladder.*'

Haltingly, I drew the yellowing sheet across the matting.

'It *can't* be… *can* it?'

'*Falling… falling… umph!*'

Anxiety erupted.

Horror consumed me.

'I was *there*…'

'Torch… meat… death.'

My bedtime perusing had been the coverage of a particularly savage triad attack – a woman and baby hacked to pieces and dumped in a shaft on one of the colony's rooftops.

I fought to calm myself, to work out how this had something to do with me. 'Did *I* cause *this*…?'

The full colour, the blood, the mutilation jumping up off the page, I felt sure I'd been there *with* them at some point.

Stephan had said, '*And do you know what happens to people who interfere with triad business… they end up DEAD!*' He knew something like this would happen.

I checked the date on the paper.

'Thank *fuck*…!'

It was *three* days before I'd arrived in Hong Kong.

I was relieved yet traumatised at the same time. Relieved the vividness had to be a figment of my fractured subconscious, yet deeply disturbed my life had descended into such drug-warped Asian chaos that the boundaries between life and death and reality and fantasy had blurred to the point of being dangerous.

I called the club to tell them I would be late. Paul Eng answered. 'Don' worry,' he said, almost cheerfully. 'Tekk the nigh' off.'

That was one problem sorted – even if I was forgetting it was Sunday, my night off anyway – but I still had another to deal with.

I wasn't going to be the laughing stock of this town. I might disrespect those clowns but I still had respect for myself and it was about time I faced up to the fact I had a problem with drugs. And if I was going to get the regard back that I had once been so proud of – the doorman that everyone knew and liked – then I had to knock the meth on the head.

With that in mind, my stash now gone, I climbed back up onto my bed, pulled the grey blanket across my midriff and, wondering how I would cope with my new resolution, drifted off to sleep.

'Drik, I might be a little tired for a couple of days. Do you know what I'm saying?'

I hoped he did – after all the shit he'd given me.

Getting up for work hadn't been too bad after almost thirty-six hours sleep, yet when I arrived at the club, the tiredness began to roundhouse me. Yawning incessantly, I had to go into the back room to try to sort it out.

Despite my intentions, my body couldn't handle it. I needed at least two or three days to replenish my reserves. I sat on a plastic drinks crate, desperately trying to get it together. I must been there for a couple of hours, my head rolling around, when Sidney entered. He said, '*Errh,* Quiss'a, the boss say, heeya is tree-tousand dollar. He say you don' nee' to work heeya anymore.'

'Sure, Sid,' I replied, thinking what a shit Drik was for not covering for me, and feeling like death, I stood up and left by the fire exit.

Walking along Lockhart Road, I came across Johnny Horsepower chatting to his fellow street dwellers. His eyes lit up and rushing towards me, he began to rabbit on in his usual taxing banter. 'I ge' you da wun,' he said, 'dat make you many hosspowers.'

It was too much. I'd had enough of trying to understand the complex riddle of Wan Chai life, and now I'd had enough of Johnny. I snapped.

'*Johnny!* Can't you see I *can't* understand what you're *saying!* Then I ran off up the road.

I found myself in a remote part of the town. Leaning against a shop wall, I slid down onto the litter-strewn pavement, not knowing *where* I was in every sense – just that I'd cocked up yet another job and this was the lowest part of my life. But *hey!* Even though I'd managed to get fired from the Last Chance Saloon, I still respected myself – so *fuck* it! Nobody said life was easy.

Squares of pink paper covered in red Chinese writing lay all around me. I didn't know what they were, but they littered the pavements all over Hong Kong – maybe lotto cards or something. I felt sure they contained the kind of esoteric information needed to work out this weird circus, so I shoved a few into my pocket and set off for home – going via Mack Zane's place first, of course.

I found Mack labouring away with Diego, Clara's brother, on a superbly built counter for Mack's DJ decks. I marvelled at how he was able to accomplish such an undertaking, particularly as he got less sleep than I did and was the marketing manager for a busy postal service.

Their construction was a thing of beauty, with chromed-steel legs, glass shelving and an electric-blue-varnished wooden top that gleamed lustrously under the spotlights in his tiny apartment.

Kay was a pretty and voluptuous Chinese acquaintance of his. We hit it off immediately. She'd laughed when I said the wick of the candle on the coffee table was a bird in flight... only I *wasn't* joking!

Having smoked some of our host's hospitality, Diego, Kay and I set off to walk back to Wan Chai – only Diego, squinting at what was left of the turquoise rings surrounding my mad pupils, insisted we take a cab.

As we left, Mack, kind as ever, told me to turn up at his office the next day as he needed a temp to do some typing for a mail shot.

When the car pulled up outside my building, Kay suggested we go inside and roll a joint. Before I knew it, we were sitting on my bunk and doing just that. 'Wow!' She tapped the bamboo. 'You live like Chiniss!'

In the morning, I suited for work and saw her to the door – under the disgusted stare of Gabriel, who I guessed to be a pick-and-choose religious fanatic, a misogynist or a eunuch. Fortunately, he and Anil slept somewhere else most nights, although I had no idea where, as I didn't care to ask.

My day at Mack's office probably didn't produce the results his employers had intended. We took a bus back to his place at midday. Mack had our lunch ready and wrapped in silver foil… which we duly unwrapped and smoked through his water pipe.

The resulting paranoia combined with my crappy typing meant any recipient of the two letters I managed to knock out would have had to be an expert code breaker to decipher whatever message it contained.

When I got back to the flat, Gabriel was crouching in the bathroom, trying to fix the blockage in the drainage hole. In the end, he stuck a length of wood down it and smacked it so hard with a hammer that the pipe outside detached from the building and now our dirty water poured into the alleyway below. So happy with achieving the dizzy heights of cowboy plumber, he pranced around the front room giggling in glee, until I blurted out, 'Great! Now that's fixed, you can *fuck* off!'

I honestly hadn't meant to, but I was still upset they were invading my privacy and it came shooting out of my subconscious.

He puffed out his pigeon chest and waddled across the room towards me. With his feet pointing outwards, he looked like a fat duck with a grievance. Bracing up to me like a prize-fighting banana, he swung the hammer to within an inch of my head, drawing it back and forward, as if lining up on a difficult nail, while trying to stare me out.

I shook my head and went on into my room.

It was weird, though. As he gave me the evils, I'd looked into his eyes and they weren't right. His pupils had cloudy bits in them, like ice floating in glasses of cola. I wondered if he might have cataracts. I remember reading something about Indians going blind from drinking homemade booze laced with methanol or some such thing. I felt guilty I'd been so hard on the little fella.

Seeing as though work at Mack's was a no-goer, that a meteoric rise to Postmaster General was indeed unlikely, I resolved to check the *Post* for teaching positions.

In my two-minute interview with Mr Lee, the owner of the Hong Kong English Language School, the major obstacle was the question: 'Are you English?'

Having navigated that one successfully, I found myself duly appointed as teacher of English to Class Nine of Kwai Chung Primary School in the New Territories. Further helmsmanship saw me steering a course towards the Big Apple that evening, looking forward to getting deep down and funky, only so high on meth I needed a ladder to think.

On the corner of Lockhart and Luard, Chee Chu stood under the awning of a convenience kiosk. 'Where you work now?' he asked, looking reticent and awkward.

'Over there,' I replied, pointing a casual arm north – in my mind, obviously in the direction of Kwai Chung Primary School, ten miles away – but noting as I drifted on by like a zombie on a conveyor belt he was staring with a bemused look at the fruit vendor's stall across the road.

The Killing House

'HELLO, CLASS NINE!' I greeted the line of six-year-olds, pulling my best monkey face. It didn't just get Class Nine giggling – like school children, as the expression goes – it got all the kids doing it as they queued in rows on the playground waiting for their teachers to lead them to class.

'My name is Mister Thrall. But you can call me Quiss!' Now that I was in charge of the Youth of Today's education, there'd be none of that draconian nonsense.

Mr Lee told me I would be teaching Monday-to-Friday for two hours in the afternoon. Arming me with a curriculum book, he arranged a meet with Josh, another of his expat teachers assigned to Kwai Chung Primary. Exiting the MTR station and walking through the high-rise blocks towards the school, we got to know one another.

Josh had been teaching at the school for over a year and seemed the type of young man who'd come to the territory for a daring work/travel experience. He certainly wasn't a Wan Chai crazy person – more the sort to take his role extremely seriously, then go for an après-work jog, write to his MP, knock up a *coq au vin*, read Hemingway, say a few prayers and go to sleep a contented man. But as it turned out, we did have one thing in common...

Josh asked how my Hong Kong experience was going. Obviously, I was hesitant to tell him about the secret brotherhood and the weird expat cabal. I thought he'd think me crazy, but it was exactly the opposite. When I said, 'I've had a few problems with triads, but you probably don't know what I'm on about,' by crikey did he snap a crank, stopping dead on the pavement and giving me the three sixes.

'*You* think I don't know about *triads*, Chris! I was in a restaurant once, yeah? Normal scenario, place packed out, people smiling, then all of a sudden, on like… some *invisible* cue, everyone stood up and threw everything they could at one guy. Chairs, tables, crockery – *everything*! It was the most horrific thing I've ever seen. So *don't* tell me about *triads*!'

I made up my mind never to tell Josh about triads. It seemed a bit of a sore point.

Not as sore as when it came to leading our classes off to their rooms. All the other teachers seemed to go for the traditional approach: say hello to class, beckon class to follow Fount of all Wisdom and march class to the school building. I couldn't see what possible benefit this had for the Future of Tomorrow, unless they were in training for the military or off to Borstal.

No, better to lead them off at a trot in the opposite direction for an impromptu lap of the playing field, our arms out and bodies weaving from side to side like kamikaze pilots, which, from their reaction of giggles and furtive glances at one another, I had a feeling no teacher had done before.

But coming back in to land at Academia Central, I caught the look Josh was giving me, and for the second time in a day, I felt it wasn't the most ingratiating one I'd ever received.

The class went well, nonetheless. As the cutest kiddywinks took their seats, I looked in the curriculum book and put some serious consideration into whether Billy the Brown Goat knew anything about verbs and nouns – being a farm animal an' all that – and reckoned if this was the case then he was a few steps ahead of me. I threw it back in my briefcase, deciding if I ever met a class of six-year-old Chinese kids that wanted to know more about English grammar than a twenty-six-year-old native speaker then I would let rip with the goat and any other farmyard beast I thought might be of assistance.

Instead, I opted for a game of 'name that mime', lining the kids up at the front of the classroom and then mimicking some easy-to-guess objects and actions – a set of chopsticks, eating a banana and so forth. The first to guess the English words could take a step backwards. It was only a game – something to gauge their understanding of the language and appreciation of teachers who do handstands in the classroom – but this didn't stop them from taking it *extremely* seriously and cheating like a bunch of linguistic criminals. When one of them got the answer right and took a step to the rear, the rest discreetly shuffled backwards. It was a terrible state of affairs. There was no honour with this lot.

One girl, La La Wing, guessed a particularly difficult mime correctly, so I said, *'Ho ho!'* and went to shake her hand.

Only shaking hands is a Western adult protocol. She looked at my palm in bemusement, until a cohort whispered that this was a *gweilo* thing. Then little La La checked herself and, timid as a mouse with issues and eyes as wide as pies, tentatively placed her tiny mitt in mine. As we shook like *real* men, a special part of history was born.

There were only two glitches in my perfect life. The first being Billy – not the goat, but Billy Chen – a slightly chubby kid, taller and more boisterous than the others, who came to my attention with his incessant talking and disregard for anything I said. If I had to deploy child psychology, I would say the rest of the class came from families that instilled a Confucian ethic of respect Teacher and Teacher will teach you the language needed to get ahead in business. Whereas I reckoned Billy's family probably told him to tell the *gweilo* to go fuck himself.

I was writing something on the blackboard when off he went, *again.* Miss Lin, the head of English, had given me strict instructions to send any misbehaving pupil to the headmaster. There was no way I would do that, though. I remembered the abuse passed off as 'punishment' in my first school – and the kid who dropped the plates in the restaurant.

Instead, I indicated with my eyes to the propeller ceiling fan whirring above our heads. Then I told him, *'Shhhh!'* and mimicked lifting him up by the waist and sticking his head into the spinning blades, adding *'Dhrdhrdhrdhrdhrdhr!'* while vibrating my head like Wile E. Coyote. It had the little tackers in stitches – except Billy who, lapping up the attention, looked around the class with the regal regard of a conquering emperor having his balls massaged and then continued his conversation from where *I'd* rudely interrupted him.

The second blot on my beautiful Hong Kong landscape was another problem child: my inner one. Despite my resolution to give up the drugs, now that I was free of Club Nemo's reproachful gaze I didn't feel the same pressure – although putting the triads to one side, there was still this global conspiracy operating all around me.

It hit me on the MTR going home that afternoon. I sat in the carriage wishing I could be inconspicuous, but as a *gweilo* higher than the Himalayas, sweat cascading like Niagara Falls, I couldn't have felt more self-conscious. I'm sure prying eyes were on me, and burying myself in my Cantonese book, I wished they weren't.

Back in the privacy of my room, the feeling of constant scrutiny lifted off my shoulders like a flock of seagulls from a rubbish dump – until I went up on the roof to practise kung fu.

Adopting a floating-fag-butt stinging-paper-cut pose, I was about to put an evil overlord to bed with a Shaolin high-kick when I happened to look at a window in the building opposite and see three lads finding my performance hilarious. I gave them a friendly wave, only it was returned with further mockery and some unbecoming – some would say offensive – hand gestures, so I motioned them to stay where they were.

Rushing into my room, I grabbed the dictionary and looked for the Cantonese word for 'belief'. It wasn't in there, so I settled for 'confident', *dzi son*, scribbling the characters in bold on a piece of cardboard with a red marker before going back up to my audience.

Strangely, they continued to laugh at stage one of my plan and carried on gesturing wildly, so I ignored their ignorance and went to stage two. After placing my hands on the three-foot-high parapet surrounding the rooftop, I casually pushed up into a handstand and held it there for twenty seconds while taking in the miniature street scene below. Then after flipping back down, I looked over to the panel of judges to see middle fingers replaced by frantically hoiking thumbs and scornful looks replaced by ones of outright astonishment.

I wasn't sure what happened during the twenty-odd hours that had passed since leaving the school – other than an edgy train journey and some aerial acrobatics. I vaguely remembered trying to put the air conditioner in my room back together, most of which now lay in pieces on the floor.

I don't know why I'd taken it apart. There wasn't anything wrong with it and I never used it anyway.

Reassembling it seemed a straightforward job: look at aircon, find non-existent problem, fix it and then put all the bits back where you found them. But as I looked inside the main unit – the part still bolted to the wall – a whole world of shenanigans was going on inside and something told me I had to check it out as it played a huge part in the global mystery.

Inspecting the unit's louvres, I suddenly understood the meaning of life and my purpose in it –

'It's all in there... the meaning of life... your purpose in it.'

– for running the length of these slats was a story playing out in shapes, textures and layers. Pure *frickin'* theatre!

Set in the near, middle and far distance along each blade was a battle scene... or it may have been a fairground... I'm not sure as they kept merging with each other and none of the protagonists would shut up and give me a break. It was like Lilliput in *Gulliver's Travels*. There were kings and queens who were fidgety, battle tanks made out of balsa, and knights without horses. The horseless bit wasn't right – not right for anyone. It was up to *me* to fix it.

'Fix the horses for the riders... or the whole thing grinds to a halt.... use logistics... bring them onto the field or the show's all for nothing... you gotta play your part... everyone's relying on you?'

It was up to me. I was in charge of bringing the whole thing together for *everyone*. It was crunch time and the world relied on me...

Now it was late morning and I had to force myself away from the air-conditioned theatre and go into the bathroom to splash some water over my body, have a shave and then dress for class. I pushed myself to focus so I didn't sidetrack to some irrelevant venture like fixing an electrical appliance I never used.

I ended up feeling a little disappointed. Not only had I spent the best part of a day with my head inside an air cooler *and* not achieved anything, but the whole circus had upped sticks and left town. I peered at the louvres to see that all of the weird and wonderful characters and astonishing scenes I'd witnessed had turned into patches of dirt, dust and grime that had accumulated over years and blended with flecks of blue paint left behind by an over-zealous decorator.

This time, having led them directly to class to avoid the wrath of Josh the Just, I stood in front of my desk, greeting each of the tots.

In came Billy Chen, looking so pleased with himself, as if he'd just strapped a firework to a cat and stuck it in the microwave, and behind him, La La Wing, the epitome of cuteness, knee-high to a pygmy and wearing brown-framed glasses with her pigtails. As the class filed to their seats, she broke away and walked over. Then, with a resolute look on her little face, she shoved her hand out.

Well, it baffled me – until she frowned at her halfwit teacher and mimicked shaking hands!

Being a beautiful summer's day in the Fragrant Harbour, I deemed it an opportune one to instigate a conspiracy of child-size proportions. As a former member of an elite fighting force, I felt it only right to instruct these tiny tots in the art of conducting covert operations behind enemy lines.

'...*Sssh!*' I put my finger to my lips. 'Who wants to play *outside?*'

After a few whispers of their own, my platoon slowly raised their hands, a mix of trepidation and animated smiles creeping across impish faces. 'Okay... leave your bags... follow me... *sssh!*'

Having peeked up and down the corridor, I instructed them to get down on all fours and we began our long march to liberty.

We made our way past the other classrooms, the kids giving each other explicit and hush-hush instructions to keep both quiet and down below the level of the windows. I had to chuckle when creeping past Justful Josh's room and hearing him bashing out Billy the Brown Goat rhetoric for all its worth.

Finally, the last of my troopers made it out of the main door and we took our first sweet breaths of freedom. Having found a spot on the school field, we did the mime game again. After that, I told them the story of how Dennis the Dragon nearly ate Billy the Brown Goat, but luckily Billy the Kid stepped in and rescued him, and even Billy listened this time, silent and wide-eyed in awe.

Everything went swimmingly during those first four days. I loved the kids and they loved me – or at least my pedagogic bent. On the Friday, though, the swimmer nearly sank.

I was standing at the front of the class when I heard a police siren in the distance. As it slowly got louder and louder, panic welled up inside me, rooting me to the spot as rivulets of terror-charged sweat exploded from my pores.

I tried not to make it obvious I was looking out of the window, but as I did, the squad car came into view over the brow of a nearby hill. It was heading straight towards the school, its blue light flashing with single-minded intent, its wailing scream informing all around… *it was coming to get the gweilo!*

And this wasn't about dissing Billy the Brown Goat or sneaking the kids outside to play. No, the coppers didn't care about brown goats, or any other coloured goat for that matter, and playing outside wasn't a crime. No, the copper's sole concern was that the devil man had broken the colony's golden rule: *Don't do the drugs!*

A little girl raised her hand. 'Teacher… *errh, Quiss'a*, are you okay?'

No, I was far from okay.

I stood there, motionless, with the fear of a man about to be executed, my mind predicting the scene about to take place… *The sound of sirens and screeching tyres filling the school car park, the frantic shouts of 'Gweilo hai bin do'a? (Where's the devil man?)' and then the Goon Squad rampaging along the corridor like a pack of relentless Rottweilers with radios blaring odiousness and evil… Josh the Just bursting out of his classroom like a hate-filled hernia, gesticulating like a football club manager on FA Cup day and screaming, 'He also took them around the playing field and he's not allowed to do that! I'll be a witness, Officer! So help me God, I will! It's hard labour for life for that fucking bastard!'*

But fortunately – *'Phew!'* – it never happened. I stood there until the sirens moved off into the distance, then went back to teaching my class.

Later that afternoon I relaxed in my room, gazing out of the window, enjoying the feeling of being high and happy at the start of the weekend. I saw a small brown bird flit from its perch on one of the exterior air-conditioning units on the building opposite to another on the adjacent high-rise, then to a window ledge below that. I watched it repeat the exact same flight path *three* times.

Something struck me as strange, something not *quite* right. The movement appeared to be mechanical, like a set routine, reminding me of an aircraft carrier game I got for Christmas as a kid, where I'd catapult a fighter jet off the ship's deck, sending it shooting along an elevated wire.

A movement in the window opposite caught my eye. It was the old bald-headed chap, the one with the feng shui mirror hanging outside his window to ward off evil spirits. Yet again, he was shuffling around his apartment, mysteriously, like a hermit.

'Ahh…!' It suddenly made sense. This bird was on a *wire*! It was *robotic*! And I bet the old boy was the *controller*! I'd uncovered a part of the puzzle I'd been blind to: *freakin'* puppets! 'Of *course!*… where did puppetry originate?'

'In Asia…'

'It *was* in Asia… wasn't it?' I reckoned it was. 'Those shadow puppets from *Malaysia…*?'

'Indonesia…'

'Wasn't it one of those places?… I saw it in a movie—?'

'The Year of Living Dangerously…!'

'Yes!… *The Year of Living Dangerously*… these people are masters at this kind of stuff—'

'Puppet masters…'

'Of *course!*… how *bloody* clever!…what else is going on here that's all a grand show for the public?'

I turned my attention to a restaurant courtyard backing onto the alleyway below.

Six cats lazed in the sun, appearing as tiny balls of fluff from this height. Only, when one of them moved it was the same set play as the bird. Instead of standing up on bended legs, effortlessly as you'd expect, their limbs appeared to be rigid, seeing them move awkwardly with an *eee… eee… eee* like Muffin the Mule. Then they would go *ziiiiiiiiiiiip* right across the courtyard at a uniform speed and in a dead-straight line, as if automated and on wires, before laying down again in the same staggered manner.

'Puppets… took you a long time to suss that one…. eh?'

'Yeah… it did!… I can't believe it!'

'Look at the restaurant worker… he chops twice at the meat then opens the back door and shuts it… twice at the meat then opens the back door and shuts it.'

'Yeah!… I see it!… he's on strings too!'

'On a loop… '

'On a loop!… that's *just* amazing!'

Intrigued, I must have watched for hours, as it was getting dark. Now I understood it was all one great big show for the public, I couldn't wait to uncover more.

Gabriel and Anil were in the flat, so I put my foray on hold until they went to bed – I didn't want them interrupting my fun. I spent the time drawing a picture of Bruce Lee on the door, copied from a magazine I'd found in the junk stash. But just as I was priding myself on my effort, I realised the nursery rhyme going around in my head had an important meaning.

'Jack and Jill went up the hill… '

'Why…?'

'Think about it… there must be a reason.'

'Ah!… they had to play their part… yeah… right!'

'That's why there's a Rhyme and a Reason… '

I started writing out the reason for Jack and Jill's hill-climbing venture on the wall, but all the other bloody nursery rhymes sidetracked me and I had to write them down too – *'…the writing's on the wall… '* – as well as the proverbs that insisted on interrupting my thought process.

I really felt as though I was onto *something*, that I was finally getting *somewhere*.

Sure that the Indians were asleep, I crept out of the flat. Excited and buzzing like a bumblebee on an electric fence, I had to go walkabout and explore my high-rise abode in order to solve this Asian odyssey once and for all.

I knew now that all around me was a show of majestic proportions: the dogs, cats, birds and chefs, people in windows, the lighting, *everything*.

The clues were there and it was up to me to piece them together. The guidebook said Hong Kong culture is black and white.

'*Simple choice... eh?*'

It seemed either you saw this thing or you didn't.

In the darkness, I edged my way up the stairs towards the roof, my body tingling with the excitement of espionage, but as I neared the top a shout of '*HO LANG LOY!*' made me jump out of my skin.

'Who the *fuck* was that?' I wondered, stopping dead. As my heart pounded, I tried to work out if it was the mysterious rooftop dweller or the old man who slept on the stairs.

Ho lang loy meant 'very beautiful girl'. Did someone think *I* was a very beautiful girl? Maybe it was the old boy talking in his sleep *about* a beautiful girl. Regardless, it frightened the life out of me, so I turned around and eased back down.

It wasn't a major problem, though, because there was plenty to check out from the windows in the hallway.

I looked over to a towering skyscraper in Causeway Bay, immediately eye-catching as it was lit up by multicoloured spotlights.

'*MGM Studios... their headquarters... maybe Universal Studios... look at the lights... the opening sequence to the movies... they know all about putting on a show... special effects... that's their job.*'

I gazed at it for ages, sure at one point I saw the lion's face appear on it – the MGM lion – but then I don't think it did.

Instead, something told me it must be the Empire State Building in *King Kong* and that Kong was going to come scrambling around it at any moment clutching Fay Wray in his powerful but adoring grip.

It was fascinating, as though the whole world, Hollywood included, was behind the scenes of this majestic and monster-sized performance, one you had to know was there before you could begin to appreciate it.

In the window opposite, a young woman sat in the glow of a computer screen. I wondered why she sat there for so long and if she was communicating with someone in my building. She never once looked up, and I wondered *why* not?

Below her, a middle-aged man sat on the bog in full view of the Hong Kong public. He looked like an inmate in a panoptic prison. With no frosted glass to provide even a token of modesty and the toilet itself appearing elevated, it gave the impression of a ruler sitting on a porcelain throne, a sovereign of the sewers. I racked my brain trying to work out what part he played in this subterranean theatre, observing him intently to see if I could see any strings.

A movement above and to the right caught my eye: a man laying a *coffin* lid against the window *while looking right at me* and laughing such a wicked laugh that it sent a shudder to join the rushes cruising up and down my spine.

The clown was an evil one. They're either good or bad, and this one was definitely the latter.

I hadn't invited him into my room. Nor had I intended to fall asleep or to emerge from a dead-to-the-world slumber lying on my back amongst the cluttered junk like a shipwrecked sailor awaking on a desert island after a storm.

Upon opening my eyes, I'd had to focus for a few moments and try to get it all into perspective. '*Who* am I?... *where* am I?... *what* must I have been doing to end up in this undignified state?'

And just as things slotted into place, this circus freak showed up – or at least his head did, rising up out of the floor and leering at me as if *I* didn't belong here.

We glared at each other, each trying to psych the other out, before I got bored of the stupid game, ran across the room and took a flying kick at his sickly-grinning mug. His head detached from his body and flew into the air... *coming down to land as the yellow-chequered rag I'd borrowed from the storage area.*

'What the *fuck* happened in here last night...?'

Scanning around, I spotted my sandals, straps akimbo like the claws of aggravated crabs. It all came flooding back: 'My *feet!*... my *massive oversized feet!*' I had feet the size of a water-retentive elephant the previous evening, the kind you see plodding along under flowery skirts in the summertime – *big ol' feet...* and ankles to match!

My sandal straps must have cut off the circulation and they'd ballooned to twice their normal size. I'd looked like a hobbit. It can't be good to take so much of a drug that you start turning into Frodo. 'Still,' I figured, 'that was last night and today's a new day... so if I smoke some more ice and remember to keep my sandal straps loose… everything should be just funky.'

Unusually, I still had the awful hunger after my fix, so I went out to buy some raisin bread and condensed milk. En route, there was a shop on Lockhart undergoing renovation. I must have passed it fifty times before, but this time it was different, for I happened to glance through the window to see yet *another* performance playing in its shadowy interior.

I peered through the glass, spellbound, unsure if it was a Wild West saloon bar, the Grand Ole Opry *or* maybe the Grand Canyon, because the scenes kept changing, sliding in and out like a fast-moving stage production.

I stood there a while, hooked and smiling at the bloody cleverness of it all. 'How come I've never noticed this kind of thing before?… and who the hell puts it all together and pulls the strings?'

It seemed that everything in Wan Chai, indeed even Hong Kong, had a secret set of pulleys, cables and motors linking it all up like an enormous pinball machine or a city-sized version of the ghost house at the fair.

A group of teenage girls walking down the pavement interrupted my daydream. They looked like Chinese locals, but when they spoke, it was in English.

'What's he looking at?' one of them asked, with a hint of ridicule.

'I don't know,' her friend replied, and giggled. 'He *always* does that.'

It was dark by the time I got back to the flat. The Indians were in their room, so I went quickly to mine, closed the door and turned on the radio.

Listening to RTHK's shows, broadcast in a mix of Cantonese and English, always gave me an eerie feeling during the nights spent alone in the half-light of my room. Out of my window, I could see the Peak and the red aircraft-warning lights along the mast on its summit. Something told me the radio station was at the base of the big antenna and that they might be observing me with a telescope through my curtainless window.

I would listen to the phone-ins, suspicious of the Cantonese conversation and wondering if people were calling in to report my movements – like in the film *The Warriors*. I didn't mind too much, didn't feel in danger, just curious as I whiled away the dark hours.

Settling down on the floor, I picked up a storybook I'd found in the junk room, picturing a poor kiddy losing their bag on the way to school. The fact it was children's literature didn't matter. The important thing was it was in English and might just contain some answers.

Another thing in my favour were the cool red sunglasses I'd come across. Now I understood the adage of seeing the world through rose-tinted spectacles. They obviously create a filter, allowing you to perceive the world as it *really* is – a bit like the 3D ones you wear at the cinema.

As I put them on, the topic on the radio changed from some bullshit phone-in asking whether the listeners preferred *maau* or *gau*, 'cats' or 'dogs' – like you saw shitloads of people coming down from thirty-floor high-rises to take their dogs for a walk in Hong Kong – to a programme about the rights and wrongs of former military personnel writing tell-all accounts of their service. The show started to discuss books written since the 1991 Gulf War, suggesting there were disputes as to the accuracy of some.

My blood ran cold…

I'd shared a room with two SAS guys on my parachute course at RAF Brize Norton, right at the time the war kicked off. They'd asked me if I knew a marine who had 'joined our lot' and was serving with the Special Forces in the Gulf. I didn't personally, but we'd all followed Bob's story as he was the first bootneck to join the Army's Special Air Service as opposed to the Royal Marines' Special Boat Service.

Back in Plymouth I happened to flick on the box to see a news clip showing pallbearers carrying a Union Jack flag-draped coffin, stunned to hear that the first casualty of the war was our comrade.

Naturally, I'd read a couple of the books the show talked about. Bob had died courageously, protecting his mates by all accounts. Now I questioned what the truth really was and how the bloke's poor family must be feeling. It spun me out. I wondered if RTHK was purposely messing with my head.

I went back to the storybook, opening it up at a chapter titled: The Children and the Sea Monster. The tale was about a boy and a girl who wanted to swim in the sea, but they were terribly afraid of a ferocious creature known to lurk in its depths.

I scanned every line for a metaphor, but it wasn't until I turned the page that I sussed the story's true symbolism *and the bottom dropped out of my world...*

An illustration depicted the two tots on the seashore, up to their knees in gently lapping waves, hugging each other in terror as tears poured down their cheeks, for out of the depths emerged a frightening beast like the Loch Ness Monster. But it wasn't the fearsome creature making me realise how unaware I'd been... *It was the children's eyes!*

'See the world through rose-tinted spectacles...'

As I looked at them with the sunglasses on, they appeared to be dark orbs, redundant of life... *for these poor kids must have been blind!*

The monster was a metaphor for the sickness in the water, the hepatitis Benny Tsang told me about, the disease endemic to Hong Kong and carried by many of its population.

'Blindness... side effect... hepatitis.'

'I see it now!... Hong Kong must be a place where people affected by blindness can seek refuge from ignorance and discrimination!'

'Poor old Benny wore glasses, didn't he?... and what about Gabriel?... the time he threatened you with a hammer... you stared into his eyes but they were clotted and lifeless... he's a part of this underground affiliation... not for any wrongdoing... but for safety and security and to be amongst his own kind... Anil's probably blind too... passed down father to son... poor sod... and Old Ron... why do you think he acts so bizarrely and gets drunk all the time and needs to belong to the Cult?... and what about your kids at school?... how many of them can't see a thing?... did you ever stop to think?'

It shamed me to think of how oblivious I had been.

'Are all the guys in Nemo's blind as well...?' I wondered.

I thought they were all in it for the cash, the kudos and the cliquishness. It never occurred to me that they banded together for the sake of their disability, all drawn to the safe haven of Wan Chai, home to the world's blind émigrés. I felt foolish I'd questioned their motives.

'But they can't *all* be blind...' I felt confused, 'otherwise what would have been the point of those hand signs?'

'Carers and the cared for...'

'*Of course!*... that's why Drik took such a dislike to me... he must have been one of the carers and thought I was ignoring these people's needs... I *have* been ignoring them... *I* was the one who was blind!'

I felt so, so remorseful. I'd thought that there was something untoward going on here, some dark conspiracy that pervaded the streets of Hong Kong and networked its way around the globe. It never occurred to me that these people might be timid souls who'd resorted to secret methods of communication to protect their vulnerability in a world that overlooked them.

'You see it now... what a clever way to communicate if you can't see someone... just give 'em the old cough!'

'So *is* Old Ron blind then...?'

'Explains a lot... why do you think he doesn't dance?'

'So he doesn't bump into people...?'

'Why do you think he dotes on Tom?... and Tom wears that red snooker ball around his neck... it's so Old Ron can see him... Tom's his carer.'

The phrase Gonzales had thrown at me went spinning around in my head: *'Wake up and smell the roses... wake up and smell the roses...'*

'Fuck it!' I was awake now.

I scanned the *Culture Shock!* book, frantic and feeling sure something written in it would validate my newfound understanding. I spent an age flicking through before hitting on a paragraph headed: *GODDESS OF THE SEA.*

> In a community dependent upon the water, the Goddess of the Sea and protector of those who sail on the waters enjoys an imposing edifice to house her image.

There it was! A community *dependent* upon the water! A goddess to protect them against the evil disease! And written in *black* and *white!*

What more proof did I need?

It was time to go and see Old Ron.

Old Ron's reaction to my visit said it all. For a start, he had Tom's red snooker ball around his neck – I assumed as a token of respect for the care Tom gave him.

'Is everything alright, mate?' I tendered.

'Fine, Chris. Why shouldn't it be?'

'Well... *you* know... is everything sort of... *clear* for you?'

'Perfectly clear. Is everything alright with you?'

'All good, man. Just sort'a been in the *dark* a bit up until now, you know? Been tryin' to *see* my way.'

I felt such sadness for Ron's situation and so wretched I hadn't sussed my dear friend's disability before.

He was tapping away on his laptop – I guess using the Braille function you can get for such machines. Only, now that I'd arrived he shuffled closer to the screen as though he didn't want me to see what was on there.

'Must be a blind thing...'

I took the opportunity of him being preoccupied to tidy the front room, picking up all the things he might trip over and injure himself on. But I felt hurt myself when he suddenly stood up and said, 'I've got to be off now, Chris. I'm meeting Tom downtown,' while waving the little snooker ball.

I *knew* he was trying to tell me I'd let him down, that I'd been too much into my own problems to see his need was greater.

After we left the flat, I stood and watched as he ran off in the direction of Clubland, marvelling at his sense of direction and the courage he displayed dodging the traffic on his own, while simultaneously feeling rejected and dumb.

I took the MTR to Quarry Bay to see Max. I needed some company and Max was one of the few people who made me feel comfortable. I didn't mention the blind thing. Not because I wanted to hide my suspicions, but because it went right out of my head, replaced by the other abstractions occupying my sorrow-filled swede.

He could see I was troubled and went over to the little transom panel on his window and unhooked a necklace hanging there. 'This one protec' you, Quiss,' he said gently.

It was a shark's tooth on a leather thong, undoubtedly the coolest pendant ever and a gift and sentiment I would treasure for life – especially as Max's window was unprotected from the spirit world now.

Back at the flat, I fell against the wall of my room and slowly sunk down amongst the crap on the floor. I was about to take five minutes off from ingesting so much information, when I saw the blood on the far wall.

I hadn't realised it was blood before, not amongst the peeling layers of paint, scuff marks and other blemishes, but there it was as plain as day – dried-up splats.

I got up to check it out. Sure as hedgehogs, it looked like blood, and wetting my finger and rubbing one of the desiccated drips… it *was* blood! It looked as though they – whoever 'they' were – had put someone up against the wall and *executed* them.

'*Who dares wins…*'

'Eh…?'

'*Hereford…*'

'Hereford…?'

'*Killing House…*'

'Really…?'

'SAS… *anti-terrorist training.*'

'No!… *here…* in *this* place?'

'*Good a place as any…*'

'Frightening place…'

'*Where frightening things happen…*'

By the time Monday morning came around, I was starting to feel the pressure. Although spending all weekend on the case, I had yet to work it out: the triads, the global cult, the puppetry, the symbolism, the blindness *and* the blood – not to mention everyone knowing who I was and that I'd been subjected to ridicule by people I'd never done a thing to.

But I would show them! I would show them *all* I could work this puzzle out. This was *my* Hong Kong and I wasn't about to up sticks and fuck off without a fight.

The previous thirty-six hours I'd spent scrabbling around on the floor, diving into books to find some meaning to it all. I'd been battling with a fair amount of confusion too – so many random and fragmented thoughts filling my head. I tried to make sense out of them, but no sooner had they arrived than they left again, like rude guests from a birthday party.

'*The road is long…*'

'*Shit*, the fucking road!… I'm meant to be getting ready for school.'

I forced a moment of lucidity and clinging onto it like the last rock before a waterfall I washed and dressed as quickly as I could. Then feeling parallel with the planet, I hurled myself towards the MTR using my sixth sense to cross Lockhart Road's four lanes of traffic without a pause. Upon exiting the station at the other end, I ran to the school.

'Fuck!'

The playground was empty.

As I stood there sweating like a racehorse, feeling so desperate as a fountain of scarabs rushed up through me, the main door opened and the distant figure of Miss Lin, the head of English, appeared and beckoned me over.

Walking the long walk, I knew I'd let them all down. I felt flustered and confused as to how this kept happening, afraid of yet another dismissal.

'Miss Lin...' I tried to catch my breath *'I'm-I'm... sorry.'*

'S'okay, Quiss. I have other teacher take your class. You can go home, come back tomorrow.'

'Oh thanks, Miss Lin! I'm really sorry. I'll see you tomorrow.'

I was so grateful and so relieved, but just as I turned to go, she said, *'Errh*, Quiss'a?'

'Yes, Miss Lin.' I saw a kindly look in her eye.

'Errh, the children say, your class is their favourite class. An' the children say, you are their favourite teacher.'

'Oh... thanks, Miss Lin,' I managed to waffle, walking away quickly so she didn't see the tears pouring down my face.

Going for a Walk

BACK IN WAN CHAI, there was a telephone call to make. My family knew things weren't right as I'd told my dad during a previous call to let the building society repossess my house and the debt collectors to do what they liked, explaining I had more pressing matters on my mind because there was a strange cult-like conspiracy going on over here, things weren't quite as they seemed, I couldn't talk too much about it and certainly not over the telephone.

I'd called another time, wanting to tell my dad that everything was okay, that I wasn't staying out in Hong Kong as some sort of vengeance for all the turmoil pushed upon us as kids – because parents have a way of distorting reality to fit their own interpretation of events.

I thought he should know I wouldn't want to be any person in this world other than the one I was and where I was, and that I'd come out to Hong Kong to make something of my life and had no reason to return to the UK. But my stepmother had answered and told me to call back when my dad was home.

So now, I went into a telephone box and dialled my dad's number. I was beginning to feel drained and it seemed the right thing to do.

'Dad? It's me. Look, I tried to tell Ellen that—'
   '*Chris!* Are you *alright?* Can you *talk?*'
   'Of course I can talk, Dad. I phoned you, remember?'
   'No, I mean have you got your *passport*, son?'
   'Of course I've got my passport. Why wouldn't I?'
   'Chris, keep a *hold* of it! You *understand* me?'

'Yeah, I hear you, Dad. But what's wrong?'

'*Chris!*' My dad lowered his voice to a whisper. 'Look out for the *washing machine*, the *washing machine*! Do you *hear* me? Don't let them get your *passport*!'

Well, I came out of the telephone box a little confused. It hadn't even occurred to me to give my father the number for the flat.

'What was Dad on about?' I wondered.

I mean, I knew what he was trying to say. He seemed to think I was being brainwashed by the Cult – despite their efforts, they'd never do that to me. I wasn't afraid of them. No, it was confusing that my dad seemed to know all about this thing. 'So it *must* be global... *fuck*!'

'*Ngoh seung lohk yuh* (I think rain),' I said to the guy selling newspapers near my building – not sure if I meant it metaphorically or literally.

'No, I think it's fine,' he replied in impeccable English, with a smile – and I wasn't sure if he meant it metaphorically or literally.

I hurried on into the lift. I had a lesson for the Cult – one Gabriel and Anil could deliver to the fuckers personally.

'*Passport!*' I shouted through the wall of their office. 'Oh *dear*! I've dropped my *passport*!'

I threw it down on the floor by their door.

'*Afraid?*' I continued. 'Let's see who's *afraid*, shall we?'

I climbed up onto the windowsill in my room and crouched there, gazing down at the multi-coloured specks of litter scattered over the tarpaulins below.

'Whad'is going on?' demanded Gabriel, standing in the doorway with Anil stuck to his side. He cast a brief but disapproving eye over the mess, maintaining his displeasure when he saw me in the open window. 'Whad'are you doing?'

'I'll show you what I'm doing,' I said, feeling a mix of anger and apathy. 'I'll show you right *nowwww*!' I dived off the ledge and into the concrete canyon.

'*Nooooooooooo!*' Gabriel screamed, having witnessed my body plummet to earth.

'No what?' I asked – looking up from where I swung like an orangutan on the washing frame bolted below the casement.

'*No*! Don't be doing these silly t'ings! *Please*, Creese. Do you hear?'

I *did* hear. I heard enough to know that whatever their little game was, they didn't want me to die. It gave me something to think about, but not as much as the little beasts did – the ones I had to annihilate later that day.

Sitting amongst the crap on the floor, I felt my hair come alive. My eyes flicked to the yellow-chequered rag I'd found out the back to wipe up a drink I'd spilt. Now, eyeing it with suspicion, I must have contracted lice from it.

A mixture of stress, anxiety and confusion rose up to swallow me, as the ocean does a sailor when his boat has a hole in it.

'Why does this shit keep happening to me…?'

Once again, I found myself swimming against the current and wishing the tide of life would for once flow in my favour, beaching me high and dry above the constant wash of misfortune.

I threw the cloth out of the window, shifted across to the mirror and began inspecting my locks like a monkey possessed. I couldn't see any nits but I reckoned the junk room teemed with the bloody things, jumping ship from the rats or the rooftop guy's dreadlocked haystack.

Just imagining the infestation made my skin crawl. I had to do something about it, and quickly. I dusted the top of my head with my fingertips. Then I tried to pick the little demons out – only I still couldn't find any. Before long, I was clawing at my crown.

Suddenly I stopped…

I drew closer to the mirror…

'Oh *NO!*'

In my panic, I'd scratched deep gouges into my scalp, some of which ran down onto my forehead. Blood began to well up. Soon they were brimming with crimson.

'*NO… NO… NO!*'

I couldn't get a grip on what was happening or what I'd done to myself. I went into the bathroom, washed my wounds in the sink, gave them a rough towel dry and rushed out to find a chemist. On my return, I emptied the bottle of insecticide over my hair, massaging it in with my fingertips to get the full effect.

It burnt a little… then a little more…. then more until it felt as though I'd poured acid into the cuts. It was agony, and as I tried to rub the liquid off my bleeding forehead, I succeeded in getting it in my eyes. On all fours in the bathroom, I tried to bear the searing pain long enough to let the stuff do its work.

Finally, unable to stand it any longer, I fumbled for the tap, letting the water run over my head for an age. Yet even after I'd washed the bug-buster out, the cuts continued to sting like the devil had peed in them.

Back in my room, still trembling, I happened to look at the label on the bottle – *'Evil fucking bastards…!'* – and shuddering with shock and outrage, I despised the devious vile Cult even more. For on the label was a cartoon stick picture of a child's head and shoulders, the kiddie screaming as tears burst from its eyes.

'This shit isn't for getting rid of head lice… it's for—'

'Torture… sadists… these people hate kids… you already know that… restaurant… plates… you fell for the chemist's trick… fucking hurts… eh?'

I should've got some sleep. When the next day came around, I knew there was something I had to do, something important.

'I've got to… I've got to—'

'Teach the kids… last chance saloon.'

I felt *sure* I had to teach the kids, but I was too confused to know whether that was true.

'Don't need to teach today… school's out… it's all in the book… it'll all come good in the end.'

For hours, I'd been engrossed in the text of *Break Through the Barriers Inside*, the personal-development book I'd bought at the three-day Eric Jansen seminar in London. Flicking through the pages and zoning in on the maxims contained in random paragraphs, I found myself hypnotised by a wealth of information that seemed to make perfect sense.

> We won't understand all the events in our lives. This is when our faith will be truly tested.

'Has my work at the school been a test…?' I wondered, as the truth sunk in.

'What do you think?… two-minute interview… you didn't think you were there to teach them, did you?'

There is no set time or place to learn the lessons of life. Positive or negative experiences are only society's constructs. In short, your most challenging times have conditioned and guided you and sent you on a journey…

'Ah…!' My business collapsing, fired from so many jobs, the experience at Club Nemo, my entire life, it was all *conditioning* and *guidance*. 'Have I been punishing myself too much?… is turning up at the school today a part of my destiny?… perhaps—'

'Something big is going to happen… something you've waited your entire life for.'

Keep in mind the proverb: 'If the student is ready, a teacher will appear'.

'My students are ready for me to appear… because *I'm* ready!… and because I'm ready—'

'They're waiting for you… it's all going to come good and you'll see why you've been put to the test… you've passed with flying colours… everyone is proud of your achievement… they're all in the stadium… you've made it through the rain… la la la la!'

'Stadium…?'

I pictured a stadium somewhere in the direction of the school. Was it a *covered* stadium because I'd made it through the rain? I felt I had to go there.

'The school… not really a school… it's a massive open-air stadium… they're all waiting for you… up there in the New Territories.'

'Who's waiting for me…?'

I had a vision of every single person I had ever met being there.

'Everyone!… your family… the kids from your class and their parents to say thank you… all the Wan Chai crazies from the clubs… the managers didn't really want to fire you… it was a test… actually they're really fond

of you… the DJs can't wait to shake your hand and congratulate you on getting through this thing… Adam and John from Gung Wan Hong… they're there… big smiles… Lim and Benny… even Liu San… you thought he was evil… his triads out to get you… we fooled you… ha!… they're waiting to greet you… Vance won't be there though… away on business in China… he's not so sentimental about this kind of thing… but Old Ron and Tom… they were in on it all along… they're looking forward to welcoming you home after the long walk… even Neil Diamond… he didn't really go back to England… he's been in Pok Fu Lam helping to organise this thing… ha-ha-ha!… it's a big surprise party and it's just for you.'

If we could foretell its events, how mundane would life be? Isn't it great that we don't know what's just around the corner? Very shortly, something could take place, something to alter the course of your life, improving it immeasurably and ratifying your very existence.

I could see it now! Everything had been for a reason – the *rhyme* and the *reason*!
'I've got to get myself to the stadium… they're all there.'
'Get yourself up there… you star!'

Understand you are ushered along a path of eternal enlightenment and love.

'That's *it*…!'
I could see the path I'd walked from birth until now, through all the challenges along the route, had all been about the love *and I had made it through!*
'I see it now…!'
I felt so happy. I knew I had to get to that stadium and see all those big smiling faces just waiting for *me!*
'But how will I know where it is…?'
'Go to class as usual… they're all in the class in the stadium.'
'Right!… I'd better leave straight away—'
'Check the Casio…'
'No…!'

My heart sank. It was nearing 3pm. I'd been so preoccupied that I'd missed the class *again*. I'd missed my one chance to get to the stadium. I could imagine my disappointed family and friends up there having to console the kids, telling them not to worry because I would be there soon... But now I never would.

I continued to sit on the floor, utterly demoralised. Everyone had been there and I'd let them down, especially the ones who'd travelled all the way from the UK. It was pointless to go up there late and expect them to be waiting. My rendezvous had to be in time with the start of the class if this thing was to go to plan.

The phone ringing in the front room shook me out of my stupor. It was Mr Lee, the owner of the language school, wanting to know why I hadn't told him I couldn't make it.

I didn't know what to say, or what was going on. I thought he would know – everyone seemed to know more than I did about everything. As I apologised to Mr Lee, I knew I would never hear from him again.

I would miss those kids, though. I hoped they weren't still waiting at the stadium. I hoped their parents would explain it to them. Maybe they could say, 'Mister Quiss isn't very well at the moment.' It would mean lying to them, but that would be better than hurting their feelings.

Outside, the sky matched my mood, growing prematurely dark as storm clouds began to build. I stood at the window watching the ominous gathering when without warning – *SMACK!* – a lightning bolt skewered the electrified atmosphere, smashing nature's full force into the roof of a nearby building. I knew what the omen meant. I remembered my conversation with the newspaper seller the day before: I think rain... and down it came.

When morning broke, it wasn't only sunlight pouring through the window filling my life with light... It was something inside.

I'd lost almost everything, but most of all the chance to claw back some self-respect and show the doubters I wasn't anyone's fool and could work this thing out. There was only one option left: it was time to go and jump off one of the forty-metre-high cranes into the harbour. That would do the trick. Ultimate confidence in one's own ability and *much* more belief than that lot had put together.

I couldn't rush into it, though – I would need some supplies. I reckoned my Eric Jansen book and boogie box would do the trick – although I'd have to find somewhere en route to buy batteries.

After a smoke from my dwindling stash, I set out with a newfound contentment and direction blossoming inside. It wasn't a bad old day for it either, the sun pure enlightenment in the calm after the storm, and as I strolled through Wan Chai heading in the general direction of the tall cranes, the warming rays complemented my sense of purpose.

I walked right the way along Jaffe Road, swapped over to Harcourt Road and passed by the gates of HMS *Tamar*, the naval base I'd stayed at when I arrived here, all those months ago.

As I crossed Edinburgh Place, home of the Star Ferry terminal and a rank of red taxicabs, a flat-bed truck sat parked in the middle. It carried a huge hoarding advertising condominiums for let on Lantau Island. The promotion featured the usual smiling Eurasian faces, and *I* knew that *they* knew all about this thing. 'There's no mistaking it for them, mate!' I said to the guy standing next to it with a microphone. 'It's all the same in the end, isn't it?'

He looked at me *slightly* sideways without saying anything in return, but *I* knew that *he* knew what I meant – there were no secrets in this place.

I carried right on through Central District and before long found myself in Sheung Wan under a sky that had turned to gloom and walking pavements somewhat more deserted.

'*Go west… my son.*'

My mission to find a crane to jump off blended with one of keeping moving, something deep inside telling me if I continued heading west, I would find my answers and it would all come good in the end.

I found myself thinking of an old matinee I'd watched called *The Swimmer*, in which Burt Lancaster plays a lonely Park Avenue executive who has one of those breakdown thingamajigs and decides that after a day spent at a friend's pool his answers lie in swimming home through all the other pools on the way.

Okay, maybe I wasn't chucking a mental as Burt had done, but I knew that I likewise had to keep moving, to keep on heading west. It was all for a reason.

I spotted a small shop selling electrical items, so I went in and bought batteries for my boogie box. I had to... although I wasn't sure why. As I thumbed through the last HK$450 in my wallet, something told me my mission wouldn't be complete without them. I loaded them into the machine, but it never occurred to me to switch it on and play some music.

I walked further through the backstreets of Western District, the buildings getting older and greyer, the roads narrower and emptier; the sky more overcast and threatening. Although feeling lonely, right out on a limb and having travelled some distance, I knew I had to press on.

Looking down an alleyway, I saw that it led to a courtyard surrounded by housing blocks. Two boys were playing football, taking it in turns to stand in a small goal they had set up.

I went inside, put my boogie box and *vade mecum* down on a bench and joined in their game. We didn't say a word. One of them passed me the ball and as we took it in turns to shoot and save penalties, it felt great to have uncomplicated company. I hoped their parents wouldn't mind them playing footy with the troublesome *gweilo*, but I didn't care. I'd always loved kids – they're more accepting than adults and you can be yourself.

Continuing on my trek, I happened across a music shop with guitars on display in the window. I peered through the glass, mesmerised by the shop's spotlessly clean interior, the well-presented guitars and, in particular, one of the manufacturer's stickers inside an instrument's soundhole. It had an alluring flowery pattern decorating its circumference, the maker's name, *The Feng Lin Guitar Company, China*, in the centre, and below that, *Satisfaction Guaranteed*.

Even though it would take most of my remaining dollars, I knew I *had* to buy it. This shop was on my route for a purpose, this guitar built especially and placed in the window so I wouldn't miss it. And the label said it all: *Satisfaction Guaranteed. That's* what I needed if I were ever to figure out this mystery.

I continued west, HK$300 lighter now I had my new toy, my key to solving the whole damn shebang. I'd walked right through the morning and into the afternoon, finding myself at the far end of the island's seafront in a place called Kennedy Town. Not having seen a crane, let alone jumped off one, I sat down on the harbour wall and tried to get my bearings.

What I did see, though, was the face of the English construction worker I'd chatted to in Club Nemo – the one who'd come over to work on the new airport with his mate, the ex-marine, who drank with him. The last time was on the morning after the murder-mystery night.

Now I spotted him, albeit fleetingly, sticking his head out from behind a yellow cargo container in a storage park on the other side of the road. He looked right at me, then turned, laughed and said something to someone out of sight before disappearing again as though he thought I hadn't seen him.

But I *had* seen him, and determined to find out who was with him, I casually walked back in the direction I'd come from. Passing behind a parked truck, I crouched behind a wheel and peered under the chassis.

Sure enough, the guy came out of his hiding place and began paralleling my route, along with his friend, who turned out to be none other than Mr Disbeliever, my fellow ex-bootneck, himself. Obviously they were involved in this bizarre conspiracy, but to be honest, as I spied them laughing at me, I thought them sad – grown men acting as if they were in the school playground.

I walked back towards the city centre, feeling despondent my mission hadn't come to much – only adding to my confusion, if I was honest. Now I had a guitar that hadn't really given me any answers and which I could only play three chords on. I didn't bother looking back at the construction workers – they could go and build themselves a sandcastle for all I cared.

Instead, I went into a petrol station. I knew how to show the critics my worth and integrity, using the few dollars I had left.

'Only money… go with your feelings.'

I went up to the counter and shoved the cash into the charity box – every last note and coin went in as the female shop assistant stood there smiling and saying, *'Dojeh! Dojeh!'*

I left feeling I had shown my true colours and if they still insisted on hating me for it, well, what else could I do? I'd spent all I could – in every sense of the word.

I wandered back along Sheung Wan's forlorn streets, wondering what it was all about, and just as I reached the part of the district that blended with Central, the sun appeared from behind the clouds and I saw something I hadn't seen before in the Fragrant Harbour: I saw someone in a wheelchair.

'The people of Hong Kong have stopped the infanticide that goes on behind closed doors and now they're giving disabled people the public profile they truly deserve…!'

I felt light pouring into my soul as I witnessed the streets grow suddenly busy and excited as if to celebrate this paradigm shift. Everything seemed so right, *right now!* Everything was all for a reason, *everything had come good in the end!*

I sat down on a bench, revelling in the glory of it all and thumbing the *Break Through the Barriers Inside* book to try to find a passage that would give me a handle on the situation. And on page 146, there it was, a paragraph expressing the similarities between religions, saying that all of them, whether founded by Jesus Christ, Mohammed, Buddha or Confucius, were working for the *common* good.

'You knew it all along…'

'I knew it all along…!'

I'd known people were generally kind. The streets now flowing with light, love, life, *and* someone with a disability, ratified this theory. I had to make my mark and let people know that I, too, was on the case and believed in all of this, and had done so from the start.

I ripped the half-page from the book and used it to wrap up my shark's tooth necklace, Max's gift and my most treasured possession. Then I walked over to a green litterbin and placed my offering on top of it, knowing as soon as I walked away someone from the Cult would look at it and see how wrong they'd been about me.

By the time I got back to Jaffe Road, it was dark. I'd been walking all day and just like Burt's character in *The Swimmer*, I too felt lonely and depressed.

As I walked into my building, the old man I'd borrowed the handcart from was sitting on the top step, chatting to a friend. He looked at the guitar, then at me and said, 'Very *goo*!'

I knew he was hinting I'd fulfilled a part of my destiny and that there were a lot of clues I could get from the instrument, but I also felt he was being a touch sarcastic, like, 'Dumb *gweilo* finally gets with programme and buys the guitar that's been waiting for him in that shop all along – *t'huh*!'

So I didn't say anything and floated on by like mist.

I exited the lift to find my floor bathed in the moon's enigmatic glow. It gave me an idea. After smoking some ice in the thankfully empty flat, I picked up the guitar and made my way back out to the landing.

Through the blind in their window, I could sense the Chinese family opposite moving around with what seemed great stealth. I wondered why I never heard them speak – I think I'd only seen them once in all the time I'd lived here.

A multitude of coloured lights on the distant harbour rebounded off its rippling water, entering through the building's decorative iron grillwork to add a jazzy aura to the moonlit mystique and giving the impression of an alien craft hovering and observing from afar.

Something told me if I could balance the instrument in the middle of the hall and align its soundhole with the lunar beams coming in through the grillwork's circular centrepiece, it would create a map on the tiled floor – a map that would give me all the answers.

I struggled for an age, but the guitar wouldn't stay upright. I should have bought a stand – as no such map appeared.

All that happened was someone in the building across the road shouted something about the *gweilo*, which sounded offensive. When I looked over, I saw the fat lady again – or at least her silhouette behind the frosted glass – not a hairbrush in her hand but most definitely a microphone.

It was all starting to make sense! I rushed back to my room and delved into my briefcase, searching for a letter I kept in there – a special letter, sent to me by my second cousin Paul.

Paul had joined the Royal Marines as a junior, rising to the rank of colonel and earning an OBE along the way. The letter was to congratulate me on joining the Corps, back in 1988. It had been touching, and I'd shown it to the lads in my room in training as it had a Whitehall letterhead.

> Lympstone will set out to pass you, not fail you – but you've got to want to pass. When it's 2am and you're walking across Dartmoor in the rain you will really wonder why you joined.

'*...But I promise you it's all for a reason... and will all make sense in the end.*'

I suddenly understood the message's subliminal meaning! Paul was referring to the commando crawl we learnt as recruits, the technique that involved edging on our stomachs along a rope suspended between two high points. It *wasn't* so we could board an enemy ship by stealing up the mooring lines, it was so I could shin across the hosepipe wire to the building on the other side of Jaffe Road.

It was simple. I *had* to see the fat lady sing.

'*Go and see her...*'

'This whole thing is...'

'*...not over until the fat lady sings.*'

I remembered reading a paragraph in the *Culture Shock!* book titled: *WILLINGNESS TO TAKE RISKS*. 'What had it said...?' It was something like:

> The price for newcomers of learning the hard way can be costly. And all the more so if a foreign newcomer chances his arm. One rule of thumb is, never enter into a big game unless you have the support of a big player.

'Christ...!' It all made *sense* now! *Everything! My* military career... the letter from my cousin – *everything!*

'*He's the big player... you've got his support.*'

Now I knew the reason why I'd come to Hong Kong.

'You had to be here at this time…'

I *had* to see the fat lady sing. I *had* to crawl across the wire carrying the water pipe, seventy metres above the ground and in the dark.

I *had* to prove it to the bastards who doubted me, bloody disbelievers who dared question my integrity and blatantly laughed at me. I would show them. I would show them all *right now!*

Up I went to the roof, peering over the edge to look down into the roof-dweller's sky-high patio. I could see the wire with the pipe attached to it, secured to the parapet and shooting out into the night to fix onto another metal ring on the fat lady's balcony, right outside the room where she continued her operatic performance.

As quietly as possible, I dropped the eight feet down, noting the length of wood jamming the exit shut and the weird bag containing dog shit, or something equally as hideous, tacked to the outside of the door. Then I climbed up to sit astride the parapet, my head reflecting on my commando training, the preparation for this thing I had to do if I was to prove myself to everyone who had mocked me.

Laying my body onto the wire, I felt excited, knowing that when I got to the other side the mystery would be over, my worth shown and this whole Hong Kong escapade done and dusted, in the bag, *ended!* I began to shin along it, wincing as the plastic ties every twelve inches scratched wickedly at my chest through the fabric of my T-shirt.

A few feet out, I stopped – my body gently swaying with the swing of the wire – to peer down at the people in the street below, wondering if they were looking up. A thought struck me: 'Will this wire take my weight?… I haven't checked it for safety… come on… marine… the seven Ps… Prior Planning and Preparation Prevents Piss Poor Performance.'

For all I knew, they might have tasked some slapdash construction worker with the job and as I got partway across it could snap, sending me spiralling down Death's greedy throat.

'Go on… Marine Boy… I've told 'em all that Chrissy Boy will do it… he's not afraid of anything… show these doubters what you're made of… I might be involved with this lot but I think the world of you… and remember… at least they'll see you're trying…'

I knew Old Ron thought a lot of me and I really didn't want to let him down, but –

'What about Ben?… best brother in the world… long way away and probably wondering what I'm up to… Ben loves me… and me him… always have done… wouldn't want me to do this… to see me like this… who's more important… the Cult or Ben?'

– my thoughts flicked to my sibling. Six years, six months and six days younger was Ben, always idolising his elder brother who'd joined the Royal Marines and gone off to serve his country.

And as if the hand of the Almighty had reached down out of the heavens to slap sense into my dumb blinkered self, *I suddenly realised what a fool I'd been!*

What the *fuck* was I *thinking?*

What the *fuck* was I *doing?*

I didn't care for this stupid cult gangster shit. As far as I was concerned they were a bunch of misfitting cowards, pathetic spineless shitbags who got their kicks from humiliating people and setting them up to be murdered. I didn't have to prove a single fucking thing to those bastards. I didn't have to prove anything to anyone in this world except my little brother and my family and friends back home, the ones who genuinely cared for me.

On our parents' final separation, Ben and I had gone to the same strange primary school way up in the North where our grandmother lived, but they'd tried to stop us seeing each other during break times because I was in the big kids' playground and him the junior and it was against their stupid fucking rules.

But I'd refused that protocol. *No one* was going to stop me seeing my kid brother, no bastard adult. So we sat next to each other on the steps between the schoolyards, and it hadn't been so lonely, homesick and desperate with all that divorce shit going on.

How would it be if Ben had to hear the news I'd become a drug addict in Hong Kong and had thrown myself off a skyscraper? Because that's how they'd report my death: a pathetic suicide by a drugged-up loser. No *fucking* way! I didn't have to prove anything to anyone, only him.

Overcome with emotion, momentarily connected to all that was important in my life and making a decision based upon my own voice, not that fucking other one and certainly not one of the Cult's insidious members, tears poured down my face, dropping into the darkness like paratroopers from a Herc.

It all seemed so clear. I'd come out to Hong Kong a determined and driven man – but now look at me.

What the hell had I done?

Who was I?

I climbed off the cable and headed back to my room, this time by the direct route, straight through the exit that the roof-dweller had wedged shut.

He could go to fuck as well.

I couldn't give a damn about him and his stupid rooftop games, or any other piss-taker for that matter. I'd been worrying about those bastards for too long. I kicked the wooden jam out of the way and after taking a glance down at the bag of peculiar shit pinned to the door, I burst on through.

Back in my room, the stark realisation of all that had happened hit home hard, washing over me like a tidal wave and reinforcing the wake-up call I should have received a long time ago.

I was *angry* now! I hadn't asked for this. Okay, maybe I took the meth – although in truth, those crafty little crystals chose me, made me feel normal for the first time in my life, the person I wanted to be, better than having ridiculously big muscles and ego-fuelled cars. But either way, I didn't deserve to end up like this, in this undignified state, in *this… this* –

'FUCKING *KILLING HOUSE! AAAAAAAAH! KILLING HOUSE! AAAARRRHHHHHHH!*'

SMASH! – the sound of my beautiful ornate box hitting the wall, the one I'd treasured so much, so happy when I found it in the market, which now lay as matchwood on the floor.

SMASH! – the mirror from the junk room followed suit.

And *CRASH!* went Chris Thrall, down amongst the broken glass, black-lacquered wood, mother-of-pearl and other crap strewn across my pitiful mess of a floor.

'I didn't *ask* for this… I didn't fucking *ask* for this… *aaaarrhhh… aarrhh… aarh… noooo… nooo… no… n'… n'…*'

Sitting there amongst the carnage, for the first time in a year missing my family and unable to stop tears of self-pity flooding down my cheeks, I must have forgotten to lock the front door because the policeman walked straight in.

'Wha' you do?' he shouted, scanning the mess and appearing angry and bewildered. 'Why you smash place up... *again?*'

'Oh... *errm*, I'm having a bit of trouble dealing with things, Officer.'

'Hmmh?' he mused, his eyes darting around like a foreman inspecting a bad job. I don't think they covered the broken-down *gweilo* scenario in the police academy.

'You know, *everyone* in Hong Kong *know who you are!* Everyone in Hong Kong *know* you do the *drug! Don' do the drug!'*

It wasn't the first time I'd heard this.

In fact, as he shook his head, more mournfully than scornfully, then about-turned and left me to my chaos, I realised it was becoming a habit... and I cried some more.

Virgin

I DIDN'T KNOW WHAT the crazy rooftop man was going on about. His Cantonese was far too rapid to understand. What I could gather, from the liberal sprinkling of '*Gweilo* this...' and '*Gweilo* that...' was that he was far from happy with me for invading his high-rise privacy.

His wailing piped up after the policeman left. It was awful. As he rampaged up and down the hallway, he sounded possessed by demons, with spiders in his ears and a hellhound snapping at his arse.

I waited for him to come knocking on my door. That would make for an interesting scenario – especially when I told him to get fucked. But his defamatory rant finally quietened and he disappeared back up to his elevated abode.

I thought I'd better check he'd gone, so I opened the front door an inch and peered through the gap.

'What the *fuuuu*...!'

Whatever *bizarre* kak had been in that bag tacked onto the exit door, he'd somehow managed to tread it all around our floor. Further investigation revealed brown foot-shaped clumps everywhere, and boy did it stink! It stunk worse than a sheep in a steam bath. It was full-on rancid, and for the life of me I couldn't work out what it was or the purpose it had served.

In the morning, Anil knocked on my door. He stood there, calm but diffident. 'Creese, you have to go now.'

'I know, mate.'

The time had come. Not only had I gone a little over the top with the restructuring of the place and waged psychological warfare on the neighbours, but I couldn't pay the rent – unless they'd accept a brand new guitar, never used... well, not to make music.

I packed my bergen, grabbed the fake-leather holdall out of the junk room to carry all the books and then went back and stashed my boogie box in the clutter as it was too much to carry.

'Goodbye, Creese,' said Anil.

'Goodbye, Anil,' said Chris, and then headed out to phone Max.

'Max, I need your help, mate. I need somewhere to stay—'

'*Mou problem*, Quiss'a!' he said. 'All the time you live in Hong Kong, I say to myself, "I hope that Quiss come live with me one day!"'

Having jumped the barrier in the MTR station, I took the tube to Quarry Bay. I found Max in his loft flat using an Apple laptop to 'chat' to a friend in Vancouver.

Max explained that Cyberspacers didn't want the authorities regulating the medium, so they employed doublespeak in their messages. The freaky thing was this underground language was the kind of deception the Cult would employ. I wondered how much Max knew about the conspiracy, but was hesitant to ask – just content to be in the calm of the storm with someone I trusted.

That evening I went to the Big Apple to see Ray about the possibility of work, but his body language told me I had a jellyfish in the desert's chance. I sensed it was because I'd developed a reputation for taking drugs, the effects of which, easy to hide in those early days, had turned me into the poster boy for the *Just Say No!* campaign. What would I do? All the doors had slammed shut behind me and I'd been powerless to stop them.

Chung, my kung-fu-teaching waiter friend, approached, brandishing a smile and a HK$500 note. I'd lent it to him a while back to cover his electric bill as he had a wife and baby at home. A week ago, I'd asked if he could repay it, my jaw dropping when he informed me, deadpan, that as we hadn't signed 'the paper', he didn't owe me anything. I'd told Chung I hadn't asked him to sign a contract because he was my mate and I liked and trusted him. He'd been unable to look me in the eye.

But here he was having understood the sentiment and paying back the loan with perfect timing. Now it was up to me to make sure I didn't use it to buy musical instruments I didn't know how to play.

I spied Old Ron at the back of the club and spent a couple of hours chatting to him in between visiting the varnish. He introduced me to Annabelle, one-half of an English couple that had moved into his apartment. As Ron and I got up to leave, she rushed over and gave me the hug of the century, holding me for an age with a fog of drunken passion in her eyes. It was touching, but a touch embarrassing, so I made a quick exit.

When we got outside, Ron said, 'Does that happen often?'

'Does what happen often?'

'Do other blokes' girlfriends hug you?'

He looked cross, somewhat spiteful.

At Ron's flat, he let me make a reverse-charge call to my dad. When my old man answered, he asked whose telephone it was.

Ron took the receiver. 'Hi, Edward.

'Yep... yep.

'Well, it's like this, Ed. His behaviour's just got *so* bizarre...

'Yes... yeah... yeah...'

'What did he say, Ron?' I felt like a schoolkid on parents' evening.

'He says you should go home, Chris. We *both* think you should.'

It hurt that people were trying to decide things for me, but I didn't say anything. I wasn't going anywhere. That was England, and I lived in Hong Kong.

In the morning, I made the trip over to Mack's with my five hundred bucks, and once again, my spirits soared as high as a condor, my finances a shot duck.

When I returned to Max's, he bugged off out, saying he had to meet his mother, so I settled down to smoke some ice. An overly loud conversation interrupted me. '*Keui mou faan gung* (He doesn't go to work).' The woman's voice came from out front and sounded scathing.

'*Been here... heard it all before.*'

Max's neighbours were having a good old gossip about me. Word must have got around – *how* surprising – and the backstabbing had started.

Why wouldn't they leave me alone? I'd never gone out of my way to cause harm or offence. All I'd ever tried to do was earn myself a place in their midst and once again they were throwing it back in my face with razorblades attached.

'*Yih chihn, keui faan gung hai Waan Jai, hai Luard Do. Yiga keui mou faan gung* (Before, he used to work in Wan Chai, in Luard Road. Now he doesn't go to work).'

'How do they know that about me?'

Then it occurred to me that Max used to work in Wan Chai… at the *Big Apple…* on *Luard Road,* and hadn't worked anywhere since.

'No!' Max replied, looking adamant.

I wondered if he was bluffing.

'You don't know enough Cantonese, Quiss'a. You get the *wrong* translation.'

'Alright, Max, just tell me what *Yih chihn, keui faan gung hai Waan Jai, hai Luard Road. Yiga keui mou faan gung* means?'

'Errh… is meaning like someone work in Wan Chai before, but not working there now.'

'On Luard Road?'

'Yeah-yeah.'

'*That's* what I'm saying, Max.'

'*No!* Mebee you juss think they say that?'

'Max, when you disappear for the day, is it because you want to make it look like you go to work?'

'*No*, Quiss.'

'Alright, in that case, can you do me a favour?'

'*Shoowah.*'

'Can you telephone Vance?'

'Whass'is number?'

I pulled the Max*Tech* Group business card from my wallet, scanned down the back and gave the number to Max.

'*Lee San!*'

I marvelled at the etiquette Max used to address 'Mr' Lee. I could tell he was explaining the situation to Vance, who I hadn't seen since leaving Hing Tak.

Max passed the phone over.

'Alright, Vance?'

'A'm okay, Quiss. A'how abou' you?'

'I'm fine, Vance. I've just got a problem. Errm… all the people going past Max's flat, well… it's like… they're talking about me?'

'Listen, Quiss'a,' he began softly, 'there's something you should know… abou' Hong Kong peepall. When you live with me… me an' Miss Lim… you only get to meet nice peepall… My friends, they all unnerstan'a *gweilo'a*?'

'Uh-huh.'

'But you don' get the *proper* idea abou' Hong Kong peepall… Hong Kong peepall, they not that nice'a?'

'Not that nice?'

'Very ol' fashion, you know? Don' unnerstan'a *gweilo'a*?'

'*Yes*! I understand, Vance. I thought it might be something like this.'

As I put the phone down, I thanked Vance from deep within. He had come good for me, just like always.

The following evening I borrowed a few bucks from my friend and hopped on one of the flying triad-operated minibuses passing his place in the direction of Wan Chai. The *maa jai* driver and his fellow little horse conductor were kind to me. I asked, '*Duk'm'duk, ngoh tsut gai hai Dai Pingwo, hai Luard Do?*' and they went a long way off their route to drop me right outside the Big Apple.

For the first time ever, I sat alone in the club, not dancing or talking to anyone. I couldn't relax. Max had told me he definitely wouldn't be having the operation to remove the tumour in his nose, needing the money to pay for his girlfriend's abortion. I felt miserable for him.

To make matters worse, when I looked over to Chan he was chatting to Ray's new Chinese barman and laughing, and I knew it was about me. The humiliation was more than I could bear. When one of the expats came over and asked if I was alright and why was I sitting on my own, I reckoned everyone in the club must be having a good old giggle too.

'No, I'm not!' I said, then got up and walked out.

But it didn't end there.

Jumping aboard a packed minibus to go back to Max's, I came under attack again, battered by a cacophony of Cantonese from people I'd never met before.

'*Laughing at you... hai Wong Gok... m'sik gong... in Mong Kok...
everybody knows you... yau pungyau hai Jakyuhchung... gweilo... has
friend in Quarry bay... Gweilo don't work Nemo's Bar... Dai Pingwo...
hohkman... hai Yinggwok yan... everyone knows you... is Englishman...
gwanyan... wahnging... gymnasium... faan gung hai Waan Jai... worked
in Wan Chai... it's all about you... Gwongdungwa... teaching... pungyau...
soldier... no money...*'

It was a bus journey through Hell, the worst night of my life. I sat
with my head down, acutely hurt to the point where I couldn't bear it
any longer –

'*Get off nowww!... just gooo!... go nowww!*'

So I got off the bus miles from Quarry Bay and started walking.

The roads at this late hour were near-deserted, the sodium-yellow
glow of the streetlights reflecting off tarmac glistening from a recent rain
shower to add a barren and sinister mood.

Scanning around, I saw people, standing in bus stops and sat outside
restaurants, all engaged in sniping conversations about me, but as I neared,
the scenes blended into lights, shadows and objects, only to come to life
elsewhere and the gossiping continue. I hurried along, beside myself with
panic, torn and twisted by shame and ostracism. I arrived back at Max's
in a right old state.

'Max, they're all talking about me, mate.'

'Who talk abou' you?'

'*Everyone*, Max! Even people I can't see!'

'*No*, Quiss! *No one* talk abou' you. You take *too* mush drug.'

Max didn't understand and I couldn't take any more. I asked if I could
phone my old man.

'Hi, Dad,' I said, fighting back a deluge befitting the time of year. 'It's all
gone wrong here, I'm afraid.'

'It's alright, Chris,' he replied calmly. 'I know it has.'

'*Uh*! How do you know?'

'My friend up the pub – he was a police officer in Hong Kong.'

'Yeah?'

'I asked him to make some enquiries... You know, after the phone
calls.'

'And?'

'He called his old colleagues and asked if they knew you.'

'What did they say?'

'They said, "*Hah*! We all know your friend's son. Everyone in Hong Kong knows your friend's son!"'

'Oh…'

'Listen, I've got an idea.'

'What's that?' I replied, thinking any idea would be welcome, as I'd long since run out of ones that worked.

'How about I call the travel agents and get you a ticket so you can come home for a while?'

'But, *Dad*! A ticket from Hong Kong is about *nine hundred quid*!'

'Don't you worry about that – I can put it on the card, can't I? Listen, give me this number.'

When the telephone rang half an hour later and he said, 'Look, son. How about you go to the airport tomorrow and take the 5pm Virgin Atlantic flight to Heathrow, and I'll be there to meet you?' it suddenly seemed my only option.

Only for a short time, though. Just to get myself sorted. But before I did, there were some things I had to do…

It was a Sunday morning in the Big Apple. Ray stood behind the bar, looking relaxed and serving drinks to the few expats sat around it – Lee Aimes being one of them.

'I'm off home, guys. Only for a while, though – just to get myself sorted, you know?'

'I think that a good idea, Chris,' said Ray, ever the kind man he'd always been during my time there.

'*No*! You *can't* go back, CJ!' said Lee, with a huge look of concern.

'I have to, mate – my dad's bought a ticket. Just for a while, though.'

'Listen, CJ. When you get yourself back 'ere, you give me a call, *yeah*? There's always a place for you to stay at mine, our kid.'

Considering our relationship had its challenges – pretend pistols, high-wired high jinks, bootlegged bubbly – Lee's words were touching. I didn't know how involved he was with this weird *gweilo*-triad business, but ever since that first bust-up, he'd been a bloody good mate. I'd never forget Lee's kind offer.

As I walked out of the Apple, a chorus of good wishes caught me up. I turned and said, 'Guys! I'm not going home because I'm a *drug addict*, you know! I'm just sick of getting crushed on the MTR!'

For some reason, it didn't get a laugh, so feeling foolish, I continued up the stairs. After sitting on the kerb for a while, I lit a cigarette and went to make my next call. I had a boogie box to pick up and a junk room to tidy.

Going back into that crazy building was a peculiar experience. Things looked different, accompanied by the you-don't-belong-here feeling, like revisiting your old school – except your old school isn't run by puppets and covered in blood splats left behind by the Special Air Service... at least mine wasn't.

I had to laugh when entering the shambles of a storage area, for the first thing I noticed was someone had pinched my boogie box. I knew who it was. As I exited the lift, an evil-sounding hag from the Chinese family shouted, *'Gweilo mou chin'a* (Devil Man no money), *ha-ha!'* through their ajar window.

I didn't mind. This was their culture, and who was I to judge? I could still look myself in the mirror... if I hadn't smashed it.

I set about putting to order the mess I'd made of the hoarded keepsakes, finding the electric lead for my boogie box in the process. 'Not as clever as you thought!' I mused, chuckling and feeling a bit sorry for my old neighbours, who obviously weren't the sharpest knives in the drawer.

Something told me it would be a nice gesture to knock up a present for the old man on the stairs using some of the junk, as a way of saying thanks for letting me help myself to bits and pieces. I'd always assumed it was his, but it may have belonged to the guy on the roof for all I knew.

'Umbrella power... wind... rainbow... bottles... tinkling.'

I began to turn an umbrella and some Coca-Cola bottles into a wind turbine-and-chime, something to hang out of the window in the hall to produce energy and a pleasant sound. I thought he would like that.

There was one slight drawback. Despite throwing myself at the project like a moose at a sliding door – for *three* hours – I didn't actually get anywhere, finally wrenching myself away because I didn't want to miss my 5pm flight and my dad to lose his money.

As I passed the Chinese family's window, the old witch jeered, '*Gweilo mou faan gung!* (Gweilo doesn't go to work!)', which produced further sniggers from the rest of her household.

With a smile, I placed the electric lead for my boogie box on her doormat, and then hurried back to Quarry Bay.

Max was at home, chatting to Jackson. We smoked some ice and I drew a picture for Mr Lu, the elderly gent who drank in the Big Apple. He hadn't been in there when I went to say goodbye and I wanted to thank him for his friendship. I'd tried to before by buying him cigarettes, but he'd refused to accept them. So now, in pencil, I sketched a scene of him dancing in the foreground in the bar area, hands waving butterflutteringly, and me on the dance floor in the background, both of us smiling, serene and supreme. It was a good likeness, and one Max promised he would deliver on my behalf.

After I'd packed and slid the packet of crystals into the lining of my boot, they helped me carry my bergen, briefbag and case, guitar and smelly bag of books to the MTR, offering to accompany me to the airport.

Only, there was a snag with our schedule. We got there for 5pm, the time my flight was due to depart. I'd forgotten you're supposed to check in two hours before.

'You fly *Virgin*, to *London*?' asked the woman at the company's ticket desk. '*No! Cannot!* Flight has gone already!'

'*Gone?* It can't be *gone!*' I replied, dumbfounded at my own stupidity. 'I *have* to get on it!'

'*Wai*', one moment.' She picked up a telephone, conducted a terse conversation in Cantonese and said, 'You're lucky. Flight is still on the ground. Flight will wai' for you, but you muss hurry. Where's your departure tax?'

'*Urrh! Departure* tax? How much is that?' I asked, not able to recall ever having paid it before and knowing my wallet was empty.

'Two hundred Hong Kong dollars (£20),' she replied, tapping on her keypad to confirm my seat.

Jackson dug deep in his pockets to come up with zilch, Max twenty bucks.

'I'm so sorry,' I said, trying to look as desperate as I felt, and unable to accept I'd fallen at the final hurdle. 'All we have is twenty dollars. *Please?*'

'Okay,' she said, pulling out a Virgin Atlantic courtesy slip and scribbling her name on it. 'When you get back to England, you send the money to me here. Okay?'

'Yeah, s-s-sure,' I stammered, my admiration for this heaven-sent angel interrupted by an official rushing across the check-in area.

'Okay, you go with him.' She thrust my passport and ticket across the counter. 'He take you through Immigration, but you muss hurry!'

'Okay,' I said, as the chap grabbed my guitar and stinking book bag off the floor.

I hugged my dear friends goodbye, unable to believe this was it and it had all gone so fast. Then I turned and rushed down the concourse after the guy. I had to smile when, in the Immigration office, he went through the protocol of asking me if I was carrying anything I shouldn't be, before dashing me onto a waiting bus, which for the first time during my stay in Hong Kong I had all to myself.

The jumbo jet stood alone on the tarmac, engines warmed, its wing and tail lights flashing expectantly. As I struggled off the bus with my luggage, I could see the strained smiles of the two Virgin Atlantic flight attendants as they waited patiently to greet me, and made up my mind to ask them to tell the pilot *and* Richard Branson I was sorry for being late. But before I did, there was one last thing I had to do…

I stopped halfway up the steps, turning for a final look out over the apron to see Hong Kong, scintillant and celestial in the distance. It was *my* Hong Kong, my *beautiful* Hong Kong, and I had to say goodbye before getting on the plane.

On that warm clear evening, the 23rd of June 1996, a wave of beloved memories washed over me as I recalled the wonderful people I'd met and the extraordinary experiences we'd shared. I didn't spare a thought for the challenges I'd faced and certainly didn't bear malice towards the beautiful people of Hong Kong, who would forever hold a special place in my heart.

I just gazed at the awe-inspiring, shimmering-in-the-dark, neon-highlighted, sky-scraping fucking wonderment, the incredibleness of which had been my extraordinary home for thirteen months, and as I turned to walk up the last few steps, I knew I would return to the Fragrant Harbour as soon as I could.

I've never been back.

About the author

In 1999, Chris Thrall fire-walked 120 feet to raise money to work with street children in post-war Mozambique. He has driven journalists from Norway to India to highlight issues of poverty and ran the London Marathon to support disadvantaged young people. Having raised thousands of pounds for projects in Africa, Chris received the Second Level Commendation of Finland, awarded to him for human generosity.

He has backpacked through eighty countries on all seven continents and led a team of explorers to Iceland in a vintage army truck. He is a keen snowboarder, a qualified pilot, skydiver and scuba diver, who in 2012 expeditioned to the Antarctic polar circle to dive with icebergs and leopard seals.

Earning a degree in Youth and Community Work, Chris has worked in mental health, learning disability and substance misuse. He lives in the UK, where he has written the opening novels in a series of thrillers and still hopes to become an astronaut, a dolphin trainer or the Milky Bar Kid.

Acknowledgements

To my family and friends for their interest and support, in particular my brother, Jenny Hoare, the Wellington Street Crew and George Buckton; to Daniel Knäble, Clayton Thomas, Innes Edridge, Tim Madge and Mike 'Rosco' Ross for their input; to Nikki Davenport and Richard Keane for prompting me to write a book – bet you didn't expect this one! – and to Tom Carter, author of *China: Portrait of a People*, for making sure this story never saw a slush pile. Thank you.

EXPLORE ASIA WITH BLACKSMITH BOOKS

From retailers around the world or from *www.blacksmithbooks.com*